THE WORLD FOOD PROBLEM

FIFTH EDITION

THE WORLD FOOD PROBLEM

Toward Understanding and Ending Undernutrition in the Developing World

Howard D. Leathers
with Phillips Foster

LYNNE
RIENNER
PUBLISHERS

BOULDER
LONDON

Published in the United States of America in 2017 by
Lynne Rienner Publishers, Inc.
1800 30th Street, Boulder, Colorado 80301
www.rienner.com

and in the United Kingdom by
Lynne Rienner Publishers, Inc.
3 Henrietta Street, Covent Garden, London WC2E 8LU

Library of Congress Cataloging-in-Publication Data
Names: Leathers, Howard D., author. | Foster, Phillips, 1931– author.
Title: The world food problem : toward understanding and ending
  undernutrition in the developing world / by Howard D. Leathers, with
  Phillips Foster.
Description: 5th edition. | Boulder, Colorado : Lynne Rienner Publishers, [2017] |
  Includes bibliographical references and index.
Identifiers: LCCN 2016041275 | ISBN 9781626374515 (pbk. : alk. paper)
Subjects: LCSH: Food supply—Developing countries. |
  Poor-Nutrition—Developing countries. | Malnutrition—Developing
  countries. | Food supply—Government policy—Developing countries. |
  Nutrition policy—Developing countries. | Food supply—Developing
  countries—International cooperation.
Classification: LCC HD9018.D44 F68 2017 | DDC 363.809172/4—dc23
LC record available at https://lccn.loc.gov/2016041275

British Cataloguing in Publication Data
A Cataloguing in Publication record for this book
is available from the British Library.

Printed and bound in the United States of America

The paper used in this publication meets the requirements
of the American National Standard for Permanence of
Paper for Printed Library Materials Z39.48-1992.

5 4 3 2 1

Contents

Tables and Figures

Tables

Figures

1

Introduction

Children dream of changing the world—achieving world peace, ridding the world of disease, ending oppression and injustice. But one of these dreams—eliminating hunger in the world—may just be a dream that comes true in the lifetimes of some readers of this book.

The progress made during the past five decades has been remarkable—about 40 percent of the world's population suffered from undernutrition in the 1960s; today that number is close to 10 percent. And it is not inconceivable that the progress will continue. This achievement has not been the work of a single individual but has come about through the efforts of multitudes—economists, plant scientists, political leaders, farmers, good-hearted people helping their neighbors—to name just a few.

Despite this progress, heart-wrenching problems of undernutrition remain. Images in the media of families migrating in search of food or babies with bloated bellies and bodies too weak to sit up have flooded our consciousness with the horror of hunger. Each decade seems to produce its own horror stories: Famine in North Korea reached such an acute stage in late 1997 that there were reports of people eating grass and tree bark. Southern Africa was the focus of an international effort to avoid widespread death from famine in 2002. In 2015, the tragedy of refugees from Syria and the Sudan leapt into newspaper headlines and political debates. One estimate puts worldwide deaths from starvation during the 1990s at 100,000 to 200,000 per year (Kates 1996).

When a person dies of hunger, what happens? Describing famine-related death, an anonymous author writing for *Time* magazine put it eloquently and succinctly:

> The victim of starvation burns up his own body fats, muscles, and tissues for fuel. His body quite literally consumes itself and deteriorates rapidly. The

1

kidneys, liver, and endocrine system often cease to function properly. A shortage of carbohydrates, which play a vital role in brain chemistry, affects the mind. Lassitude and confusion set in, so that starvation victims often seem unaware of their plight. The body's defenses drop; disease kills most famine victims before they have time to starve to death. An individual begins to starve when he has lost about a third of his normal body weight. Once this loss exceeds 40 percent, death is almost inevitable. (Anonymous 1974:68)

Although the drama of famine tends to capture our attention, most hunger-related deaths do not occur in famines. They happen daily—quietly and largely unchronicled—all around the world. Figures vary, but one estimate (Katona and Katona-Apte 2008), using data provided by the World Health Organization (WHO) of the United Nations, says that some 3 million children die annually from hunger. This amounts to one death every ten seconds.

In previous editions of this book, we asked readers to imagine the media coverage that would ensue if a 747 jet crashed, killing all 220 children on board. The deaths attributable to hunger are equivalent to 37 of these jet crashes every day. After the terrorist attacks of September 11, 2001, in New York City and Washington, DC, we no longer have to imagine the media coverage, or the grief, or the universal resolve to never let it happen again. The tragedy of undernutrition fails to stir such outrage or determination. The world hunger problem is too pervasive, too commonplace, too remote.

Of course, as these numbers make clear, not all hunger is fatal. Consider this common scenario, played out again and again in developing countries: Picture a loving but poorly educated, poverty-stricken mother with several children. Food is scarce. Her youngest child has not grown for months because of undernourishment, and the baby's resistance to disease has fallen to a very low level. The family's supply of water is unsanitary. The older members of the family can handle the microorganisms in the water, but the baby develops diarrhea. He loses interest in eating. He seems more willing to take liquids, so the mother removes solids from his diet. Because liquids cannot provide enough nourishment to conquer his illness, the diarrhea continues. Finally, in a desperate but seemingly logical attempt to stop the diarrhea, his mother removes liquids from his diet as well. By now, the boy is feverish, and limiting liquids accelerates the baby's loss of fluids. Severe dehydration follows, with death not far behind.

While adult males do die of hunger during times of famine, most hunger-related deaths, whether from famine or from chronic undernutrition, occur among preschoolers. Pregnant and lactating women are also at substantial risk, although less so than children. Malnutrition in children takes many forms. Undernourished children may be crippled by vitamin D deficiency, blinded by vitamin A deficiency, or stunted by protein deficiency. But the most common form of child undernutrition results simply from a lack of sufficient calories, with disease and death too often the result.

The purpose of this book is to provide a general introduction to the world food problem, its causes, and possible ways of addressing it. Our intention is to encourage the reader to be objective and analytical. We try to avoid advocating any particular point of view while also avoiding turning a blind eye to inconvenient facts. As the past few paragraphs suggest, the pages that follow are replete with statistics and with inferences drawn from those statistics. We invite the skeptical reader to contend with us, to point out other inferences that can be drawn or other factual information that leads in a different direction.

Part 1 of this book presents some factual background. What is undernutrition? How does being undernourished affect a person? How can we determine whether a person is malnourished? What do we know about the extent of undernutrition in different periods of time and in different geographical areas?

Factors Influencing Food Supply and Demand in the Future

Part 2 deals with factors that influence the extent of undernutrition. The framework we use to outline these factors is the framework of economics: supply and demand. As we look to the future, global quality of life will hinge on whether world food supply grows faster or slower than world food demand. If supply grows more rapidly than demand, average quality of life in the world will almost certainly improve—food prices will fall, making it easier for poor people to afford an adequate diet and freeing up income for the rich to spend on other goods and amenities. By the same token, if demand outpaces supply, quality of life is likely to deteriorate.

In analyzing future prospects for food supply and demand, there are four particularly critical factors, which we refer to as the four Ps:

- Population
- Prosperity
- Pollution (or environmental resource quality)
- Productivity in agriculture

The impact of population growth on food demand is obvious. More mouths to feed means more demand for food.

Widespread economic prosperity means that more people can afford adequate diets and that people are more likely to have access to healthcare, a sanitary water supply, and education. Income levels also affect food demand—as people attain higher income levels, they tend to buy more food and a wider variety of it, including meat and animal products. So 7 billion relatively affluent people require significantly more agricultural production than do 7 billion relatively poor people.

Pollution, environmental quality, and the availability of land and water resources needed for agricultural production are critical factors in analyzing the future of agricultural production. To what extent can a population expand the area it devotes to agricultural production? Will soil erosion or water pollution result in land that is less arable or less irrigable? How will global climate change affect agricultural production?

Agricultural productivity refers to the amount of food produced on a given area of agricultural land. Regardless of environmental quality and land and water resources, the food supply will continue to grow if productivity grows quickly enough. Productivity per acre may increase when farmers apply more fertilizer, or use more labor. Productivity can also increase because of new technology, such as new seed varieties.

Population, prosperity, pollution, and productivity interact with each other in complex ways. Some examples of these interactions:

• As population grows, urban and industrial water users compete with agriculture for scarce water.
• Population growth slows as people become more prosperous.
• As agricultural productivity increases, economic prosperity improves for the entire economy.
• Increased use of agricultural chemicals may improve productivity while harming the environment.

Government policies can influence the long-term supply-and-demand balance of food. However, the complexity of these interactions illustrates how difficult it can be to decide among various policy alternatives. Appropriate policy changes are the subject of the last part of this book.

The Main Nutrition Policy Alternatives

Part 3 of the book focuses on policy interventions that may help alleviate the world hunger problem. For the most part, the policy interventions we examine are aimed at the factors identified in Part 2. Undernutrition can be reduced by increasing hungry people's access to food.

The most important actions a government can take to alleviate malnutrition are to promote general economic growth and to promote agricultural research. These contribute significantly to a second tier of government objectives: reducing population growth and maintaining or improving natural resource quality. Governments have repeatedly attempted to address the world food problem by regulating prices or by redistributing food between rich and poor countries or by food distribution programs aimed at the poor, but have been largely unsuccessful.

Part 4 then provides an analytical framework for looking into the future. What are reasonable assumptions about the underlying forces influencing the extent of world hunger? What might the world food problem look like in the year 2050?

Part 1
The Facts About Malnutrition

2

Famines:
The Historical Context

Famines get the spotlight. The television specials and the historical controversies and the sad Irish songs are about famines. But famine is a fairly small part of the world food problem. If through some magical intervention we could end famines, we would still have an enormous problem of widespread, pervasive, and permanent undernutrition. Although most of this book is focused on this pervasive and permanent condition, this chapter discusses famine.

In the popular press, the word *famine* is used to describe any newsworthy food shortage. Here we reserve the term to refer to localized, temporary, and severe food shortages. Famines are almost always the result of a confluence of forces that include natural disaster and poor policy response. Of course, there is a connection between the permanent state of widespread undernutrition and the crisis of famine: in countries where undernutrition is a serious and common problem, it does not take much of a natural disaster to create a famine.

Brief descriptions of present and historical famines illustrate how natural disasters and policy responses have interacted to create or exacerbate famines. These examples also illustrate some of the ways that economists have studied famines and policy approaches to famine.

The Irish Potato Famine

The Irish potato famine of the late 1840s is fairly well known in the West because it spurred a wave of Irish emigration to the United States, transforming US culture in ways that continue to be seen, especially on St. Patrick's Day, and because the famine became emblematic of the British repression of Ireland.

Ireland of the 1840s was a country of deep and widespread rural poverty. Seventy-two percent of the Irish people were illiterate (Johnston 2003), and 37 percent lived in mud houses with a single room (Johnston 2003; Donnelly

7

2001:2). Per capita income in Ireland in the early 1840s was only about 60 percent of the level in Britain (Mokyr 1985).

Poverty was especially prevalent in rural areas. About two-thirds of the Irish population depended on agriculture for their livelihoods (Kinealy 2002:18), and 40 percent of these were landless laborers (Donnelly 2001:9). Much of the land in the Irish countryside was owned in large tracts by landlords. Landless laborers acquired plots of land from the landlord and in return either worked in the landlord's fields (primarily growing grain or flax for linen for export, or producing butter for sale in urban areas) or paid a rent to the landlord. A social structure that trapped Irish labor in the agricultural sector caused labor productivity in that sector to be about half that of British agricultural workers (Donnelly 2001:9).

In this environment of poverty, a third of Irish households depended almost exclusively on potatoes for food (a farmer in pre-famine Ireland might have consumed twelve or more pounds of potatoes per day). Potatoes have a number of advantages as a low-cost food source in Ireland: they can be grown in relatively poor soil; they yield a high number of calories per acre; and they are rich in protein, carbohydrates, vitamins, and minerals. A diet of potatoes and buttermilk (a low-value by-product of producing butter) provides better nutrition than a diet consisting primarily of wheat or maize.

Because of the potato-based diet, and despite the widespread poverty, "the Irish poor were among the tallest, healthiest and most fertile population in Europe" (Kinealy 2002:32). (See Box 2.1 for a more general assessment of the importance of the potato to European economic development.) The cheap and nutritious potato diet served as a foundation for low-wage agriculture; cheap food exported from Ireland in turn fueled the industrial revolution in Britain. In addition, the low-wage labor provided a cushion protecting some landlords from the consequences of their inefficient farming practices.

Box 2.1 The Importance of Potatoes in European Development

Research by economists Nathan Nunn and Nancy Qian demonstrates the importance of the potato in European development more generally: "[T]he introduction of the potato was responsible . . . for approximately one-quarter of the growth in [European] population and urbanization between 1700 and 1900" (2011: 593). Nunn and Qian are able to attribute causality because of geographical differences in the degree to which the potato was a suitable crop and because of differences in when the potato was introduced to different areas. (The potato is a South American crop, unknown in Europe before Columbus's voyages, and introduced widely in Europe in the seventeenth and eighteenth centuries.)

The potato blight—a fungus that causes potatoes to turn black and rotten as they grow in the ground—had appeared in small areas prior to 1845. But the blight hit about half the crop in 1845, and destroyed nearly the entire crop in 1846, 1848, and 1849 (the 1847 crop was partially successful). Estimates of famine-related deaths range from 290,000 to 1,250,000 compared to Ireland's pre-famine population of about 8 million (Johnston 2003).

Once the severity of the potato blight was understood, a tremendous amount of attention was devoted to the appropriate "policy response": What could or should the government do? Throughout the nineteenth century, Ireland was governed by Great Britain. The choices made by the British government, and the criticisms of these choices, illustrate a philosophical or ideological debate about the appropriate relationship between government action and private action. The policy decisions fall into three categories (identified here with today's nomenclature): technology policy—what the government should do to encourage better scientific understanding of the causes and consequences of the potato blight; trade policy—what the government should do to increase food imports or reduce food exports during a time of famine; and poverty alleviation policy—what the government should do to help the poor.

The British government recognized the possibility of ending the famine with a technological fix, but its efforts never came to fruition. The government instituted a board of scientific experts to draw conclusions about how to save potatoes that had been infected by the blight. The board's recommendations involved complex chemical procedures requiring materials and training unavailable to the starving Irish masses. Even if followed, the program promised little hope of success. The government also appealed to the private sector by promising to purchase and donate to all farmers any treatment that would kill the blight. No successful antifungal treatment was discovered until years after the Irish famine.

Trade policy in the mid-nineteenth century was the subject of intense ideological debate. The individuals in power during much of the famine were ardent proponents of free trade, or laissez-faire—a policy of minimal government intervention in markets. The Irish famine put pressure on both sides of the debate over free trade. On the one hand, the famine provided the impetus for repeal of the Corn Laws that restricted imports of food into Ireland. On the other hand, exports of food from Ireland continued. The rigidity of the position in favor of free trade is reflected in an exchange between Randolph Routh, an official in Ireland administering food distribution, and Charles Trevelyan, the permanent head of the treasury for the British government (quoted in Donnelly 2001:69):

> Routh: "I know there is great and serious objection to any interference with these [food] exports, yet it is a most serious evil."

Trevelyan: "We beg of you not to countenance in any way the idea of prohibiting exportation. The discouragement and feeling of insecurity to the [grain] trade from such a proceeding would prevent its doing even any immediate good; and there cannot be a doubt that it would inflict a permanent injury on the country."

Some scholars point to evidence of substantial reductions in grain exports to conclude that "even if exports had been prohibited, Ireland lacked sufficient food . . . to stave off famine" (Gray 1982:46). Kinealy notes that exports of other food commodities remained high, and concludes: "The Irish poor did not starve because there was an inadequate supply of food within the country, they starved because political, commercial, and individual greed was given priority over the saving of lives" (2002:116).

If trade policy illustrates the role of ideology in policy, poverty assistance or relief policy illustrates the law of unintended consequences. Policies to help the poor during the famine were under constant discussion and revision. The government policies included such aspects as:

• Importation of grain from the United States.
• "Work houses" where poor families could live.
• Public works programs to provide incomes to the jobless.
• Soup kitchens distributing prepared food.

The cost of these programs was financed in large part through a tax on Irish landlords. The amount of the tax depended on how many poor households or tenants lived on the landlord's property. Landlords realized that they could reduce their tax burden by evicting tenants from their farms and destroying the tenant cottages. In this way, the policy intended to help the poor actually ended up separating many poor people from their shelter and from their means of growing food.

The evictions had the impact of consolidating landholdings into larger farms. Between 1841 and 1851, the number of small farms (5 acres or less) dropped from over 300,000 to less than 100,000. The number of large farms (30 acres or more) tripled (Johnston 2003). Many landlords, having lost their rent-paying tenants, went bankrupt. Over the next decades, the landlord-tenant system died out, and it became commonplace for Irish farmers to own the land that they worked.

Some of the better-off tenants who lost their homes to eviction had sufficient resources to emigrate to the Americas. During the 1840s, an estimated 1.3 million Irish people emigrated. The conditions of their voyages were harsh: perhaps as many as 40 percent of the emigrants died during the passage to the Americas (Abbot 2003).

Mike Davis (2001), in his book on late–Victorian era holocausts, describes a set of circumstances and ideologies that led to and exacerbated the Bengal famine of the 1870s that are quite similar to those described here for the Irish famine.

Famines Created by Government Policies

Two of the worst famines in the past century occurred in centrally planned economies: the famine in the Ukraine of the 1930s and the Great Leap Forward famine in China of the 1950s. If the Irish potato famine illustrates that a famine can occur in a country governed by those who embrace a laissez-faire ideology, these two famines illustrate that state socialism is not immune to poor policy choices that cause or exacerbate famine conditions.

The Ukrainian Famine, 1932–1933

By the early 1930s, the urban industrial regions of the Soviet Union had been transformed into a collectively state-owned, centrally planned system. In 1929, Stalin introduced a policy of compulsory collectivization of agriculture. Under the collectivization plan, all of the productive assets—land, machinery, cattle, and so forth—of 25 million farmers were to be aggregated into 250,000 collective and state farms.

Even if collectivization had been enthusiastically embraced by Soviet farmers, the process of reorganization would no doubt have been awkward, and aggregate agricultural production may have decreased. There were difficulties obtaining agricultural machinery and managing the transportation of agricultural goods, as well as inexperienced managers of the new large farms.

In addition to these problems, the collectivization process was resisted by farmers. For example, farmers slaughtered their horses and cattle rather than surrender them to the collective. This resistance was especially strong in the Ukraine, where peasants had always cultivated their own land and therefore "had a much stronger sense of private ownership and deeper feeling of freedom and independence" compared to Russian peasants (Dolot 1985:xiv).

The objectives of the central Soviet government during the early 1930s were therefore to maintain ample food supplies for the urban industrial sector while completing the transformation of agriculture to a collective system. In the Ukraine, these objectives were pursued by giving farmers a quota of grain that had to be shipped. Farmers who resisted joining the collectives were forced to ship their entire crops:

> Stepan Schevchenko was a poor farmer . . . like the rest of us [but different] from us in only one way: he had categorically refused to join the collective farm. He paid off all his taxes for the year 1932, and apparently thought that the government would leave him alone. . . . But he was overly optimistic.

One day he received a requisition order demanding him to deliver 500 kilograms of wheat to the state. He delivered it in full. But no sooner had he done so when he received another order. This time they demanded twice as much wheat, . . . [even though] he had none left. . . . The officials . . . threatened him with Siberia, . . . [and] he was forced to sell everything he had of value, including his cow, to buy the order of wheat. . . . He soon received the inexorable third order: 2,000 kilograms of wheat immediately! . . . The Bread Procurement Commission paid him a visit. . . . He and his family were ordered to leave their house. . . . All that belonged to the Shevchenkos was confiscated and [became] "socialist property." (Dolot 1985:146)

The seizure of all available stocks of food in the Ukraine caused widespread starvation among the very people who produced the food in the first place. The most extreme famine conditions were suffered in the Ukraine for several reasons: the more active resistance to collectivization in the Ukraine, a nationalistic or ethnic bias against Ukrainians on the part of the Russo-centric decisionmakers in Moscow, and a desire to hide evidence that the agricultural collectivization experiment was less than perfectly successful.

An estimated 6–8 million Ukrainians died during the famine (of a prefamine population of about 34 million) (see Mace 1984:vi). This leads some

---

Box 2.2 Global Climate Change and Famine in the 1600s

In 1600, Huaynaputina—a volcano in Peru—erupted. The eruption lasted for two weeks, and spewed enough ash to fill a box 3 miles wide, 3 miles long, and 3 miles deep. The ash and the sulfur dioxide emitted by the volcano caused severe weather thousands of miles away in Europe. Sweden had record snowfalls. Estonia had the coldest winters in 500 years of recordkeeping.

But in Russia, the cold weather was just part of the climate disaster. The summer of 1601 had such heavy rain that crops failed. Boris Godunov, who had become tsar in 1598 following the death of Ivan the Great's invalid son, attempted to deal with famine. He permitted serfs to leave their masters and move to other farms or to cities; he financed public works (notably the erection of the Bell Tower dedicated to Ivan the Great), paying workers with grain drawn from government stores.

But those efforts fell short. In 1602 crops failed again. And in 1603, they failed again. The crop failures resulted not just from floods but also from drought and from freezing.

During the period 1600–1603, one-third of the Russian population died of famine. A Dutch merchant traveling in Russia during these years wrote: "So great was the famine and poverty in Moscovia that even mothers ate their children."

Sources: Mataev 2001: Perkins 2008

historians to compare it to the holocaust of the Nazi concentration camps. James Mace draws these sobering conclusions: "The Great Famine of 1932–33 is unique in the annals of human history in that it was wrought neither by some natural calamity nor even by the unintentional devastation created by warring armies. It was an act of policy, carried out for political ends in peacetime. It was deliberately man-made" (1984:i). (See Box 2.2 for a story of famine in Russia in the 1600s.)

The Chinese Great Leap Forward Famine, 1959–1961

The most destructive famine in terms of human lives lost occurred in China during Mao's Great Leap Forward. During this period, a large number of social and economic changes were being instigated by the central government. In the agricultural sector, collectivization began in 1952 and was successful in increasing agricultural output through 1958. Beginning in 1958, the government insisted that farmers undertake untested production methods based on unorthodox (and as the Chinese experience was to prove, flawed) science. The government forced a reorganization of smaller group or cooperative farms into larger communes (see Box 2.3). In addition, a commitment to an ideology of regional self-sufficiency led to a program that forced farm workers to divert some of their working hours to industrial production such as small-scale steel plants. China was also seeking to establish its economic independence from the Soviet Union, so food exports were increased during 1959 and 1960 to repay debts.

Simultaneous with these changes in government policies, poor weather conditions occurred in the years 1959–1961; conditions were especially poor in 1960 and 1961, with 15–20 percent of agricultural land being hit by natural calamity. Agricultural production, which had risen by 28 percent from 1952 to 1958, fell back below 1952 levels. A paper by Houser, Sands, and Xiao (2009) looks at regional data to see whether higher mortality rates were uniform throughout the country (as we would expect if policy caused the famine), or whether there were geographical differences (as we would expect if weather problems caused the famine). They conclude that policy mistakes are a more important cause than bad weather. More than 30 million people died prematurely as a result of the Great Leap Forward famine. The enormity of the problem emboldened political leaders in the provinces to abandon the policies imposed by Mao's central government. The famine can be said to have had political as well as demographic consequences, as power devolved to the provinces until the Cultural Revolution in the late 1960s reasserted the primacy of the central government. Chen and Zhou (2007) find that the famine had long-term consequences reducing the stature, health, labor supply, and earnings of those exposed to the famine in early childhood.

Scholarship about the Great Leap Forward famine has accelerated as more and more records from the era become public. Two books (*Tombstone* by Yang

Box 2.3 Incentives in Chinese Agricultural Communes

One of the changes that accompanied the Great Leap Forward campaign was a change in the way group farms were organized. Economist Justin Yifu Lin (1990) examined the details of farm organization and concludes that the changes in the rules of these organizations contributed to the famine of 1959–1961.

After the revolution of 1949, many Chinese farmers voluntarily formed cooperatives of different types. In "mutual aid teams," a handful of neighboring families would share tools and draft animals and would help on each other's plots when needed. Each farm household continued to own land, tools, and animals; each family made its own decisions about which crops to plant; each family received the output from its land for consumption or sale. In "elementary cooperatives," twenty to thirty households agreed to combine into a single farm. Here, each family continued to own land, tools, and animals, but the decisions were communal, and output was shared. The sharing of output depended on how much land, tools, and animals the household contributed to the cooperative, and on how much work each household contributed. In "advanced cooperatives" the cooperative itself owned the land, tools, and animals, and members shared in output based solely on their labor contribution.

Each of these three kinds of organization provided an incentive for people to work hard: the harder you work, the more you earn. Even in the most "communal" of these organizations—advanced cooperatives—each farm household received a bigger share of the commune's output if it contributed more labor. What is more, Lin points out, the fact that membership was voluntary created an additional reason for families not to be laggards. If one family became known as a lazy household, the other, hardworking households could form a new cooperative the following year, leaving out the lazy household. The initial collectivization effort in China was quite successful; agricultural output increased 28 percent from 1952 to 1958.

In 1958, the central government disbanded existing agricultural cooperatives and forced all farmers to join large communes of about 5,000 households and 10,000 acres. As well as these communes being larger than previous cooperatives, the rules of organization were different in two important respects. First, peasants were paid "based mainly on subsistence needs and only partly on worked performed" (p. 1236). Second, membership in the communes was no longer voluntary, and peasants were forbidden from withdrawing from the commune. With this change, it became "impossible to use withdrawal [from the commune] either as a way to protect oneself or as a means to check the possibility of shirking by the other members. . . . Since supervision in agricultural production is extremely difficult, . . . incentives to work in a compulsorily formed . . . collective must be low. A peasant will not work as hard as on the household farm. Therefore the productivity level of a collective will be lower than the level reached on the individual household farm" (p. 1242).

Lin notes that the downturn in production coincided exactly with the adoption of these new rules for cooperatives. The rules were abandoned in 1961, again coinciding exactly with the rebound in agricultural production.

Jisheng and *Mao's Great Famine* by Frank Dikotter) detail the hardship brought about by famine conditions and the cruelty of local party leaders and law enforcement officials. Yang Jisheng (2012) estimates 36 million died in the famine; Dikotter (2010) puts the number at 45 million.

Recent Famines

The famines described here were in a sense national problems. In none of the cases was there much discussion about how the world community could or should respond to the famine. More recent experiences with famine illustrate an evolving internationalist perspective.

Previous editions of this book have included more extensive descriptions of the famines in North Korea and Zimbabwe. Those countries continue to appear on lists of food-crisis countries. But the very fact that these countries have been in crisis for a decade or more illustrates a difference between the famine situations of today and those historical famines described earlier that have lasted two or three years. Here, we condense our discussion of North Korea and Zimbabwe (focusing on southern Africa in general in the latter case) and begin with an added description of the situation in Sudan.

Sudan

A serious famine threat has arisen from the conflict in South Sudan. The conflict is both personal/political (the president of South Sudan in conflict with his former deputy) and ethnic (the Dinka tribe in conflict with the Nuer tribe). As one side of the conflict gains military advantage in an area, supporters of the losing side become landless, homeless (and foodless) refugees, with the conflict taking place against a background of extreme poverty and food insecurity: people spend 80–85 percent of their income on food. The food security situation depends on three factors: (1) the degree of economic and geographical dislocation caused by the internal conflict, (2) local agricultural conditions (weather, extreme events) that influence the size of the locally produced food supply, and (3) policy—especially the size of food aid deliveries to the region.

In early 2015, the Food and Agriculture Organization (FAO) of the United Nations estimated that more than 1.3 million people had been forced out of their homes by the fighting. Three and a half million people—40 percent of the Sudanese population—are in need of emergency food aid. The armed conflict also reduces crop production by making it impossible for farmers to keep to a regular schedule of planting, weeding, and harvesting. Farm animals are killed or stolen, or weakened by forced movement away from conflict zones (see FAO 2015b).

The root cause of the Sudanese famine is the internal political conflict. Efforts at peacekeeping have led to the signing of a series of ceasefire agreements, going back as far as 2005, but these agreements have not been effective in ending the conflict.

The United Nations has been active in trying to force the parties to find a more permanent end to the hostilities, and has in the interim been coordinating outside assistance to shelter refugees and provide food aid. Between January 2015 and June 2015, the World Food Programme (WFP) of the United Nations distributed 178,000 metric tons of food and $31 million in cash vouchers in southern Sudan. The WFP acts as the coordinating agency, with funds from donor countries such as the United States, the European Union, and Japan. But the conditions of war have made it difficult to move food aid to the areas of greatest need.

North Korea

Since the 1990s, North Korea (the Democratic People's Republic of Korea) has suffered from famine conditions of varying intensity. The roots of this famine are found in the Cold War. During the Cold War, North Korea was closely allied with the Soviet Union and China, often playing one of those superpowers off against the other to get increased aid. With the breakup of the Soviet Union and the end of the Cold War, this aid dried up. Not only did food donations dwindle but domestic agriculture in North Korea, which had been designed to utilize subsidized imports of energy and fertilizer, now required radical restructuring. Drought struck in 1995, and an estimated 2–3 million people (about 10 percent of the population) died from famine-related illness in the 1994–1998 period.

The response of the government undoubtedly made things worse. Prior to the famine, nearly all grain in North Korea was produced on state or communal farms. The workers on these farms were given a grain ration out of the harvest that was nutritionally sufficient. As grain yields began to fall because of poor weather and insufficient inputs, the central government cut peasant worker rations by over a third. The intention was to preserve more of the grain harvest for shipment to hungry urban areas. The unintended impact was to reduce the grain harvest even further, for two reasons (Natsios 1999). First, farm workers secretly "preharvested"—taking grain out of the communal fields before it was ready for harvest—and hid the grain for their own consumption. Because the grain was harvested before it was fully ripe, the grain yield was lower than it would have been if harvested according to plan. Second, farmers diverted effort from communal fields to legal and illegal private plots. These private plots were often in poor terrain and so the yields were lower than on the collective farms, but the output did not have to be shared.

The international response to the famine was substantial. Shipments from all sources averaged over 1 million metric tons per year from 1995 to 1998 (Natsios 1999). (To put this in context, the World Food Programme estimated that in 2001, North Korea would produce 3 million metric tons of food, but would require 4.8 million metric tons to feed its population [Struck 2001].)

Reliance on food donations from abroad has created pressure on the North Koreans to bring their foreign affairs and military policies into conformance with demands by countries making the food donations. For example, in 2002 the United States suspended food aid to North Korea (see Dao 2003). Observers suspected that the suspension was a reaction to North Korea's refusal to halt its nuclear weapons program, although US officials denied that this was the reason. Support for aid to North Korea was also undermined by reports of corruption in the aid distribution system and fears that the aid was not helping those most in need. (For more detailed accounts of the continuing North Korean food crisis, see Natsios 2001 and Haggard and Noland 2007.) The *New Yorker* magazine ran an article describing the life of one woman's suffering and escape from the North Korean famine (Demick 2009).

Southern Africa

International response also played a major role in ameliorating the impacts of famine conditions in southern Africa in the years 2002–2003. By June 2002, it was obvious that poor weather conditions (a drought followed by heavy rains during the harvest season) would devastate crop production in a large part of southeastern Africa, affecting Zimbabwe, Zambia, Lesotho, Malawi, Mozambique, and Swaziland.

The situation in Zambia was one of unusually poor weather occurring in an extremely poor country where much of the population suffers from undernutrition during "normal" or nonfamine times. Production of Zambia's staple crop—maize—fell in 2002 to a level about half that of the average output over the previous four years. Between mid-2002 and early 2003, the World Food Programme directed shipments of 130,000 metric tons of food to Zambia, helping to feed 1.7 million people. The weather conditions improved considerably for the 2003 crop, with maize production double that of 2002. Zambia faces ongoing problems of poverty, AIDS, and undernutrition, but the acute crisis of the 2002 famine has ebbed.

The weather situation in 2001–2002 in Zimbabwe was similar to that in Zambia. But in Zimbabwe food output was suppressed further by a government program to redistribute agricultural land. During Zimbabwe's period as a colony of Britain (when it was known as Southern Rhodesia), prime agricultural land along the railway line was given over to white commercial farmers. After independence in 1980, these farmers continued to farm the land, but the government was under increasing pressure from its supporters to seize the white-owned land and distribute it to indigenous supporters of the ruling party.

The land redistribution proceeded slowly from 1980 to 1998, but then accelerated. In addition to a formal process of government purchases of white-owned farms, an extra-legal process of farm invasions forced white farmers to give up their farms. The area planted with maize on large commercial farms fell from 163,000 hectares in 1998 to 61,000 hectares in 2000. Much of the land remained in cultivation in smaller parcels by the recipients of the land reform, but yields dropped precipitously. Zimbabwe's cereal production in 2002 was less than one-quarter of the peak production of 1996.

The Zimbabwean government purchased substantial amounts of food, but additional help was needed from the international community. The ruthlessness of the land reform activities and the impression that the Zimbabwean government was turning a blind eye to lawless farm invasions created a reluctance on the part of developed-country donors to provide assistance. Ultimately, the World Food Programme did make substantial amounts of food aid available (in 2002–2003 amounting to about 500,000 metric tons of food). However, as of the summer of 2003 nearly half of Zimbabwe's population continued to face the specter of famine.

Over the next five years, little changed. The actions of the Zimbabwean leadership were widely condemned (Lynch 2008). Rural violence and land seizures continued (Dixon 2008). Price controls kept farm prices low, discouraging food production (Lynch 2008). Annual maize production in the five years prior to 1998 was about 2 million metric tonnes; in the most recent five-year period, it was about half that amount. In 2015 the FAO's famine early warning system projected that 16 percent of the rural population of Zimbabwe would suffer from food insecurity during the "peak lean" season of January to March 2016 (FEWS 2015).

* * *

These recent examples illustrate the difficulties in making a clear distinction between famine and the problem of permanent undernutrition. Famine is a shock or a disaster—it is a disturbance to the normal condition. There is both good news and bad news in this. The good news is that the needed policy response to famine is a temporary (though urgent) response. The bad news is that existing institutional frameworks (laws, power structures, social mores) often lack the flexibility to respond and thus exacerbate the impact of the natural disaster. The failed responses of the governments of North Korea and Zimbabwe, and of the two sides in the Sudanese conflict, have made famine conditions last so long that it is hard to characterize them as temporary. The solution to these difficulties does not rely on food production and distribution—the main focus of this book—but will depend on political or military solutions to the underlying problems of governance.

Famine and Disaster Relief

In times of famine, domestic and international disaster relief agencies respond as best they can to get food into the hands of the starving. Sometimes, the best efforts get excellent results.

Singh (1975) describes a successful effort to address potential famine in

India in 1967. The district of Bihar suffered severe drought—the worst in a century. Crop production fell to half the normal amount. An effort by the national government created jobs for food—employing 18,000 people and paying them with food drawn from government stocks. As a result, there was no starvation.

More recently, there was a huge international outpouring of charity in response to the Indian Ocean tsunami of 2004. Aid donations from governments and private individuals and organizations amounted to $7,100 per affected person (Telford, Cosgrave, and Houghton 2006). And the World Food Programme can point to successes, as in the Zambian emergency described earlier. The emergence over the past decade of the WFP as an organizing entity for international assistance to famine-struck countries has resulted in better coordination of disaster assistance to fight famine.

But sometimes the relief can be a mixed blessing. The authors of a well-documented and detailed Oxfam report warn that poorly supervised or uncontrollable distribution of food aid can do more harm than good. To quote one example, a field worker helping out in a drought relief food aid program (where the food handouts were supposed to be free of charge to the recipients) wrote,

> In Haiti we had . . . a problem of theft and mishandling. In [a] town . . . fairly near to us and very badly hit by drought, the magistrate [appointed mayor] was known to sell PL480 [international relief] food for $7.00 a 50 pound bag. At other times the CARE food distributors were so desperate that they would just throw bags of food off the truck and drive on, so that the food would go to the strong and the swift. (Jackson and Eade 1982:9)

When disaster has created the need for assistance, but the local food supplies are adequate, supplying emergency food relief can be counterproductive. It depresses the local price of food, in turn depressing the income of the local farming community, and may lead to other socially undesirable results (see Box 2.4).

In areas where food aid has become a yearly occurrence, food aid "dependency" can develop. Thielke (2006) describes the situation in Kenya:

> Only as a result of regular food deliveries by the United Nations World Food Program can the people in Kenya's harsh northern region avoid starvation. . . . According to [a German expatriate], the aid has become a threat to the entire region. "People just hang about, waiting for food deliveries from Nairobi," he says. "They are losing traditional survival strategies. The area is pretty much made up of only dependent recipients of charity." [A] Swiss biologist . . . who headed the ICIPE ecology research institute in Kenya for many years agrees. "Northern Kenya is hopelessly overpopulated," he says, "and this overpopulation is the result of years of western aid shipments to areas that really don't have the potential to feed so many people." . . . [A for-

Box 2.4 When Food Aid Is Not Needed

Tony Jackson and Deborah Eade

Imported food may not be necessary at all, despite a major disaster, and its arrival may do more harm than good. The classic example of this comes from Guatemala where the earthquake in 1976 killed an estimated 23,000 people, injured over three times as many and left a million and a quarter homeless. The earthquake occurred in the middle of a record harvest. Local grain was plentiful and the crops were not destroyed but left standing in the fields or buried under the rubble but easy to recover.

During the first few weeks, small consumer items—salt, sugar, soap, etc.—were in short supply and temporarily unavailable in the shops. Some of these small items, such as salt, were lost when the houses collapsed. People expressed a need for these food items in the short period before commercial supplies were resumed. However, during that year, about 25,400 tons of basic grains and blends were brought in as food aid from the US. A further 5,000 tons of US food aid already stored in Guatemala were released and supplies were also sent in from elsewhere in the region.

Catholic Relief Services (CRS) . . . field staff objected to the importing of food aid but they were overruled by their headquarters in New York. . . . The Coordinator of the National Emergency Committee of the Government of Guatemala asked voluntary agencies to stop imports of food aid. . . .

Finally, the Government of Guatemala invoked a presidential decree to prohibit imports of basic grains from May 1976 onwards. Yet after this decree, quantities of food aid were still imported in the form of blended foodstuffs. One article refers to these blends as "basic grains in disguise."

Field staff and local leaders identified three negative results. Firstly, they considered that food aid contributed to a drop in the price of local grain that occurred soon after the earthquake and continued throughout 1976. As to the need for basic grains, a peasant farmer explained: "There was no shortage. There was no need to bring food from outside. On the contrary, our problem was to sell what we had.". . .

An OXFAM–World Neighbors official reported: "Virtually everyone in the area is selling more grain this year than he does normally. Furthermore, emergency food shipments have drastically curtailed demand for grains. Thus the prices of the farmers' produce have plummeted."

Later, the then Director of CRS in Guatemala was to tell the New York Times: "The general effect was that we knocked the bottom out of the grain market in the country for nine to twelve months.". . .

The second negative effect of the continuing supply of free food was to encourage the survivors to queue for rations instead of engaging in reconstruction or normal agricultural work.

Thirdly, it brought about a change in the quality and motivation of local leadership. The OXFAM–World Neighbors official, quoted above, noted:

> Immediately after the earthquake, we tended to see the same leaders whom we'd seen before the earthquake—people [with] a high degree of honesty and personal commitment to the villages. But gradually . . . I

began seeing fellas who I knew were totally dishonest. They'd go into the different agencies and . . . say that theirs was the most affected village in the Highlands, and they'd get more food. So largely because of the give-aways, the villages started to turn more to leaders who could produce free things like this, whether they were honest or dishonest, rather than to the leaders they'd been putting their trust in for years.

With larger and larger quantities of free food coming in, there are increased incentives to corruption. . . . Groups that had worked together previously became enemies over the question of recipients for free food.

Source: Jackson and Eade 1982:9–11.

mer health commissioner explains:] "There are more and more people and there is less and less water. . . . The desert is expanding. . . . In the past people slaughtered their animals for food during difficult times. . . . But ever since the World Food Program began feeding us, hardly anyone does this anymore. Everyone just waits for the next delivery."

General Studies of Famines

The magazine *The Economist* has compiled data on worldwide famine deaths by decade since the beginning of the twentieth century. These numbers are shown in Table 2.1. The incidence of famine has declined precipitously from its peak mid-century—a peak undoubtedly caused by the Great Leap Forward famine in China, described earlier. By this table, one might conclude that the era of famines is over. But as mentioned, the phenomenon of famine has changed, now also requiring political solutions, with immediate needs able to be addressed to a considerable extent by international aid efforts.

Famine does not affect a country's population equally. Reutlinger and his colleagues (1986:27) list the groups most likely to fall victim to a famine:

- Small-scale farmers or tenants whose crops have failed and who cannot find other employment in agriculture (the Wollo in Ethiopia in 1973).
- Landless agricultural workers who lose their jobs when agricultural production declines (Bangladesh in 1974) or who face rapidly rising food prices and constant or declining wages (the great Bengal famine of 1943).
- Other rural people, including beggars who are affected by a decline in real income in the famine regions (almost all famines).

Table 2.1 Deaths from Famine Worldwide, by Decade

	Thousands of Deaths from Famine	Number of Deaths per 100,000 Population
1900–1910	541	3
1910–1920	162	9
1920–1930	16,280	814
1930–1940	7,200	343
1940–1950	9,400	409
1950–1960	15,950	578
1960–1970	16,650	500
1970–1980	3,820	94
1980–1990	1,400	29
1990–2000	4,820	84
2000–2010	200	3

Source: The Economist 2013b.

- Pastoralists who get most of their food by trading animals for food grains; their herds may be ravaged by the drought, or animal prices may collapse relative to food-grain prices (the Harerghe region of Ethiopia in 1974 and the drought-stricken Sahel in 1973).

Martin Ravallion (1997) did a thorough review of the economics literature regarding famines. He cites examples of failed policy responses to famine: "The British government's . . . non-intervention in food markets during [nineteenth-century] famines almost certainly made matters worse. . . . At the other extreme, . . . food procurement policies implemented [by] . . . the Soviet Union . . . resulted in severe famine in the Ukraine in the 1930s" (p. 1225). Ravallion draws the following lessons for policies in response to famine:

- *Better governance.* Greater democratization and freer flow of information in a society make it more difficult for a government to ignore famines.
- *Early warning and rapid response.* Policy interventions are likely to be more effective if they take place before famine conditions are firmly entrenched.
- *Increased aggregate food availability.* Policies to increase the total amount of food available in famine areas include food aid, policies to discourage hoarding in private or public storage, and policies to encourage domestic food production.
- *Distribution policies.* "Although the case is often strong for increasing aggregate food availability during a famine, food handouts need not be the best form of intervention from the point of view of minimizing mortality. Cash or coupon payments to potential famine victims can provide

more effective relief than the usual policy of importing and distributing food" (p. 1230).

- *Stabilization policies.* "An effective but affordable . . . stabilization policy in famine-prone economies . . . will probably combine buffer stocks and . . . a relatively open external trade regime" (p. 1233). Buffer stocks are programs in which the government purchases food in periods when it is plentiful and sells food out of their stocks when shortages occur.
- *Other policies.* Ravallion argues that there are potential synergies between policies to address famines and other policies to spur economic development, including credit programs, improved infrastructure, and assignment of property rights.

For students of history interested in Europe and Asia, Mabbs-Zeno (1987) has reviewed the famines on these continents.

Finally, no discussion of famines can ignore the Nobel Prize–winning work of economist Amartya Sen. Sen grew up in a family of intellectuals and was ten years old when the Bengali famine of 1943 occurred. Although Sen's family was not affected by the famine, it inspired him to take a professional interest as an adult in the study of famine. Sen is famous for the dictum "no famine has taken place in the history of the world in a functioning democracy" (Sen 1999:180). Recent experiences (for example Zambia, described earlier) seem to provide counterexamples to Sen's rule. Daniel Davies (2005), in a blog post, discusses the validity and meaning of Sen's dictum, and concludes: "So, 'democracies don't have famines' should really read 'there is no excuse for having a famine if you are a government which cares about its population and is in control of its territory.'"

3

Defining Malnutrition

One common definition of malnutrition is "overconsumption or underconsumption of any essential nutrient." This chapter is devoted to exploring this definition.

Four Types of Malnutrition

Internationally famous nutritionist Jean Mayer (1976) identifies four types of malnutrition: (1) overnutrition, (2) secondary malnutrition, (3) dietary deficiency or micronutrient malnutrition, and (4) protein-calorie malnutrition.

Overnutrition

When a person consumes too many calories, the resulting condition is called *overnutrition.* Overnutrition is the most common nutritional problem in high-income countries such as the United States, although high-income people in low-income countries also suffer from this type of malnutrition. The diet of the world's high-income people is usually overladen with calories, saturated fats, salt, and sugar. Their diet-related illnesses include obesity, diabetes, hypertension, and atherosclerosis. Overnutrition is a serious problem. For example, Martorell (2001) reports research showing that in Latin America, 35 percent of women age fifteen to nineteen are either overweight or obese. Another report shows that the percentage of the Chinese population who are obese rose from 16.4 percent in 1992 to 22.6 percent in 2002 (Luo, Mu, and Zhang 2006). The problem of overnutrition in the developing world is being addressed through an international effort coordinated by the World Health Organization (WHO 2002). The WHO (2015b) estimates that in 2014, 39 percent of adults worldwide were overweight, and 13 percent were obese.

This book will have relatively little to say about the problem of overnutrition. It is an important and serious public health problem, but it is not the subject of this book. Here we will be concerned with problems that are primarily addressed by actions that influence the production and distribution of food.

Secondary Malnutrition

When a person has a condition or illness that prevents proper digestion or absorption of food, that person suffers what is called *secondary malnutrition*. It is called "secondary" because it does not result directly from the nature of the diet, as do the other types of malnutrition, which are termed "primary." Common causes of secondary malnutrition are diarrhea, respiratory illnesses, measles, and intestinal parasites. The following mechanisms cause secondary malnutrition:

- *Loss of appetite (anorexia).*
- *Alteration of the normal metabolism.* For example, when the body shifts some of its attention to fighting infection, among other things, production of disease-fighting white blood cells may be increased and body temperature raised.
- *Prevention of nutrient absorption.* For instance, diarrheal infections irritate the lining of the gastrointestinal tract, creating difficulty in absorbing nutrients and at the same time causing it to shed contents before full digestion has had time to occur.
- *Diversion of nutrients to parasitic agents.* Parasites such as hookworms, tapeworms, and schistosome worms rob the body of nutrients it would otherwise retain (Briscoe 1979; Martorell 1980; Brooker, Hotez, and Bundy 2008).

Public health measures such as providing sanitary human-waste disposal and clean water are especially important in reducing secondary malnutrition. A worldwide effort has increased the number of people with access to safe drinking water by 1.6 billion since 1990. In 2006, 84 percent of the population of all developing countries had access to an improved drinking water source (United Nations 2008:42).

Low-income people in developing countries are at risk for undernutrition (insufficient calories), which is commonly exacerbated by secondary malnutrition (especially parasites and diarrhea caused by unsanitary drinking water). Because of the strong link between the two, undernutrition and secondary malnutrition are commonly grouped together and called, simply, *undernutrition.*

Dietary Deficiency or Micronutrient Malnutrition

A diet lacking sufficient amounts of one or more essential micronutrients, such as a vitamin or a mineral, results in dietary deficiency. Although a deficiency of any micronutrient can become a serious problem, most nutritionists are primarily concerned about deficiencies in vitamin A, iodine, and iron. In recent years, this category of malnutrition is usually referred to as *micronutrient malnutrition* or *micronutrient deficiency*. The four most significant micronutrient deficiencies are for vitamin A, iodine, iron, and zinc:

- *Vitamin A.* Deficiency of vitamin A can cause "xerophthalmia," or night blindness. It is also associated with increased mortality from respiratory and gastrointestinal disease. One study (Gopalan 1986) suggests that vitamin A supplements could reduce deaths of children age six months to five years by 23 percent. Vitamin A may also play a role in maintaining the immune system and in fighting cancer.
- *Iodine.* Iodine deficiency causes goiter and leads to a reduction in mental abilities. Babies born to iodine-deficient mothers can suffer from "cretinism," which can result in learning disabilities in children. One study indicates that even mild iodine deficiency can reduce intelligence quotient (IQ) by 10–15 points (Ma, Wang, and Chen 1994). Iodine deficiency is the greatest single cause of preventable brain damage and mental retardation. The WHO (2007) estimates that one-third of the world's people live in iodine-deficient environments.
- *Iron.* Iron deficiency, or anemia, causes reduced capacity to work, diminished ability to learn, increased susceptibility to infection, and greater risk of death during pregnancy and childbirth. Using extensive country surveys for the year 2011, the WHO (2015c) estimates that 43 percent of children, 38 percent of pregnant women, and 29 percent of nonpregnant women have anaemia.
- *Zinc.* Zinc deficiency causes impaired immune function—making the person more susceptible to disease. The WHO reports that zinc deficiencies are responsible for 18 percent of malaria cases, 16 percent of respiratory infections, and 10 percent of diarrhea cases. About 800,000 deaths annually can be attributable to zinc deficiency. Severe zinc deficiency can also lead to cognitive dysfunction (WHO 2002; see Chapter 4 in this volume).
- *Other micronutrients.* Other diseases caused by micronutrient deficiencies include rickets (soft bones), caused by vitamin D deficiency; scurvy, caused by vitamin C deficiency; and beriberi and pellagra, caused by deficiencies in B-vitamins. Some research (Tang et al. 1993) indicates that the risk of contracting AIDS is substantially lower among those who consume very high levels of niacin (a B-vitamin), vitamin A, and vitamin C. Some research has emphasized the importance of folic acid in reducing the incidence of spina bifida (Erickson 2002) and the importance of vitamin D in fighting cancer, diabetes, and heart disease (Holick 2004).

When compared with underconsumption of proteins or calories, the problem of underconsumption of micronutrients appears relatively easy to solve. The missing elements are inexpensive, and programs to provide them are relatively easy to initiate. In the United States, iodized salt (salt to which iodine has been added) protects us from iodine deficiency, specially fortified milk provides vitamin A (and vitamin D), and iron pills (or vitamin supplements) are a common source of iron.

In 2008, a Danish university gathered together eight world-famous economists and asked them to make joint recommendations about how (the relatively small sum of) $75 billion could be spent to improve the world. Three of the ten recommendations made by this group involved micronutrient malnutrition: vitamin supplements for children, zinc and iodine fortification of salt, and plant-breeding efforts to increase micronutrients in crops ("biofortification"). (A fourth recommendation—deworming—would address secondary malnutrition described earlier.)

There are many examples of successful micronutrient interventions in the developing world:

- In Guatemala, dietary anemia was greatly reduced in a rural community after the inhabitants were persuaded to substitute iron cooking pots for aluminum pots.
- Also in Guatemala, fortification of sugar with vitamin A has been effective, and experiments are now under way to fortify sugar with iron.
- In Brazil, a school's drinking water was fortified with iron, creating a noticeable improvement in students' iron levels at a cost of about 15 cents per student per year.
- In China, iodine deficiency was treated by dripping potassium iodate solution into the water of an irrigation canal. Iodine intake by people in the area increased significantly.

The World Bank estimated in 1994 that it would cost about $3 per year to meet a person's entire needs for vitamin A, iron, and iodine. (Other micronutrients are not so inexpensive: an antioxidant formula of vitamin E, beta-carotene, and vitamin C may cost $60 per person per year.)

Despite the apparently easy solution to these vitamin and mineral deficiencies, the problems have remained surprisingly persistent, though progress is being made. For iodine: "Out of . . . 130 countries . . . there are only 47 countries where [deficiency] still remains as a public health problem [in 2006], compared to 54 in 2004 and 126 in 1993" (WHO 2007:14). By 2011, the number of countries had fallen further to 32 (UNICEF 2013:24). In 2002, under the multinational Micronutrient Initiative, 300 million children under the age of five were given a high-dose vitamin A supplement. The United Nations Children's Fund (UNICEF 2007:9) reports that the proportion of children receiving the full (two-doses per year) treatment for vitamin A deficiency increased from 16 percent in 1999 to 72 percent in 2005. By 2011 the proportion had increased to 75 percent, and to 82 percent in the least developed countries. (UNICEF 2013:23). According to the World Health Organization's most recent estimates, anemia affects about 25 percent of the world's population, compared to 37 percent of the world's population in the early 1990s, although it still affects almost 50 percent of preschool-aged children and 40 percent of pregnant women (WHO 2001, 2008). By 2011, slight progress was reported, with 47 percent of preschool-aged children and 42 percent of pregnant women suffering from anaemia (UNICEF 2013:23).

Policies to reduce micronutrient malnutrition will continue to be important because of the huge impact on public health that relatively small expenditures can have. As we shall see in the next chapter, the health impacts of micronutrient deficiencies are significant. However, the solutions to these deficiencies are more likely to come from fortification programs, supplementation, and research into biofortification such as the efforts described earlier, and less likely to come from additional food consumption and production.

Protein-Calorie Malnutrition

The underconsumption of calories or protein—known as *protein-calorie malnutrition* (PCM) or *protein-energy malnutrition* (PEM)—is a problem that can be solved only by increasing the amount of food that an individual eats. A person suffering from PCM is not obtaining enough of the protein or calories needed for normal growth, health, and activity. PCM hardly ever occurs in families with enough income to satisfy their basic needs for food, shelter, clothing, and heat; it is found predominantly in low-income countries where poverty is widespread.

In extreme forms, PCM manifests itself as the potentially fatal nutritional disorders known as kwashiorkor and marasmus. Kwashiorkor results from protein deficiency, usually as the child is weaned from breast milk, which provides adequate protein to newborns. In fact, *kwashiorkor* is a Ghanaian word meaning "the evil spirit which infects the first child when the second child is born." Children with kwashiorkor exhibit swollen bellies, or edema, and depigmentation of hair (black hair turns a reddish hue). Marasmus is a condition of both protein and calorie deficiency. The term derives from a Greek word meaning "wasting away," and the physical effects are just that—low body weight, or emaciation. One observer described children with marasmus as "wizened little old people . . . , just skin and bones" (Whitney and Hamilton 1990). As daily food intake is inadequate to meet requirements for protein and calories, the body begins to use reserves stored in the fat cells. As those reserves are used up, the person enters the end stages of starvation, a condition known as catabolysis (Zeigler 2012:343–345).

Calories and Protein

Because protein-calorie malnutrition is a major source of nutrition-related disease, and because reducing it requires increasing food consumption, much of this book will focus on this form of malnutrition. These two elements—calories and protein—are both derived from food and are both necessary for growth, health, activity, and survival. But their nutritional roles are different. More important, calories and proteins are derived from foods in different ways, and a diet must be carefully planned if it is to be adequate in both.

Nutritional Role of Calories and Proteins

Calories are a measure of the energy contained in food (see Box 3.1). The body obtains energy from carbohydrates (e.g., sugar and starch) and fats (e.g., oil and butter). Calories are used by the body to provide energy for various needs:

- Involuntary functions such as breathing, blood circulation, digestion, and maintaining muscle tone and body temperature.
- Physical activity.
- Mental activity.
- Fighting disease.
- Growth.

The human body makes the millions of different proteins that it needs from some twenty amino acids, which are the building blocks of the body's proteins. Proteins function in ways other than providing a source of calories:

- They are necessary for building the cells that make up muscles, membranes, cartilage, and hair.
- They carry oxygen throughout the body.
- They carry nutrients into and out of cells and help assimilate food.
- They contribute to the development of antibodies that fight disease.
- They work as enzymes that speed up the digestive process.

Simple organisms such as yeasts and algae can synthesize almost all of the amino acids they need. But humans cannot synthesize or make sufficient quantities of some amino acids. To live, therefore, we must consume enough *essential amino acids* (those that the body cannot produce in sufficient quantities). Of the approximately twenty amino acids needed, nine are essential. Because the body cannot manufacture them, we must consume them as part of our diets. All of these amino acids are found in eggs, milk, and meat—proteins from these dietary sources that contain all the essential amino acids are referred to as *complete proteins*.

Proteins from vegetable sources tend to be deficient in at least one of the essential amino acids and are therefore "incomplete." To understand the im-

---

Box 3.1 Calories and Kilocalories

In physics, chemistry, and engineering, a calorie is the amount of heat energy required at sea level to raise the temperature of 1 gram of water by 1 degree centigrade. A kilocalorie (abbreviated Kcal) is the energy it takes at sea level to raise the temperature of 1,000 grams of water (a kilogram—also a liter) by 1 degree centigrade.

Nutritionists always quote their data in kilocalories, but unfortunately they commonly shorten the word to "Calories"—capitalized to indicate kilocalories as distinguished from calories. But the convention is not always observed. Regardless, in nutrition literature the lowercased word calorie usually means kilocalorie.

---

portance of this for diet, we need to understand the way that the human body takes the amino acids from protein in food and constructs protein for the body's use. Protein molecules in food are composed of fixed proportions of amino acids. A balanced protein is one in which the essential amino acids appear in the same ratio to each other as the body needs them for constructing its protein molecules. (Information about dietary reference intakes for essential amino acids can be found in National Academy of Science 2002:10-65–10-66).

If you consume more amino acids than you need, your body cannot use them for making proteins; instead, it burns the amino acids for energy. If you consume less of an amino acid than you need, a portion of other amino acids goes to waste for want of the "matching" part needed to manufacture protein molecules. Whitney and Hamilton provide a delightful analogy:

> Suppose that a signmaker plans to make 100 identical signs, each saying left turn only. He needs 200 L's, 200 N's, 200 T's and 100 each of the other letters. If he has only 20 L's, he can make only 10 signs, even if all the other letters are available in unlimited quantities. The L's limit the number of signs that can be made. The quality of dietary protein depends first on whether or not the protein supplies all the essential amino acids, and second on the extent to which it supplies them in the relative proportions needed. (1990:92)

Complete proteins can be obtained from animal products such as meat, milk, eggs, and cheese, but not from most grain and vegetable products. However, complete proteins can be obtained by combining different *types* of grains and vegetable products. For example, a person living on a diet of beans might be getting plenty of the amino acid lysine, but might be deficient in the amino acids methionin and cystine. A person living on a diet of wheat might be getting enough methionin and cystine, but not enough lysine. A diet that combines wheat and beans would give the appropriate balance of these amino acids. (See Scrimshaw and Young 1976 for more detail.)

The Chemical Process of Producing Dietary Calories and Protein

The energy that the human body uses comes from the sun, but the body cannot absorb solar energy directly and use it for physical growth and activity. The chemical process by which plants transform solar energy into a form of energy (in plants) that can be absorbed by humans or animals is known as *photosynthesis:* carbon dioxide plus water plus radiant energy from the sun yields (in the presence of chlorophyll) a carbohydrate plus oxygen plus water. Using enzymes, a plant can rearrange the carbon, hydrogen, and oxygen atoms of the carbohydrate, or sugar, to form starch or fat.

The conversion of sugar into starch is energy-efficient: practically all the energy in the original sugar can be released in burning the starch made from it. The conversion of sugar to fat, however, is about 77 percent energy-efficient, so we can say that most of the energy in the original sugar can be released in burning the fat that is made from it.

Making amino acids is not so easy. Like carbohydrates and fat, amino acids contain carbon, hydrogen, and oxygen, but they also contain nitrogen; and nitrogen in the form that can be used to build amino acids is scarce. In the process of photosynthesis, plants can use carbon dioxide (CO_2) straight from the atmosphere. But in making amino acids, nitrogen cannot be used as N_2, the gaseous form in which it is found in the atmosphere. It has to be converted to more complex forms, such as ammonia (NH_3), before the plant can use it.

Converting atmospheric nitrogen to usable nitrogen is called *nitrogen fixation.* It can be done in a commercial fertilizer plant, where energy is combined with some raw organic stock such as naptha. Or it can be done by nature, which provides three other ways of fixing nitrogen: lightning storms, nitrogen-fixing bacteria, and blue-green algae. For the most part, the nitrogen fixed by blue-green algae is not available to plants useful to humans. Leguminous plants, such as beans, peas, and alfalfa, provide a suitable environment on their roots for nitrogen-fixing bacteria and thus have an extra boost of nitrogen available.

The fixed nitrogen taken up by plants becomes available in the food chain to make amino acids and, ultimately, proteins. Plants and animals must spend energy (use up sugar) to synthesize amino acids. They spend still more energy to recombine these amino acids into enormous molecules of protein. As a result, the energy available from burning a protein is substantially less than the energy used to produce that protein. By contrast, the amount of energy released in the burning of a carbohydrate or fat is closer to the amount of energy it took to make it in the first place.

Which Is the Bigger Problem:
Protein Deficiency or Calorie Deficiency?

The chemistry involved in producing calories and proteins helps explain why proteins are scarce relative to carbohydrates and fats. The relative scarcity implies that putting adequate protein into our diets will be more expensive than consuming adequate calories. And, generally speaking, we do pay a premium for protein-rich foods. For instance, hamburger, which is a richer source of protein than rice, costs more per pound than rice (and in contrast, rice provides about twice as many calories per pound compared to hamburger).

Because protein is more expensive than carbohydrates, the question arises: Should we show more concern about the protein intake of poor people than we do about their calorie intake? Until the 1970s, nutritionists believed that protein was the central concern.

No doubt, protein deficiency can and does occur. However, the experience of the past three decades demonstrates that calorie deficiency is a more widespread problem. For example, a study (Gopalan 1970) of 15,000 Indian preschool children in the 1960s found that 35 percent showed evidence of both calorie and protein deficiency, 57 percent showed evidence of calorie deficiency but not protein deficiency, but virtually none showed evidence of protein deficiency without an accompanying calorie deficiency.

Recent data on food availability also indicate that calorie deficiency is likely to present a bigger problem than protein deficiency. In its food balance sheets, the Food and Agriculture Organization showed that in Africa, food available per capita would provide 2,618 calories and 69 grams of protein per person per day in 2011. If we compare this to the average requirements listed in Table 3.1 for adults, we see that available protein is substantially higher than the requirements for all groups, but that available calories are lower than the requirements for most adult men.

Nevin Scrimshaw, a renowned advocate of the importance of protein in the diet, puts it like this: "It is true that adult protein needs are met by most traditional developing country diets when they are consumed in sufficient quantity to meet normal energy needs" (1988). A review of studies of protein intake in developing countries reached the same conclusion: "At the habitual levels of intake, only 75 to 80 percent of the . . . requirement for energy is satisfied, while more than the current safe level for dietary protein is supplied" (Rand, Uauy, and Scrimshaw 1984: sec. 5.1).

How Much of a Nutrient Is Enough?

Before describing what can happen when a person does not get enough of a nutrient, we need to explore what "enough" means. Of course, no single standard applies to everyone. Each person is different. Growing children have different nutritional needs than mature adults. Men have different nutritional

Table 3.1 Dietary Reference Intakes for Calories and Protein

Category	Age (years) or Condition	Calories Estimated Average Requirement (EAR) (Kcal per day)	Protein (grams per day) Estimated Average Requirement (EAR)	Recommended Daily Allowance (RDA)
Males	0–1/2	570	9.1[b]	9.1[b]
	1/2–1	743	9.9	13.5
	1–3	1,046	10.6	13.0
	4–8	1,742	15.2	19.0
	9–13	2,279	27.4	34.0
	14–18	3,152	44.5	52.0
	19–30	3,012[a]	46.2	56.0
	31–50	2,852[a]	46.2	56.0
	51+	2,607[a]	46.2	56.0
Females	0–1/2	520	9.1[b]	9.1[b]
	1/2–1	676	9.9	13.5
	1–3	992	10.6	13.0
	4–8	1,642	15.2	19.0
	9–13	2,071	28.1	34.0
	14–18	2,368	38.3	46.0
	19–30	2,345[a]	37.6	46.0
	31–50	2,253[a]	37.6	46.0
	51+	2,081[a]	37.6	46.0
Pregnant	1st trimester	+0	+12	+25
	2nd trimester	+300	+12	+25
	3rd trimester	+300	+12	+25
Lactating	1st 6 months	+500	+22	+25
	2nd 6 months	+500	+22	+25

Sources: Protein RDA: National Academy of Science 2002. Protein EAR: National Academy of Science 2003: summary tab. 1. Calories EAR: Thomson-Wadsworth 2003 (developed from National Academy of Science 2002).

Notes: a. For 19-year-olds: 3,067 calories for males, 2,403 calories for females. For each year above age 19, subtract 10 calories for males and 7 calories for females. Calories shown are for individuals 24.5 years old, 39.5 years old, and 65 years old for the three age groups.

b. For infants under 6 months, adequate intake of protein is reported.

needs than women. Active people have different nutritional needs than sedentary people. Box 3.2 describes how energy requirements can be different for two people of the same sex and age. And some people are different for other reasons. For example, we all know someone who can eat and eat yet never gain weight; that person has a higher metabolism, or a higher daily need for calories, than the rest of us.

Nutritionists have several different ways of describing the nutritional needs of a group. The recommended daily allowance (RDA) shows the nutrient level at which 97–98 percent of the group will be adequately nourished. RDAs are useful as targets for an individual: an individual who gets his or her

Box 3.2 How Many Calories Do I Need Each Day?

Table 3.1 shows the dietary reference intakes for people in different groups. But not everyone in each group is the same. To obtain an absolutely accurate calculation of how many calories you burn each day, you would need to undergo a complicated and expensive clinic assessment. But you can make a good estimate by using the following formulas (applicable to people over age 19 who are not excessively over- or underweight).

For men:
$$661.8 - 9.53 \times AGE \text{ (yrs)} + PAC \times$$
$$[(15.92 \times WEIGHT \text{ (kg)}) + (539.6 \times HEIGHT \text{ (m)})]$$

For women:
$$354.1 - 6.91 \times AGE \text{ (yrs)} + PAC \times$$
$$[(9.36 \times WEIGHT \text{ (kg)}) + (726 \times HEIGHT \text{ (m)})]$$

Plug in your age, weight (1 pound = 0.4536 kg), and height (1 inch = 0.0254 m).
  The physical activity coefficient (PAC) takes on one of four values, depending on how active you are:

Daily Exercise Level	PAC	Example of Daily Exercise
Sedentary	1.00	None
Mildly active	1.12	30 minutes of moderate walking
Active	1.27	30 minutes of moderate walking, 25 minutes of moderate bicycling, and 40 minutes of tennis
Very active	1.45	45 minutes of moderate cycling, 25 minutes of jogging, and 60 minutes of tennis

Depending on height and weight, calorie requirements can vary widely for different people in the same PAC category. Consider two 21-year-old men. One is 5 feet 3 inches tall, weighs 104 pounds, and has a sedentary lifestyle. His daily calorie requirement is about 2,000. The other is 6 feet 3 inches tall, weighs 199 pounds, and has an active lifestyle. His daily calorie requirement is about 4,000.

RDA of a nutrient can be quite confident of obtaining an adequate level of that nutrient. However, "RDAs are not useful in estimating the prevalence of inadequate intakes for groups" (National Academy of Science 2002:13-7). Nor are they appropriate as targets for the *average* intake of a group. For these purposes, a better measure is the estimated average requirement (EAR) (for calories, the EAR is often referred to as the estimated energy requirement). The

Figure 3.1 Distribution of Nutrient Requirements in a Typical Population of Healthy Individuals

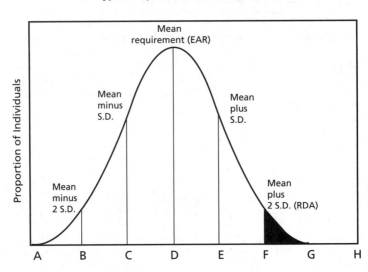

EAR is the daily intake amount that will be adequate for half the individuals in the group. Thus the EAR is always lower than the RDA (compare the EAR and RDA values for protein shown in Table 3.1). The RDA for calories is no longer reported, since it might encourage people to consume too many calories (Trumbo et al. 2002).

The difference between the EAR and the RDA is shown in Figure 3.1. This bell-shaped curve shows the distribution of people in a certain group— say, men age nineteen to twenty-two—according to how much of a certain nutrient—say, calories—each person needs. Some men in this age group need few calories (near point A); some need a lot of calories (near point G). On the curve, point D is the mean (or average) requirement. This is the EAR. The degree to which the bell curve is spread out around the mean is measured by a statistic called the *standard deviation* (S.D.)—a large standard deviation means that the curve is a relatively flat, wide bell; a small standard deviation means a tall, skinny bell. An intake level at point F is calculated by taking the standard deviation, multiplying it by two, and adding the result to the mean. Statisticians have shown that point F, calculated in this way, will show the following characteristics: nearly all (97.5 percent) of the people in the group will have a requirement that is less than F; only 2.5 percent of the population will have a requirement greater than F. The RDA for a nutrient in a given age-sex

group is set at point F by adding two standard deviations to the mean requirement for the group.

RDAs and EARs for micronutrients (vitamins and minerals) can be found
in National Academy of Science 2003. A general description of the process of
determining calorie and protein requirements is contained in WHO 1985.

4

Measuring Undernutrition

In the previous chapter, we identified underconsumption of calories, micronutrients, and protein as the most serious types of malnutrition. We now turn to the question of how we can measure the extent of undernutrition in a group. In this country, or city, or village, is undernutrition rare or is it commonplace? Because resources for coping with undernutrition are scarce, they must be spent wisely, and this requires that we accurately identify where the problem is most serious.

Measuring the Nutritional Status of the Individual

Measurements of undernutrition in a group will be based on determinations of nutritional status, individual by individual. The common methods of direct assessment of the nutritional status of an individual are clinical, biochemical, dietary, and anthropometric. Each method has shortcomings and each may result in a somewhat different assessment of the nature and extent of nutritional disorders.

Clinical Assessment

Clinical assessment of nutritional status relies on the examination of physical signs on the body that are symptomatic of nutritional disorders (Jelliffe 1966 or WHO 2009). For example, kwashiorkor might be diagnosed by loss of pigment in the hair. A national Philippine nutrition survey (Philippines National Science and Technology Authority 1984) that examined schoolchildren for goiter (a generalized swelling at the base of the neck above the collarbone) and found that 3.1 percent of children over the age of nine suffered from iodine deficiency. Researchers examined the extent of vitamin A deficiency among preschool children in Mali by giving eye tests and diagnosing xerophthalmia (Schemann et al. 2003).

Correct identification of nutritional disorders using physical signs depends not only on the training and skill of the clinician but also on how significantly the signs are manifested in the particular individual. Clinical signs are difficult to quantify and are usually obvious only in the advanced stage of the disease; for this reason, clinical assessment can be used in only the most severe and specific types of nutritional disorders.

Biochemical Assessment

Biochemical assessment requires examination of bodily fluids such as blood or urine for the complex metabolic changes that accompany nutritional disorders. For example, in the Philippines, when 14,000 blood samples were drawn and analyzed, 27 percent of the total population, 51 percent of young children, and 49 percent of pregnant women were found to be anemic (Philippines National Science and Technology Authority 1984).

Biochemical tests provide an accurate indication of short-term nutritional problems (especially micronutrient deficiencies), but their complexity and expense are impediments to widespread use in field surveys. Imagine the problems associated with persuading a sample of over 14,000 individuals living throughout the Philippines to submit to having blood drawn, and then transporting these samples to appropriate laboratory apparatus for analysis before they deteriorated in the heat.

Dietary Assessment

Dietary surveys are often employed to assess nutritional status. Two approaches are used: (1) dietary recall, in which the subject is asked to remember what he or she ate, such as during the past twenty-four hours or the past seven days; and (2) dietary record, in which someone records the amount of food consumed at mealtimes, often by weighing it. Both methods have their advantages and drawbacks.

Dietary recall (see Box 4.1) is advantageous in that researchers can interview subjects when they are not expecting to be surveyed; they are less likely to adjust their consumption because of the survey. Yet it is often difficult for people to remember exactly what they or members of their family ate during the past twenty-four hours, much less during the past week. And estimates of quantity consumed are particularly prone to error in recall surveys. Dietary-recall surveys have historically relied on educated and trained interviewers—making these kinds of surveys expensive, and possibly infeasible in many developing contexts. For richer countries where home computers and smart phones are common, a computer program can take the place of a human interviewer to prompt the individual to recall and record diet (see Subar et al. 2012 for a description).

When keeping food records, especially if every portion of food must be weighed, the cook tends often to simplify the diet to make recordkeeping easier (Quandt 1987). Subjects in food-recordkeeping surveys are especially

---

**Box 4.1 Use of a Dietary-Recall Survey to Evaluate the
Impact of a Financial Crisis on Nutrition in Indonesia**

A study of the prevalence of undernutrition among pregnant women in Indonesia (Hartini et al. 2003) used a dietary-recall survey. Four hundred fifty women in their second trimester of pregnancy were interviewed repeatedly (up to six times) and asked to recall their food intake in the twenty-four hours preceding the interview. The results were averaged to estimate each woman's typical dietary intake. From this, daily nutrient intake (how many calories, how many grams of protein, etc.) was estimated using coefficients about the nutritional composition of the food items. The daily nutrient intake for each woman was compared to the estimated average requirement for the nutrient in Indonesia. The study ran from 1996 to 1998, spanning the Indonesian financial crisis that began in 1997. Therefore the study was able to analyze the impact of the crisis on nutrition. Urban consumers suffered the most from the crisis: protein intake declined from 52 grams per person per day before the crisis to 44 grams during the crisis; iron intake dropped from 17 grams to 12 grams. In rural areas, nutrient intakes held steady, or even increased, during the crisis.

---

likely to adjust their diets so that things will "look better" to the surveyor, especially if the surveyor is in the household for the sole purpose of making and recording the measurements. As with dietary-recall surveys, computer-based surveys (or surveys based on photos) may help improve and reduce the cost of food records in places where computers and smart phones are common, but it is unlikely that these technologies will make a big impact in the poorest areas of the world.

In both types of surveys, measuring the quantity of food consumed by breast-fed babies presents difficulties. And in both cases, seasonal variation in consumption may confound the data unless appropriate adjustments are made. For instance, the Philippine survey was conducted from February through May, a time when access to the countryside is easier because of the relative absence of monsoon rains and typhoons. The retail price of tomatoes, for example, is typically 250 percent higher in November than in April. Similarly, the price of rice tends to be low from February to May, while the price of corn tends to be high (Philippines Ministry of Agriculture 1981a, 1981b). The unadjusted survey data thus probably overestimated annual consumption of tomatoes and rice, which were in abundant supply during the survey period, and probably underestimated the consumption of corn. A 2014 paper (Smith, Dupriez, and Troubat) reviews the research on the accuracy of food surveys and strategies to increase the accuracy.

In either case (dietary recall or dietary record)—and subject to the limitations discussed here—results of the survey can be used to determine amounts of various nutrients consumed; these amounts can then be compared to a dietary standard appropriate to the particular country being observed, to determine nutritional status.

Dietary assessment is useful in studies relating consumption and income, or in determining food allocation patterns within the family. But care must be taken in interpreting the results of such surveys. Food intake is not always a good index of nutritional status. For instance, secondary malnutrition (worms, diarrhea) can substantially degrade the nutritional status of an otherwise appropriately fed individual.

Anthropometric Assessment

Anthropometry is the science of measuring the human body and its parts. It serves as the most commonly used measure of nutritional status. To understand how anthropometric assessment works, we must first understand how human physical growth and development are responsive to nutritional status.

Impact of Undernutrition on Physical Growth and Development

Because calories and protein are necessary for the growth of the human body, the most obvious physical effects of undernutrition manifest in the individual's size. In considering this impact, we should discriminate between *acute undernutrition* and *chronic undernutrition*. Acute undernutrition is short-term, severely inadequate food intake, such as one might see during famine or war. The human body can recover from a relatively short bout of acute undernutrition; people who lose weight in a famine can gain it back when the famine ends. In some cases, children whose growth has slowed during a famine will regain their normal size when the famine ends. Chronic undernutrition refers to long-term inadequacy of protein or calories or both, and causes physical effects even when the inadequacy is moderate. The physical effects of undernutrition manifest in various ways.

Low Height-for-Age, or Stunting

An individual whose height is low for his or her age is said to be *stunted.* Low height-for-age is a symptom of past undernutrition; the person may or may not be undernourished today. Gomez and colleagues (2013) explain the use of stunting as a measure of undernutrition: "Stunting is caused primarily by maternal undernutrition, which leads to poor fetal growth, and by poor nutrition and repeated infections in the first 2 years of a child's life. Stunting is a key indicator of undernutrition because it causes permanent impairments to cognitive and physical development that lowers attained schooling and reduces adult income" (2013:130).

The link between nutrition and height is the focus of a small group of economic historians (see Fogel 2004; Steckel 1995; Komlos 1989; for a nontechnical overview, see Bilger 2004; for an example of how anthropometric history is practiced, see Box 4.2). In a 2015 paper, Hoddinott and Horton explain why stunting—as an indicator of child nutritional status, which can influence life-long health and development—has rightly been included as a target of the Sustainable Development Goals framework. (The world community, acting through the United Nations, has identified 17 Sustainable Development Goals with specific targets to be achieved or actions to be taken during the period 2015–2030. These goals follow up on the Millennium Development Goals adopted in 2000 specifying targets and actions to be taken by 2015.)

Evidence of the link between nutrition and height is found in a large number of sources. Average height in nations increases over time as nutritional sta-

---

Box 4.2 An Anthropometric Mystery

In 1850 the average American man was 3 inches taller than the average Dutchman. A century later, the average Dutchman was 1 inch taller than the average American (Steckel 1995:1919). Since the 1950s, average height of Europeans has increased an extra three-quarters of an inch per decade, and average height in some Asian populations several times more, compared to Americans, who haven't grown taller in the past half century. Even the Japanese—once the shortest industrialized people on the planet—have nearly caught up with Americans, and Northern Europeans are now 3 inches taller than Americans on average (Bilger 2004).

Economic historians attribute the early American advantage in height to abundant sources of protein from farm animals and wild game. But why hasn't the United States maintained its "lead"? Per capita incomes have grown in Europe, but they've grown in the United States too. Food consumption has increased in Europe (calories per capita per day grew by 4 percent in the Netherlands between 1961 and 2011), but it has increased faster in the United States (by 26 percent over the same time period).

Could the explanation have something to do with immigration? Perhaps the US height average is brought down by immigration of shorter adults from Central America and Asia. But analysts have checked, looking only at heights of native-born men of European ancestry, and the height disparity still exists (Bilger 2004).

Students of anthropometric history are now considering other explanations. Perhaps growing income inequality in the United States is creating a new, shorter economic underclass. John Komlos of the University of Munich is examining heights of different demographic groups (college-educated whites, for example) to see if that provides any evidence about this possibility. Richard Steckel of Ohio State University notes that, relative to Europeans, Americans grow more slowly in infancy and adolescence; perhaps, then, inferior pre- and postnatal care, or too much junk food in teenage diets, is stunting growth in the United States (Bilger 2004).

tus improves (see Tanner 1977:349; Steckel 1995). At a local level, in 1981 in the Indian village of Bagbana, studied by Phillips Foster and colleagues (unpublished study; Foster was a coauthor of previous editions of this book), 61 percent of adult sons were taller than their fathers by an average of 3.1 centimeters (1.25 inches). John Strauss and Duncan Thomas (1998) present data on height increases over time for the United States, Côte d'Ivoire, Brazil, and Vietnam. In the United States, the average man born in 1930 was 4 centimeters taller than the average man born in 1910, reflecting a marked improvement in nutrition; but the increase from 1930 to 1950 was only 1 centimeter, perhaps because there was less room for improvement in nutritional status.

Other data reported in Strauss and Thomas (1998) show that in periods of war or economic depression, when nutritional status declines, average height stagnates or declines. In Vietnam, average height increased with birth year from 1920 to the late 1950s, when the Vietnam War started. From the late 1950s through the 1970s there was little change in height, reflecting the impact of war on nutritional improvement. In what amounts to a kind of naturally occurring controlled experiment, Alderman, Hoddinott, and Kinsey (2003) examined the impact of the 1982–1984 drought in Zimbabwe. In comparing the height-for-age of children before and after the drought, they found an average loss of stature of 2.3 centimeters.

Low Weight-for-Height, or Wasting

People who are currently undernourished are thin. In scientific jargon, they exhibit low weight-for-height, or *wasting*. This fact is known to anyone who has tried to lose or gain weight by changing their food intake. Low weight-for-height is a symptom of current undernutrition and is used to identify individuals who are currently suffering from acute malnutrition. A paper by Chotard and colleagues provides an example of how wasting is used as a measure of undernutrition: "Malnutrition in preschool children, usually measured as wasting, is widely used to assess possible needs for emergency humanitarian interventions. . . . [We find that] among pastoral child populations average prevalence of wasting was 17%, 6–7 percentage points higher than the rates among agricultural populations, or populations with mixed livelihoods" (2010:s219). In other words, this research found that the problem of childhood undernutrition was much more severe among livestock-farming populations (pastoralists) than among crop-farming populations (agriculturalists).

Body mass index (BMI). Body mass index is a variant of weight-for-height. BMI is calculated as weight in kilograms divided by the square of height in meters. BMI is used widely as a measure of undernutrition (or overnutrition) among adults: it is easy to calculate (there are many BMI calculators online) and the interpretation of BMI is extremely simple. According to the FAO (1996b), a BMI below 18.5 is regarded as lower than normal and thus indicative of undernutrition. A person who is 6 feet tall and has a BMI of 18.5 would weigh about 135 pounds. In the United States, the National Institutes of Health (NIH) have set the ideal ranges for BMI at 21 to 23 for women and 22 to 24 for men. A 2012 study of health and nutrition in Asia reported that 36 percent of adult women in India had BMIs of less than 18.5; for China the figure was 9 percent (OECD 2012:47).

Low Weight-for-Age, or Underweight

Low weight-for-age is a symptom of either past or present undernutrition. Individuals with low weight-for-age are referred to as *underweight.* Low weight-for-age is a composite measure—it might reflect low weight-for-height, or low height-for-age, or both. For example Pelletier and colleagues (1993) found that 45–83 percent of malnutrition related to deaths among children occurred to children in the mild to moderate range (60–80 percent of the median—a fuller explanation follows). This implies that policymakers should not focus solely on severely undernourished children.

A special case of low weight-for-age is *low birthweight.* Low birthweight is a strong indicator of health problems in the early weeks and months of life, and is caused by malnutrition in the mother during pregnancy.

Fat Composition of the Body: Mid-Upper Arm Circumference

The human body stores excess calories as fat. In periods when calorie intake exceeds requirements, fat is added, and in periods when calorie intake is deficient, fat is depleted. No single part of the body represents the fat content of the whole body. Even a careful calculation of total body density (by weighing people and then comparing their weights to the weight of the water they displace when submerged in a tank) may not estimate accurately the percentage of the entire body that is fat. Nevertheless, the mid-upper arm is considered to be fairly representative of the body as a whole and is used as an indicator of nutritional status. It has the great advantage of being easy to measure: surveyors can be trained quite quickly to take measurements of individuals using a tape measure with three colored areas (green for a "healthy" upper arm, yellow for a "warning" level, and red indicating an upper-arm circumference in the "danger" range).

As developed by Shakir (1975) the "reference standard" for a child ages one to five years is 16.5 centimeters. A circumference of greater than 14.0 centimeters (85 percent of standard) is considered normal. A circumference of 12.5–14.0 centimeters (76–85 percent of standard) is classed as undernutrition. A circumference of less than 12.5 centimeters (less than 76 percent of standard) is classed as severe undernutrition.

The system is highly accurate for severe cases of undernutrition, and moderately accurate for mild cases. Nevertheless, because of its simplicity and because it works on preschoolers without age data, it has become an important screening tool. As Cogill writes:

Mid-upper arm circumference (MUAC) is relatively easy to measure and a good predictor of immediate risk of death. It is used for rapid screening of acute malnutrition from the 6–59 month age range (MUAC overestimates rates of malnutrition in the 6–12 month age group). MUAC can be used for screening in emergency situations but is not typically used for evaluation purposes. MUAC is recommended for assessing acute adult undernutrition and for estimating prevalence of undernutrition at the population level. (2003:12)

Nature vs. Nurture, or Heredity vs. Environment

Of course, nutrition is not the only determinant of body size. We observe differences from country to country, or ethnic group to ethnic group. For example, a 1967 study of body weights in the United States and seven Latin American countries showed that boys in all eight countries started life with similar average weights, but that there was considerable variation among countries in average adult weights, with US adults being heavier than adults in the Latin American countries by as much as 20 kilograms (44 pounds) (White House 1967). Foster's unpublished 1981 study of the Indian village of Bagbana shows that median adult height in that village was about the same as the height of a person in the shortest 5 percent of Americans. Even more striking, the average weight of a seventy-year-old woman in Bagbana was about half the average weight of her counterpart in the United States. Are Indian women underweight? Are US women overweight? Are these weight and height differences attributable to nutrition?

Some ethnic groups have reputations as being unusually small or unusually large. Weiner (1977:419–420) reports a number of studies indicating that protein composition of a group's diet may explain size. The meat-eating Sikhs of northern India are noticeably larger than the vegetarian Madrassi of southern India. In Kenya, the farming Kikuyu tribe live on cereals, tubers, and legumes. The Masai tribe—also in Kenya—are nomadic cowherds. Their diet includes meat and milk; in addition, Masai get high-protein nutrition from blood drained from living cattle. On average, Masai men are 7.5 centimeters (3 inches) taller and 10 kilograms (22 pounds) heavier than Kikuyu men.

Although studies of twins show that "heritability of height" is about 0.9 (out of a maximum of 1.0). Heritability of 0.9 means that 90 percent of the differences in height among individuals in a sample can be explained by genetics. Bowles and Gintis (2002) help put this number into perspective:

It is sometimes mistakenly supposed that if the heritability of a trait is substantial, then the trait cannot be affected much by changing the environment. The fallacy of this view is dramatized by the case of stature. The heritability of height estimated from U.S. twin samples is substantial (about 0.90 . . .). Moreover there are significant height differences among the peoples of the world: Dinka men in the Sudan average 5 feet and 11 inches—a bit taller than

Norwegian and U.S. military servicemen and a whopping 8 inches taller than the Hadza hunter-gatherers in Southern Africa. . . . But the fact that Norwegian recruits in 1761 were shorter than today's Hadza shows that even quite heritable traits are sensitive to environments. What can be concluded from a finding that a small fraction of the variance of a trait is due to environmental variance is that policies to alter the trait through changed environments will require non-standard environments that differ from the environmental variance on which the estimates are based. (2002:13)

Stephenson, Latham, and Jansen compared growth data from US children, privileged African children, and underprivileged African children and concluded that ethnic differences were less important than other factors as determinants of growth: "Poverty, poor food intakes, infectious and parasitic diseases, and other environmental factors combine to prevent children from realizing their growth potential" (1983:53). There are of course genetic influences that lead to differences of body size, and especially of stature, but it seems that in prepubescent children, heredity is a much less significant cause of below-average growth than are other factors

The contributions of nature and nurture can be understood most easily by considering a person's height. Nature (or genetics, or heredity) determines the person's maximum potential height; nurture (or environment, and to a considerable extent nutrition) determines the degree to which the person attains the maximum potential height. So if we had two groups—one that had been well nourished during childhood and one that had been poorly nourished during childhood—we very likely could find some individual in the poorly nourished group who was taller than some individual in the well-nourished group. The taller person in this example had a greater genetic height potential but didn't fully reach it, while the shorter person had a lesser genetic height potential and did fully reach it. But if we were to measure *average* heights in the two groups, the average for the well-nourished group would be higher: though the two groups, on average, may have had about the same height potential, the well-nourished group, on average, would have achieved more of that potential. The fact that environmental influences are major determinants of the average body-size characteristics of a population provides the basis for anthropometric measurement of malnutrition.

Anthropometric Assessment of Nutritional Status

As discussed previously, human physical growth and development are responsive to variations in calorie and protein intakes. Because of this, measurements of the human body, when compared to a reference standard, provide clues as to protein and calorie nutrition. This is especially true during youth, when growth is so rapid, but to some extent is also true during adulthood, when various dimensions change gradually with aging. Thus anthropometry can be used to suggest the protein and calorie nutritional status of adults as well as children.

An anthropometric assessment of an individual's nutrition status has three steps: (1) take measurements of the individual; (2) compare that individual to a "reference group"—the measurements of other individuals of the same age, sex, and ethnic group, for example; and (3) make a determination of nutritional status based on that comparison.

How Is Anthropometry Used?

As noted, nutrition is not the only influence on bodily growth and development. Growth and development can also be affected by such variables as genetic disposition, health, hormonal abnormalities, or deficiencies in micronutrients (e.g., zinc deficiency is associated with poor growth). Because anthropometry does not provide particularly useful clues as to dietary deficiencies (micronutrient shortages), it is not normally used to measure them. Nevertheless, because nutritional status is by far the most common variable influencing bodily growth and development, and because deficiencies in calories and protein are by far the most important causes of subnormal growth and development in the third world, anthropometry is generally assumed to provide strong clues as to protein and calorie nutrition.

Despite substantial genetic variation in height and weight within any population, the growth trajectories of infants and very young children are much more uniform than those of older children. Therefore, anthropometric measurements can be particularly accurate in identifying nutritional problems at very early ages.

In developed countries, anthropometry is used most often as a measure of overnutrition, which is the most common nutritional problem among high-income people. Adults who are trying to keep their weight down are using the anthropometric measure weight-for-height as a reference standard, although they seldom think of their activities in such technical terms.

Since 1966, when the World Health Organization published a monograph by D. B. Jelliffe titled *The Assessment of the Nutritional Status of the Community,* which provided a set of standardized measurements, anthropometry has become the most widely used tool in nutritional assessment. The most common measures used for anthropometric assessment of nutritional status are height, weight, and arm circumference. They are usually used in conjunction with sex and age (as in weight-for-age or height-for-age) and sometimes in combination with each other (as in weight-for-height).

Low cost and ease of data collection combine to make anthropometric assessment such a widely used way to measure undernutrition. Training time for field surveyors is minimal. The measurements are relatively easy to take, and the tools required are simple to use: scales, tape measures, measuring boards, and skin-fold calipers. Intelligent amateurs can be trained in a matter of days to take accurate measurements. By contrast, training technicians to recognize and diagnose undernutrition from clinical symptoms can take weeks or months.

From the point of view of accuracy, age data may be the biggest problem in using anthropometry. Adults in developing countries often have only a vague idea of how old they are, and illiterate mothers sometimes have difficulty telling the age of their children. In some circumstances, where there are age cutoffs for qualifying for assistance programs, parents may deliberately lie about their children's ages in order to get the children into the program.

Capital requirements for anthropometry are minimal. Compared to the laboratory apparatus involved in biochemical analysis, anthropometric tools are inexpensive. And anthropometry measures the results of nutrition (the size and shape of the body) rather than nutritional inputs (as in dietary intake). Because of its quantitative nature, anthropometry can be used to judge varying degrees of undernutrition—not just its presence or absence. And by using a mix of anthropometric indexes, researchers can make judgments about a nutritional disorder (protein or caloric) as well as the time dimension of the disorder (past or present).

Reference Groups

A person's size can only be evaluated by comparing it to the sizes of other people (the *reference population*). These comparisons lead to statements such as "Tommy is shorter than average," meaning that Tommy is shorter than the average person in the reference population. Or we might say, "Adele is in the 95th percentile of height," meaning that 95 percent of people in the reference population are shorter than Adele.

The purpose of a reference population is to provide a standard against which the growth and maturation of particular individuals can be judged. By observing how much one person deviates from others of a similar status (age and sex, for example), we can draw inferences about the subject's nutritional status.

Similarly, whenever you try to guess someone's age, you use the person's body size and configuration (among other clues). That is, your life experience teaches you what to expect in the way of variations in height and weight as people grow and develop, and from this (and other clues, such as amount of gray hair and wrinkled skin) you deduce age.

In setting up a reference population, it is important to control for as many variables as possible that might influence the observed variables. For example, if an individual is much shorter than the reference group, we don't learn much if the individual is four years old and the reference group is composed of teenagers. Therefore, reference groups are chosen so that we can compare persons of approximately the same age and of the same sex.

The curves in Figure 4.1 show how the reference population can be described. The top part of the figure shows the distribution of height (length) among girls age three years and younger. The bottom part of the figure shows the weight-for-age of the same reference group. A twenty-four-month-old girl who weighs 12 kilograms is at the 50th percentile (in other words, 12 kilograms

**Figure 4.1 Height-for-Age and Weight-for-Age Percentiles
for Girls Age 0–36 Months, United States, 2000**

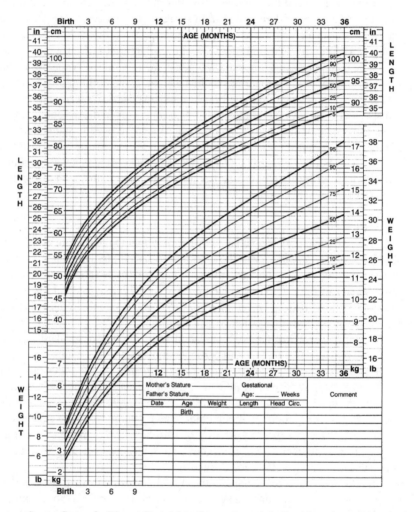

Source: Centers for Disease Control, http://www.cdc.gov/nchs/data/nhanes/growthcharts/set1 clinical/cj411018.pdf.

is the median weight for girls this age). A twenty-four-month-old girl who weighs 10.2 kilograms is at the 5th percentile, meaning that about 95 percent of girls in the reference population weigh more than 10.2 kilograms. A similar set of curves can plot weight against height and serves as a description of the reference population for the measure weight-for-height.

As noted, there may be systematic genetic differences among people of different ethnic backgrounds. Where those differences are substantial, reference populations for different ethnicities or countries-of-origin may be necessary.

Classification System for Identifying Undernutrition

Choosing a classification system for undernutrition involves selecting an appropriate anthropometric measure or measures in conjunction with an appropriate set of criteria (deviations from the reference standard) for identifying undernutrition, or various levels of it. If we have measured the body-size characteristics of the individual, and know the body-size characteristics of the reference population, what can we conclude about nutrition by comparing the individual to the reference group? When is the individual's height or weight so low that it indicates undernutrition? No matter which system is chosen, the aim is to identify those most in need of help, either because they are undernourished or because they are in danger of becoming so.

Table 4.1 shows five commonly used classification systems. The first three can be used with any measure (height-for-age, weight-for-age, or weight-for-height). The whole point of using a reference population is to decide, roughly, whether an individual's height or weight is abnormally low for that

Table 4.1 Anthropometric Classification Systems for Comparing Individuals to Reference Groups

Classification System	Range	Malnutrition Category
World Health Organization	Z-score of –1 to –2	Mild
	Z-score of –2 to –3	Moderate
	Z-score lower than –3	Severe
"Road to Health" (RTH)	Greater than 80% of median	Normal
	60–80% of median	Mild-to-moderate
	Less than 60% of median	Severe
Gómez	Greater than 90% of median	Normal
	75–90% of median	Mild
	60–75% of median	Moderate
	Less than 60% of median	Severe
Body mass index (BMI)	Greater than 18.5	Normal
	17–18.5	Grade I
	16–17	Grade II
	Less than 16	Grade III
Mid-upper arm circumference (MUAC)	Less than 18.5 centimeters	Moderate
	Less than 16 centimeters	Severe

Source: Cogill 2003:42, 72–73.

group. If an individual's height or weight is below a certain amount (referred to as a *cutoff point*), then he or she may be presumed to have a nutritional problem. The three most commonly proposed candidates for cutoff points are each based on deviation from the *median score*. "Median" means that half the reference population is larger and half is smaller. Thus, if the median weight of a reference population is 90 pounds, then half the people in that group weigh more than 90 pounds, and half weigh less. The three candidates for cutoff points are percentile, percentage of the median, and standard deviation unit. For the purposes of explanation, we use weight as the variable being measured and compared to the reference population. The terms can also be applied to any other variable, such as height.

Percentile indicates the percentage of the reference population who weigh less than the individual. Thus, if the individual's weight is at the 30th percentile, this indicates that 30 percent of the reference population weighs less than the individual. The 50th percentile is the same as the median. In discussing the reference-groups chart in Figure 4.1, we noted that a twenty-four-month-old girl who weighs 10.2 kilograms is at the 5th percentile.

We calculate percentage of the median by dividing the individual's weight by the median weight for the reference population. The 10.2-kilogram girl in our example is at 85 percent of the median weight, since median weight for girls this age is 12 kilograms.

Standard deviation unit, or "Z-score," is a statistical measure of dispersion away from the mean. For example, a weight measurement that is two standard deviation units below the mean will be approximately at the 2nd percentile, meaning that only 2 percent of the reference population will weigh less than this amount. For measures of height and weight, experience shows that two standard deviations below the mean is usually fairly close to 75 percent of the median. Experience also shows that the average weight (and height) of population groups is usually quite close to the median (Krick 1988:326–328). Our reference chart (Figure 4.1) does not tell us the standard deviation of the sample, but an estimate allows us to calculate a Z-score of -1.65 for the 10.2-kilogram girl we have been using as an example. This means that a twenty-four-month-old girl weighing 10.2 kilograms is 1.65 standard deviations below the mean weight for girls of this age. (Recall that the girl in our example was at the 5th percentile of weight for age. In a standard bell-shaped curve such as that shown in Figure 3.1 (on page 36), about 5 percent of the area under the curve is to the left of the line drawn at 1.65 standard deviations below the mean.)

As mentioned, these three categorizations can be used for any anthropometric measure. Waterlow and colleagues (1977) suggest that a more complete picture of a person's nutritional status can be obtained by combining weight-for-height (which identifies present undernutrition) and height-for-age (which identifies past undernutrition). The beauty of this system is that it is likely to correctly identify individuals who are presently at risk for undernutrition, and to eliminate from consideration those who merely have been undernourished in the past.

The remaining two categorizations shown in Table 4.1 are body mass index and mid-upper arm circumference. Those measures have their own generally accepted standards for categorizing nutritional status of the individual.

The FAO's 2001 *State of Food Insecurity in the World* report contains a lengthy explanation of the use of anthropometric measurements, and includes some examples of how anthropometry has helped guide policymakers.

Measuring Nutritional Status of Large Groups

In addition to determining the nutritional status of individuals, policymakers also need to learn about the nutritional status of large groups. They need to know the extent of undernutrition on a continent or subcontinent, in a country, in a state or region of a country, or among demographic or ethnic groups.

Drawing Inferences from a Sample

If we can measure the nutritional status of a number of representative individuals in a country or in a group, we can draw inferences about the extent of malnutrition in the whole group. The science of statistics deals with the problem of how to determine the characteristics of an entire population (in this case, the extent of malnutrition in a country or among a group) by observing the characteristics of a sample from that group. So if we have anthropometric evidence categorizing, say, 11,000 children under the age of five years in Nigeria that tells us that 34 percent of these children are undernourished, this might allow us to deduce that 34 percent of all children in Nigeria are undernourished.

Mortality or Disease Rates

A second way of drawing inferences about the incidence of malnutrition in a country or other large group is to examine aggregate data about effects of malnutrition and to draw inferences from those data. For instance, low birth weights or high infant mortality rates in a country or region are assumed to indicate high rates of undernutrition. Aggregate data such as these can provide a good initial approximation of where substantial numbers of undernourished people are likely to be found. Because undernutrition and poor health often occur together, aggregate data on morbidity can also provide indirect measures of the incidence of undernutrition in a country or region.

For example, India has conducted its National Family Health Survey in four time periods dating back to 1992–1993 (http://rchiips.org/nfhs). The national rate of tuberculosis was 467 per 100,000 individuals in the 1992–1993 survey and had fallen slightly to 445 per 100,000 in the 2005–2006 survey. If this were the only information available on which to base a judgment on undernutrition, it would lead us to conclude that only slight progress had been made over this thirteen-year period. Or we can compare disease incidence across geographical areas. The percentage of under-age-five children with anemia is 38.2 in the Indian state of Goa, but 73.9 in Uttar Pradesh. If this were the only factual basis, we would likely conclude that undernutrition is much more severe in Uttar Pradesh than in Goa.

As we will see in the next chapter, high infant and child mortality rates, or high morbidity rates, are suggestive of high rates of undernutrition in a population, but these variables do not measure nutritional status directly. Rather, undernutrition is inferred from the nonnutritional aggregate data. As the preceding examples from the Indian survey suggest, factors other than nutrition (notably access to healthcare) will influence these indirect measures, so they are imprecise measures of undernutrition.

Food Balance Sheets or Food Availability Measures

Another indirect approach to identifying regions or countries with nutritional problems is to look at aggregate nutrient intake or average per person nutrient intake. These data are available on a country-by-country basis in food balance sheets published annually by the FAO. The food balance sheet shows sources and uses of over a hundred separate food items on an annual basis. Listed sources of food include beginning stocks, production, and imports; uses include ending stocks, exports, animal feed, and human consumption. The term *balance sheet* refers to the fact that total supply of each food item equals the total use: sources and uses are in balance. A condensed balance sheet for India in 2011 is shown in Table 4.2. This version aggregates many individual food items into groups, and also aggregates several sources and uses.

Once human consumption is estimated for every food commodity in a country, the food consumed can be converted into calorie and nutrient measurements, and per capita consumption figures can then be derived. If a country's per capita consumption turns out to be below amounts recommended by nutritionists, we have good cause to assume that a substantial block of its population is undernourished.

Measures derived from food balance sheets—in particular, calories per capita per day—have become perhaps the most widely used measures of malnutrition. The big advantage of such measures is that they are readily available from the FAO for almost every country for a number of years or time periods (see FAOSTAT food balance sheets).

However, the measures are not free of problems. We have emphasized that calories are not the sole nutrient of concern in identifying malnutrition. In addition, as noted in Chapter 3, there is no single level of nutrient requirement that applies to all people. And if we are looking at national data (for a population that includes infants, children, and adults), we see an especially wide variation in nutritional requirements. In addition, the information on food avail-

Table 4.2 Food Balance Sheet for India, 2011

	Production (thous. tons)	Stock Variations (thous. tons)	Imports Exports (thous. tons)	Domestic Supply Quantity (thous. tons)	Feed, Seed, and Nonfood Uses (thous. tons)	Food (thous. tons)	Food Supply (kilograms, per Capita per Day)	Food Supply (kilocalories per Capita per Day)	Protein Supply (grams per Capita per Day)	Fat Supply (grams per Capita per Day)
Grand total								2,459	60.1	51.8
Plant products								2,232	48	36.7
Animal products								228	12.1	15.1
Cereals, excluding beer	235,279	−9,629	−10,112	215,538	18,115	185,770	152.1	1,394		
Starchy roots	51,462	0	−285	51,179	3,048	39,207	32.1	62		
Sugar and sweeteners	31,773	481	−2,901	29,353	2,470	26,883	22	214		
Pulses	17,647	0	3,031	20,677	2,634	17,325	14.2	135		
Tree nuts	1,189	0	501	1,690	0	1,673	1.4	8		
Oil crops	52,028	−708	−1,409	49,911	40,146	7,829	6.4	35		
Vegetables	107,376	0	−2,202	105,174	0	98,658	80.8	56		
Fruits, excluding wine	73,912	24	−226	73,712	242	62,905	51.5	66		
Meat	6,228	0	−1,065	5,163	9	5,156	4.2	17		
Eggs	3,490	0	−66	3,425	152	2,924	2.4	9		
Milk, excluding butter	123,400	0	219	123,619	21,013	98,160	80.4	124		
Fish, seafood	8,870	0	−987	7,882	681	7,201	5.9	11		

Source: FAOSTAT.

ability shows us only the average nutrient intake. Some people in the country or region consume less than the average, and some consume more. So even if average caloric intake is greater than average caloric requirement, a country can still suffer significant undernutrition. Therefore, comparing caloric intake to caloric requirement does not always give an accurate view of the extent of undernutrition. For example, the FAO (in their data-rich FAOSTAT website) reports that during the 1990–1992 period, India and Senegal had virtually the same calories available per person per day (2,310 in India, 2,320 in Senegal). However, anthropometric data for the two countries in the late 1980s found that the percentage of children who were underweight was 63.9 percent in India, but only 21.6 percent in Senegal.

Aggregate food intake measures can also be used to estimate the percentage of a population who are undernourished. The FAO's *Sixth World Food Survey* (1996b) uses the following method: average caloric intake per capita is calculated from food balance sheets, and an estimate of the statistical variance of caloric intake per capita is derived from studies of individuals. These two statistics (average and variance) give an estimate of the distribution of food intake—for example, what percentage of the population has an intake below 2,000 calories per day, what percentage has an intake below 2,500 calories, and so on. Thus, once a minimum food requirement has been identified for the population, we know what percentage of the population is undernourished. Minimum food requirements are identified for different age and sex classes (e.g., children under ten, males over ten). Minimum requirements are calculated in two ways. First, we can determine the number of calories that would give a person of average height a minimally healthy weight. A minimally healthy weight is determined as a BMI of 18.5 (see prior discussion of body mass index). A second method is to determine the *basal metabolic rate* (BMR) for the population. The BMR shows the number of calories needed for survival when the body is at rest. The minimal food requirement is calculated by multiplying the BMR by a constant (e.g., 1.56 was the constant used in the *Sixth World Food Survey*).

An innovative approach to measuring undernutrition is described in Box 4.3.

Box 4.3 Using People's Food Choices to Make Inferences About Their Nutritional Status

A paper by economists Robert Jensen and Nolan Miller (2010) proposes an innovative way to "measure" undernutrition: measure the percentage of calories in a person's diet that come from the "staple" food.

People eat for two reasons: they eat to survive, and they eat for pleasure. A person who is severely undernourished (facing starvation) will choose a diet that depends heavily on the cheapest source of calories ("staple foods" such as rice, maize, potatoes, plantains). As a person becomes better nourished, and less concerned with short-term undernutrition, the person will begin increasingly to eat for pleasure and will replace the cheap form of calories with more expensive (but presumably better-tasting) sources of calories.

Jensen and Miller provide an example for a person in China. Rice is the cheapest common source of calories (the staple). Rice, however, is a poor source of protein. They calculate the minimum-cost diet for a person to get adequate calories and adequate intake of all essential proteins. To calculate "adequacy" they use formulas such as those presented in Box 3.2. For an active man 67 inches tall, weighing 121 pounds, the daily calorie requirement is 2,554. The minimum-cost diet to provide this level of calories (and also to provide adequate protein) is 586 grams of rice, 134 grams of bean curd, and 11.4 grams of cooking oil. With this minimum-cost diet, 84 percent of the calories come from rice.

Jensen and Miller argue that by looking at the percentage of calories that come from rice, we can make inferences about the individual's nutritional status. An undernourished individual will be choosing a diet quite close to the minimum-cost diet, and will have a percentage of calories from rice very close to the 84 percent in that diet. But as the person becomes better and better nourished, and the person begins to eat more for pleasure rather than for survival, that percentage will fall.

According to the paper, the results of this approach to measuring undernutrition can be quite different from the typical approach of measuring the percentage of a population that falls below an average calorie requirement. For a sample of households in China in 2000, 67 percent of households were undernourished using the typical calorie-count approach, but only 32 percent were undernourished using the "calories from staple" approach.

5

Why Does It Matter?

Throughout this book we use the term *undernutrition* to refer to a physical condition, and we reserve the term *hunger* to refer to the subjective feeling that comes from not having enough food. But undernutrition does not just make a person feel hungry; it stunts their growth (as we saw in the previous chapter), makes them more susceptible to disease, reduces their capacity to do physical work, and interferes with their intellectual growth and achievements. In all these ways, it reduces the person's ability to be economically productive, and in the aggregate—when undernutrition is widespread in a country—it can reduce the pace of economic growth.

Undernutrition and Mortality Risk Among Adults

The connection between nutrition and health is widely and intuitively understood. Hundreds of Internet websites include BMI calculators that can tell you whether your weight is outside the ideal range for your height (see Chapter 4 for discussion of body mass index). Economic historians (see Fogel 2004 for a comprehensive review) have confirmed the relationship. Costa and Steckel (1997) used medical records of US Civil War veterans to investigate their relative risks of dying during the twenty-five years following their initial evaluations (veterans varied in age from forty-seven to sixty-four at their initial evaluations). Their results track out a U-shaped curve. The veterans with BMIs in the mid-20s had the lowest risk of dying (bottom of the curve). Those with BMIs less than 20 (underweight) and those with BMIs greater than 30 (obese) were about 50 percent more likely to die than the mid-20 group. (For more on the U-shaped relationship between BMI and mortality-risk, see Box 5.1.)

The nutrition-health link has been studied in more detail by Norwegian epidemiologist Hans Waaler. He mapped the heights and weights of soldiers in the Norwegian army and discovered clear relationships between body shape and risk of dying. The general shape of a Waaler surface is a "basin," as shown

---

Box 5.1 BMI and Mortality

The U-shaped relationship between mortality risk and body mass index has been confirmed in modern research. A couple of points emerge from these studies:

• Typically, the lowest-mortality BMI is a little higher than the normal range. Costa and Steckel (1995) reproduce a curve for Norwegian males that reaches the lowest mortality at BMI of 25—the cutoff point between normal and overweight. A 2010 study by de Gonzalez and colleagues shows the lowest-mortality BMI is above 25 for men, and between 22.5 and 25 for women. (The standard categories for BMI are underweight, less than 18.5; normal, 18.5 to 25; overweight, 25–30; and obese, above 30.)

• Being too thin can raise mortality risk as much as being too fat. For example, a Norwegian male at the low end of the normal BMI has the same mortality risk as one at the low end of the obese BMI range.

A review article in the journal Nature (Hughes 2013) points out that the U-shaped relationship between mortality and BMI becomes more pronounced as age advances. Again it is worth noting how sharply mortality increases as BMI moves lower than the optimal BMI. A seventy-year-old woman who is 5 feet 6 inches tall and weighs 118 lbs (BMI = 18.1, at the low end of the normal range) has the same mortality risk as a seventy-year-old woman who is 5 feet 6 inches tall and weighs 250 lbs (BMI = 40, in the morbidly obese range).

For people under the age of forty, the mortality risk associated with low BMI is relatively small.

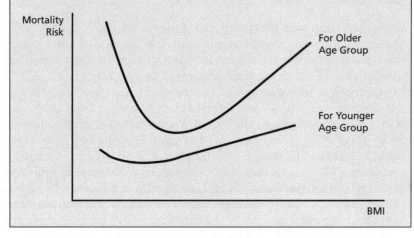

---

in Figure 5.1. The low point (the darkest spot) shows the height-weight combinations at which mortality risk is the lowest. As we move to individuals of lower heights and weights (reflecting a history of undernutrition, on the sides

Figure 5.1 Waaler Surface and Cross-Sections

a. Waaler Surface

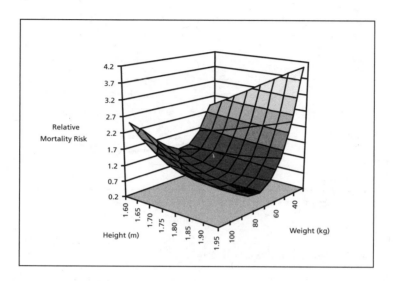

b. Mortality Risks of Men Standing 1.7 m Tall

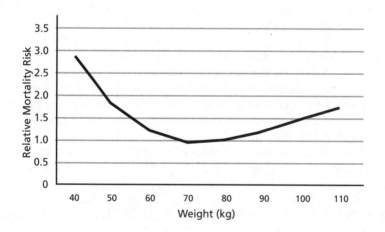

(continues)

Figure 5.1 continued

c. Mortality Risks of Men Weighing 70 kg

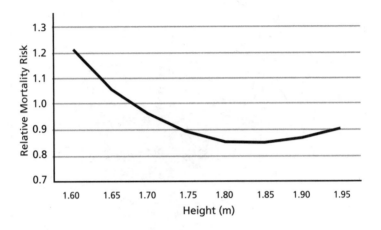

Source: Derived from data in Fogel 2004.

of the basin), the mortality risk increases. (Relative mortality risk measures the risk of dying for men of a particular height and weight compared to the average for the entire population. For purposes of illustration, suppose that 15 percent of all men in a group die between the ages of fifty and sixty-four. Men who are 1.85 meters tall and weigh 80 kilograms have a relative mortality risk of 0.69; this means that their probability of dying between ages fifty and sixty-four is 15 × 0.69 = 10.35 percent. Men who are 1.6 meters tall and weigh 50 kilograms have a relative mortality risk of 1.62; their probability of dying between ages fifty and sixty-four is 15 × 1.62 = 24.30 percent, compared to 15 percent for all men in the age group—15 percent is an assumed number for the purpose of this illustration.)

If we look at a cross-section of the Waaler surface for individuals of a particular height—say, all men standing 1.7 meters tall—we see a picture that looks very much like the Costa-Steckel result (see Figure 5.1b; since this is a cross-section of the Waaler surface at a specific height, everyone in this sample is the same height; therefore, those with low weight also have low BMIs, and those with high weight have high BMIs). This kind of result is the basis for a doctor advising a patient to modify their diet in order to achieve a more healthy weight.

A more surprising result from the Waaler surface is that mortality risk also varies in a predictable way with height. If we look at a cross-section of the Waaler surface for individuals of a particular weight—say, all men weighing

70 kilograms—we see generally that mortality risk declines as height increases (see Figure 5.1c). This indicates that mortality risk is influenced not only by current nutritional status (weight as an adult) but also by nutritional status during the developmental years of childhood, which is an important determinant of adult height. (At the top heights in Figure 5.1c, we find individuals who are currently undernourished and therefore have low weight considering how tall they are; this accounts for the upturn in the mortality risk among the tallest people in this weight category.) (See Box 5.2 for a warning about correlation and causation.)

Box 5.2 Correlation Is Not Causation

In this chapter we show a *correlation* between mortality risk and measures of undernutrition (height, weight, BMI), and we (implicitly) invite the reader to infer that undernutrition *causes* increased risk of death. Here, and throughout the book, we often show graphs and tables showing correlations.

A word of warning is in order: generally speaking, discovery of a correlation does not demonstrate anything about the underlying cause. A website (http://www.tylervigen.com/spurious-correlations) and a related book (Vigen 2015) illustrate a number of clearly ridiculous (or "spurious") correlations. For example, suicides by hanging in the United States are almost perfectly correlated with federal spending on space and science; but no one would argue that we could reduce suicide by cutting the space budget.

Sometimes spurious correlations are found in variables following similar long-term trends: life expectancy in the United States increased over the twentieth century, and so did automobile ownership, so those two variables are positively correlated. But no one would regard the correlation as evidence that automobile ownership is a healthcare treatment.

Sometimes there is a causative relationship between two variables, but the causation runs "in the opposite direction." Is it possible that mortality risk is correlated with undernutrition of individuals because when individuals are threatened by death they divert resources away from food consumption and toward medical care?

Sometimes there is a third factor influencing both of the variables that are correlated. For example, possibly lack of education results in undernutrition, and lack of education results in poor healthcare. This would account for a correlation between undernutrition and mortality risk; but the policy implication would be quite different—reduce mortality risk by improving education, not by fighting undernutrition.

Economists use theory to tease out the direction of causality. The theory suggests that a correlation must exist between the causative variable and the outcome. A failed empirical search for that correlation can prove that the theory is wrong; but a successful search only indicates that the data are consistent with the theory—but perhaps are also consistent with other competing theories.

In addition, econometricians have developed statistical techniques to investigate causality and the existence of spurious correlations. See Box 5.4 for an example.

Box 5.3 The "Hunger Winter"

Scientists like controlled experiments. If a scientist wants to measure the impact of a new drug, he or she will split a group of patients into two subgroups and give members of one subgroup the new drug and members of the other subgroup a placebo. But nutritionists who want to learn about the impacts of starvation cannot deliberately starve one subgroup to compare to the normally fed subgroup.

The starvation conditions that existed in the Netherlands during World War II provided scientists with a kind of controlled experiment. At the end of the war, the Nazi-occupied Netherlands experienced severe food shortages (the hongerwinter, or "hunger winter"); average food intake was about 1,000 calories per person per day, with some people surviving on as few as 400–800 calories per day. The famine, which began in late 1944, was short-lived, ending abruptly with the Allied victories in May 1945. This situation, and the existence of precise birth records, created an unplanned "controlled experiment": children born, or who were in utero, during the famine, could be compared to children born before and after the famine.

The Dutch Famine Birth Cohort has generated a number of studies that identify the impacts of maternal undernutrition on unborn children. For example, children who were in utero during the hunger winter had a higher rate of infant mortality, but also had higher rates of cardiovascular disease and late-onset diabetes during adulthood.

(More information about the Dutch Famine Birth Cohort is available at http://www.dutchfamine.nl/index_files/study.htm and in the book *The Hunger Winter* by Henri van der Zee [1998]. A description of the research that has grown out of the hunger winter cohort can be found at http://ihome.ust.hk/~lbcaplan/dutchfamine.html and in the book *Famine and Human Development* by Zena Stein [1975]. Readers interested in an experiment in which humans [volunteers from a group of conscientious objectors during World War II] were deliberately starved can look up the starvation experiment of Ancel Keys at the University of Minnesota discussed later in this chapter.)

The link between adult height and mortality risk indicates that childhood undernutrition has repercussions throughout life. Such repercussions have been discovered in analyses of medical histories of children born during the "hunger winter" in the Netherlands during World War II (see Box 5.3).

Undernutrition and Disease

Undernutrition makes an individual more susceptible to disease. Sometimes this leads to death, explaining the mortality-undernutrition correlation described previously. But more often, the disease runs its course without resulting in death. Undernourishment weakens a person's immune system, making the person more likely to develop a disease in the first place, and less able to recover from the disease. Undernutrition weakens a person's muscles, including the heart and muscles that assist in breathing, making the person more susceptible to heart and lung diseases. Undernourished people have a lower capacity to fight dehydration, caused (for example) by diarrhea. As a result, undernourishment results in more frequent disease, longer and more serious bouts of a disease once present, and more complications arising from disease. This section relates some studies on this subject.

A group of adult males in Kolkata, India, were asked to self-report the incidence of disease over the previous month and over the previous four months (Chakraborty, Bose, and Bisai 2009). Respondents were divided into three "nutritional status" groups according to their mid-upper arm circumference (MUAC). The incidence of illness was 40.4 percent in the lowest MUAC group, 22.9 percent in the in the middle MUAC group, and 19.0 percent in the high MUAC group.

Correia and Waitzberg (2003) studied a random sample of 709 records of adult patients in twenty-five Brazilian hospitals. Of course, everyone in the sample was sick enough to require hospitalization. But the authors looked to see if the hospitalization records showed evidence of complications and whether the complications were correlated with nutritional status. (Nutritional status of patients in this study was determined using an evaluative process used by medical professionals called the Subjective Global Assessment of Nutritional Status. See Detsky et al. 1987 for details.) Overall the rate of complications was 16.8 percent among well-nourished patients and 27.0 percent among moderately and severely malnourished patients. (If we look only at severely malnourished patients, the figure is 42.8 percent.) As Table 5.1 shows, this correlation between nutritional status and complications held for infectious complications (such as infections of the lungs or urinary tract) and noninfectious complications (such as respiratory failure or cardiac arrest).

As this example indicates, there is ample evidence linking undernutrition to the incidence and severity of disease as well as to premature death. Analysts of health policy have introduced a concept called disability-adjusted life years

Table 5.1 Complications and Deaths Among Adult Hospital Patients in Brazil

Type of Complication	Incidence Among Patients with Normal Nutrition	Incidence Among Patients with Moderate or Severe Malnutrition
Infectious	10.1%	19.4%
Noninfectious	8.4%	20.5%
Death	4.7 %	12.4%
Average length of hospital stay	10.1 days	16.7 days

Source: Correia and Waitzberg 2003.

(DALYs), which measures total amount of healthy life lost, whether from premature mortality or from temporary or permanent disability. DALYs are the sum of years lost to premature death, and years lived with an illness or disability. The World Health Organization estimates that poor nutrition is responsible for 46 percent of DALYs lost to children (WHO 1996). However, this measure attributes to malnutrition any DALY lost to a disease or condition where malnutrition played a part. A malnourished person who dies or is disabled by measles, for example, contributes to the count of DALYs caused by malnutrition *and* to the count of DALYs caused by measles.

A recent study (Murray et al. 2013) attempts to end this double counting by using WHO data on the global burden of disease and attributing DALYs to single specific and nonoverlapping conditions. The results of this are shown in Table 5.2, where out of a total of 291 diseases and conditions, five are malnutrition conditions. The seriousness of undernutrition is illustrated by the fact that those five conditions (1.7 percent of the 291 reported) account for 3.4 percent of all DALYs lost. The table also illustrates the progress that has been made over the past decades—lost DALYs attributable to malnutrition dropped from 4.5 percent of the total to 3.4 percent of the total.

Box 5.4 illustrates how economists use sophisticated statistical techniques to explore the relationship between disease and undernutrition in children.

Undernutrition and Child Health

Undernutrition is an especially serious problem for infants and children because their immune systems are less fully developed than those of adults. They are therefore more susceptible to diseases than are adults. Undernourished children are especially susceptible because their bodies are already weakened.

Table 5.2 Disability-Adjusted Life Years Lost to Nutritional Deficiencies, 1990 and 2010

Cause	Disability-Adjusted Life Years Lost and Percentage Total from All Causes			
	1990		2010	
Protein-energy malnutrition	60,542,700	(2.4%)	34,874,500	(1.4%)
Iodine deficiency	3,243,100	(0.1%)	4,026,700	(0.2%)
Vitamin A deficiency	739,800	(0.01%)	806,400	(0.03%)
Iron-deficiency anemia	46,792,300	(1.9%)	45,338,200	(1.8%)
Other nutritional deficiencies	438,600	(0.02%)	294,700	(0.01%)
All nutritional deficiencies	111,786,500	(4.5%)	85,340,600	(3.4%)
All causes	2,502,601,200		2,490,384,900	

Source: Murray et al. 2013.

**Box 5.4 An Econometric Analysis of the Relationship
Between Disease and Undernutrition in Children**

Alok Bhargava (1996), an expert in the intersection of health and undernutrition, conducted a study of the relationship between disease and undernutrition among children using data from surveys of households.

One difficulty with using household surveys is that even if they are very large (say 10,000 people surveyed), only a small portion will include observations on children under age five (say 15 percent or 1,500), and only a small portion of those households will have had experience with a particular disease in the month preceding the survey (say 2 percent of the 1,500 households with children, or 30 households in the survey, have had a child with measles in the last month). Therefore, it is hard to conduct a statistical analysis of a single disease.

Bhargava proposed a measure of "morbidity" or disease burden that would be a simple count of the number of days a child had experienced any of a long list of symptoms—fever, upset stomach, headache, vomiting, and the like. The measure would be higher for children who had a disease for a longer time period (because each day with a symptom was counted), and would be higher for children with more severe illnesses (because each symptom was counted).

In Box 5.2 we noted that correlation can exist between two variables even when neither of the variables is causing the other; this can happen when a third "confounding" variable causes both of the other two. (Better education causing both better nutrition and better healthcare could explain why nutrition and mortality are correlated.) Use of multivariate regression allows us to take these confounding factors into account in the statistical analysis.

Bhargava's analysis of 312 Filipino children finds a (statistically significant) negative relationship between a child's weight (or BMI) and the child's morbidity, suggesting that children with poor nutrition get sick more often and have more severe bouts of disease.

A second problem in determining causality is the *direction* of causality. "Note, however, that the underlying causality can also run in the reverse direction, i.e., sicker children had lower BMI" (Bhargava 1996:59). This would especially be a problem if BMI were measured at the end of the disease-reporting period. A second dataset of 103 Kenyan children allowed Bhargava to investigate the relationship between BMI at the *beginning* of a period and morbidity during the period; he found results similar to those for the analysis of Filipino children. This implies that the direction of the causation is from undernutrition (first) to disease (second), not the other way around.

Increased Disease Incidence and Severity

Undernourished children are more likely to develop diseases, and suffer more serious bouts of diseases once present. Nandy and colleagues (2005) studied Indian children under the age of four years, dividing them into groups depending on anthropometric measures of undernutrition. The group of children who were undernourished (suffering from all three conditions of stunting, wasting, and underweight) had an incidence of diarrhea that was 72 percent higher than the incidence in the healthy group (suffering from none of the three conditions). The undernourished children had an incidence of acute respiratory infection that was 39 percent higher than the healthy children.

The severity of disease is also higher among undernourished children. The Nandy study found that the incidence of diarrhea was 72 percent higher in the undernourished group, but that incidence of severe diarrhea was 95 percent higher compared to the healthy group. Caulfield, Richard, and Black (2004a) studied the global burden of malaria among children under the age of five. They examined the underlying nutritional status of young children who had bouts of malaria serious enough to require a visit to the local clinic. Eight percent of clinical attacks of malaria were attributable to protein-energy malnutrition, 20 percent were attributable to zinc deficiency, and 20 percent to vitamin A deficiency.

As with the adults in the Brazil hospital study, undernourishment in children also leads to complications. Undernourished children in Africa who caught measles had a much higher chance (compared to well-nourished children) of subsequently developing pneumonia (Chandra 1980).

High Infant and Child Mortality Rates

Death is the most dramatic of undernutrition's adverse effects. As mentioned in Chapter 1, deaths from acute undernutrition—such as those that occur in famines—are not nearly as big a worldwide tragedy as are deaths in which chronic undernutrition weakens the ability of people to resist diseases. This form of fatal undernutrition is an especially large problem among children.

A few facts illustrate the seriousness of childhood mortality. The annual number of deaths worldwide is about 57 million people. Not surprisingly most of those people were old—over the age of sixty-five. That group accounted for 64 percent of the deaths but represents only about 9 percent of the population. But children under the age of five are also overrepresented in the deaths, accounting for about 12 percent of the deaths but representing only 9 percent of the population. (The story here is not quite as dramatic as in previous editions of the book: a worldwide effort to reduce child mortality—part of the Millennium Development Goals effort—reduced deaths in this age group from 12.7 million in 1990 to 6.3 million in 2013.)

The death rate is especially high for third world children. The World Health Organization has reported: "Children in sub-Saharan Africa are more than 15 times more likely to die before the age of five than children in developed regions" (WHO 2015a).

Childhood diseases, to which undernutrition contributes by weakening the immune system, are major killers in developing countries (Dever 1983). Intestinal disorders that lead to diarrhea are the leading killers of children in these

Table 5.3 Deaths Among Children Under Age Five Worldwide

Immediate Cause of Death	Percentage of Under-Five Deaths
Neonatal causes	36.9
Acute respiratory infections	19.1
Diarrheal diseases (post-neonatal)	16.6
Other diseases and injuries	12.5
Malaria	8.0
Measles	3.7
AIDS	3.0

Source: Katona and Katona-Apte 2008.

countries, but other diseases associated with malnutrition, such as pneumonia, influenza, bronchitis, whooping cough, and measles, are also deadly. The diseases causing death in young children and the relative importance of each cause are shown in Table 5.3.

The article from which Table 5.3's data are drawn also concludes, "More than half of these deaths [of children under age five] are associated with malnutrition" (Katona and Katona-Apte 2008:1582). That figure echoes an earlier WHO report: "Malnutrition has been found to underlie more than half of deaths among children in developing countries" (1997:13–14). Another study (Pelletier, Frongillo, and Habicht 1993), of fifty-three developing countries, came to a similar conclusion: 56 percent of child deaths are caused by weakening of the immune system resulting from undernutrition. In addition, this study found that 83 percent of nutrition-related child deaths are caused by mild to moderate malnutrition; only 17 percent are caused by severe malnutrition.

This finding—that most of the deaths caused by undernutrition are in the group of children who are mild-to-moderately undernourished—might lead the reader to think that if we want to reduce childhood deaths from undernutrition, we should focus on the mild-to-moderately undernourished group. That would be a mistake. Death predominates in the mild-to-moderately malnourished group because that group is so much larger than the severely malnourished group. There is abundant evidence that probability of death increases dramatically with the severity of undernutrition.

This is shown in Table 5.4. Caulfield and colleagues (2004b) looked at under-age-five deaths by proximate disease cause. They divided the children into four groups, based on weight-for-age. Children who were higher than the mean, or below the mean, but close enough to be within one standard deviation, were categorized as well nourished. (See discussion in Chapter 4 of Z-scores for a more detailed explanation of this type of measure.) The children with lower weight-for-age than the well-nourished group were further divided depending on how far below the mean they were. The least severely malnourished group (category I in Table 5.4) were children who were between one and two standard deviations below the mean. The most severely malnourished group (category III in the table) were more than three standard deviations below the mean. An intermediate group (category II) were between two and three standard deviations below the mean. (As Chapter 4 makes clear, category II children are in fact severely malnourished, and category III children might best be called very severely malnourished.)

The study then looked at the relative mortality rates for children suffering from these diseases. If 3 percent of the well-nourished children with a disease died, and 6 percent of the category I children with the same disease died, the relative mortality rate for category I would be 2 (because 6 percent is double 3 percent). With this in mind, we can see how mortality risk escalates as severity of undernutrition increases. For most diseases, category I mortality risk is about twice as high as the well-nourished group. But category II mortality risk is three to five times higher, and category III mortality risk is six to twelve times higher. As an illustration, if 3 out of 100 well-nourished children die of these four diseases, 26 percent of children in category III malnutrition die of the diseases (because 3 percent $\times$ 8.72 = 26.16 percent).

When discussing the most cost-effective ways of reducing the impacts of undernutrition worldwide, we should keep in mind the fact that many deaths can

Table 5.4 Mortality Risk Among Undernourished Children Compared to Well-Nourished Children

Cause	Mortality Risk		
	Category I (least severe undernutrition)	Category II	Category III (most severe undernutrition)
Diarrhea	2.32	5.39	12.50
Pneumonia	2.01	4.03	8.09
Malaria	2.12	4.48	9.49
Measles	1.73	3.01	5.72
All causes	2.06	4.24	8.72

Source: Caulfield et al. 2004b.

Notes: Nutritional status is measured by comparing the child's weight to the mean weight-for-age; well-nourished children are those above mean weight-for-age or less than one standard deviation below the mean. Category I is defined as one to two standard deviations below the mean, Category II as two to three standard deviations below the mean, and Category III as more than three standard deviations below the mean. The mortality risk numbers show the multiple of mortality risk for the group compared to well-nourished children; for example, a risk of 2.32 means that children in this group have a risk of mortality from the condition listed that is 2.32 times higher than the risk for children in the well-nourished group.

be avoided by relatively low-cost interventions that move children from the mild-to-moderate undernutrition category to the adequately nourished category.

Keilmann and McCord (1978) showed that infant mortality doubles with each 10 percent decline below 80 percent of the median weight-for-age. Looking at a sample of children in Punjab, India, collected by Galway and colleagues (1987), they found a 1 percent mortality rate in children who were well nourished (80 percent of median weight-for-age or higher), 5 percent mortality in children who were 70–79 percent of median, 6 percent mortality among children who were 60–69 percent of median, and 12 percent mortality in children who were less than 60 percent of median.

The risk of death from nutrition-related disease in the third world decreases dramatically after the second year of life. This is shown in Table 5.3, which lists neonatal conditions as by far the leading cause of death of young children (the term *neonatalal* refers to deaths in the days and weeks following birth). One study (de Zoysa et al. 1985) looked at deaths per year for the developing world as a whole and found about 22 per 1,000 children in the first year of life, about 20 per 1,000 in the second year, and about 6 per 1,000 in each of the third through fifth years.

When we compare developed and developing countries in terms of child mortality, the differences are startling. For example, in Table 5.5, compare the data for the developing countries with the highest rates of infant mortality (top four rows) to the rates for representative developed countries (bottom three rows). Again, these differences are strongly related to differences in nutrition.

Table 5.5 Neonatal, Infant, and Child Mortality, Selected Countries, 2013

	Percentage Who Die in First Month of Life	Percentage Who Die Before First Birthday	Percentage Who Die Before Fifth Birthday
Angola	4.7	10.2	16.7
Sierra Leone	4.4	10.7	16.1
Chad	4.0	8.0	14.8
Somalia	4.6	9.0	14.6
Nigeria	3.7	7.4	11.7
Afghanistan	3.6	7.0	9.7
India	2.9	4.1	5.3
China	0.8	1.1	1.3
Brazil	0.8	1.2	1.4
United States	0.4	0.6	0.7
Japan	0.1	0.2	0.3
Sweden	0.2	0.2	0.3

Source: UNICEF 2014.

Mothers' Nutrition, Breast-Feeding, and the Health of the Baby

Mothers who are undernourished during pregnancy are likely to give birth to babies with low birth weights. These babies start life malnourished and are significantly more likely to die in the first year of life; in fact, during the period shortly after birth, low-birth-weight babies die at a rate forty times that of normal babies (Samuels 1986; Overpeck, Hoffman, and Prager 1992). Low birth weight for an infant indicates that the infant was malnourished in the womb or that the mother was malnourished during her own infancy, childhood, adolescence, or pregnancy. The malnourishment is typically due to underconsumption of calories and protein; however, it can also result from underconsumption of micronutrients such as iron (Levinger 1995).

Even poor nutrition early in a girl's life can affect the health of the babies she bears as an adult. One study in Guatemala (Stein et al. 2003) followed the lives of girls who were given nutritional supplements during their early childhoods in the 1960s and 1970s. Some girls were given a high-protein, moderate-energy supplement, and others were given a low-energy supplement with no protein. The girls who received the more nutritious supplement grew up to be larger women, on average, and when they gave birth their babies were larger on average.

If the baby is breast-fed, the child's health is significantly improved. Breast milk contains all the nutrients a child needs during the first months of life. Breast milk also helps the baby fight infection. In developing countries, breast-feeding contributes to infant health in two indirect ways. First, breast-feeding provides the baby with a guaranteed food supply; the infant does not have to compete with other family members for scarce food. Second, breast-feeding ensures that the baby will have a clean food supply; babies who do not breast-feed are exposed to diseases caused by unsanitary food and water. According to one 2001 estimate, 1.5 million children in the developing world die because they are not breast-fed (UNICEF 2001: map 1, 68). Even women who are suffering from mild to moderate undernutrition are able to produce sufficient milk to feed their infants, although severe undernutrition, such as that resulting from a famine, does compromise a woman's ability to produce breast milk (Prentice, Goldberg, and Prentice 1994).

One physical effect of undernutrition has important implications for population growth. Undernourished women are less fecund, because they begin ovulation later in life, and because the resumption of ovulation after childbirth is postponed, relative to well-nourished women. The resumption of ovulation after childbirth can be further postponed by breast-feeding, which puts additional nutritional demands on the nursing mother.

The female sex hormone, estrogen, is produced from cholesterol, a fat (Pike and Brown 1984:42). The higher a woman's percentage of body fat, the more estrogen she is likely to produce. An undernourished girl is likely to produce less estrogen than a well-nourished girl of the same age; therefore, the well-nourished girl is likely to begin menstruation at a younger age. A study by Thomas and colleagues (2001) looks at the average age of menarche in various countries and finds the kind of pattern we would expect. Most of the countries with the youngest ages of menarche are relatively high-income countries (Italy at age 12.2 years, the United States at 12.8 years) and most of the countries with the oldest ages of menarche are poor countries (Bangladesh at 15.8 years, Senegal at 16.1 years, and Nepal at 16.2 years). But there are examples that seem to defy the pattern—Congo-Brazzaville at 12.0 years and South Korea at 13.9 years.

In addition to the benefits of breast-feeding for the baby, breast-feeding also postpones the recurrence of menstruation after childbirth. The same hormone (prolactin) that stimulates the production of breast milk also suppresses ovulation. In addition, the production of breast milk tends to use up the body's supply of fat, reducing estrogen production and impeding ovulation. The use of breast-feeding to postpone ovulatory cycles after childbirth is referred to as the lactational amenorrhea method of birth control. The method is at least 98 percent effective if three conditions are met: (1) the mother has not experienced the return of her menstrual periods; (2) the mother is fully or nearly fully breast-feeding; and (3) the baby is less than six months old. Studies in developing countries confirm the effectiveness of breast-feeding as a birth control method. In Chile, for example, according to one study, only 1 of 422 breast-feeding women became pregnant during the six months after childbirth; in Pakistan, there was 1 pregnancy among 391 women; in the Philippines, there were 2 pregnancies among 485 women. The experience in Pakistan and the Philippines showed 98–99 percent birth control effectiveness for a full year after childbirth among women meeting the first two of the preceding three conditions (Family Health International 1996). Another study estimates that breast-feeding is by far the most widely used contraceptive method in India—six times greater use than the birth control pill, four times greater use than sterilizations and intrauterine devices, and nearly two times greater use than condoms (Gupta and Rohide 1993).

Impacts of Undernutrition on Intellectual Development and Educational Attainment

The impact of undernutrition on a person's physical characteristics (weight, most obviously, but also, as we have seen, height, health, and mortality) may be intuitively obvious. But there is significant evidence that undernutrition also has an impact on intellectual capacity and development. That impact can be seen in the very short run (undernourished today so mentally confused or unable to concentrate today) and over a much longer time period (undernourished during childhood so mentally less able during adulthood). In this section, we briefly review some of the evidence on this.

Impact on Intellectual Development

Nutritionist Ancel Keys (Keys et al. 1950) wanted to study the impacts and treatment of severe undernutrition that was occurring during World War II. He sought out conscientious objectors who wanted to contribute to the war effort without violating their belief that fighting and killing was wrong. These conscientious objectors volunteered to be subjected to starvation-type diets (under the care of medical professionals). Keys found that male adults subjected to diets that led to measurable undernutrition experienced intellectual problems as the first symptom. (Later, as their undernutrition continued, the men suffered problems with physical dexterity.)

Since Keys's work, nutritionists have found, in a wide variety of settings, that poor nutrition has a negative impact on cognitive ability. The negative impact in the early years of life can have a negative impact on intellectual development (Grantham-McGregor, Fernald, and Sethuraman 1999a, 1999b). This more recent research has tended to focus on the potential effect of childhood undernutrition on later intellectual development and achievement.

For example, if a mother suffers from undernutrition during pregnancy, her baby can suffer from reduced intellectual capacity and cognitive functioning. When malnourished women are given protein supplements during pregnancy, improvements in their children's cognitive functioning can be observed through age six or seven (Hicks, Langham, and Takenaka 1992). If pregnant women are given adequate calories and protein, the effects on their offspring can be sustained into adolescence and even young adulthood (Pollitt et al. 1993).

Chronic malnutrition in children—especially during the first two or three years of life—can impair mental development directly (undernourished, and therefore smaller children have smaller brains) and indirectly (undernourished children are less active, and therefore their brains are less stimulated) (World Bank 1997).

In a study conducted in Hyderabad, India, children who had previously suffered from the type of protein-energy malnutrition known as kwashiorkor scored an average of 35 points below their matched controls on IQ tests administered up to six years after their recovery. (Since the average score on IQ tests is 100, and since only 2 percent of the general population have IQs less than 70, a 35-point deficiency is huge.) However, the authors of the Hyderabad study note that it was difficult to determine "to what extent this is a result of the episode of kwashiorkor and to what extent it is due to other factors" (Champakam, Srikantia, and Gopalan 1968:844). A different study in Barbados (Galler 1986) matched 183 children who had a history of kwashiorkor, with 129 classmates who had no such history but who were of similar age and sex, and who were from the same socioeconomic group. Both sets of children were followed from ages five to eighteen years. By sexual maturation, the previously undernourished children had essentially caught up with the matched group in terms of physical growth, but they still demonstrated small deficits in IQ.

UNICEF, in its 1998 *State of the World's Children* report, found evidence to support the conclusion that poor nutrition reduces intelligence: iron deficiency during infancy and early childhood reduced IQ by 9 points on average; two-year-old children who were severely stunted (an anthropometric indicator of poor nutrition) had IQs 5–11 points below those of two-year-olds of normal height; and low-birth-weight babies (born to mothers who had been poorly nourished during pregnancy) had IQs 5 points below those of normal children. (Again, to put this in context, 50 percent of the overall population have IQs less than 100, and about 35 percent of the population have IQs less than 85, and 2 percent have IQs less than 70. So undernourishment could move a child from the middle of the distribution to well down in the low part of the distribution.)

Iodine deficiency is the most significant avoidable cause of mental retardation worldwide. An overview of eighteen studies shows that iodine-deficient groups have IQs that are 13.5 points below those of non-iodine-deficient groups (Bleichrodt and Born 1994). To understand how important a difference of this magnitude can be, consider that a person with an IQ of 100 is at the median score for intelligence (half the population scores less than 100, half scores greater than 100); a person with an IQ of 86.5 (100 – 13.5) scores higher than only about 20 percent of the population, and lower than 80 percent. Deficiencies in other micronutrients, such as iron and vitamin A, are also associated with impaired intellectual abilities (Levinger 1994).

Of course, IQ is not the only or even the best metric for determining mental ability. But other measures give a similar result. Using the Bayley scales for cognitive skills, Gretl Pelto (1987), professor of nutritional science at the University of Connecticut, in a seven-year longitudinal study of nutrition and cognitive development among seventy-eight Mexican preschool children, tested short-term memory, responsiveness to stimulus, attention and distractibility, abstract categorization skills, and sedentary passivity. She found that children with little animal food in their diets were short in stature and delayed in cognitive development, and that delays in intellectual development resulted from nutritionally induced growth stunting. And Nassar and colleagues (2012) found that language development is slower among children who had suffered from poor nutrition.

Chavez and Martinez (1982) studied child development among poor Mexican peasant families. They set up a controlled experiment in which one set of families were given supplemental food for the child through three years of age, and for the mother while she was pregnant and lactating. The control group was a set of families matched to the treated group to have similar genetic and socioeconomic characteristics, but were given no food supplements. Of the many tests for neurological maturation and mental performance given to each set of children, in virtually every instance—walking, control of bladder, and language development—the control children lagged behind the treated children. The better-nourished children were found to be more precocious in constructing three-word sentences.

Chavez and Martinez stressed that it is not possible to determine the ultimate significance of the gap between undernourished and better-nourished children; undernourished children (they speculated) may catch up later in life. There is some evidence that intellectual impairment is at least partially reversible if nutrition is improved. Winick, Meyer, and Harris (1973) tracked severely undernourished Korean orphans and found no signs of mental impairment years after their adoption by US families. On the other hand, a study that followed Filipino children through the first years of life also found that IQ deficiencies resulting from infant malnutrition persisted in children up to the age of twelve (UNICEF 1998: panel 3). And the Nassar study found language deficiencies among undernourished children that persisted for at least five years.

Overall, Lynn and Vanhanen conclude: "Rises in intelligence that occurred in Western populations during the twentieth century are largely attributable to improvements in nutrition" (2002:185). Research into the relationship of nutrition to IQ continues; see Nisbet et al. 2012 and Schoenmaker et al. 2014 for two recent examples.

Impact on Educational Attainment
Not surprisingly, given its impact on intellectual development, undernutrition can also impact the educational achievements of children.

In the United States, it was found that children who had low birth weight had problems succeeding in school. They were more likely to need special education services and more likely to repeat a grade (Levinger 1995).

The Barbados study mentioned earlier (Galler 1986) found that the most striking difference between the undernourished and well-nourished groups was a fourfold increase in the frequency of attention deficit disorder among the previously undernourished. This syndrome is characterized by decreased attention span, impaired memory, high distractibility, restlessness, and disobedience, and was found to reduce educational progress among the previously undernourished children to a far greater extent than the slight deficit in IQ they experienced.

Recent studies in the Philippines (see Box 5.5) and Kenya found a significant relationship between nutritional status and educational attainment as measured by test scores (Glewwe, Jacoby, and King 1996; Bhargava 1996).

But the impact of undernutrition on mental capacities is not just a long-term issue. Other research shows that if children miss breakfast—if they fast for sixteen hours or more—their school performance suffers. In particular, students suffer from poorer memory and reduced ability to pay attention.

Box 5.5 The Cebu Longitudinal Study

Another example of nutritional research is the Cebu Longitudinal Study, led by Linda Adair of the University of North Carolina. It began as a study of about 3,000 pregnant women in Cebu, Philippines, who gave birth during the year spanning May 1983 to April 1984. The original plan was to study the infant-feeding practices of these women (how long they breast-fed, when they introduced different kinds of solid food, etc.). From 1991 to 1992, 2,400 of the families were located and revisited, and both mothers and children were interviewed and evaluated anthropometrically. The younger siblings of the 1983–1984 babies were also measured and evaluated. In 1994 and in 1999, the families were again revisited for interviews and tests. Thus the impact of nutritional practices in the first years of life could be traced through the children's first sixteen to seventeen years of life. (Studies of the data collected include Glewwe, Jacoby, and King 1996. For a more complete description of the study and analyses of its data, see http://www.cpc.unc.edu/projects/cebu.)

World Bank nutrition specialist Alan Berg (1973) points out that children's education also suffers from missed days of school due to nutrition-related illnesses. He cites the case of four Latin American countries where illness caused children to miss more than fifty days of school a year. A study of children born during the 1982–1984 drought in Zimbabwe found that those children started school an average of 3.7 months later than children born in a nondrought period; the children of the drought also finished fewer grades of schooling (Alderman, Hoddinott, and Kinsey 2003).

Recall our discussion of anthropometric results showing that nutrition is positively related to height-for-age (see Chapter 4). If nutrition also affects educational attainment, does this mean that we can find a correlation between height of an individual and years of schooling? Strauss and Thomas (1998) show that, in fact, taller individuals finish more years of schooling, both in the United States and in Brazil.

Effects of Undernutrition on Labor Productivity

In this chapter as in the previous chapter, we have seen evidence that undernutrition has negative effects on physical growth and development, health, intellectual capacity, and educational attainment. For all of these reasons, we might expect that undernutrition can reduce labor productivity. A number of studies have analyzed this effect (see Strauss and Thomas 1998 for a good review of the literature):

• A study of Chinese cotton-mill workers (Li et al. 1994) found that the women were able to do 14 percent more work for each 1-gram increase in their hemoglobin; these increases were attained by giving the workers iron supplements.

• A study of agricultural workers in Colombia and the United States (US Department of State 1976) found a high correlation between nutritional status and physical work capacity. Among undernourished Colombian sugar cane cutters, physical work capacity was reduced by 50 percent.

• A survey of smallholder farmers in Sierra Leone (Strauss 1968) discovered that a 50 percent increase in calories per capita was associated with a 16.5 percent increase in farm output. When nutrition levels were extremely low, the impact of improved nutrition was higher: for families whose average intake was less than 1,500 calories per person per day, a 50 percent increase in calories led to a 25 percent increase in farm output.

Again, relying on the anthropometric measure height-for-age as an indicator of poor nutrition, studies have found that smaller adults are less productive workers in many jobs—they cannot lift and carry as much heavy weight, for example, as larger adults. Strauss and Thomas (1998) show that in a test of physical capacity, taller people are more likely to be able to carry a heavy load. The World Bank, in its 1995 *World Development Report,* estimates that this stunting causes an economic loss of $8.7 billion per year worldwide.

In that same 1995 report, the World Bank finds that an increase in a person's height by 1 percent is associated with an increase in that person's wages by 1.38 percent. Strauss and Thomas (1998) show that positive correlations exist between wages and height and between wages and body mass index in Brazil, where undernutrition is fairly widespread, but not in the United States. This is consistent with the explanation that lower wages are tied to undernutrition. Strauss and Thomas also show that lower wages are not just a result of less education; when the authors limit the comparison to Brazilians with no education, they still find that wages are higher for taller people or for people with higher BMIs.

Paul Schultz (1999) examined the impact of nutrition on wages in Ghana and Côte d'Ivoire. In Ghana, he found a positive correlation: greater body heights and higher BMIs were associated with higher wages. However, in Côte d'Ivoire, the nutritional indicators were not found to have a statistically significant impact on wages. Schultz concludes that the reason for this disparity is that nutrition was much worse in Ghana than in Côte d'Ivoire during the period studied; the implication is that undernutrition ceases to be a cause of low wages once the problem has been reduced to a certain level. This conclusion is buttressed by the findings in the previous paragraph about the lack of correlation between wages and nutrition in the United States.

Strauss and Thomas (1998) find that poorly nourished people are more likely to be unemployed. Among urban males in Brazil who were at least 165 centimeters tall, the average unemployment rate was less than 5 percent. For individuals who were 155 centimeters tall, the average unemployment rate was 10 percent. Likewise, for people who had BMIs of at least 24, the average unemployment rate was 4 percent, compared to 10 percent for individuals who had BMIs of 18.

In the previously cited study of the impact of drought on Zimbabweans born between 1982 and 1984, Alderman, Hoddinott, and Kinsey (2003) conclude: "We present calculations that suggest that this loss of stature, schooling and potential work experience results in a loss of lifetime earnings of 7–12 percent and that such estimates are likely to be *lower* bounds of the true losses."

In recent years, economists have found considerable evidence that nutrition in early life has impacts on economic well-being in adulthood. For example, Case and Paxson (2008) conclude: "There are substantial returns to height in the labor market in both the United States and Britain. For both men and women, an increase in height of four inches is associated with an earnings premium of approximately 10 percent. The estimates shown . . . imply that an American man who is 6 feet 2 inches tall is 3 percentage points more likely to be an executive and 2 percentage points more likely to be a professional than is a man who stands 5 feet 10. The evidence we present is consistent with the hypothesis that economic returns to height are the result of correlation between height and cognitive ability—a correlation that is evident early in life and remains throughout" (2008:528). (Case and Paxson have written numerous other articles on various aspects of this relationship. See also Black, Devereaux, and Salvanes's 2007 study, which focuses on the relationship between maternal nutrition [and birthweight] on adult economic outcomes.)

How Nutrition Shaped the History of Western Civilization

The preceding discussion on the relationship between nutrition and economic productivity has implications for one of most important lessons of the book. Policies that improve nutrition and reduce the prevalence of undernutrition can change a downward cycle of despair for an economy or nation (poverty causing undernutrition causing low productivity leading to more poverty) to an upward cycle of hope (improved nutrition leading to increased productivity leading to lower levels of poverty leading to even further improvements in nutrition).

Economic historians have examined the link between nutrition and productivity. Nobel Prize–winning economist Robert Fogel concluded that food shortages were so severe in Europe in the eighteenth and early nineteenth centuries that "the bottom 20 percent subsisted on such poor diets that they were effectively excluded from the labor force" (1994:373), being too weakened from hunger to work. Fogel estimates that improved nutrition accounts for 30 percent of the growth in income per capita in Britain between 1790 and 1980 (Fogel also reviews other studies linking nutrition to economic development in Europe and the United States).

Kelly, Mokyr, and O'Grada (2013) make the argument that the industrial revolution began in Britain because the British labor force were better nourished. "We will argue that better nutrition made British males grow up on average to be healthier and taller than their continental counterparts. Health and height meant both more physical strength and in all likelihood higher cognitive ability, and hence higher labor productivity." In this context, improved nutrition helps explain not just the geography of the industrial revolution but also the emergence and strength of the British Empire, and arguably the British victories in twentieth-century European wars.

As described in Chapter 2 in Box 2.1, Nunn and Qian (2011) make a similar kind of argument focusing only on the timing and extent of introduction of potatoes in different parts of Europe. Potatoes were unknown in Europe until the sixteenth century, when they were introduced from the Americas by European sailors and missionaries. And potatoes have huge nutritional advantages over cereal crops—an acre of potatoes produces three to four times as many calories as an acre of oats, wheat, or barley. A family of five could feed itself on half an acre of potatoes, but would need 1.4–1.7 acres of cereal crops. (Potatoes have other advantages over cereal crops nutritionally and agronomically.)

But potatoes became incorporated into diets of different parts of Europe at different times, appearing in Spain in 1573, Italy in 1586, England in 1596, and Germany in 1601. There are also geographical differences in the extent to which soil and climate are suited to potato cultivation; eastern Europe and northern parts of Europe extending from Ireland and Denmark into central Russia appear to be the areas of highest suitability for potatoes. Nunn and Qian conclude: "According to our estimates, the introduction of the potato explains 25–26 percent of the increase in Old World population between 1700 and 1900 and 27–34 percent of the increase in urbanization. . . . Our findings contribute to the historical debate about the importance of nutritional improvements in explaining part of the rapid population increase over the past three centuries. They provide evidence that nutrition matters. . . . [O]ur results suggest that the availability of potatoes also played an important role in spurring economic growth in the 18th and 19th centuries" (2011:644).

6

Who, When, Where?

In Chapter 4, we explored a number of ways to measure under-nutrition. Given that some measures are based on somewhat arbitrary cutoff points, we should not be surprised to find that the extent of undernutrition can only be approximated.

Nevertheless, we know enough about undernutrition to put the severity of the problem into perspective. In this chapter we consider the following questions: How widespread is undernutrition? How has the extent of undernutrition changed over time? What are the demographic and geographic characteristics of the problem? What time of year is worst for undernutrition?

Global Trends in Long-Term Perspective

Table 6.1 presents estimates of the number of people worldwide who are affected by undernutrition-associated conditions. For technically advanced readers, descriptions and criticisms of the method used by the Food and Agriculture Organization to measure the extent of undernutrition can be found in Svedberg 1999 and Gabbert and Weikard 2001.

Over time, the number of undernourished people has declined. This is illustrated by Table 6.2. For the developing world as a whole, the number of undernourished people dropped from 960 million in the early 1970s to 908 million at the turn of the century to 780 million in the 2014–2016 period. Expressed as a percentage of the population, the drop has been more dramatic; over one-third of the developing world's population was undernourished in the early 1970s; by the turn of the century, the proportion had dropped to 18 percent; and by 2014–2016 it had dropped to under 13 percent. However, these declines have not been spread evenly throughout the developing world over this period. During the last thirty years of the twentieth century, progress in Asia has been remarkable—the percentage of undernourished people dropped from 41 percent to 18 percent. During the same thirty years, progress in sub-

Table 6.1 World Population Affected by Various Types of Malnutrition

	Prevalence (millions of people)	Percentage of World Population Affected
Iodine deficiency (2007)	2,000	30
Vitamin A deficiency (children under age five, 1995–2005)	190	33
Iron deficiency (women ages fifteen to nineteen, 2011)	521	29
Prevalence of undernutrition (2014–2016)	795	11
Stunting among children (under age five, 2007–2014)	155	24

Source: WHO 2008, 2009, 2015a; FAO 2015a.

Saharan Africa was very slow, from 36 percent to 30 percent. However, the past fifteen years have seen Africa making the same kind of progress that Asia made in the twentieth century.

Additional evidence of a long-term trend toward an improving food situation is shown in Figure 6.1, which shows that worldwide food production per capita increased steadily from 1960 to 2013. Notice that the growth in food production *per capita* means that food production is growing faster than population.

Earlier editions of this book pointed to price trends as additional corroborative evidence of the improving food situation. As Figure 6.2 shows, world food prices fell overall from the early 1960s through the mid-1980s before flattening out for the remainder of the twentieth century. Food prices were more volatile than food production. Prices increased dramatically between 1972 and 1974 (see Johnson 1975 for a discussion of the reasons—unusual weather due to an El Niño, the entry of the Soviet Union into world commodity markets), and then fell sharply. But even with this volatility, the long-term downward trend in prices is clear over the 1960–2000 period. As we will see in Chapter 7, this downward price trend is what we expect when food supply is growing faster than food demand.

However, the experience of food prices in the twenty-first century is quite different from that of the earlier period. The sharp price increases between 2005 and 2008, and then again between 2009 and 2011, are more consistent with growing food shortages than with growing food availability. And there was widespread conjecture that what we were seeing was the beginning of a new era of ever increasing prices: "The End of Cheap Food?" asked *The Economist* in late 2007.

But there are reasons to think that this type of conjecture was overly alarmist. First, we can see from Figure 6.2 that the upward trend has failed to continue in the years since 2011. Second, we see from Figure 6.1 and Table 6.2 that even during the years of price spikes, the data on food production and

Table 6.2 Trends in Number and Percentage of People Undernourished, by Continental Area, 1969–2016

	1969–1971	1979–1981	1990–1992	2000–2002	2010–2012	2014–2016
Number of Undernourished (millions)						
Sub-Saharan Africa	92.8	127.0	175.7	203.6	205.7	220.0
Near East and North Africa	42.8	20.8	16.5	23.1	33.9	33.0
Asia and the Pacific	769.9	730.0	726.2	617.2	525.4	490.1
Latin America and Caribbean	55.1	46.0	66.1	60.4	38.3	34.3
All developing countries	960.7	923.8	990.7	908.4	805.0	779.9
Percentage of Population Undernourished						
Sub-Saharan Africa	36	37	33.2	30.0	24.1	23.2
Near East and North Africa	24	9	6.6	7.5	8.3	7.5
Asia and the Pacific	41	32	24.3	18.0	13.7	12.3
Latin America and Caribbean	20	13	14.7	11.4	6.4	5.5
All developing countries	37	28	23.3	18.2	14.1	12.9

Source: FAOSTAT; FAO regional reports for 2015: Near East and North Africa, http://www.fao.org/3/a-i4644e.pdf; Latin America and the Caribbean, http://www.fao.org/3/a-i4636e.pdf; Africa, http://www.fao.org/3/a-i4635e.pdf; Pacific Asia, http://www.fao.org/3/a-i4624e.pdf.

Figure 6.1 Index of Worldwide Food Production per Capita, 1961–2013

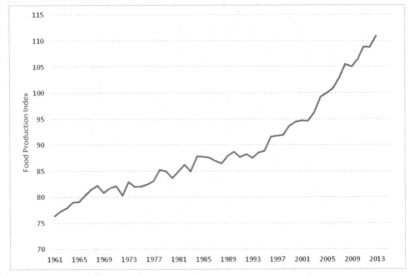

Source: FAOSTAT.
Note: 2004–2006 = 100.

Figure 6.2 Index of Real (Inflation-Adusted) Food Prices, 1961–2015

Source: FAO, *World Food Situation*, various years..
Note: 2002–2004 = 100.

prevalence of undernutrition did not show the kind of bad news that the high prices might imply.

A number of papers (see Masters and White 2008 or Herman, Kelly, and Nash 2011) have suggested that the apparent disconnect between rising food prices and stable food availability can be explained as an example of a "price bubble" caused by market psychology. A price bubble can occur as follows. An investor notices that food prices have risen rapidly and speculates that this trend is likely to continue. Based on this observation, our investor decides to buy futures contracts for agricultural commodities—investments that will make money if prices continue to rise. And if other investors reach the same conclusion slightly *after* our investor does, and also rush to buy futures contracts, they will bid up the price, and our investor *does* make money. However, at some point investors lose their optimism and the bubble bursts—prices, having been driven up to levels that are unrealistically too high, suddenly fall back to levels more consistent with underlying conditions. Econometric tests of this bubble explanation have generally found only weak evidence to back it up (see Irwin 2013 for a review of the literature).

Since 2011, food prices have fallen back to levels that existed before the spikes of 2008 and 2011. But it is too soon to tell whether this downward trend will continue. The general level of food prices as of mid-2016 is at about the level of the early 1960s. However, because per capita incomes have grown substantially over the past five decades, constant prices mean that food is much more affordable to the average person today, and this explains the much lower prevalence of undernutrition of today compared to the 1960s. Box 6.1 discusses a situation thousands of years ago when nutrition did not improve.

The Seasonality of Undernutrition

People at risk for undernutrition are not usually at risk all the time; it tends to come in fits and starts. We are all aware of the periodicity of famine—the word connotes a time of extreme food scarcity as contrasted with normal times when food is less scarce. But we are less aware that third world hunger usually follows the rhythm of the seasons. In the third world, a strong seasonality variable is usual in the production, price, and availability of food, as well as in the availability of employment (Sahn 1989). All these factors can influence the nutritional status of a family at risk for undernutrition.

The seasonality of undernutrition is often linked to the agricultural year, which in the tropics is usually heavily dependent on rainfall patterns. In monsoon Asia, for instance, rice is planted at the beginning of the wet season, which typically starts in July. Harvest begins about four months after planting. With irrigation, farmers can harvest more than one crop per year, but most of the rice is still grown during the wet season. Likewise, in the Sahel region of Africa (including parts of Chad, Niger, and Mauritania), crops mature in September and October, but the food supply begins to run out in May, and the hungry season can run for four months, from May through August (FAO 1997b).

Box 6.1 Nutrition, the Natural Environment, and the Development of Agriculture

It is tempting to presume that the improvements in worldwide nutrition seen over the past half century are simply an extension of a long history of gradual improvement in human nutrition. But some anthropological evidence indicates that precivilized hunter-gatherers obtained good nutrition with relatively little effort.

Angel (1975) found that, 30,000 years ago—before the birth of agriculture—the average adult male was 177 centimeters (5 feet 11 inches) tall, but that, 20,000 years later, average height was only 165 centimeters (5 feet 6 inches). Other information from Angel (1984) indicates that residents of the eastern Mediterranean at the beginning of the age of agriculture were taller than modern Greeks. Harris notes that it is "hard to reconcile [a view of starving hunter-gatherers] with the enormous quantities of animal bones accumulated at various Paleolithic kill sites. . . . The skeletal remains of the hunters themselves bear witness to the fact that they were unusually well-nourished" (1977:10). Cohen (1984) notes that skeletal evidence indicates low rates of anemia and infection among hunter-gatherers.

Other evidence that hunter-gatherers had good nutrition comes from studies of modern hunter-gatherer societies. Lee (1968a, 1968b, 1969, 1972) studied the !Kung bushmen of Africa and found that they consumed 93 grams of protein per day, mostly from meat and nuts. The composition of the diet of many hunter-gatherers is varied and more likely to contain sufficient quantities of a broad array of nutrients.

An even more remarkable finding from Lee's study of the !Kung is that they achieved this nutritious diet with relatively little effort—less than three hours per day per adult, despite the fact that the !Kung lived on the edge of the Kalahari desert. The rest of the time was spent resting, visiting with others, doing embroidery, playing games, and the like. Similarly, Sahlins (1968) found that the aborigines of Australia worked for two days and took the third as a holiday. These observations are consistent with studies of great apes, which spend about half their time grooming, playing, and napping, and the other half foraging for food. "As collectors of food . . . [Paleolithic populations] were certainly no less effective than chimpanzees" (Harris 1977:10).

Why—if hunting and gathering was so nutritionally efficient—did agriculture ever develop? After all, Diamond (1987) refers to the development of agriculture as "the worst mistake in the history of the human race." According to Harris, the answer is global warming:

As long as . . . exploitation of [naturally occurring animal and plant resources] is kept relatively low, hunter-collectors can enjoy both leisure and high-quality diets. . . . Then, about 13,000 years ago, a global warming trend [began, and] . . . forests invaded the grassy plains which nourished the great herds [of large animals, known as 'megafauna']. . . . The collapse of the big-game hunting cultures . . . was followed by . . . [a system of] preying on smaller species . . . called . . . 'broad spectrum' hunting and collecting. . . . [H]unters then intensified predation of [smaller species], and these too soon became extinct. . . . As they fought their long and futile delaying action against the consequences of the depletion of animal species, [they] . . . shifted their primary subsistence effort away from animals toward plants. . . . It seems clear that the extinction of the Pleistocene megafauna triggered the shift to an agricultural mode of production. (1977:10–25)

Consequently, the price of rice is lowest just after harvest and rises gradually as supplies dwindle. During the growing season, supplies may become short and prices may rise more sharply. The pattern of seasonal variation in food price and food consumption in the Philippines is shown in Table 6.3. Consumption is at its lowest in September, when the price has been high for three months, and picks up during the following months, when the rice is harvested and price falls below the annual average. Similar seasonal price patterns occur throughout the developing world. For example, millet prices in Niger rose 80 percent between July and August of 1996 (FAO 1997b).

A detailed study of dietary intake in Mozambique (Rose et al. 1999) vividly illustrates the impact of the hungry season. As shown in Table 6.4, average calories per person per day in the village of Montepuez drop from 91 percent of requirements (about 2,000 per person per day) in the harvest season, to 63 percent (about 1,430 calories) during the hungry season. During the hungry season, the calorie intakes of 30–40 percent of the villagers are insufficient to replace the calories they expend in normal daily activity. Maize—the source of 60 percent of calories in the average diet during the harvest season—disap-

Table 6.3 Seasonal Prices and Food Consumption in the Philippines

	Food Consumption (annual kilograms per capita)	Index of Food Price
March	97	108
June	100	110
September	110	98
December	92	104

Sources: Adapted from Philippines Ministry of Agriculture 1981a, 1983.

Table 6.4 Nutrient Intakes for Harvest Season and Hungry Season for Smallholders in Montepuez, Mozambique, 1995–1996

	Percentage of Requirements Met	
	Harvest Season	Hungry Season
Calories	91	63
Protein	148	79
Vitamin A	23	88
Niacin	103	64
Calcium	42	42
Iron	92	64

Sources: Rose et al. 1999.

Box 6.2 The Hungry Season in Zambia and Malawi

Data such as those presented in the accompanying text give us some idea of the quantitative aspects of the hungry season. But a more complete picture emerges from some vivid descriptions.

A *Washington Post* reporter visiting Zambia during the hungry season found this: "When the people by the lake began to starve, they fell back on the knowledge of their ancestors. They picked poisonous fruits from the bush and boiled them for three days to eliminate the toxin concocting a barely palatable dish. But sometimes hungry children would sneak a taste early . . . and the poison would make them ill. Kebby Kamota, father of 11, could take it no longer. 'Three days! Three days!' He shouted explaining how long his children would sometimes go without food" (Gillis 2003:A1).

A Peace Corp volunteer in Zambia describes the onset of the hungry season like this: "I can tell the change of season by signs rather than months. When there are mangoes, rain, disease, funerals and kids crying at night, it's the hungry season" (Kluender 2003).

A report by the Centro Internacional de Mejoramiento de Maize y Trigo describes how Agness Pungulani, a single mother in Malawi, copes: "During the . . . hungry season, markets were devoid of grain [and] local traders were selling maize at [two-and-a-half times the normal price]. When the food stocks disappeared, Pungulani . . . foraged, drank tea from wild occra leaves in place of evening meals, and pounded banana tree roots into a crude flour approximating their preferred maize staple. . . . A neighbor . . . says, 'This flour tastes sour, but we eat it because we have no choice.' The hungry season normally arrives during January–February in this part of Malawi, but lately families have run out of grain as early as September and must survive until the March harvests" (CIMMYT 2003).

A *New York Times* reporter describes the joyful end of the hungry season in Malawi like this: "Late one afternoon, during the long melancholia of the hungry months, there was a burst of joyous delirium in Mkulumimba. Children began shouting the word 'ngumbi,' announcing that winged termites were fluttering through the fields. These were not the bigger species of the insect, which can be fried in oil and sold as a delicacy for a good price. Instead, these were the smaller ones, far more wing than torso, which are eaten right away. Suddenly, most everyone was giddily chasing about; villagers were catching ngumbi with their fingers and tossing them onto their tongues, grateful for the unexpected gift of food afloat in the air. . . . Most every year, Malawi suffers a food shortage during the so-called hungry months, December through March. . . . Families often endure this hungry period on a single meal a day, sometimes nothing more than a foraged handful of greens" (Bearak 2003:33).

---

pears from the diets of many during the hungry season; it is replaced by manioc, peanuts, and sorghum—less desirable substitutes that are not eaten as much when maize is available.

One nutritional bright spot for the hungry-season diet described in Table

6.4 is the abundance of vitamin A, due to an increase in consumption of fruits and vegetables such as pumpkin squash. Such increases in consumption of wild fruits and vegetables during the hungry season appear to be a widespread phenomenon. Falconer (1990), in a review of the literature, finds a number of studies that stress the importance of wild plants and animals as sources of food during the hungry season in different parts of the developing world. In one Zambian village, wild foods make up 42 percent of the diet during the hungry season, compared to 7 percent during the rest of the year. In rural Bangladesh, people eat almost no wild plants—an average of 1 gram per person per day—during the ten months following the rice harvest; then, during the May–June hungry season, this increases to 191 grams per person per day. (See Box 6.2 for descriptions of the hungry season.)

Who Is Undernourished?

In which countries is the problem of undernutrition the worst? Tables 6.5, 6.6, and 6.7 show that the answer to this question depends on the way in which the extent of undernutrition is measured.

Many countries rank high in terms of both calorie deficiency and prevalence of undernutrition: North Korea, Haiti, Ethiopia, Tanzania, Chad, Zimbabwe, and Madagascar appear on both lists in Table 6.5. Nearly all the countries in Table 6.5 are sub-Saharan African countries. But in Table 6.6—which

Table 6.5 Countries That Rank High in Undernutrition Based on Dietary Intake and Requirements, 2014

Average Calories per Capita per Day as Percentage of Average Daily Requirement, 2014		Percentage of the Population Suffering from Undernutrition, 2010–2014	
North Korea	87	Haiti	52
Haiti	91	Zambia	48
Zambia	91	Central African Rep.	38
Zimbabwe	93	North Korea	38
Madagascar	96	Namibia	37
Ethiopia	97	Chad	35
Chad	98	Ethiopia	35
Afghanistan	99	Tanzania	35
Kenya	102	Rwanda	34
Yemen	102	Republic of Congo	32
Tanzania	105	Tajikistan	32
Bangladesh	107	Zimbabwe	32
Pakistan	107	Madagascar	31
India	108	Liberia	30
Mozambique	108	Timor-Leste	29

Sources: Calories per capita per day from FAOSTAT food balance sheets. Calories per capita per day requirements calculated from population by age and sex according to the US Census Bureau for 2000 (http://www.census.gov) and calorie requirements in Table 3.1. Percentage of population suffering from undernutrition from FAO, *State of Food Insecurity in the World 2013*.

ranks the "worst case" countries by looking at nutritional outcomes of *children*, we see many countries that do not appear in Table 6.5. What is more, there is less consistency among the three different measures in Table 6.6. Seven countries appear as worst-case countries according to all three measures of child undernutrition, and thirteen countries appear on two of the three lists, but thirteen countries appear on one of the three lists, but not the other two. Furthermore, the ranking according to anthropometric indicators of childhood undernutrition is quite different from the ranking (in Table 6.7) according to under-five mortality or low birthweight.

Again, most of the worst-off countries in all these lists are sub-Saharan African countries. However, the lists of low-birth-weight babies and anthropometrically small (stunted) children contain a number of Asian countries near the top. Ramalingaswami, Jonsson, and Rohde (1996) suggest that this phenomenon may be explained by a combination of factors:

- "Girls and women in South Asia are less well regarded and less well cared for than in sub-Saharan Africa" Poor nutrition among pregnant women causes low-birth-weight babies.
- "Differences in standards of hygiene between the two regions [South Asia and sub-Saharan Africa] are very pronounced. . . . This all-round poor hygiene increases the burden of illness, and [causes] significantly higher levels of malnutrition among South Asia's children"
- Quality of childcare is higher in sub-Saharan Africa than in South Asia.

Recent literature has given a good deal of attention to the second of these explanations. "This report suggests that a key cause of child undernutrition is a subclinical disorder of the small intestine known as tropical enteropathy; . . . tropical enteropathy is caused by faecal bacteria ingested in large quantities by young children living in conditions of poor sanitation and hygiene; that provision of toilets and promotion of handwashing after faecal contact could reduce or prevent tropical enteropathy and its adverse effects on growth; and that the primary causal pathway from poor sanitation and hygiene to undernutrition is tropical enteropathy and not diarrhoea" (Humphrey 2009:1032).

It is interesting that the small size of babies and children in South Asia does not translate into high rates of child mortality.

Several organizations have developed multidimensional measures of food insecurity combining some of these measures, as well as other variables. The Economist Intelligence Unit publishes an annual Global Food Security Index, which includes measures of food affordability (six indicators such as food consumption as a percentage of average household expenditures), food availability (eleven indicators such as average food supply and dependence on food aid), and food quality and safety (ten indicators such as micronutrient availability and the existence of a national agency for food safety). The worst-off countries

Table 6.6 Countries That Rank High in Undernutrition Based on Anthropometric Measurements of Children Under Age Five

	Percentage of Children Stunted (low height-for-age)		Percentage of Children Underweight (low weight-for-age)		Percentage of Children Wasted (low weight-for-height)
Timor-Leste	57.7	Timor-Leste	45.3	South Sudan	22.7
Burundi	57.5	Eritrea	38.8	Djibouti	21.5
Eritrea	50.3	Niger	37.9	Sri Lanka	21.4
Papua New Guinea	49.5	Yemen	35.5	Timor-Leste	18.9
Madagascar	49.2	Bangladesh	35.1	Niger	18.7
Guatemala	48.0	Sudan	32.2	Bangladesh	18.1
Yemen	46.6	Pakistan	31.6	Nigeria	18.1
Pakistan	45.0	Nigeria	31.0	Sudan	16.4
Rwanda	44.3	Chad	30.3	Chad	15.7
Laos	43.8	Djibouti	29.8	Eritrea	15.3
Mozambique	43.1	Burundi	29.1	Papua New Guinea	14.3
Niger	43.0	Nepal	29.1	Indonesia	13.5
Democratic Republic of Congo	42.6	Papua New Guinea	27.9	Yemen	13.3
Tanzania	42.5	South Sudan	27.6	Mauritania	11.6
Malawi	42.4	Laos	26.5	Syria	11.5
Liberia	41.8	Sri Lanka	26.3	Nepal	11.2
Cambodia	40.9	Ethiopia	25.2	Comoros	11.1
Central African Republic	40.7	Burkina Faso	24.4	Burkina Faso	10.9
Nepal	40.5	Mauritania	24.4	Pakistan	10.5
Ethiopia	40.4	Cambodia	23.9	Maldives	10.2

Source: UNICEF, http://www.childinfo.org, data for various years, mostly in the 2005–2013 range.
Note: Afghanistan and Somalia are excluded here because comparable information is not available for all of Tables 6.5–6.7.

Table 6.7 Countries That Rank High in Undernutrition According to Infant and Child Health

	Under-Five Mortality Rate (per thousand)		Low Birth Weight (percentage of births)
Angola	167.4	Mauritania	34.7
Sierra Leone	160.6	Pakistan	32.0
Chad	147.5	Yemen	32.0
Central African Republic	139.2	India	28.0
Guinea-Bissau	123.9	Nauru	27.0
Mali	122.7	Niger	27.0
Democratic Republic of Congo	118.5	Comoros	25.0
Nigeria	117.4	Haiti	23.0
Niger	104.2	Bangladesh	22.0
Guinea	100.7	Philippines	21.0
Côte d'Ivoire	100.0	Ethiopia	20.0
South Sudan	99.2	Chad	19.9
Lesotho	98.0	Senegal	18.6
Burkina Faso	97.6	Mali	18.0
Equatorial Guinea	95.8	Marshall Islands	18.0
Cameroon	94.5	Nepal	17.8
Mauritania	90.1	Côte d'Ivoire	17.0
Zimbabwe	88.5	Sri Lanka	17.0
Zambia	87.4	Mozambique	16.9
Mozambique	87.2	Madagascar	16.0

Source: UNICEF, http://www.childinfo.org, data for various years, mostly in the 2005–2013 range.
Note: Afghanistan and Somalia are excluded here because comparable information is not available for all of Tables 6.5–6.7.

by this measure are shown in Table 6.8. (For other examples, see IFPRI's Global Hunger Index, or the Maplecroft Food Security Risk Index.)

The general lessons from these multidimensional measures are the same that we have seen earlier in the chapter. Most of the worst-off countries are in sub-Saharan Africa. Haiti too is among the worst-off countries. (North Korea is not included in this list because of lack of available data.) And most of the

Table 6.8 Global Food Security Index for Selected Countries, 2014

	Food Security Index (out of 100)
Democratic Republic of Congo	24.8
Chad	25.5
Madagascar	27.7
Togo	28.4
Burundi	28.8
Tanzania	29.9
Haiti	30.2
Niger	30.5

Sources: Economist Intelligence Unit 2014.

countries are showing improvements according to this index (though this is not shown in Table 6.8).

Some readers may wonder if we have forgotten to consider undernutrition in the developed world. But the incidence of undernutrition in the developed world is generally so close to zero that it does not contribute much to world-wide numbers. A comparison of Tables 6.1 and 6.2 reveals that, of the 795 million undernourished people worldwide, 780 million are in developing countries. The situation in the United States is described in Box 6.3.

Box 6.3 Undernutrition in the Developing World

All of our attention here has been focused on poor countries. What about rich countries such as the United States? Perhaps you have heard claims that thousands of children in this American city or that American state go to bed hungry every night. The source of those claims, and of the most in-depth study of hunger in the United States, is a food security report by the US Department of Agriculture (Coleman-Jensen et al. 2015).

That report concludes that food insecurity afflicts 15.4 percent of people and 20.9 percent of children in the United States. But what is food insecurity? The report based its definition on a ten-question survey (plus an additional eight questions for households with children). Some of the questions are rather subjective, such as: "In the past 12 months, did you worry that your food would run out before you got money to buy more?" Other questions are more concrete, such as: "Did you lose weight in the last year because there wasn't enough money for food?" or "Did you ever not eat for a whole day because there wasn't enough money for food?"

A household that answered yes to more than two of these questions was labeled "food-insecure." A household with children could be categorized as "food-insecure" if they "couldn't afford balanced meals" and "relied on a few kinds of low-cost food." If the household answered yes to more of the questions, the household could be labeled as having "low or very low food security." This most severe form of food insecurity (very low food security) afflicts 5.5 percent of people and 1.2 percent of children in the United States.

Of all households, only a small percentage (0.19 percent) reported that their children went without eating for a whole day at any time during the preceding thirty days, and only 2.6 percent reported that adults went without eating for the whole day during the preceding thirty days.

For poor families in the United States, running out of food and having no money to buy more can be difficult. But compare the descriptions in this box to the descriptions of the "hungry season" in Box 6.2. By international standards, the undernutrition problem in the United States is almost undetectable. The incidence of hunger is low because incomes in the United States—even incomes of the poor—are high by world standards, and because of public programs (such as food stamps) and private efforts (such as church-run food pantries) to help poor families.

What Groups of People Are Undernourished?

Of course, hunger knows no boundaries: it afflicts the young, the old, the healthy, the sick, the working, the unemployed. But there are groups of people among whom undernutrition is more common.

Within any given country, malnutrition is likely to be more prevalent in rural areas. The World Bank, in its 1990 *World Development Report,* calculated that, among the forty-two countries it classified as low-income in 1988, rural people represented 65 percent of the population. Because rural incomes are usually considerably lower than urban incomes, and because undernutrition is so closely associated with low-income populations, a strong argument can be made that the majority of the world's hungry are rural. Because of this, and because so many policies affecting the price and availability of food to both rural and urban consumers impinge on the rural sector of the economy, we place heavy emphasis in this book on policies affecting the rural sector. The tension that exists between the rural and urban sectors of developing countries is discussed in more detail in Chapter 21. As the world moves further into the twenty-first century, developing economies are expected to become increasingly urban, but even then, rural-oriented policies will remain especially significant among those aimed at undernutrition.

Children as a group are by far the most vulnerable to undernutrition, especially at weaning time—that transitional period during which an infant's diet is changed from 100 percent breast milk to 100 percent other foods. Though this transition can be abrupt, in the third world it often takes place during an eighteen-month time span, such as between six months and two years of age. While infants are being moved from breast milk toward other foods, their requirements for a calorie- and protein-dense diet are still very high, and in cultures where the diet is dominated by grains, providing an appropriate diet for weaning children takes a special effort.

Pregnant women and lactating mothers are the next most vulnerable to undernutrition, perhaps followed by elderly women. During times of extreme food shortages or famines, these groups are almost always the most at risk, but during such times a broader segment of the population, including large numbers of able-bodied men, is likely to be affected also.

A number of studies have attempted to identify the determinants of undernutrition. For example a paper by Masibo and Makoka (2012) found that childhood undernutrition in Kenya (as measured by stunting in the 2008–2009 period) was a bigger problem for children who are (1) boys, (2) between the ages of one and three years, (3) in larger families, (4) in the poorest families, (5) in households with nonimproved toilet facilities, and (6) in families where the mother has no secondary education. Variables that were found to have no significant impact on stunting include rural/urban status, age of mother, and child size at birth.

Part 2

Addressing Causes of Undernutrition

7

Supply and Demand

To this point, we have focused on the effects, measurement, and prevalence of undernutrition. We now begin to describe the factors that influence the occurrence and extent of undernutrition. Economics serves as the organizing framework for this discussion. This chapter is intended to be a very brief introduction to economic principles.

An Elementary Example of Supply and Demand

Alfred Marshall, a nineteenth-century British economist, is the father of modern economics. He used a simple example of a boy gathering raspberries to illustrate the concepts of supply and demand. Imagine a boy walking through the woods who spots a patch of raspberry bushes. The boy reaches out and plucks a raspberry and pops it into his mouth. He gets a burst of pleasure: he was hot, thirsty, and hungry; the raspberry refreshes him. As he continues to eat raspberries, two things occur. First, the pleasure from eating additional raspberries subsides; the pleasure he gets from eating the twentieth raspberry is less than the pleasure he got from that first raspberry. This may be because he is no longer as hungry, hot, and thirsty, or because the novelty of eating raspberries has worn off, or because the twentieth raspberry is not as ripe as the first one. Second, the boy discovers it is harder and harder to find raspberries to pick. He has to kneel on the ground, or reach into the brambles, to find additional raspberries.

If we were to graph this experience, it would look like Figure 7.1 (we use straight lines rather than true curves for simplicity). The downward-sloping curve shows the pleasure the boy gets from each successive raspberry: he gets a lot of pleasure from the first berry, slightly less additional pleasure from the second, still less from the third, and so forth. The upward-sloping curve shows the amount of effort needed to obtain each successive berry: the first requires very little effort, the second requires a little more, the third even more, and so on.

Figure 7.1 The Boy in the Berry Patch

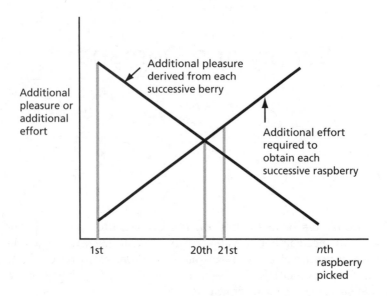

We can also use the graph in Figure 7.1 to track the boy's reasoning. Should I eat the first raspberry? Yes: the pleasure from that is very high and the cost of obtaining it is very low. Likewise for the second, and the third. When he gets to the twentieth berry, the pleasure from that berry has dropped, and the cost of obtaining it has increased, but it is still (just barely) "worth it"—the pleasure derived exceeds the effort needed to obtain it. When he considers the twenty-first berry, he realizes that this berry is no longer worth the effort. In terms of the graph, the intersection of the "additional pleasure" curve and the "additional effort" curve shows the point at which the boy stops.

We can characterize the boy's decision as an "optimal" decision in the following sense. The boy's decision is one that maximizes his "surplus pleasure," defined as the pleasure from consuming berries, minus the discomfort of gathering them. This illustrates a fundamental principle of economics: an optimal decision is one in which the "marginal benefit"—in our example, the additional pleasure gained from eating one more berry—equals the "marginal cost"—the additional effort needed to pick that berry. Note that in the raspberry example, there is no money—the boy does not put a dollar value on his pleasure or on his effort. Yet there is an implicit comparability: the boy can say, "The pleasure from the berry is worth (or not worth) the additional effort."

A Producer's Supply Curve and a Consumer's Demand Curve

The fundamental concepts of economic behavior are contained in the story of the boy and the raspberries. The only difference when it comes to modern economics is that pleasure is calculated explicitly in monetary terms: Figure 7.2 is exactly like Figure 7.1 except that the Y-axis is now labeled "price" to indicate cost per unit of the good.

The downward-sloping curve is an individual consumer's *demand* curve. It shows how much of a good the person will want to consume at all the different possible levels of price. An alternative interpretation is that the demand curve shows the maximum amount per unit the person is willing to pay for all the different possible levels of consumption. The downward slope of the demand curve means that as the price of a good falls, a consumer will want to consume more of that good. (See Box 7.1 for an example of a downward-sloping demand curve.)

The upward-sloping curve in Figure 7.2 is an individual producer's *supply* curve. It shows how much of a good the producer will produce at all the different possible levels of price. Alternatively, it shows the minimum amount per unit that the person will require to produce at each of the different possible levels of production. The upward slope of the supply curve means that as the price of a good increases, a producer will produce more of that good. The concepts of costs of production and the technical relationships between input and output are discussed in Box 7.2.

Figure 7.2 Supply and Demand Curves

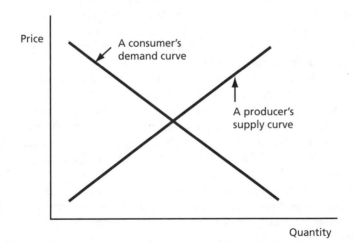

Box 7.1 Demand Curve Slopes Down

The city of London has a problem: too many people driving too many cars. Economists have a solution: increase the costs associated with driving in the city. In February 2003, a congestion fee of 5 pounds (about $8) was imposed on all cars driving during weekdays (Monday through Friday) in a particular zone of central London. Cameras recorded the license plate numbers of cars that entered the zone to ensure that drivers paid the required fee. The hoped-for result was that automobile traffic would be reduced by 15 percent by 2010. Economists estimated that the fee would reduce traffic by 12–17 percent. But by early April 2003, traffic loads appeared to have stabilized at 20 percent lower than previous levels. The demand curve for driving in central London was flatter (economists would say, "the elasticity of demand was higher, in absolute value") than economists predicted. But the economists were right in the direction of their prediction: if you want people to consume less of a good, raise the price of the good.

Sources: Blow, Leicester, and Smith 2003; Transport for London 2003.

Aggregate Supply, Aggregate Demand, and Markets

Of course, in real-world markets, the number of consumers does not equal the number of producers. A single potato farmer grows enough potatoes to feed hundreds of people, and a single consumer buys different kinds of food produced by many different farmers. But the market serves as a place where many consumers and many producers can interact in a process that sets an equilibrium price at the point where the *aggregate supply curve* intersects the *aggregate demand curve,* illustrated in Figure 7.3. Recall that the individual producer's supply curve shows how much of a good the producer will produce at different price levels. If we add up (aggregate) those quantities for all producers, we have a picture showing the total quantities that will be produced at different price levels. Likewise, we add up quantities demanded by individual consumers to obtain the aggregate demand curve.

The point at which the aggregate supply and demand curves intersect shows the equilibrium price and aggregate quantity. If the price is above this equilibrium price, producers want to sell a greater quantity than consumers want to buy. Producers who cannot find a buyer for their output will try to attract buyers by offering a lower price. If the price falls below the equilibrium price, some buyers will be unable to buy the quantities they want, and the price will increase.

In a complex economy with many consumers, many producers, and many goods, the prices determined by the interaction of aggregate supply and aggregate demand for each good serve to organize or direct consumption and production patterns. Under certain restrictive assumptions, the consumption and

Box 7.2 Why the Supply Curve Slopes Upward

There is a physical basis and also a cost basis for the relationship between price and the amount that a farmer will try to produce. Let us start with the underlying physical relationship, using as our example the relationship between the amount of seed planted in one field (say, a hectare of land) and a crop yield. The raw data we assume are given in Table A and plotted in Figure A. The top curve in Figure A represents the total yield from varying amounts of fertilizer (total physical product or production function). The bottom curve represents the yield added by each successive increment of ten units of seed (marginal physical product).

Table A: Hypothetical Yield Response to Varying Amounts of Seed

Seed	Yield	Marginal Physical Product
0	0	39
10	39	13
20	52	9
30	61	5
40	66	0
50	66	-2
60	64	

Figure A

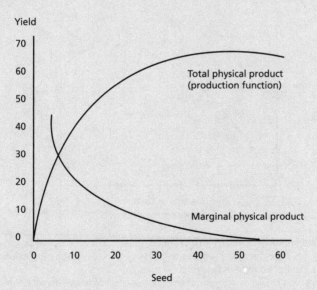

continues

Box 7.2 continued

What we have in Figure A is a graphic representation of the fact that, as we increase the amount of an input used, holding other inputs constant, we experience diminishing returns to successive inputs (thus the downward-sloping marginal physical product curve—which is often called diminishing marginal returns). These functional relationships are based on observations that have been made in the real world.

Now let us combine the variable inputs commonly used to increase production on our hypothetical hectare of land. As we increase production, we add not only more seed but also more fertilizer, more labor, and maybe more of other inputs such as irrigation water and pesticides. These things cost money. As we increase production, we could, at various amounts produced, add up the costs of the things we are using to increase production and plot these sums to obtain a cost curve.

The cost curve would show very much the same thing that Figure A shows, except that it would measure costs, instead of seed, along the horizontal input. (The relation between cost and production is based on the underlying physical relationships between inputs and production.) We diagram our cost curve in Figure B. Because the fixed cost of land is not included in our set of costs, we identify the costs in this diagram as variable costs.

Figure B

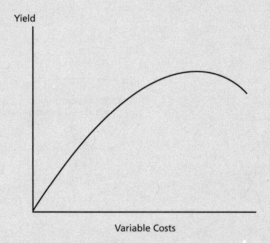

Although not specifically diagrammed, notice in Figure B that as yield increases, there are diminishing marginal returns to costs, just as there were diminishing marginal returns to seed in Figure A.

It is a convention of economics to draw cost curves with the cost on the vertical axis and the yield on the horizontal axis. So let us redraw Figure B in the conventional way, namely as shown in Figure C. (To see what happens to the cost curve when this is done, trace Figure B and then flip it over and look at it from the back side, to obtain Figure C.)

Figure C

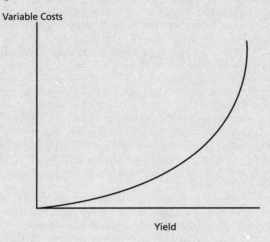

Variable Costs

Yield

Figure D

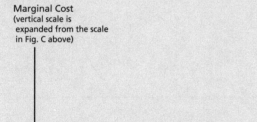

Marginal Cost
(vertical scale is
expanded from the scale
in Fig. C above)

Marginal cost

Yield

continues

Box 7.2 continued

With Figure C, instead of thinking about what happens to yield as we increase costs by one unit, we can think about what happens to costs as we increase yield by one unit. In Figure C we see that we produce under conditions
of increasing marginal cost. For each additional unit of yield from our hectare
of land, we have to spend somewhat more on our bundle of variable costs. These
increasing marginal costs are diagrammed in Figure D.

Thus we see that we are producing under diminishing marginal returns,
which results in producing with increasing marginal costs. The two are based on
the same underlying physical relationship.

For an individual producer, the marginal cost curve (Figure D) is the price
schedule at which they are willing to produce various amounts of goods for the
market. They are willing to produce up to the point where the price equals their
marginal cost of production. If they are producing at this point and we want to
motivate them to produce more, barring a shift in technology or a reduction in
the costs of some of their inputs, we will have to pay them more. This is represented in Figure E as shifting production from A to B, which is motivated by an
increase in price from P1 to P2.

Adding up the marginal cost curves (individuals' supply curves) for all the
individual producers yields the supply curve for the industry. Increasing the
price of the product will motivate the industry to produce more.

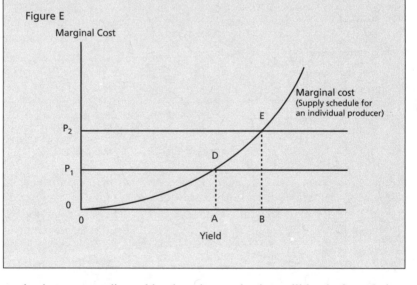

Figure E

production patterns dictated by the price mechanism will be the best choices
in the following sense:

• Each consumer tries to obtain the most pleasure possible out of the
money he or she has to spend. The consumer does this by trying to obtain the

Figure 7.3 Aggregate Supply and Demand

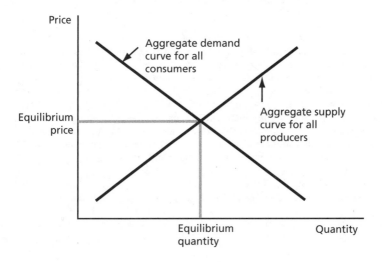

same amount of pleasure from the last dollar spent on each good. To understand what this means, suppose that this were not the case; instead, suppose
that the last dollar spent on bananas, for example, provides the consumer with
very little pleasure, compared to the last dollar spent on tomatoes. In this case,
the consumer would get more pleasure if he or she spent that last banana dollar
on tomatoes instead.

• Each producer produces at the point that gives the highest profits (revenue minus cost). The producer does this by producing units only as long as
the received price exceeds the additional cost of production, and by refusing
to produce any additional units.

This description of how a competitive market equilibrium, in which each
producer and consumer acts in his or her own self-interest, resulting in an allocation of goods that is (in the sense described here) optimal for the group as
a whole, is at the heart of Adam Smith's image of an "invisible hand" guiding
economic activity (see Box 7.3). This concept will be discussed more fully in
Chapter 16, which explores criticisms of the "economics approach" to policy
analysis.

Combining Goods into Groups

In many economic discussions, and frequently in this book, the commodities
referred to are not actually single goods. We have some idea of what it means
to talk about the price of a tomato, or the price of a banana, or the price of a

---

Box 7.3 Adam Smith's Invisible Hand

"[E]very individual . . . neither intends to promote the public interest, nor knows how much he is promoting it. . . . [B]y directing that industry in such a manner as its produce may be of the greatest value, he intends only his own gain, and he is in this, as in many other cases, led by an invisible hand to promote an end which was no part of his intention. Nor is it always the worse for the society that it was no part of it. By pursuing his own interest he frequently promotes that of the society more effectually than when he really intends to promote it. I have never known much good done by those who affected to trade for the public good. It is an affectation, indeed, not very common among merchants, and very few words need be employed in dissuading them from it."

Source: Adam Smith, *Wealth of Nations* (1776), Book IV, http://socserv2 .socsci.mcmaster.ca/~econ/ugcm/3ll3/smith/wealth/index.html.

---

bushel of corn or a pound of chicken wings. But when we talk about the price of "food" or the quantity of "food," this is an abstract concept. In the rest of this chapter, we refer to "aggregate supply" and "aggregate demand" as shorthand terms meaning aggregate supply and demand of food.

How Demand Changes over Time

One important aspect of our study of the world food problem is to understand how supply and demand for food have changed in the past and how they might be expected to change in the future. In this section we examine factors that shift the aggregate demand for food.

Recall that aggregate demand for food shows the total quantity of food demanded at every level of price. The total quantity of food demanded at any given price might increase for any of the following reasons: (1) the number of people in the economy increases; (2) people in the economy have more money to spend on all goods, so part of the additional income is spent on food; (3) people's tastes change, such that they get more pleasure out of food compared to other nonfood goods. (Economics students will recognize that we have failed to mention an additional factor: [4] prices of other nonfood items increase, such that the pleasure per dollar of additional expenditure on those nonfood goods declines.)

Population Growth Shifts the Aggregate Demand Curve

Aggregate demand for food depends on how many individual consumer demand curves we are aggregating. This is the usual departure point for discussions of the world hunger problem: Can food supplies keep up with population growth? In other words, how many people are there to feed? This will be the focus of Chapter 8, and population policy will be discussed in Chapter 18. For now, we simply note that an increase in population causes an outward shift in the aggregate demand curve for food. At any particular price level, the aggregate quantity demanded is higher because there are more people contributing to the aggregate demand. Holding all other factors constant (and in particular assuming that the aggregate supply curve remains constant), the effect of the outward shift in aggregate demand is to increase the price, and the higher price induces farmers to produce more food, so that the aggregate equilibrium quantity increases.

Changes in Income or Income Distribution Shift the Aggregate Demand Curve

Aggregate demand for food is not the same thing as quantity of food that will provide every individual a healthy diet, nor is there any implicit promise that the equilibrium price will guarantee that the average individual (or all individuals, or even most individuals) will have sufficient food. Aggregate supply and demand can describe famine conditions or conditions of great plenty.

An individual's demand curve for food shows how much food he or she will want to buy at every price level, *given his or her income.* A person with a low income will have a demand curve that reflects low quantities. For most goods (so-called normal goods), if the person gets more income to spend, his or her demand curve will shift up and to the right, as shown in Figure 7.4: at every price, the person will demand a higher quantity.

How big will the shift be? Economists use the concept of "income elasticity of demand" to measure this. This concept and some measures of the income elasticity of demand will be discussed in more detail later in this chapter, where we will show that the size of the shift is different for a poor person than for a rich person. If a poor person's income increases by 10 percent, the person will spend a lot of the increase on food and the person's demand curve for food will shift a relatively large amount. If a rich person's income increases by 10 percent, the person will spend little of the increase on food and the person's demand curve for food will shift a small amount. This fact has implications for the relationship between changes in aggregate demand for food and changes in income distribution.

If everyone's income grows, each person's demand for food will shift out and aggregate demand will also shift out. If average income stays the same, but income is redistributed from a rich person to a poor person, the aggregate demand curve for food will also shift out, since the poor person's demand for food will shift out by a large amount, while the rich person's demand for food shifts back (in the opposite direction of the arrow in Figure 7.4), but by a smaller amount.

Figure 7.4 Outward Shift in Demand

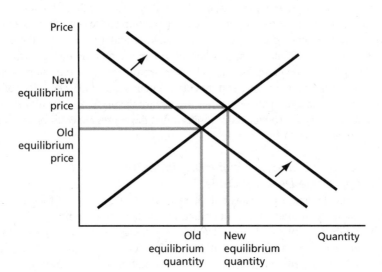

*Changes in Tastes and Preferences Can Shift
the Aggregate Demand Curve*

A final factor that may shift the aggregate demand curve for food is worth mentioning, even though it may seem obvious: changes in people's tastes and preferences over time. To see how this works at the level of the individual, let us return to our analogy of the boy and the raspberries and imagine that the same boy revisits the same raspberry patch the following summer, except that this year he is wearing braces on his teeth. As he begins to eat the raspberries, he discovers that the tiny seeds get stuck in his braces in an annoying way. The pleasure he derives from eating the berries is less. In economics terminology, his individual demand curve has shifted down and to the left.

A change in tastes and preferences is not the same thing as a change in quantity of food a person wants to buy. As the price of food changes, the quantity of food a person wants to buy will change as the person moves along their (constant) demand curve. As a person's income changes, the quantity of food the person wants to buy will change as their demand curve shifts. A change in tastes and preferences causes a change in the quantity of food a person wants to buy even as prices and income remain constant. For example, a person who decides to lose weight by eating less food will have a shift in demand.

In the aggregate, some trends in general behavior may cause a detectable shift in aggregate demand for food in developed countries: an increasing concern with obesity and overeating, an increasing interest in diets low in carbohydrates, an increasing interest in food produced "organically," and a shift toward a more vegetarian diet.

How Supply Changes over Time

We next look at two types of changes that may cause shifts in the aggregate supply of food over time: changes in availability (or price) of resources used to produce food, and changes in technology or in efficiency of resource use.

Changes in Availability of Resources Used to Produce Food

If the resources used to produce food become more readily available—if the price of those resources falls—then at any level of output price, farmers will be willing to produce more. In the berry patch analogy, this is equivalent to an increase in the density of berries on the bush, or a decrease in the density of the thorns. Because it is less costly to produce an additional unit, more units are produced. An increase in production at every price level means an outward shift in supply, such as that illustrated in Figure 7.5.

Some simple examples illustrate this. If a farmer obtains more land, then at every price level he will produce more output; his individual supply curve will shift out. If the farmer has more children able to work in the field, the extra labor will cause the farm's supply curve to shift out. If a dry creek begins to run with water so that the farmer can irrigate, the supply curve will shift out. If the general weather pattern changes to be more conducive to agricultural production, the supply curve will shift out. If the soil on the farm is eroded, or

Figure 7.5 Outward Shift in Supply

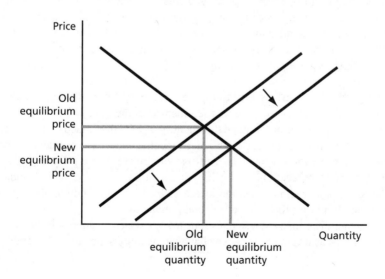

soil nutrients deplete, the supply curve will shift back (in the opposite direction of the arrows in Figure 7.5). All of these—land, labor, water, weather, soil—are examples of productive resources; changing their availability shifts the supply curve.

When productive resources are bought and sold on a market, changes in general availability are reflected in the level of price for the resources. If fertilizer becomes more plentiful, the fertilizer price drops, and the supply of agricultural output shifts out. Similarly (as we will see later in the book), a government program to reduce fertilizer price (or to reduce the price of any other productive resource) has the same effect: it reduces farmers' production costs and causes an outward shift in the supply of agricultural output. During 2007–2008, oil and gasoline prices more than doubled; during that period (as noted at the end of Chapter 6) the supply curve for food shifted back (up and to the left) and contributed to the increase in food prices.

Changes in Technology or in Efficiency of Resource Use

The amount of food produced from a given set of resources also depends on the efficiency with which the resources are used. Available water can be used efficiently to irrigate, or some of it can be wasted in runoff. Labor hours of a second worker can (inadvertently or intentionally) undo the work of the first worker. Anything that systematically improves the efficiency of resource use will have the same impact as an increase in resource availability.

A technological improvement is some kind of new knowledge that allows farmers to produce more output with the same resources. Often the new knowledge is embodied in some piece of equipment (such as the invention of the plow) or other input (such as a new variety of seed). But the concept is broad enough to encompass improvements in the ability to predict weather patterns, or a better understanding of agronomic processes. A technological improvement is similar to a reduction in the price of a productive resource: both reduce the cost to the farmer of producing an additional unit of output, and both shift the supply curve out.

Using the Concept of Elasticity to Quantify Economic Changes

So far in this chapter we have focused mainly on the direction of changes: as price goes up, consumers reduce the quantity of food demanded and producers increase the quantity of food supplied; as income goes up, consumers increase the quantity of food demanded. But by how much? If the price of food increases by 3 percent, how much will quantities supplied and demanded change? If a household's income increases by 12 percent, how much will the household increase the quantity of food purchased?

Economists answer these questions using a concept called "elasticity." An elasticity measures the percentage change in quantity supplied or demanded in response to a 1 percent change in price or income. Here we will limit our attention to three types of elasticity. *Income elasticity of demand* measures the extent to which a demand curve shifts out in response to an increase in income. *Price elasticity of demand* measures the steepness of the demand curve: How much does quantity demanded fall as price increases (or how much does quantity demanded rise as price decreases) as we move along a demand curve? *Price elasticity of supply* measures the steepness of the supply curve: How does quantity supplied change in response to a change in price as we move along a supply curve?

Income Elasticity of Demand

In simplest terms, income elasticity of demand is the percentage change in the consumption of something, such as rice, when a 1 percent change occurs in income. How this elasticity will change depends on income level. If a poverty-stricken Indian villager suffers a 1 percent decrease in income, he might decrease his consumption of rice by half a percent or so. But a wealthy stockbroker who suffers a 1 percent decrease in income might not change her rice consumption at all (she might spend less on recreational travel, for instance, but this is getting ahead of our story).

Let us look at some general ways in which food consumption changes as income rises or falls. Studies of how food consumption changes in countries as their average per capita incomes grow show consistently that food consumption increases as income increases, but that the rate of increase in consumption falls off as incomes reach higher and higher levels. This is because the proportion of the household budget spent on food decreases as income increases. The first person to write about this was Ernst Engel, and the phenomenon has become known as Engel's law.

Figure 7.6 provides an illustration from Indonesia of how food is related to income. Only the families in the top half of the income groupings (the right-hand half of Figure 7.6a) consume a minimally sufficient number of calories. Figure 7.6b provides a second illustration of Engel's law: as income rises, the percentage of income spent on food declines, from 75 for the lowest-income families in the sample population, to 60 for the highest-income families. Figure 7.6c shows how the food expenditure mix changes as income increases. As income grows, the East Javanese spend a smaller proportion of their food budget on starchy staples—cassava, rice, maize, and wheat flour—and a larger proportion on other items, especially animal products. This phenomenon is called Bennett's law (after agricultural economist Merrill Bennett; see Bennett 1941), which states that the *starchy staple ratio* (the ratio of starchy foods such as cereals and root crops to other foods in the diet) falls as income increases. Figure 7.6d shows how the energy derived from various food sources shifts as income rises.

**Figure 7.6 Relationships Between Income Level
and Nutritional Status, East Java, Indonesia, 1977–1978**

a. Energy (Kcal)

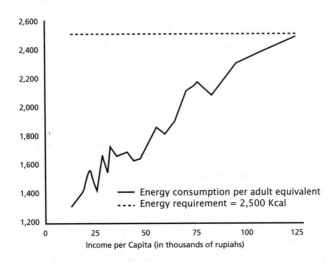

b. Food Expenditures (percentage of income)

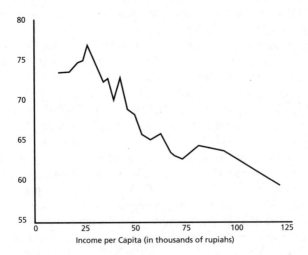

(continues)

Figure 7.6 continued

c. Percentage of Food Budget

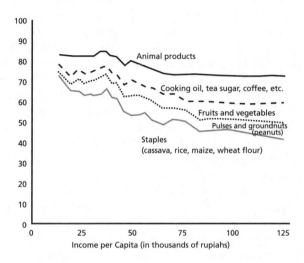

d. Percentage of Total Energy Consumption

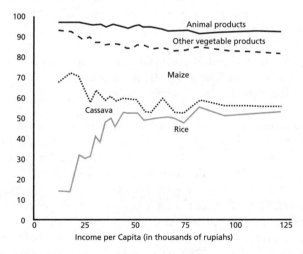

Source: Ho 1984.
Note: An income of 125,000 rupiahs in 1977–1978 was worth something over $200. The study region included Madura and the nearby regency of Sidorajo.

One aspect of Figure 7.6d deserves special attention. Notice that for people in this survey, starting at the very lowest levels of income, additional income leads to an *increase* in cassava consumption; but for only slightly higher levels of income, increased income leads to a *decrease* in cassava consumption. In a situation like this, as a person's income rises, instead of demand shifting out (as shown in Figure 7.4), the demand curve shifts in the opposite direction—quantity demanded at any given price is lower than it was before the income increase.

Commodities like this—of which people consume less as their incomes rise—are known by the ignominious name of *inferior goods*. A study of maize consumption in South Africa (Alderman and Lindert 1998:221) showed a similar pattern. At very low income levels, households used additional income to *increase* their maize consumption, but as income reached higher levels, households used additional income to *reduce* their maize consumption and replace it with consumption of other, more palatable foods. In the United States, during the recent economic slowdown, grocery stores reported large increases in sales of the meat product Spam (Martin 2008). This implies that as incomes fall (during a recession), demand for Spam shifts out; so, in the United States, Spam is an inferior good—it has a negative income elasticity of demand

The explanation for this behavior is that inferior goods (like cassava in Indonesia or maize in South Africa) provide the most calories per dollar spent but are not the tastiest foods available. For very poor people who have insufficient calories in their diets, increased income provides an opportunity to reduce the extent of undernutrition in the household through purchase of the most efficient source of calories. But for slightly richer households where undernutrition is less of a problem, increased income provides an opportunity to add tastier food to the household diet without significantly harming nutritional status. (An extreme example of inferior goods is discussed in Box 7.4.)

In Figure 7.7, we see that, for the world as a whole, changes in diet are consistent with Bennett's law. Carbohydrates make up about 70–75 percent of the dietary calories of the lowest-income countries, and only 45–50 percent of the dietary calories of the highest-income countries.

Quantifying income elasticities. As discussed earlier, income elasticity of demand is the percentage change in the consumption of something, such as rice or calories or "all food," when there is a 1 percent change in income, holding all other variables (such as price) constant. Reading this definition, one might think that it would be a fairly simple matter to estimate an income elasticity: observe a change (or difference) in consumption, such as "per capita milk consumption increased 2 percent between 2004 and 2008"; observe a comparable change (or difference) in income, such as "per capita income increased by 4 percent between 2004 and 2008"; and then divide the first number by the second number. But such a procedure would fail to give a good estimate of an income elasticity because it would fail to hold other things constant—prices and

---

Box 7.4 An Economic Experiment to Verify the Existence of Giffen Goods

---

Earlier in Chapter 7, we mentioned Alfred Marshall as the father of modern economics. Marshall credited his colleague, Robert Giffen, with the following insight: "[A] rise in the price of bread makes so large a drain on the resources of the poorer labouring families, . . . that they are forced to curtail their consumption of meat and the more expensive . . . foods; and, bread being still the cheapest food which they can get and will take, they consume more, and not less of it." Marshall (1920, book III, chapter VI, page 17). In other words, Giffen posited that for very low-income consumers, an increase in price could actually cause an increase in consumption of inferior goods.

Economists have long recognized the theoretical possibility that Giffen pointed out. However, they have looked in vain (until recently) for a real-world example of a "Giffen good." Introductory economics textbooks sometimes suggest that potatoes during the Irish famine might be an example, but careful consideration (Rosen 1999) raises serious doubt. "It is unlikely that consumption of potatoes could have increased when the price rose during the famine, at least in the aggregate, precisely because the price rise was caused by a blight that destroyed much of the crop" (Jensen and Miller 2008:1553–1554).

A problem with finding real-life examples of Giffen goods is that if we look at aggregate changes in quantity consumed when the price of a staple good rises, we combine in that aggregate the consumption responses of very low-income people (for whom the staple good is a normal good) with the consumption responses of higher-income people (for whom the staple good is an inferior good). One way around this problem is to construct artificial situations in which people with the same income levels face different prices. These artificial situations are know as "economic experiments."

Jensen and Miller went into the Chinese countryside (Hunan province) and conducted an economic experiment designed to test whether Giffen behavior could be observed in the real world. They handed out coupons that entitled the holder to buy rice at reduced prices. In return, the coupon recipients agreed to be interviewed about their incomes and consumption patterns. Based on this experiment, Jensen and Miller conclude: "For the group consuming at least some substantial share (20 percent) of calories from sources other than rice, i.e., the poor-but-not-too-poor, we find very strong evidence of Giffen Behavior. . . . When faced with an increase in the price of the staple good, these households do indeed 'consume more, and not less, of it'" (2008:1566).

---

tastes also changed between 2004 and 2008. In the real world of constantly changing incomes and prices, estimating elasticities is a lot more difficult than this. We leave descriptions of how this is done to others (e.g., Deaton and Muellbauer 1980; Huang 1985; Johnson, Hassan, and Green 1984), accept their elasticity estimates, and concentrate on the meaning and implications of these estimates for policy planners.

Figure 7.7 Percentage of Calories Derived from Fats, Carbohydrates, and Proteins, by Annual GNP per Capita, 2001

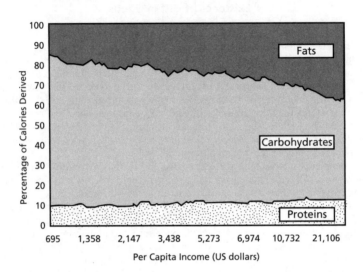

T. J. Ho (1984) calculated income elasticity for the East Javanese consumers whose food consumption patterns are outlined in Figure 7.6. She found the income elasticity of expenditure on food to be 0.58. That is, for this community, a 1 percent increase in income will produce a 0.58 percent increase in spending for food.

For purposes of illustration, let us hypothesize that this community spends half its income on food and, to make the computations simple, let us assume that its total income is $100. A 1 percent increase in income raises income to $101. If food spending increases by 0.58 percent, these people will spend 29 cents more on food, for a total of $50.29. The remaining 71 cents of increased income will be spent on nonfood items, bringing the total for that category (housing, clothing, paying off debts, etc.) to $50.71. We can deduce, therefore, that the income elasticity of demand for nonfood items in this community is 1.42. Had this community increased its spending on food by exactly the same percentage (and in this case exactly the same dollar amount) as its spending on nonfood items, this would indicate that the income elasticity of demand for both food and nonfood items is exactly 1.0.

Bouis and Haddad (1992), in a review of the literature, report a wide range of calorie-income elasticities, from 0.01 in Nicaragua to 1.18 in India. They argue that the wide range is attributable in large part to the different methods that different studies use to collect data on calories, and to different conceptual measures of "income." They conclude that if appropriate measures are used, elasticity estimates fall in the 0.08–0.14 range.

Ho (1984) estimates the income elasticity of demand for calories to be 0.28 and for protein to be 0.52. These elasticities condense some of the information in Figure 7.6d. Review this graph and notice again how the East Javanese are substituting rice for cassava as their incomes increase. To a lesser extent, they are substituting animal products and other vegetable products for cassava at the same time. Calories from cassava are cheaper than calories from rice, other vegetables, or meat. Therefore, as the East Javanese increase their spending on food, they buy fewer calories per rupiah and more of other food properties such as protein content and flavor. This is what the income elasticity figures (low for calories and high for protein) are telling us.

Here is another way of looking at those elasticity figures for calories versus protein. A 1 percent increase in income yields only a 0.28 percent increase in consumption of calories but a more generous 0.52 percent increase in protein consumption. That is, as income changes, the East Javanese change their consumption of protein more (in terms of percentage) than they change their consumption of calories. While it is easy to arrive at this conclusion without the aid of the elasticity figures, those figures allow us to calculate how much the people of East Java change their consumption of these two nutrients when income changes. This is the beauty—and the importance—of elasticity. It quantifies things.

Of course, people do not go to the market and buy nutrients like calories and protein. They buy food. So let us look at some income elasticity figures for particular commodities and see how these elasticities change with income. A detailed table of income elasticities in various countries for a variety of food groups and nutrients can be found at the website of the US Department of Agriculture (USDA) (see http://www.ers.usda.gov/data/internationalfooddemand).

How income elasticity changes with income. Table 7.1 shows some income elasticities for three income groups in rural Brazil. Notice that, except for cassava flour, the income elasticity figures are positive. That is, for most foods, consumption increases as income increases. Cassava flour, with a negative income elasticity, is an inferior good. Notice also that the absolute values of these elasticity figures (i.e., their values regardless of negative/positive sign) tend to decrease from low- to high-income consumers. That is, food consumption among low-income consumers is considerably more responsive to changes in income than it is among high-income consumers. This phenomenon is found among all third world populations.

When the low-income consumer in the Brazilian sample receives a 1 percent increase in income, he or she tends to increase rice consumption by about 2 percent. But the high-income consumer tends to change his or her consumption of rice by less than 0.2 percent when income changes by 1 percent. We call the low-income family's consumption response own-price *elastic.* That is,

Table 7.1   Income Elasticities for Calorie Intake, Selected Foods, by Income Group, Rural Brazil, 1974–1975

	Income Group		
	Lowest 30 Percent	Middle 50 Percent	Highest 20 Percent
Cassava flour	–3.50	–1.590	–.356
Rice	1.99	.172	.173
Milk	2.27	.147	.172
Eggs	1.93	.630	.114
Mean per capita calorie intake	1,963	2,432	2,771

Source: Gray 1982:26.

Note: The 1974–1975 National Household Expenditure Survey (ENDEF) of the Brazilian Geographical and Statistical Institute was used as the database from which to calculate these income elasticities.

a 1 percent change in its income yields a greater than 1 percent change in consumption. On the other hand, we call the high-income family's consumption response own-price *inelastic*. That is, a 1 percent change in its income produces a less than 1 percent change in consumption. If a family changed its consumption of rice by exactly 1 percent when its income changed by 1 percent, we would say it had an income elasticity of demand for rice of 1.0—neither elastic nor inelastic.

Remember that the elasticity figures show percentage change in consumption following a 1 percent change in income. The income elasticity of de-

Table 7.2   Changes in Calorie Consumption Resulting from a 1 Percent Increase in Income, Selected Foods, Lowest 30 Percent of Consumers by Income, Rural Brazil, 1974–1975

	Daily Kilocalories from Food Source	Percentage of Total Kilocalories Consumed	Income Elasticity	Change in Kilocalories Consumed Resulting from a 1 Percent Increase in Income
Cassava flour	440	22.4	–3.50	–15.4
Rice	296	15.1	1.99	5.9
Milk	41	2.1	2.27	.9
Eggs	7	.5	1.93	.1
Other	1,152	59.9		17.4
Total kilocalorie intake	1,936		.46	8.9
Estimated kilocalorie intake after 1% increase in income	1,945			

Source: Calculated from Gray 1982:20, 26.

mand for rice in rural Brazil is about the same as the income elasticity of demand for eggs. But because rice makes up 15 percent of the total calories consumed among this income group, and eggs only 0.5 percent, a 1 percent change in income results in a far greater change in actual consumption of rice than of eggs (see Table 7.2). The nutritional significance of an elasticity, therefore, depends not only on the magnitude of the elasticity but also on the magnitude of consumption of the goods under consideration.

Price Elasticity of Demand

How food consumption changes with price. As Figures 7.2 and 7.3 show, quantity demanded normally increases in response to a price decrease. But by how much? The consumption response to a decline in the price of a food item can be complex. Let us think about what might happen to consumption among a group of poor people if the price of rice were to fall substantially.

A fall in the price of rice would likely result in the consumption of more rice. But it might well be that not all the increased purchasing power that results from a fall in the price of rice will be spent on rice. Some of it might be spent on purchasing more of other foods, such as eggs, and some of it might be spent on purchasing nonfood items, such as entertainment.

This percentage change in rice consumption as a result of a 1 percent change in the price of rice (holding all other variables constant) is its *own-price elasticity.* The percentage change in the consumption of a good resulting from a 1 percent change in the price of *some other good* is the *cross-price elasticity* of demand.

Cross-price elasticities tend to be small. A change in the price of rice, for instance, will probably have little impact on the quantity of movie tickets a person buys. Data on cross-price elasticities are harder to obtain and may be less reliable than income and own-price elasticities. Furthermore, much sound analysis of the nutritional impact of policy alternatives can be done with what we know about income and own-price elasticities. Therefore, in this book we will not deal much with cross-price elasticities.

Quantifying own-price elasticities. Remember that price elasticity of demand is the percentage change in consumption of something, like rice, when a 1 percent change occurs in its own price, holding all other variables constant.

As with income elasticity of demand, estimating these elasticities is a lot more difficult than the preceding equation suggests. So again we leave descriptions of how this is done to others. A comprehensive set of demand elasticities in various countries for a variety of food groups and nutrients have been calculated by the USDA (see http://www.ers.usda.gov/data/international fooddemand), which obtained values of between –0.2 and –0.4.

Table 7.3 shows a set of income and own-price demand elasticities for major food groups in Indonesia. These figures are for the complete spectrum

Table 7.3 Income and Price Elasticities for Selected Foods, Indonesia

	Income Elasticity	Own-Price Elasticity
Corn and cassava	0.3	−.26
Spices	0.3	−.25
Rice	0.7	−.63
Coconut	1.1	−.88
Tea and coffee	1.1	−.90
Vegetables and fruits	1.2	−.97
Prepared food	1.2	−1.01
Fish	1.3	−1.04
Sugar	1.4	−1.15
Drinks	2.1	−1.71
Livestock and livestock products	2.2	−1.73

Source: Boediono 1978:362.

of incomes, not broken down by income groups. Notice that for Indonesian society as a whole, all the income elasticities are positive and all the own-price demand elasticities are negative. This is exactly what the theory leads us to expect: income elasticities are positive, meaning that an increase in income causes an outward shift in demand, as in Figure 7.4—the goods here are "normal goods," not "inferior goods"; price elasticities are negative, meaning demand curves are downward-sloping.

Elasticities show the relative importance consumers attach to the various foods in their diets. Items considered essential or necessary tend to have price and income elasticities below 1.0. Think of it this way: When income falls by 1 percent, consumption of necessities falls by less than 1 percent. Or, if the price of a necessity rises by 1 percent, people do not cut their consumption very much. From Table 7.3, it appears that Indonesians generally regard corn and cassava, spices, and rice as necessities.

Conversely, items considered luxuries tend to have price or income elasticities above 1.0. If income falls by 1 percent, the consumption of luxuries falls by more than 1 percent, as people cut back on luxuries and concentrate what income is left on necessities. Or, if the price of a luxury rises by 1 percent, people are more likely to cut back substantially on consumption of that good. Table 7.3 shows that Indonesians generally regard livestock and livestock products as luxuries. This is commonly the case in poor consumers in developing countries.

How price elasticity changes with income. Pinstrup-Andersen and colleagues (Pinstrup-Andersen et al. 1976; Pinstrup-Andersen and Caicedo 1978) were the first to show that one could estimate price (and income) elasticities by income groups as well as by the community as a whole. They di-

Table 7.4 Estimated Direct Price Elasticity of Demand by Income Group, Cali, Colombia, 1969–1970

	Low Income			High Income		
	I	II	III	IV	V	Average
Cassava	−0.23	−0.28	−0.25	−0.00	−0.00	−0.19
Potatoes	−0.41	−0.42	−0.31	−0.00	−0.00	−0.26
Rice	−0.43	−0.40	−0.40	−0.26	−0.18	−0.35
Maize	−0.63	−0.55	−0.44	−0.00	−0.00	−0.44
Bread/pastry	−0.65	−0.56	−0.32	−0.24	−0.00	−0.31
Beans	−0.82	−0.78	−0.64	−0.45	−0.25	−0.60
Peas	−1.13	−1.13	−0.76	−0.59	−0.52	−0.70
Eggs	−1.34	−1.23	−1.26	−0.75	−0.35	−0.92
Oranges	−1.39	−0.96	−0.79	−0.64	−0.29	−0.69
Milk	−1.79	−1.62	−1.12	−0.64	−0.20	−0.77
Pork	−1.89	−1.61	−1.12	−0.82	−0.70	−1.01
Daily calorie intake as percentage of requirement	89	99	117	132	1,718	119

Source: Pinstrup-Andersen et al. 1976:137–138.

vided their Cali, Colombia, sample population into five income groups, and estimated elasticities for each income group as well as for their entire sample. Some of the elasticities calculated in their groundbreaking study are shown in Table 7.4.

Notice how responsiveness to change in price generally diminishes when moving from low-income to high-income consumers. Table 7.4 shows that high-income consumers in Cali do not react at all to small changes in the price of cassava, potatoes, maize, or bread. And items like pork or milk are luxuries for low-income households (price elasticities greater than 1 in absolute value), but necessities (price elasticities less than 1 in absolute value) for high-income households.

Since this pioneering study, a number of other studies have been conducted that relate food price elasticities to income. A useful survey of those studies can be found in Alderman 1986. In a 2015 paper, Cornelsen and colleagues did a "meta analysis" (or study of previous studies) of seventy-eight papers that had estimated demand elasticities for food. Some of their results are shown in Table 7.5, and reinforce the general points discussed here: (a) food demand is "price inelastic"—all of the elasticities in Table 7.5 are less than 1 in absolute value; (b) demand for animal-derived products (meat and dairy) is more elastic, or more responsive to price changes, than is demand for crop-derived products (cereals and oils); (c) food demand in poor countries is more inelastic (less responsive to price changes) than is food demand in rich countries.

Table 7.5 Own-Price Demand Elasticities by Country Income Group

	Low-Income Countries	Middle-Income Countries	High-Income Countries
Fats and oils	−0.60	−0.54	−0.42
Cereals	−0.61	−0.55	−0.43
Fruits and vegetables	−0.72	−0.65	−0.53
Meat	−0.78	−0.72	−0.60
Dairy	−0.78	−0.72	−0.60

Sources: Cornelsen et al. 2015.

Price Elasticity of Supply

The final elasticity we will look at is the supply elasticity, which measures the percentage change in quantity of output in response to a 1 percent change in price of output. Estimates of supply elasticities find that supply is also "inelastic": a 1 percent increase in price will induce less than a 1 percent increase in quantity supplied. López (1980), for example, estimates a supply elasticity of 0.010 for crops and a supply elasticity of 0.472 for animal products.

Table 7.6 shows some estimates of supply elasticities for important crops in a number of important producing countries and worldwide. Table 7.6 confirms the assertion that supply of agricultural commodities is inelastic—all of the numbers in Table 7.6 are well below 1.0.

Some earlier research implied that agricultural supply elasticities are somewhat higher in the developed world than in the developing world (Askari

Table 7.6 Estimates of Own-Price Supply Elasticities for Various Countries, Regions, and Crops

	Wheat	Corn	Soybeans	Rice
South Africa	0.09	0.28	0.03	0.03
China	0.09	0.13	0.45	0.16
India	0.29	0.21	0.36	0.11
Argentina	0.41	0.70	0.32	0.24
Brazil	0.43	0.42	0.34	0.07
European Union	0.12	0.08	0.19	0.24
United States	0.25	0.17	0.30	0.35
Canada	0.39	0.18	0.32	n/a
Australia	0.33	0.23	n/a	0.17
Global				
Roberts and Schlenker 2013	0.10	0.27	0.55	0.03
Haile, Kalkuhl, and von Braun 2014	0.10	0.23	0.34	0.05

Source: Calculated from Gray 1982:20, 26.

and Cummings 1976; Herdt 1970:518–519), indicating that farmers in developing countries are somewhat less responsive to changes in prices than are farmers in the developed world. But the more recent estimates in Table 7.6 (or see also Hochman et al. 2014) fail to find systematic differences in supply elasticity depending on the income level of the producing country.

Similar results are obtained for long-run aggregate supply elasticities (evaluations of the "long run" allow all inputs, including land and major capital items, to vary in quantity when the output price changes). Because all inputs are allowed to vary, long-run supply elasticities are generally higher than short-run supply elasticities. Estimates of long-run supply elasticities for agricultural commodities range from 0.3 to 0.9 (Chhibber 1988).

Economic Analysis of Food Price Increases in the Twenty-First Century

At the end of Chapter 6, we described the rapid increase in food prices during 2007–2008 and 2011. The tools of economic analysis described in this present chapter can help us better understand the possible economic causes of that price increase. A number of potential interrelated causes of the high prices have been identified by economic analysis (e.g., Glauber 2008a; IFPRI 2008; OECD and FAO 2007; Hochman et al. 2014).

One set of economic explanations for a price spike is a rapid growth in demand for agricultural commodities. This could happen if the people of China and India reach of level of prosperity where they rather suddenly begin to incorporate meat into their diets to a greater extent. This explanation of a shift in demand for food—illustrated by the shift as shown in Figure 7.4—is discussed in more detail in Chapter 10. (We should note that economic theory does not view the incorporation of meat into diets as incomes grow as a kind of seesaw with sudden and rapid changes as incomes reach some tipping point; rather, meat will be added incrementally as incomes rise.) Demand for grain will also shift out as policies encourage "biofuels" such as ethanol, which use food commodities (corn, sugarcane) for nonfood uses.

A second set of explanations of a price spike is that agricultural supply was shifted back (up and to the left) suddenly. This can happen if there is poor weather that reduces crop yields, or increases the costs of farm production because of high energy prices. On global markets, policy decisions by countries that restrict exports can also cause a backward shift in supply. In the 2008–2011 period, both India and China restricted exports. In a period of rising food prices, exporting countries may desire to insulate their domestic consumers from those high prices by limiting exports—increasing the domestic supply of food (and therefore keeping food prices relatively low), but reducing the supply of food and increasing the price on the world market.

Notice that some of the explanations advanced here differ from the standard shifters of supply (technology, cost of inputs) and demand (population, income, tastes) presented earlier in the chapter. Government policies can have important influences on supply and demand of agricultural commodities. Government policies that encourage or require use of biofuels (in the United States and European Union, for example) have undoubtedly caused aggregate demand for those commodities to shift out and to the right. And government policies that restrict exports (in India and China, for example) have undoubtedly caused aggregate supply on the world market to shift back and to the left.

In addition, remember that both aggregate supply and demand of food is price *inelastic*. An inelastic demand curve is one that is closer to vertical than to horizontal—quantity demanded stays about the same even as the price changes substantially. But this means that even fairly small backward shifts in the aggregate supply curve can cause large price increases. An inelastic supply curve is also one that is closer to vertical than to horizontal—quantity supplied stays about the same even as the price changes substantially. But this means that even fairly small outward shifts in demand can cause large price increases. The inelastic nature of supply and demand for food is an underlying explanation for why food prices are so volatile and how those prices can shoot up so quickly, as described in Chapter 6.

8

It's Not
Food vs. Population

Land, unlike people, . . . does not breed.

—Heilbroner 1953:82 (paraphrasing Malthus)

Thomas Malthus

The debate over food versus people started with an argument between the young reverend Thomas Robert Malthus and his father. The elder Malthus was enthusiastic about a recently published book that promised a future world devoid of "disease, anguish, melancholy, or resentment" (Godwin 1793). Young Thomas was not impressed. In fact, he was so skeptical about such a utopian future that he wrote down his objections. The father was so struck with Thomas's words that he encouraged his son to publish them (Heilbroner 1953:69–70). First issued anonymously in 1798 as *An Essay on the Principle of Population As It Affects the Future Improvement of Society,* Malthus's "essay" was never short and by its sixth edition, still claiming to be an essay, covered some 600 pages of detailed argument. For Malthus in his own words, see Box 8.1.

The Malthusian thesis postulated that the reproductive capacity of humans must put continual pressure on the "means of subsistence." Human numbers, he said, could increase by "geometric" progression: 2, 4, 8, 16, 32, 64, 128, 256 (we now call this progression *exponential*). Malthus did not see how subsistence could increase any faster than an "arithmetic" progression: 1, 2, 3, 4, 5, 6, 7, 8, 9 (we now call this progression *linear*). Unlike people, land does not breed, and Malthus thought that the potential for human numbers to increase exponentially must therefore put continuous pressure on our food supply.

Malthus enumerated a long list of checks to population growth, including war, "sickly" seasons, epidemics, pestilence, and plague. Humans themselves, Malthus thought, would be unable to check their own population growth because the only way he knew how to limit family size was through, as he put it,

---

Box 8.1 Excerpts from "An Essay on the Principle of Population" by Thomas Malthus (1798)

"It has been said that the great question is now at issue, whether man shall henceforth start forwards with accelerated velocity towards illimitable, and hitherto unconceived improvement, or be condemned to a perpetual oscillation between happiness and misery, and after every effort remain still at an immeasurable distance from the wished-for goal. . . ."

"I think I may fairly make two postulata. First, That food is necessary to the existence of man. Secondly, That the passion between the sexes is necessary and will remain nearly in its present state. . . ."

"Assuming then my postulata as granted, I say, that the power of population is indefinitely greater than the power in the earth to produce subsistence for man. Population, when unchecked, increases in a geometrical ratio. Subsistence increases only in an arithmetical ratio. A slight acquaintance with numbers will shew the immensity of the first power in comparison of the second. . . ."

"By that law of our nature which makes food necessary to the life of man, the effects of these two unequal powers must be kept equal. . . ."

"This implies a strong and constantly operating check on population from the difficulty of subsistence. This difficulty must fall somewhere and must necessarily be severely felt by a large portion of mankind. . . ."

"Taking the population of the world at any number, a thousand millions, for instance, the human species would increase in the ratio of—1, 2, 4, 8, 16, 32, 64, 128, 256, 512, etc. and subsistence as—1, 2, 3, 4, 5, 6, 7, 8, 9, 10, etc. In two centuries and a quarter, the population would be to the means of subsistence as 512 to 10: in three centuries as 4,096 to 13, and in two thousand years the difference would be almost incalculable, though the produce in that time would have increased to an immense extent. . . ."

"No limits whatever are placed to the productions of the earth; they may increase for ever and be greater than any assignable quantity. Yet still the power of population being a power of a superior order, the increase of the human species can only be kept commensurate to the increase of the means of subsistence by the constant operation of the strong law of necessity acting as a check upon the greater power. . . ."

Source: The full text of this excerpt can be found at http://socserv2.socsci .mcmaster.ca/~econ/ugcm/3ll3/malthus/popu.txt.

"moral restraint." (The technology of contraception was next to nonexistent at the time.) And in Malthus's view, given the "passion between the sexes," moral restraint was not strong enough to effectively limit human fertility. Therefore, lurking in the shadows, always ready to impose the ultimate check on population growth, would have to be famine. "Famine stalks in the rear, and with one mighty blow, levels the population with the food of the world" (Heilbroner 1953:83).

There was plausibility to the Malthusian argument. It was, in fact, a precursor to the now widely accepted ecological principle that any population will expand until it fills the ecological niche available to it. What Malthus did not foresee was that there would eventually be other checks to human population growth besides war, pestilence, and famine; that changing attitudes about family size—a kind of "small is beautiful" philosophy—could combine with a new technology in the form of effective and simple contraception to limit population growth. Nor did he foresee the enormous increases in agricultural production that would accompany the application of science to farming.

Important as Malthus's book was for the thesis it espoused, it was more important as a stimulation to thinking among people who read it. Charles Darwin, for instance, reports that he happened to read Malthus "for amusement," yet this reading inspired the theory of natural selection and survival of the fittest that would dominate his *On the Origin of Species* (Bettany 1890; Herbert 1971).

Others were not amused. As one biographer put it, "Malthus was not ignored. For thirty years it rained refutations" (James Bonner, as quoted in Heilbroner 1953:76). In the storm of protest that followed the publication of his essay, Malthus was compared to Satan and denounced as an "immoral, revolutionary, hard-hearted, and cruel atheist" (Bettany 1890:ix). But the strongest refutation of the seeming inevitability of a perpetual tendency toward famine that Malthus postulated lies in what has happened since he wrote his essay.

Since 1800 the population of the world has, in fact, grown exponentially—or nearly so (Figure 8.1). And more remarkably—as a tribute to

Figure 8.1 World Population, 0–2000

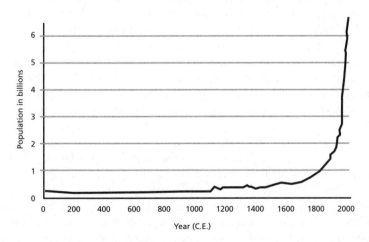

Source: US Bureau of the Census, "Collection of Historical Estimates of World Population" (10,000 B.C.E. to 1950) and "Census World Population Estimates" (1950–2008), http://www.census .gov/ipc/www/idb/worldpopinfo.html.

Malthus—his treatise in 1798 was at the very beginning of the exponential-type growth trend. On the other hand, the growth of world population seems destined to slow and to stop eventually through a process demographers call the demographic transition.

The Theory of Demographic Transition

The world appears to be going through a pattern of growth known as the *demographic transition*. Originally described by Frank Notestein (1945), the literature contains a number of ways of defining the term. We adopt and paraphrase from a conceptualization by Carl Haub (1987:19) of the Population Reference Bureau in Washington, DC.

The theory of demographic transition offers a general model for the gradual evolution of a population's birth and death rates (see Box 8.2) from the preindustrial to the modern pattern, which results in an S-shaped curve of population growth through time. According to the theory, population growth goes through four stages, illustrated in Figure 8.2:

Stage I. Preindustrial stage: Birth rates are high and fertility uncontrolled, with the birth rate exceeding the death rate and generally within the range of 25 to 45 per thousand. Periodic famines, plagues, and wars cause brief periods of population loss. Population grows, but slowly. Population growth rates in stage I are close to zero and stay relatively constant over time.

Stage II. Mortality decline before fertility decline: With better public health services and more reliable food and water supplies, death rates fall and life expectancy increases. If no accompanying decrease in the birth rate occurs, the population growth rate rises and population grows rapidly. In stage II, therefore, population growth rates become higher and higher over time.

Stage III. Fertility decline: At some point, usually as the country urbanizes and industrializes, the birth rate decreases in response to desires to limit family size. Population continues to grow rapidly for a while. But eventually birth rates approach death rates, and population growth slows. In stage III, population growth rates are still positive, but the rate is slowing over time. As we reach the end of stage III, population growth may have fallen to near zero.

Stage IV. Modern stage: By this point both the birth rate and death rate are low. After the birth rate falls as low as the death rate, population stabilizes. A population that is stable over a number of generations implies that the life expectancy is stable (each generation lives as long as the last, and as long as the next) and that fertility rate is at the "replacement fertility rate" of 2.1 children per woman (2.1 rather than 2.0 to account for childhood mortality and other factors that would keep some small percentage of the population from reproducing).

Box 8.2 Terms Commonly Used by Demographers

Crude birth rate, or birth rate: The number of births per year per thousand individuals in the population.

Crude death rate, or death rate: The number of deaths per year per thousand individuals in the population.

Gross reproductive rate: The number of female children a newborn female will have during her lifetime if current levels of fertility by age of female continue through time.

Life expectancy at birth, or life expectancy: The average expected age of death of newborns who follow a given age-specific mortality schedule.

Net reproductive rate: The expected number of daughters per newborn female, after subjecting those newborn females to a given set of mortality rates. (Net reproductive rate is lower than gross reproductive rate because some of the newborn females will die before completing their reproductive years.)

Total fertility rate, or fertility rate: The total number of births a female has during her lifetime.

The experience of fertility rates in the advanced economies of Europe in recent decades has caused some demographers (Haupt and Kane 2004) to speculate that the theory of demographic transition will have to be expanded to include a fifth stage—one in which fertility rates fall *below* the replacement

Figure 8.2 The Theory of Demographic Transition

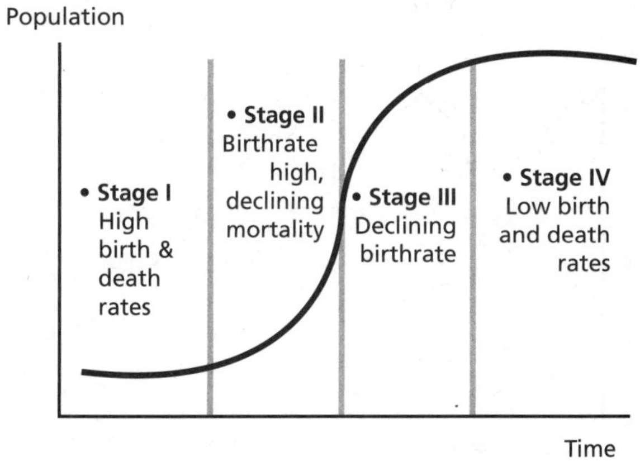

rate, and population dwindles rather than grows. According to the US Census Bureau (http://www.census.gov), the current fertility rate in eastern Europe as a whole is 1.51, in western Europe as a whole is 1.72, and for some countries (Italy, Japan, Germany, Slovenia, for example) is 1.40 or less.

There is abundant evidence to support the validity of the theory of demographic transition. First, we can find developed countries in which all four stages of demographic transition have occurred. The experience of Sweden, for example, is shown in Figure 8.3. In the decades before 1805, Sweden was in the last phase of stage I, with birth rates and death rates approximately equal, but high. Stage II in Sweden covered the seventy years between 1805 and 1875, as death rates began to fall, but birth rates stayed high. Stage III in Sweden covered the hundred-year period between 1875 and 1975, as birth rates declined faster than death rates. Sweden is now in stage IV, with birth and death rates approximately equal, but low (in fact, currently the birth rate in Sweden is slightly below the death rate).

A second source of evidence supporting the theory of demographic transition is a comparison of population growth rates in developed countries to those in developing countries. For example, in the period 2000–2015, the population of Africa (where many of the poorest countries of the world are) grew at a rate of 2.43 percent per year; the population of Asia (where there are many developing countries) grew at a rate of 1.08 percent per year; and the population of Europe grew at a rate of only 0.14 percent per year. In what are today's developed countries, the demographic transition is essentially finished: according to the US Census Bureau, for "more developed countries" birth rates are now just slightly higher than and death rates; and death rates are expected to match birth rates in the year 2019.

Figure 8.3 Birth and Death Rates in Sweden, 1751–2008

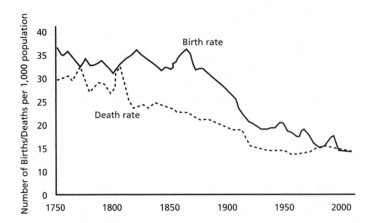

In developing countries, the process of demographic transition is still under way. Compare the demographic transition as shown in Figure 8.3 (with Sweden as representative of the developed world) and Figure 8.4 (with Mexico as representative of the developing world). The death-rate decline in Sweden began shortly after 1800 and took approximately 150 years to fall from 30 to 10 per thousand. The more dramatic death-rate decline in Mexico did not begin until about 1915 and took only 40 years to fall to 10 per thousand. Birth rates in Mexico remained above 40 per thousand until the early 1970s, when they began a rapid decline. Consequently, by the early 1970s, Mexico's population growth rate was above 3 percent, yielding a doubling time of fewer than twenty-three years.

Figure 8.5 makes this point a little more generally: population growth is higher in less developed countries. The countries with high population growth rates are bunched at the left of the figure in low per capita incomes. The rich countries generally have lower rates of population growth. This has two implications. First, economic growth, or improved economic prosperity, can be a powerful policy mechanism for reducing population growth. This will be discussed in more detail in Chapter 18. Second, since population is growing fastest among groups of people who have low incomes, the growth in demand for food may lag behind population growth. When we get to future projections in Chapter 23, we will assume that a 50 percent increase in population translates into a 50 percent increase in demand for food; in reality this may overstate the impact on demand.

A final piece of evidence supporting the theory of demographic transition is shown in Figure 8.6. For the world as a whole, the growth of population is slowing down. The actual growth—numbers of people added to the world's

Figure 8.4 Birth and Death Rates in Mexico, 1895–2005

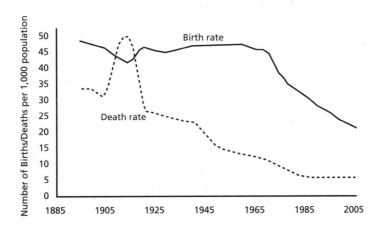

Figure 8.5 Population Grows Faster in Countries with Lower per Capita Incomes: Evidence from 165 Countries, 2001

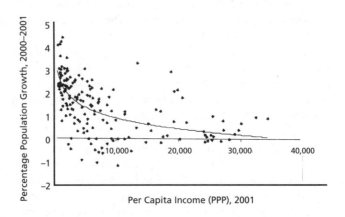

Source: World Bank 2003, *World Development Indicators.*

population every year—peaked in the late 1980s. The *rate* of growth—actual growth as a percentage of total population—peaked in the late 1960s. At that point in time, the world as a whole moved from stage II to stage III. Note that the rates of growth are still positive—world population continues to grow, but the *rate* of growth is slowing over time. In addition, the US Census Bureau predicts that the rates of growth in population will continue to decline for the next fifty years. (One interesting aspect of Figure 8.6: the sharp dip in population growth rates in the late 1950s and early 1960s corresponds with the Great Leap Forward famine in China, discussed in Chapter 2.)

Lester Brown and Hal Kane point out a less happy road to population stabilization. Criticizing the optimistic view of demographic transition, they say,

> As we approach the end of the twentieth century, a gap has emerged in the [demographic transition] analysis. The theorists did not say what happens when second stage population growth rates of 3 percent per year begin to overwhelm local life-support systems, making it impossible to sustain the economic and social gains that are counted on to reduce births. Unfortunately, trends that lead to ecological deterioration and economic decline are also self-reinforcing: Once populations expand to the point where their demands begin to exceed the sustainable yields of local forests, grasslands, croplands, or aquifers, they begin directly or indirectly to consume the resource base itself. . . . This . . . reduces food production and incomes, triggering a downward spiral in a process we describe as the demographic trap. All countries will complete the demographic transition, reaching population stability with low death and birth rates, or will get caught in the demographic

**Figure 8.6 Annual Growth Rate of World Population,
Historical and Projected, 1950–2050**

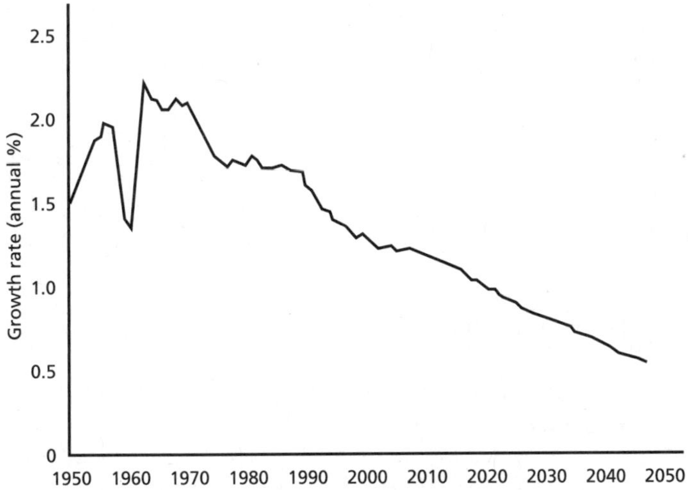

Sources: US Bureau of the Census, International Database, 2008.

trap, which eventually will also lead to demographic stability—but with high
birth rates and high death rates. (1994:55–56)

If the world's population growth does, in fact, stop as projected, humans
will have succeeded in controlling their own numbers without war, pestilence,
and famine—the things that Malthus thought would be necessary to curb population growth.

Projections of Future World Population

As we consider the future prospects for world food supply and demand, we
think first of population. How many mouths will there be to feed? The US Census Bureau, basing its statistics on the growth rates shown in Figure 8.6, projects that by the year 2050, world population will be about 9.41 billion, 30 percent higher than the current (2015) population of 7.26 billion (see Table 8.1).

The UN has also made population projections into the future. The UN
projections are based on assumptions about how life expectancy will change
in the future, and about how fertility rates will change. See UN Population Division 2015a, b) for a description of these assumptions.

Life expectancy at birth is assumed to increase as average nutrition continues to improve and as average incomes continue to rise. The improvements

Table 8.1 World Population for 2050: Four Projections

	Population Size in 2050 (billions)	Percentage Increase from 2015	Average Annual Rate of Growth, 2015–2050 (%)
UN low variant	8.701	18	0.51
UN medium variant	9.725	32	0.91
US Census Bureau	9.408	30	0.85
UN high variant	10.801	47	1.34

Source: US Census Bureau, International Database, http://www.census.gov/data/developers/data-sets/international-database.html; UN Population Division 2015b.

are assumed to be greatest in countries where life expectancy is the lowest, and therefore where potential for improvement is the greatest.

These assumptions mean that life expectancies are projected to increase substantially in some parts of the world. Babies born in many African countries in 2060 are expected to live over ten years longer than babies of their grandparents' generation born in 2000 (UN Population Division 2015a). This may sound like quite a dramatic increase. But life expectancy has increased by substantial amounts in other areas. Life expectancy in Saudi Arabia increased from 55.5 years in the early 1970s to 71.6 years in the late 1990s; in Indonesia, the increase over the same period was 12.3 years, from 54.1 to 66.4; in South America as a whole, the increase was from 62.9 to 70.2 over the same period (UN Population Division 2012b is correct). The UN's assumption is therefore within the range of historical experience.

It is more difficult to make assumptions about future levels of fertility. As a result of this difficulty, the UN presents possible scenarios, or *variants*. The *medium variant* assumes that fertility in each declines (from its current level of about three children born to an average woman of childbearing age) until it reaches a level of 1.85 children per woman. (This is below the "replacement level"—the number of children each woman would need to give birth to, on average, to ensure that two children survived to puberty. Even if the fertility rate fell to the replacement level, population would continue to grow because of increases in life expectancy.) In the *high variant,* fertility is assumed to be 0.5 percent above the medium variant. In the *low variant,* fertility is assumed to be 0.5 percent below the medium variant.

Again, to put these projections in historical context, let us examine recent experience. According to the US Census Bureau, for the world as a whole, fertility rates dropped from 4.5 children per woman in 1970–1975 to 2.42 in 2014–2015. In Asia, where economic growth has been exceptionally strong in the past two decades, fertility rates dropped from 5.1 in the early 1970s to 2.16 in 2010–2015. In Europe, fertility was at the replacement rate of 2.1 in the early 1970s, by 2010–2015 the number dropped to 1.59. Thus, the UN's low-variant assumption is that fertility worldwide will drop to levels currently observed in Europe.

Based on these assumptions, the UN's three population projections are shown in Table 8.1. The medium variant is quite close to the US Census Bureau's prediction. How good are the projections? Table 8.2 shows UN projections of world population in 2000 made at different points in time. Several things are notable:

• For obvious reasons, near-term projections are more accurate than long-term projections.

• However, the projection made in the early 1960s was remarkably close to the actual population that existed in 2000; the 1963 projection was off by only 3 or 4 percent.

• All of the projections (except the last one) overestimated the actual population. For the most part, projections of future population have shrunk over time. But this is not a hard-and-fast rule. For example, the second edition of this book reported the 1996 projections of the population in year 2050; the US Census projection was 9.35 billion and the UN medium variant was 9.85 billion. The third edition of the book reported a 2002 Census projection of 9.084 billion and a UN medium variant of 8.919 billion. By 2008, we have the Census projection at 9.539 billion and the UN's at 9.191 billion.

Looking back through older editions of this book, and related material, we find that the Census projections for the year 2050 have bounced around a bit.

Table 8.2 Past Projections of World Population for 2000: How Good Were They?

Year of Projection	Projected Population in 2000 (billions)
1957	6.28
1963	6.13
1968	6.49
1973	6.25
1980	6.12
1984	6.12
1988	6.25
1990	6.26
1992	6.23
1994	6.16
1996	6.09
1998	6.06
Actual 2000 population	
US Census Bureau	6.07
United Nations	6.12

Source: National Research Council 2000.

Table 8.3 Percentage of Adult Population (Age 15–45) Infected with HIV, 2015

	Percentage Infected with HIV
Swaziland	27.7
Botswana	25.2
Lesotho	23.4
South Africa	18.9
Namibia	16.2
Zambia	12.4
Mozambique	10.4
Malawi	10.0
Eastern and southern Africa	7.4

Source: UNAIDS 2014.

The projection in 2002 was quite a bit lower than the current projection (a 2050 population of 9.08 billion was projected in 2002 compared to the 9.41 billion projection in 2015). But in 2008, the projection was somewhat higher (9.54 billion). And in 1996 (9.39 billion) and 2006 (9.40 billion) the projections were very similar to the current projection.

A report published in the journal *Nature* (Lutz, Sanderson, and Sherbov 2001) criticized the UN's methods of projection and made a set of projections to the year 2100. The median projection of that report tracked closely with the UN medium variant through 2050. The median projection published in *Nature* estimates world population peaking at about 9 billion during the decade of the 2060s and then declining.

AIDS (acquired immunodeficiency syndrome) has received considerable attention but is unlikely to be a major factor in future population size. Over the past decade, the AIDS epidemic has stabilized or even begun to decline in some areas. UN estimates of the number of people with AIDS were 33 million in 2007 and 35 million in 2015. However, the problem remains severe in parts of sub-Saharan Africa (see Table 8.3).

Aging of the World's Population

One obvious implication of the increasing life expectancy and declining fertility that underlie the projections of future population is that future populations will be older on average. As this aging occurs, there will be change in the age structure. The large cohorts of children born in recent years will reach working age, and the new cohorts of children will be smaller in number. Overall, it is expected that the percentage of the population of developing countries who are working-age will grow over the next few decades (the US Census Bureau projects that in Africa, the working-age population will grow from 56.5 percent of the total in 2016 to 62.8 percent in 2050). This fact is referred to as the "demographic dividend." The Population Reference Bureau (2013) describes the concept as follows: "The demographic dividend is the accelerated economic growth that may result from a rapid decline in a country's fertility and the subsequent change in the population age structure. With fewer births each year, a country's working-age population grows larger in relation to the young dependent population. With more people in the labor force and fewer young people to support, a country can exploit the window of opportunity for rapid economic growth."

The changing age structure will also have an impact on the average food needs of the population—since adults have greater needs than children. This impact on food demand will be discussed in more detail in Chapter 10.

Current Trends in per Capita Food Production

Not only did Malthus not expect humans to be able to control their own population size, but he also did not expect our food supply to keep up with a dramatic, exponential growth in our population. The last half of the twentieth century experienced the most rapid growth of population in the entire history of the world, yet during this period of breakneck population growth, food production grew even faster, so per capita food production gradually increased.

The factors contributing to growth in food production will be discussed in Chapters 11–13. Here we simply note the facts: food production has continued to grow faster than population. As Table 8.4 shows, worldwide food production per capita has increased steadily since 1961. However, this growth is not evenly spread throughout the world. In the poorest countries, per capita food production declined from 1961 to 2001 and in 2011 was only slightly above the 1961 level. Southern Africa's experience was also poor—declining sharply in the 1980s and 1990s, and still (in 2011) below the level of 1961. In developed countries (illustrated by the European Union in Table 8.4) per capita food production has remained quite stable between 1981 and 2011.

Table 8.4 Index of Net Food Production per Capita for Selected Areas and Years, 1961–2011

	Southern Africa	European Union	Least Developed Countries	World
1961	122.98	79.12	104.78	73.65
1971	130.64	89.09	102.82	78.59
1981	131.16	101.07	96.88	82.27
1991	107.22	105.46	90.18	86.24
2001	95.46	100.84	93.95	94.00
2011	106.84	99.66	111.81	109.10

Source: FAOSTAT.
Notes: 2004–2006 = 100. See Box 14.3 for a description of index numbers.

Figure 8.7 Worldwide Calories per Capita per Day, 1961–2011

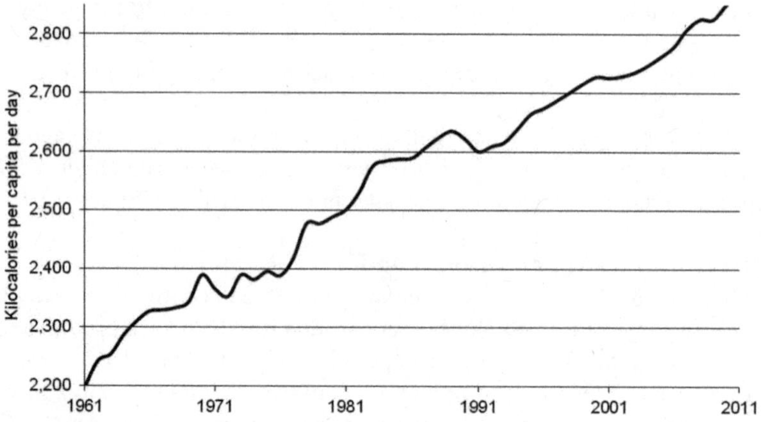

Source: FAOSTAT.

A World Bank study (Mundlak, Larson, and Crego 1996) concludes that (for the period 1967–1992) worldwide food supply is growing faster than food demand: median growth rate in agricultural production was 2.25 percent per year. (*Median growth rate* means that one-half of the world's food production takes place in countries with agricultural growth rates of less than 2.25 percent.) The study confirms that in most countries, per capita agricultural production grew—food became more plentiful.

FAO data on nutrient availability per capita also show steady improvement. As Figure 8.7 shows, since 1961 worldwide calories per capita have increased over 30 percent, from 2,196 calories per person per day to 2,870 calories per person per day in 2011. Similarly, protein availability increased about 27 percent, to 80 grams per person per day in 2011.

These levels of nutrients are sufficient for an adequate diet for the average person. One interpretation of this states that *if the world's food supply were evenly divided among the people of the world, there would be enough food for everybody.* The interpretation and implications of this fact will be discussed in greater detail in Chapter 20. People are undernourished not because the aggregate food availability is inadequate, but because their individual household incomes are inadequate. In the next chapter, we look at purchasing power—and its components, income and food prices—as the immediate problem explaining why certain people in the world are unable to afford adequate nutrition.

9

The Problem
of Income

"Get off this estate!"
"What for?"
"Because it's mine."
"Where did you get it?"
"From my father."
"Where did he get it?"
"From his father."
"And where did he get it?"
"He fought for it."
"Well, I'll fight you for it!"
                    —Carl Sandburg 1936:75

Income is central to the problem of undernutrition. A family is hungry
because the family is poor. In this chapter we look at two closely related issues. First we look at the distribution of income in the world. Which countries
are poor? How poor are they? How is income distributed within countries?
How are these things changing over time? Second, we look at how changes in
income affect the aggregate demand for food.

Who Are the Poor?
The World Bank (2015a: tab. 1.1) lists three countries with per capita income
of less than $365 and twenty countries with per capita income of less than
$730. It is hard for most of us to imagine how a person could feed herself on
a little over $2.00 per day. And people have needs besides food.

Who are the poorest of the poor? They live in the third world. They are
landless or nearly so. If they do have a bit of land, typically they earn more
than half their livelihood working for others. Whether they live packed tightly

into city slums or scattered across the countryside, they are poorly educated, often illiterate, and commonly superstitious. When employed, they accept the most menial of jobs. Some are subsistence fishermen. Some live in relative isolation in remote farming areas. Often they are squatters, neither owning nor renting the land on which they put up their huts. Their food larder is usually almost empty.

Their households are often fragmented, with one or more members away trying to find work so they can send money home. They may be in debt—to wealthier relatives, to friends, to employers, to local moneylenders. The household head is often young, not yet having found good employment, but already burdened with the responsibility of raising children. (For a good essay on the lives of the poor in a number of countries, see Banerjee and Duflo 2007.)

Comparing Average Incomes in Different Countries

In an international economy, prices are influenced by consumption in all countries. The affordability of food for poor people in one country is influenced by the consumption patterns of affluent people in other countries. As we look at the distribution of income in the world, we note that average per capita incomes are very different from one country to another (see Table 9.1). To pick the most dramatic example, in 2014 per capita income in Malawi was $250 per year, while per capita income in Norway was $103,630. The average Norwe-

Table 9.1 GNP per Capita, Selected Countries, 2014

	GNP per Capita ($)	
	Exchange Rate Comparison	Purchasing Power Parity Comparison
Malawi	250	790
Burundi	270	770
Central African Republic	320	600
Liberia	370	700
Democratic Republic of Congo	380	650
Chad	980	2,070
Cambodia	1,020	3,080
India	1,570	5,360
China	7,400	13,170
Brazil	11,530	15,590
Japan	42,000	37,920
Germany	47,640	46,850
Singapore	55,150	80,270
United States	55,200	55,860
Switzerland	88,120	57,960
Norway	103,630	66,330

Source: World Bank 2015a.

gian earned over 400 times the amount earned by the average person in Malawi (World Bank 2015a: tab. 1.1.)

Incomes, as the term is used here, refers to the gross national product (GNP) or the closely related concept gross domestic product (GDP) or gross national income (GNI), which measure the total value of goods and services produced in the economy. The richest twenty-four countries in the world have about 10 percent of the world's population but produce over 45 percent of the world's goods. The poorest fifty countries support more than a third of the world's population but produce less than 5 percent of the world's goods.

An Alternative Way of Comparing Incomes in Different Countries: Purchasing Power Parity

Some economists have expressed doubt about whether the usual method of comparing GNP per capita in different countries gives an accurate view of the quality of life in those countries. The usual method—as reflected in the previous numbers—translates the value of goods and services in a country from the local currency to US dollars by using the market exchange rate. In effect, this measure translates local currency into dollars by considering how many units of the local currency it would take to buy a dollar on the foreign exchange market.

An alternative method translates local currency into a dollar equivalent by comparing the purchasing power of the local currency to the purchasing power of the dollar. In effect, this measure translates how much it would cost in the local currency spent in the local market to buy the same quantity of goods that could be purchased in the United States with one dollar.

The two conversion methods can change the relative positions of countries in the ranking of income per capita. For example, using the exchange rate conversion, the per capita incomes of Chad and Cambodia are almost the same; but using the purchasing power parity (PPP) conversion, Cambodia's per capita income is higher than Chad's by about 50 percent. Or, using the exchange rate conversion, Switzerland's per capita income is higher than that of the United States; using the PPP method, the two countries are about the same.

With only a few exceptions (see Singapore in Table 9.1), using the PPP conversion makes rich countries appear to be a little less rich, and makes poor countries appear to be a little less poor. In effect, the cost of living is relatively high in high-income countries and is relatively low in low-income countries. To illustrate: using either conversion method, Norway is one of the richest countries and Malawi is one of the poorest. However, with the exchange rate comparison, average income in Norway is 415 times the average income in Malawi. Using the PPP conversion method, average income in Norway is a mere (!) 84 times the average income in Burundi. This relationship between per capita income and cost of living is documented clearly in the World Bank's *China Quarterly Update* (World Bank 2008a). It shows that countries at the very low end of the income scale have costs of living that are about 70 percent lower than the cost of living in the United States.

It is difficult for readers who grew up and live in the United States or other developed countries to wrap their minds around a number that says the average income per person in a country is $300 a year, or $600 per year. Box 9.1 describes the life of a poor person who lives in Malawi.

Some may dismiss the description of a single household in Box 9.1 as "anecdotal." However, "data is the plural of anecdote," as political scientist Raymond Wolfinger once said (see Shapiro 2004). Data from fourteen surveys of households in the poorest parts of the world was reviewed by Banerjee and Duflo (2007) to see if any general lessons could be drawn. We cannot hope to describe here all the results of their review, but a number of things are worth noting:

• Households are large and young. Median household size is between seven and eight people. There are six children under age eighteen years for each adult over age fifty-one.

Box 9.1 Life in Rural Malawi

The figures in Table 9.1 tell us that Malawi is one of the poorest countries in the world; average income per capita (PPP method) is about $2 a day. But what does this really mean? How can a person live on $2 a day? It is difficult—perhaps impossible—to convey the depth of poverty experienced by people in rural Malawi. Reporter Barry Bearak (2003), writing for the New York Times Sunday Magazine, visited the Malawian countryside and describes the life of Adilesi Faisoni, a grandmother in the village of Mkulumimba.

A photograph accompanying the article shows her "worldly goods": a cup, three bowls, a cooking pot, some hearth stones and stirring sticks, a cleaning rag. That's it. No electricity, no furniture, nothing else. She owns a single set of clothes. Her grandchildren wear used T-shirts from the United States with pictures of Power Rangers and Teenage Mutant Ninja Turtles. The clothes are ragged and worn. Her house is a 9-by-12-foot mud hut. She lives here with her daughter and ten grandchildren. How do they all fit? "We squeeze like worms."

Her diet is almost exclusively nsima, a thick porridge made from maize meal. During the hungry months, she may eat only a single bowl each day. "There is no way to get used to hunger," she tells the reporter. "All the time something is moving in your stomach. You feel the emptiness. You feel your intestines moving. They are too empty and they are searching for something to fill up on."

Last year, the maize meal ran out, and her family had to eat pumpkin leaves and wild vegetables. Her husband starved to death. "There was nothing to do but beg, and you were begging from others who needed to beg."

• The poorest households spend between 56 and 78 percent of their money on food. If household income increases by 1 percent, expenditures on food increase by two-thirds of 1 percent. About half the increased expenditures on food is devoted to increasing available calories (by buying more of the cheapest form of calories), and about half of the increased expenditures on food is devoted to increasing food variety and palatability.

• Almost all of the poorest households spend some money on things like tobacco, alcohol, and festivals and celebrations, but very few households spend anything at all on movies, theater, or video entertainment.

• There is considerable variation in the different countries surveyed in the ownership of assets by poor households. In Mexico, according to the survey, only 4 percent of poor households owned land; in one area of India, 99 percent of households owned land; in all countries the amount of land owned was small. In Peru, 70 percent of households own a radio; in one area of India, the corresponding number was 11 percent.

One of the surveys included in the Banerjee and Duflo paper is of extremely poor people in Udaipur, India. In that survey,

• Nearly half of the poorest households reported that at some time during the year, adults had to reduce meal size and in one-third of the households adults had to go an entire day without eating. About 12 percent of households reported that children were forced to cut meals. "Happiness" (see Box 9.2 later) was also measured in this survey and was found to have a strong negative correlation with cutting meals.

• Sixty-five percent of adults were undernourished (have a body mass index BMI of less than 18.5); 55 percent had anemia.

• Most households had a bed or cot; about half had a watch or clock; 10 percent had a stool or chair; 5 percent had a table. Almost no households in the survey had an electric fan, a sewing machine, a bullock cart, a motorized bicycle, or a tractor.

Does Income per Capita Measure What Is Important?

Some readers may at this point be a little skeptical about exactly what these average per capita numbers mean. And there are some legitimate concerns. In the following sections we will take up the issue of income distribution. Related to that, other indicators of quality of life, or depth of poverty, in different countries have been developed.

The World Bank tabulates data on the number of people in each country who live in extreme poverty measured by incomes of less than $1 or less than $2 per day. To make these comparable over time, the $1 poverty line is adjusted for inflation. The "$1 a day" standard refers to 1985 dollars; adjusted for inflation, it is equivalent to about $1.90 in the 2010–2014 period. The

United Nations Development Programme (UNDP) compiles an index (the Human Development Index, or HDI) of indicators of quality of life. This index includes per capita income, but also includes measures of health and education.

Table 9.2 allows us to compare income per capita with these other indicators. Several points emerge:

- The very high income countries also have high HDI scores and no people living on less than $1 per day.
- The countries with low HDI scores and high poverty rates also have very low incomes per capita.
- Countries (compare South Africa to Nicaragua) can have similar HDI scores even though they have very different incomes.
- Countries (compare Kyrgyzstan to Lesotho) can have very different HDI scores even though they have similar incomes per capita.

Despite the fact that income per capita rankings differ from HDI rankings or poverty-rate rankings, income per capita is in fact an important indicator of quality of life in a country. Figure 9.1 shows that countries with higher per capita income for the most part have better "quality of life"—their citizens live longer, poverty and undernutrition are less prevalent, and (not shown here, see Hayward 2006: fig. 8) environmental quality is better. Box 9.2 explores some recent research about whether people in higher-income countries are "happier" than people in poor countries.

Table 9.2 Alternative Measures of Quality of Life, Selected Countries, 2014

	Income per Capita Comparison	Human Development Index	Percentage of Population Living on Less Than $1.90 per Day
Norway	66,330	.944	0
United States	55,860	.915	0
Indonesia	10,190	.684	2.9
Nicaragua	4,790	.631	3.6
South Africa	12,700	.666	4.9
Lesotho	3,150	.497	59.7
Kyrgyzstan	3,220	.655	0.7
Haiti	1,730	.483	42.2
Democratic Republic of Congo	650	.433	77.2

Source: UNDP 2015; World Bank 2015a.

Figure 9.1 Income Matters

Poor people are better off in high-income countries

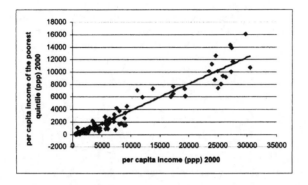

People live longer in high-income countries

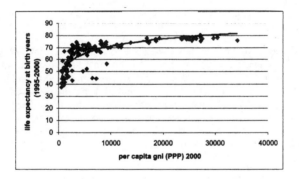

Fewer people are undernourished in high-income countries

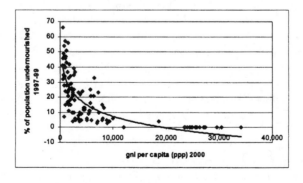

Box 9.2 Income and Happiness

Money can't buy happiness. (Or as American humorist Leo Rosten modifies it: "Money can't buy happiness, but neither can poverty.") In the 1970s, economist Richard Easterlin investigated this proposition empirically, and his conclusion—that there is no link between income and happiness—became known as the "Easterlin paradox." A paper by Betsey Stevenson and Justin Wolfers (2008) of the University of Pennsylvania uses information from opinion polls in which people are asked questions about how happy they are to reinvestigate the issue. Their conclusion:

> [W]e establish a clear positive link between average levels of subjective well-being and GDP per capita across countries, and find no evidence of a satiation point beyond which wealthier countries have no further increases in subjective well-being. We show that the estimated relationship is consistent across many datasets and is similar to the relationship between subject well-being and income observed within countries. Finally, examining the relationship between changes in subjective well-being and income over time within countries we find economic growth associated with rising happiness. Together these findings indicate a clear role for absolute income and a more limited role for relative income comparisons in determining happiness.

The issue of whether poverty is an absolute or a relative situation continues to engage economists. If one accepts the notion that there is an absolute standard, then one is led to conclude that there is virtually no poverty problem in the United States (see Boxes 9.1 and 9.4 especially, but also Box 9.3). On the other hand, if one accepts the notion that poverty is a problem of relative wealth, then the problem is defined in such a way that it is impossible to solve—some households are always in the bottom 10 or 20 percent of income, no matter what happens to the overall distribution of income.

Measuring Income Distribution Within a Country

Another legitimate criticism of average per capita income as an indicator of quality of life is that it is an average. Some people in the country have incomes above average and some have incomes below the average. This point is made by the Lesotho-Kyrgyzstan comparison in Table 9.2. The two countries have nearly identical *average* per capita incomes, but Lesotho has a much greater poverty problem, because income distribution is much more unequal in Lesotho. In this section, we look at measures of how income is distributed within a country.

Pareto's Investigation of Income Distribution

In the late 1800s the Italian mathematician-economist-sociologist Vilfredo Pareto examined income distribution in a number of countries and found a remarkably consistent pattern. Pareto's work on income distribution stimulated others to think about alternative methods of measuring it. (For a concise discussion of Pareto's work on distribution, see Steindl 1987.)

The Lorenz Curve

In 1905 the US statistician Max Lorenz proposed a method of comparing distributions of income and wealth through a cumulative income or wealth curve, the Lorenz curve, an example of which is shown as the dashed line in Figure 9.2. The vertical axis, OC, represents percentage of total income for the group under analysis. The horizontal axis, OE, represents the percentage of individuals (or families) in the group.

To conceptualize how a Lorenz curve is constructed, imagine a group of 100 individuals, each with a different income. Find the total amount of income for the group as a whole. Then line everyone up in order of income from lowest to highest. Starting from the person with the lowest income, add up the total incomes of the poorest 10 people, and calculate that total as a percentage of total income for all 100 people. (The poorest 10 percent of the population will have less than 10 percent of the total income, because, after all, they *are* the poorest.) Then repeat the process for the poorest 20 people, the poorest 30 people, and so forth. The "poorest 100"—that is to say everyone in the entire

Figure 9.2 A Lorenz Curve

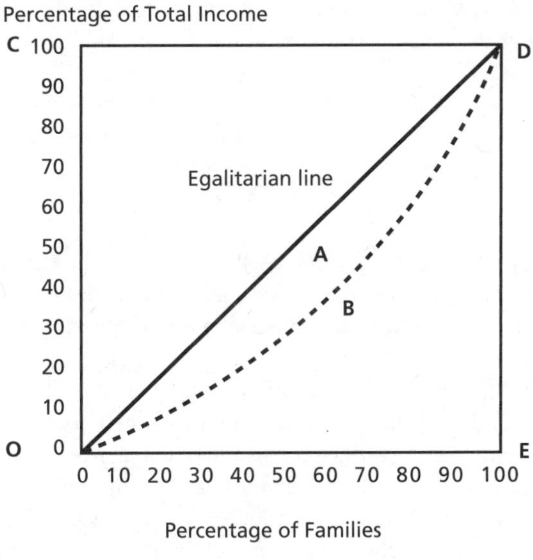

Percentage of Families

Source: Adapted from Kakwani 1987:244.

group—will, as a group, have 100 percent of the group's income. We now have ten data points: the poorest 10 percent have x percent of the total income, the poorest 20 percent have y percent of the total income, and so on. Connect the ten data points with a smooth line and you have a Lorenz curve (Cowell 1977:23).

The straight diagonal line, OD, in Figure 9.2 is called the *egalitarian line*. If everyone in the group under analysis had exactly the same income, the Lorenz curve would correspond to the egalitarian line. (The poorest 10 percent in this case would have 10 percent of the income, the poorest 20 percent would have 20 percent, and so forth—because everyone has the same income.) At the other extreme, if all the income accrued to one individual, the Lorenz curve would be the right angle represented by OED in Figure 9.2. (The poorest 10 percent would have 0 percent of the income, the poorest 20 percent would have 0 percent of the income, and even the poorest 90 percent would have 0 percent of the income, but the poorest 100 percent would have 100 percent of the income, again by definition.) Examining these two extremes illustrates that the more the Lorenz curve bends away from the egalitarian line, the greater the inequality of income.

The Gini Coefficient

The search for a better method of measuring income and wealth distribution did not end with Lorenz. In 1912 the Italian economist Corrado Gini proposed yet another measure of inequality, the Gini ratio, often called the Gini coefficient (Dagum 1987). Gini used the Lorenz curve as the basis of his ratio. He simply compared the area of the triangle OED (see Figure 9.2) with the area of the lens-shaped piece taken out of that triangle by the Lorenz curve. Labeling the lens-shaped part A and the remainder of the triangle B, the Gini ratio is:

$$\frac{A}{A+B}$$

If one individual in the group has all the income, the Gini ratio becomes 1. If the size of A approaches 0, the Gini ratio approaches 0. The range of the Gini is thus from 0 to 1. Often the ratio above is multiplied by 100 and the Gini is reported on a scale of 0 to 100.

Although popular, the Gini coefficient is open to criticism (see Paglin 1974 or Deltas 2003). It shows nothing about the location of the concentration of income inequality among high- versus low-income groups. The shape of the Lorenz curve could conceivably change (with the poor better off and the middle class worse off, for instance) without any change in the Gini coefficient.

Furthermore, neither the Lorenz curve nor the Gini coefficient take account of expected variation in income as people age. Imagine a country consisting of working adults with ages distributed evenly from twenty to fifty years and with everyone in his twenties paid the same, everyone in her thirties paid the same but more than those in their twenties, and everyone in his forties paid the same but more than those in their thirties. In this case, the Gini would be greater than zero, even though every individual in the country has exactly the same income pattern over his/her lifetime. Now imagine the same country twenty years in the future: income by age is still exactly as it was twenty years ago, but now there are more people in their twenties and forties, and fewer people in their thirties. The Gini coefficient for the country would be higher than before, indicating greater inequality, even though lifetime income patterns have not changed at all—every individual's lifetime earning pattern is exactly the same as that in the preceding generation. Lemieux (2006) estimates that demographic changes may account for 69–95 percent of observed changes in income distribution.

Relative Income Share

Lorenz curves and Gini ratios make for useful comparisons and appear frequently in the literature of income and wealth distribution, but they may be hard for the layperson to understand and time-consuming to explain to politicians. The underlying data may provide a more intuitively appealing description of income distribution. For example, from Table 9.3, rather than saying, "The Gini coefficient of expenditure distribution is 33 for Ethiopia and 43 for Nigeria," one could say, "The richest 10 percent of the population in Ethiopia accounts for 27.4 percent of the total income, while in Nigeria the richest 10 percent accounts for 32.7 percent of the total expenditures." Sometimes the ratio of the percentage earned by the richest 10 percent compared to the percentage earned by the poorest 10 percent is reported as a measure of income dispersion: "In Ethiopia the richest 10 percent spend (on average) 8.5 times as much as the poorest 10 percent, while in Nigeria the richest 10 percent spend 16 times as much as the poorest 10 percent."

Income Distributions in Different Countries and Changes over Time

Information on income distribution is collected and published by the World Bank. Some of this is presented in Table 9.3 for the world's twelve largest economies and the world's eighteen most populous countries. Together these countries account for 69 percent of the world's economic output and 68 percent of the world's population.

We can see from the table that there is quite a wide variation in the degrees of income equality. Of the countries reported in the table, the most equal distribution, as reflected by the lowest Gini coefficient, is in Pakistan (Gini = 29.6); the most unequal distribution is in Brazil (Gini = 52.9). The poorest 20

Table 9.3 Income, Population, and Income Distribution, Selected Countries, 2008–2014

	2014 GNI ($ billions)	% of World Total	2014 Population (millions)	% of World Total	Survey Year	Gini Index	Percentage Share of Income or Consumption			
							Poorest 10%	Poorest 20%	Richest 20%	Richest 10%
China	17967	16.6	1364	18.8	2010	42.1	1.7	4.7	47.1	30
United States	17813	16.4	319	4.4	2013	41.1	1.7	5.1	46.4	30.2
India	7293	6.7	1295	17.8	2009	33.9	3.5	8.2	44.2	30
Japan	4821	4.4	127	1.8	2008	32.1	2.7	7.4	39.7	24.8
Germany	3790	3.5	81	1.1	2011	30.1	3.4	8.4	38.6	23.7
Russian Federation	3610	3.3	144	2.0	2012	41.6	2.3	5.9	48.3	32.2
Brazil	3213	3.0	206	2.8	2013	52.9	1	3.3	57.4	41.8
France	2623	2.4	66	0.9	2012	33.1	3.1	7.8	41.2	26.8
Indonesia	2592	2.4	255	3.5	2010	35.6	3.4	7.6	43.7	28.2
United Kingdom	2518	2.3	65	0.9	2012	32.6	2.9	7.5	40.1	24.7
Italy	2128	2.0	61	0.8	2012	35.2	1.9	6.2	41.7	26.3
Mexico	2086	1.9	125	1.7	2012	48.1	1.9	4.9	54.1	38.9
Nigeria	1014	0.9	178	2.4	2009	43	2	5.4	49	32.7
Pakistan	941	0.9	185	2.5	2010	29.6	4.2	9.6	39.5	25.6
Philippines	838	0.8	99	1.4	2012	43	2.5	5.9	49.6	33.4
Bangladesh	530	0.5	159	2.2	2010	32	3.9	8.9	41.4	26.8
Ethiopia	145	0.1	97	1.3	2010	33.2	3.2	8	41.7	27.4
Vietnam	485	0.4	91	1.2	2012	38.7	2.6	6.5	45.7	30.1

Source: World Bank.

percent of the population controls 8.4 percent of the income in Pakistan, but only 3.3 percent in Brazil. The richest 20 percent of the population controls 38.6 percent of the income in Pakistan, but 57.4 percent of the income in Brazil.

Since the 1980s, there appears to be a trend toward greater inequality of income in many countries. The increase in inequality has been especially pronounced in formerly socialist (Soviet-bloc) countries since the end of the Cold War and the breakup of the Soviet Union. For example, the Gini coefficient in Hungary went from 21.0 in 1988 to 36.6 in 2012; in Russia it increased from 23.8 in 1987 to 41.6 in 2012. The increase for China (from the mid-20s in the 1980s to mid-30s in the 1990s) probably represents reforms in the general economic system. In addition there is a growing gap between rural and urban incomes in China. Geographer Matt Hartzell shows that average incomes along the Pacific coast of China are generally higher than the national average—in the province of Zhejiang, average income is twice the national average, and in Gansu and Guizhou provinces, average incomes are about half the national average.

However, the increases in inequality have not been limited to countries replacing a socialist system with a more market-oriented economy. In the United States, Canada, and Australia, inequality has increased gradually but substantially over a period going back to the late 1980s (and, using different data, back to the 1960s). From the mid-1980s to 2012, Gini coefficients increased from 37.7 to 41.1 in the United States, with similar increases in Canada and Australia. The World Bank's website on income distribution (World Bank 2015c) provides an excellent overview of the literature and data on income distribution.

Because of data availability, income distribution in the United States has been studied in considerable detail. Among the findings of that research are

• Income distribution is becoming more unequal over time. Piketty and Saez (2006) show that percentage of income earned by the top 1 percent of earners in the United States increased from about 8 percent in the early 1970s to about 14 percent in the late 1990s.

• Changes in the distribution of *wealth* are more ambiguous. Kennickell (2006) finds that the Gini coefficient of wealth increased from 0.784 in 1995 to 0.805 in 2004 in the United States, indicating an increase in concentration of wealth. At the same time, however, he finds that the percentage of wealth held by the wealthiest 1 percent declined from 34.6 percent in 1995 to 33.4 percent in 2004.

• But distribution of expenditures is considerably less unequal than is distribution of income. People go into debt to finance consumption during low-income years of their lives (in their twenties and thirties, for example) and pay off that debt by constraining consumption during high-income years of their lives (in their forties and fifties). Cox and Alm (2008) show that the average household in the highest 20 percent of income has an income that is fifteen times higher than the average household in the lowest 20 percent of income; but the average household in the highest 20 percent of *expenditures* spends less than four times as much as the average household in the lowest 20 percent.

The overall income distribution and changes in that distribution mask the fact that there is considerable movement of individuals from one level of the income distribution to another level over time. The US Department of Treasury (2007) found that among people in the bottom 20 percent of income distribution in 1996, half had moved out of that bottom group by 2005. Among people who were in the top hundredth of 1 percent of income distribution (the richest of the rich) in 1996, 75 percent had dropped out of this group by 2005. The median incomes of these 1995 "super rich" actually declined over the next decade.

Factors Influencing Income Distribution
The causes of income distribution are complex and not fully understood.

The "Lucky Rich" or the "Worthy Rich"?
People are more likely to favor policies to redistribute income if they believe that the rich are just "lucky" and the poor "unlucky." Wages and salaries in the general economy are set by a process that is opaque, and sometimes seems arbitrary.

One may be inclined to view Tiger Woods's high income as justified, since one can see how television ratings climb when he is playing, and at the same time be suspicious of high compensation for a corporate executive if one suspected that the executive could be seamlessly replaced with any of hundreds or thousands of other, lower-paid candidates. Tiger Woods is worth his millions, in this view, while the executive is simply the lucky one who got the plum job.

In the world of economic models of perfect competition, every worker is paid a wage equal to her or his marginal productivity, so in some rudimentary way, every person is "worth" exactly what they earn. But even the most doctrinaire free-market economist would recognize that compensation of rare-skill jobs is not set in a competitive market. What is more, even a competitively determined income can be perceived as having an element of luck insofar as it depends on the worker's physical capital (tools and equipment, for example) and human capital (health and education, for example) and whether innate or acquired skills are the skills that are currently in high demand.

Technology Adoption and the Kuznets Curve
In his 1954 presidential address to the American Economic Association, Harvard economist Simon Kuznets hypothesized that during the early phases of

development, third world countries might experience increasing income inequalities before "leveling forces become strong enough to first stabilize and
then reduce income inequalities" (1955:24). His idea that the path of income
equality through time in the third world would trace a U-shaped curve became
known as the Kuznets curve (see Figure 9.3).

The importance of the Kuznets curve relationship, should it exist, is described by Thomas Piketty, a leading researcher on inequality. "In a nutshell,
the hypothesis simply says that income inequality should follow an inverse-U
shape along the development process, first rising with industrialization, and
then declining, as more and more workers join the high-productivity sectors of
the economy. This theory has strong—and fairly optimistic—policy consequences: if LDCs [less developed countries] are patient enough . . . they
should soon reach a world where growth and inequality reduction go hand in
hand and where poverty rates drop sharply" (2006:63).

Empirical studies have found some support for the Kuznets hypothesis.
For example, Ahluwalia (1976a) used cross-sectional data of a sample of sixty
countries (forty poor countries, fourteen developed countries, and six socialist
countries) to investigate how relative income shares as per capita income
changed. The result of one of his regressions is shown in Figure 9.3, which
shows the income share of the poorest 40 percent for countries at different levels of development. For very poor countries, as income rises, the income share

**Figure 9.3 Estimated Relationship Between Income Share and
per Capita GNP, Sixty Countries, Various Years Prior to 1975**

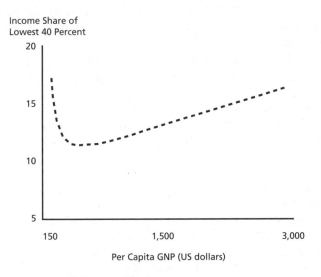

Source: Adapted from Ahluwalia 1976a:133.

of the poorest 40 percent declines; but for richer countries, as income rises, the income share of the poorest 40 percent increases.

More recent studies raise some questions about whether the Kuznets hypothesis holds in all circumstances. See Fields 2002 for a review of the literature. But see Brueckner, Norris, and Gradstein for a recent paper that finds empirical support for the idea that increasing income can go hand-in-hand with reductions in inequality: "[Our results] show that increases in national income have a significant moderating effect on income inequality: a 1% increase in real GDP per capita reduces the Gini coefficient by around 0.08 percentage points on average" (2015:149).

The Kuznets hypothesis is more of an observation of historical patterns than it is an economic theory. However, it seems reasonable to postulate that in early stages of development, the poor may benefit less from development than the rich. As development takes place, those in the more advanced sector of the economy are likely to be the first to take advantage of it. Therefore, they reap the first gains. After all, when the new productive techniques come along, they often require new knowledge and substantial amounts of capital. The railroads and canals and electric companies, which were originally privately owned, are a case in point. It was difficult for the poor even to imagine "making a killing" in these areas.

Modernization could conceivably make the poor worse off. As Ahluwalia puts it: "An aggressively expanding technologically advanced, modern sector, competing against the traditional sector for markets and resources (and benefiting in this competition from an entrenched position in the institutional and political context) may well generate both a relative and absolute decline in incomes of the poor" (1976b:330–331). He concludes from his research, however, that though the initial stages of development are likely to make the poor worse off relative to the rich, these same initial stages are not necessarily inclined to making the poor worse off in absolute terms.

Other Factors influencing Income Distribution

Ahluwalia's study, which estimated a type of Kuznets curve of income distribution (shown in Figure 9.3), also produced evidence of how some variables besides per capita income affect income distribution. Ahluwalia found the following:

- Education (measured by literacy or years of schooling) led to more equal income distribution.
- Rapid population growth led to less equal income distribution, as greater numbers of people put downward pressure on wages in the low wage sectors.
- A shift in population and production from rural/agricultural to urban/industrial also appeared to reduce inequality.

Empirical evaluations of the Kuznets curve and factors influencing income inequality have continued to be made using expanded datasets and improved empirical methods. One 2013 paper (Jaumotte, Lall, and Papageorgiou) found that inequality was lower in countries that had policies that encouraged foreign trade (openness to imports and exports), but that inequality was higher in countries that encouraged foreign investment ("financial openness").

Why Income Distribution Matters to the Problem of Undernutrition

In the world as a whole, low-income people tend to underconsume food while high-income people tend to overconsume it. Reutlinger and Selowsky (1976) pointed out that increased inequality of income hurts the nutritional status of the poor in two ways. The first, and obvious, way is that increased inequality means that the poor have less income, their food consumption declines, and their chances of being undernourished increase. The second way that increased income inequality hurts nutritional status of the poor is that increased incomes for the rich translate into increased demand for meat and dairy products. As discussed in more detail in the next chapter, the more the price of grain is bid up to satisfy the wealthy's demand for animal products, the harder it is for the poor to buy the grain they need for minimal nutrition.

Does Income Equality Promote Growth?

A study in the late 1970s answered this question with a tentative yes. Ahluwalia, Carter, and Chenery (1979) examined twelve countries for which they had data on growth and income shares for a ten-year period. They found that the countries most successful in reducing income inequality were also the countries with the highest rates of growth in per capita incomes.

However, a more comprehensive study by the World Bank (Deininger and Squire 1997) failed to find a strong correlation between growth and income inequality. Of the eighty-eight countries whose per capita GDP grew for a decade, income inequality improved slightly in about half the cases and worsened slightly in the other half. However, the study found that the distribution of *wealth* (as measured by landownership) does strongly affect growth. Countries having great inequality of wealth grow more slowly than countries with less inequality. For example, fifteen developing countries in the World Bank study had a Gini coefficient (for land distribution) higher than 70. Of these fifteen countries, only two showed growth rates higher than 2.5 percent per year during the period 1960–1992.

Global Redistribution: Do Incomes Grow Faster in Poor Countries?

No matter how large the income disparities that exist *within* a country, those differences are dwarfed by the differences in income between rich and poor countries. Remember the comparison of average incomes in Norway and Malawi earlier in this chapter? How can such enormous differences exist between countries? One obvious answer is that much more investment in productive capital occurs in rich countries; people in those countries are more productive because they have more and better capital, better equipment in their workplaces, better roads and communications, and better education. Many economists believe that as time passes, income per capita in poor countries will catch up with income in rich countries—in other words, incomes per capita will *converge*. Investors will discover that investing in poor countries with low levels of capital has a higher payoff than investing in rich countries where there are high levels of capital; this investment will increase the capital stock in poor countries and therefore increase production per person in those countries.

Looking at 200 years of experience in currently developed (rich) countries, we see clear evidence of convergence. The Maddison (2001) data provide the best evidence. In 1820, the United Kingdom and the Netherlands were, by a considerable margin, the richest countries in the world (measured by GDP per capita). Average per capita income in those two countries was $1,718, almost three times higher than the average income of $676 in five countries (Canada, Australia, Japan, Finland, and New Zealand) near the bottom of the per capita income list. By 1998, the five countries that were "relatively poor" countries in 1820 had more than caught up with the leaders: average income in the Netherlands and the United Kingdom was $19,030, and average income in Australia, New Zealand, Finland, and Japan was higher—$20,034.

For developing countries in modern times, there is mixed evidence about whether this convergence theory is correct. In 1980, per capita income in high-income countries was $8,350—about fifteen times higher than the $553 average income in low- and middle-income countries. By 1998, this ratio had increased to over nineteen times higher—incomes were *diverging*. However, in the years since 1998, the ratio as fallen, until by 2014 it was at about eight.

Table 9.4 gives more insight into the convergence (or lack thereof) of incomes. Incomes in China and India have increased faster than those of rich countries since 1973. Between 1973 and 1998 (Maddison data), average income in high-income countries grew by about 60 percent; India's per capita income more than doubled, and China's per capita income nearly quadrupled. Between 1998 and 2014 (World Bank data), rich-country income rose by 24 percent, while India's rose by about 135 percent and China's nearly quadrupled. Overall, the pace of per capita income growth in Asia provides strong evidence for the convergence hypothesis.

However, other parts of the developing world have not fared as well when it comes to income growth. Latin America showed a period of convergence with high-income countries in the period 1870 to 1950. However, in the years

Table 9.4 Evidence of Convergence: Annual per Capita Incomes, 1870–2014

	Maddison Data (constant 1990 dollars)				World Bank Data (constant 2005 data)		2014 as Multiple of 1998
	1870	1950	1973	1998	1998	2014	
Rich countries	1,894	5,663	13,141	21,470	25,128	31,106	1.24
China	530	439	839	3,117	983	3,863	3.93
India	533	619	853	1,746	525	1,234	2.35
Other Asia	620	757	1,486	3,328			
South Asia					518	1,127	2.18
East Asia					1,019	3,254	3.19
Latin America	698	2,554	4,531	5,795	4,358	5,703	1.31
Africa	444	852	1,365	1,368	791	1,045	1.32
World	867	2,114	4,104	5,709	6,369	8,009	1.26

*Source:*Maddison 2001; World Bank 2015a.

Note: For East Asia and Latin America, World Bank numbers are for developing countries only; for Africa, World Bank numbers are for developing sub-Saharan African countries only.

since 1998, Latin American incomes have grown about the same as those of rich countries. The same is true in Africa. The ratio of average incomes in rich countries to average incomes in Africa was about four to one in 1870, about ten to one in 1973, and is now about thirty to one.

Paul Collier in his 2008 book *The Bottom Billion* describes the situation this way:

> These differences between the bottom billion [mostly in sub-Saharan Africa] and the rest of the developing world [China, India, and other success stories in Asia] will rapidly cumulate into two different worlds. Indeed, the divergence has . . . already pushed most of the countries of the bottom billion to the lowest spot in the global pile. It was not always that way. Before globalization gave huge opportunities to China and India, they were poorer than many of the [bottom billion] countries. . . . But China and India broke free . . . whereas other countries . . . didn't. For the last two decades this has produced a growth pattern that appears confusing. Some initially poor countries are growing very well, and so it can easily look as if there is not really a problem. Over the next two decades the true nature of the problem is going to become apparent. . . . By 2050, the development gulf will no longer be between a rich billion in the most developed countries and the five billion in the developing countries; rather it will be between the trapped billion and the rest of humankind. (pp. 10–11)

The new century has seen new evidence of hope for a growth resurgence in sub-Saharan Africa. The magazine *The Economist* in early 2015 described this as follows: "Over the past decade Africa was among the world's fastest-growing continents—its average annual rate was more than 5%—buoyed in

Table 9.5 Annual per Capita Incomes for Selected High-Growth Countries, 2000 and 2014

	2000	2014	2014 as Multiple of 2000
China	1,127.73	3,862.92	3.43
India	572.06	1,233.95	2.16
Ethiopia	136.63	315.76	2.31
Ghana	445.87	763.94	1.71
Mozambique	276.24	535.73	1.94
Nigeria	552.19	1,098.04	1.99
Zambia	582.62	1,032.80	1.77
Rich countries	26,715.98	31,106.39	1.16
World	6,682.76	8,008.63	1.20

Source: World Bank Development Indicators, http://data.worldbank.org/indicator.
Note: Constant 2005 dollars.

part by improved governance and economic reforms" African countries are also expected to reap the "demographic dividend" described in Chapter 8—as fertility rates fall, the proportion of the population who are "dependent" (too young or too old to work) shrinks, so output divided by total population grows.

Per capita income growth for a sample of fast-growing Asian and African countries is shown in Table 9.5. Growth in China and India has been rapid for a long period of time. But per capita income in most sub-Saharan Africa counties was stagnant or negative during the last part of the twentieth century. Since then, however, African countries have begun to show signs of their growth rates approaching those of "Asian miracle" countries. (Note also the evidence of income convergence in this table.)

This promise—that African prosperity can begin to grow as fast as Asian prosperity—gives us an additional source of expectation that convergence will continue to be a dominant force in the twenty-first century.

Growth Rates in per Capita Income

The last chapter of the book will make some projections about the future, and that will require (among other things) assumptions about the rate of growth in per capita incomes. Figure 9.4 shows the annual growth rates in per capita income worldwide since 1960. The average annual growth rate during this more than five-decade period is 1.8 percent. It is almost always positive (per capita income one year is higher than that in the preceding year), with occasional dips into negative territory—notably the "great recession" of 2008–2009. The high growth rates of the 1960s and early 1970s have not been reached again, but the quadratic line fitting the data seems to indicate that the decline in growth rates has bottomed out in the 1–1.5 percent range.

Figure 9.4 Worldwide Annual Growth in per Capita Income, 1960–2014

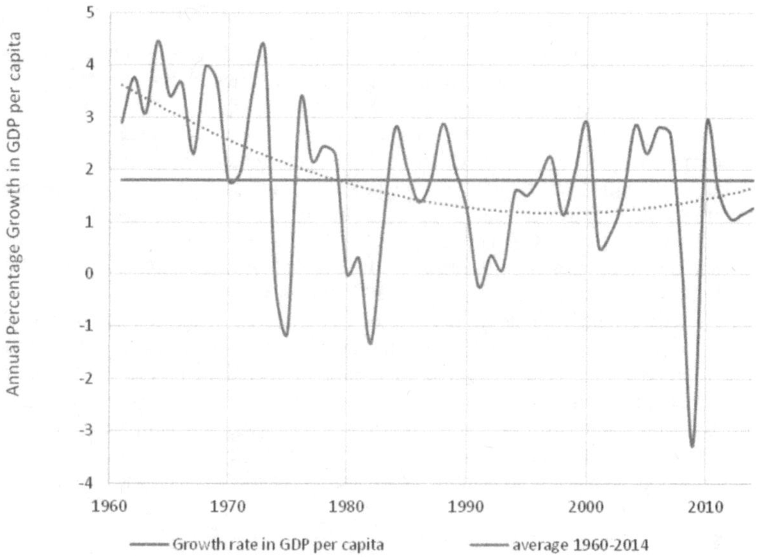

Growth rate in GDP per capita — average 1960-2014

Source: World Bank Development Indicators.

World Distribution of Income and How It Has Changed over Time

So far we have talked about two sources of income disparity: income disparity within countries that appears to be growing in many countries over the past decades, and income disparity between countries that may be declining due to convergence. What does this mean to the overall distribution of income in the world?

A description of the world distribution of income is found in Box 9.3. Notice that most incomes in the United States are at the top end of the world distribution. For example, if a college student spends $42,000 a year on tuition, room, and board, that student spends more than the annual incomes of 95 percent of the world's population. A single person at the poverty line in the United States earns more than about 75 percent of the world's population. See Box 9.4 for a more detailed picture of poverty in the United States.

A paper by Sala-i-Martin (2002) estimated the world distribution of income and how it changed over time (Sala-i-Martin's estimate of world distribution of income is similar to the distribution reported in Box 9.3). He concluded that income is becoming more equally distributed over time. He estimated Gini coefficients that fell from about 0.66 in the 1970s to 0.65 in the 1980s to 0.63 in the 1990s. Another analysis, by Lakner and Milanovic (2015),

Box 9.3 World Distribution of Income: Who Is Rich?

Who is rich? Would you say that all people in the top half of the income distribution are rich? Or do you have to be in the top quarter, or the top 10 percent, or the top 5 percent? Or would you say that only the richest 1 percent of the population are the rich? This is a subjective judgment, and well-intentioned, well-informed people can come to different conclusions. Once you have decided how you would define "rich," use the table below to find out how much a rich person earns (according to your definition). We predict you will be surprised.

Using data such as that shown in Tables 9.1 and 9.3, we constructed an estimated world distribution of income. In the table below, we show the world distribution of income in 2007 using the PPP comparison.

As described in the text, this method of comparing incomes attempts to adjust for different costs of living, so that a person making $5,000 in one country has approximately the same standard of living as a person making $5,000 in another country. The countries used for our exercise account for 94 percent of the world's population and 92 percent of the world's income in 2014. Therefore, the countries omitted are relatively rich countries, and our estimate of the distribution may be slightly biased in the downward direction—perhaps people are not quite as poor as we make them out to be.

So . . . are you one of the rich?

World Distribution of Income, 2014

This percentage of the world's population . . .	Earns less than this annual income
50	$2,500
65	$5,700
75	$8,500
80	$10,150
85	$13,000
90	$17,500
95	$26,000
98	$40,000
99	$55,000
99.9	$105,000

reached a similar conclusion: worldwide Gini ratios in the 70+ range, declining by about 2–3 points between 1988 and 2008.

The declining worldwide Gini has translated into a reduction in poverty worldwide (measured by the percentage of people living on incomes of less than $2 per day, adjusted for inflation). Sala-i-Martin found that this poverty rate declined from 40 percent in 1970 to less than 20 percent by the late 1990s. China's poverty rate fell from about 75 percent in 1970 to 20 percent in 1998.

Box 9.4 Poverty in the United States

Box 9.3 suggested that a person at the poverty line in the United States would have higher income than 80 percent of the people in the world. How does the life of a poor person in the United States compare to the life of Malawian Adilesi Faisoni described in Box 9.1?

In 2016, a single person is categorized as "poor" in the United States if her or his income is below $11,770 a year; for a family of four, a family income below $24,250 makes them poor.

In the United States:

- 97.7 percent of poor households live in houses or apartments with complete indoor plumbing.
- 80.7 percent of poor households have air conditioning.
- 99.4 percent of poor households have a refrigerator.
- 97.3 percent of poor households have a color television; 54.6 percent have more than one color television; 62.7 percent have cable or a satellite dish.

Sources: US Census Bureau 2007; US Energy Information Administration 2001.

The reduction in poverty was found in every geographical area, except for Africa, where poverty rates increased from 53 percent in 1970 to 64 percent in 1998.

An update of Sala-i-Martin's paper found that the worldwide trend had continued and even accelerated. "World poverty is . . . disappearing faster than previously thought. From 1970 to 2006, poverty fell by 86% in South Asia, 73% in Latin America, 39% in the Middle East, and 20% in Africa. Barring a catastrophe, there will never be more than a billion people in poverty in the future history of the world" (Pinkovskiy and Sala-i-Martin 2010).

10

Other Factors
Influencing Demand

Chapter 8 presented some projections about the size of the world's population—it could grow by 30 percent by 2050. Does this mean that if food supply grows by 30 percent we will have enough extra food to feed those extra mouths? To answer this question we must first examine the factors that influence food consumption per person. In Chapter 9, we discussed how demand for food increases as income increases, and we examined some trends in per capita income levels and the distribution of income. In this chapter, we ask the question: What other factors influence the amount of food and the types of food consumed per capita?

Population Characteristics and Calorie Requirements
How does average demand for food change as a result of characteristics of the population? We saw in Chapter 3 that nutrient requirements depend on age, sex, pregnancy and breast-feeding status, and physical activity level.

Age Structure
The age composition of a population reflects the underlying demographic conditions of the past and at the same time is an important determinant of demographic conditions of the future.

Population pyramids. The most convenient way to visualize the age structure of a population is through a graph of population distribution according to age and sex, called a *population pyramid.* Conventionally, population pyramids represent age cohorts by five- or ten-year intervals, and place males on the left of a vertical line and females on the right, with the youngest cohort at the bottom. The graphic representation of the age cohorts can be either the actual numbers or the percentage distribution. Figure 10.1 shows a numerical population pyramid for the industrialized nations versus the third world in the year 1985, with projections to 2025.

Figure 10.1 Population Pyramids for Less and More Developed Countries, 1985 and Projections to 2025

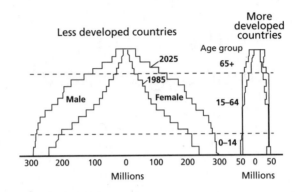

Source: Adapted from Merrick et al. 1986:19.

The 1985 version of the pyramid for less developed countries illustrates why they are called "pyramids." Because there are high birth rates in poor countries, the largest age groups are the youngest groups at the bottom of the graph. There are more children under the age of five than there are children aged five to nine, and more in the five-to-nine range than in the ten-to-fourteen range, and so forth. But notice that the graphs for more developed countries resemble rectangles more than pyramids. Because birth rates in these countries are so low, we do not see a "broad base" of large cohorts of the youngest groups. For less developed countries, as time passes (shown as the 2025 projection graph), the pyramid resembles more and more a rectangle.

In Figure 10.1, the horizontal lines mark the dividing lines that are commonly, but arbitrarily, placed to separate the dependent age categories (in this case, younger than fifteen years or older than sixty-five years) from the working-age population. Such numerical population pyramids do a nice job of illustrating the differences in actual population size, third world versus developed world. They can also show demographic features such as the higher survival rate of older women (notice the difference between the numbers of men and women in the oldest cohort for the 2025 projection for the developed world).

Age structure is of interest to demographers because, as we have noted above, it provides clues about past and future demographic patterns. It is important to policymakers because of its impact on two things we will discuss next: momentum in population growth and dependency ratios.

Momentum in population growth. Over a long period, a population would just reproduce itself if individual couples produced exactly the right number of children to replace themselves, allowing for some children to die before they arrived at childbearing age. In most populations this number comes to just over two children (that is, about 2.1) per couple (or per woman). In this discussion, we use the usual assumption that the replacement fertility rate is 2.1 (Merrick et al. 1986:6). If a population has remained constant for a couple of generations and then its fertility rate rises above 2.1, population will grow; if fertility falls below 2.1, the population will decline. (We are assuming no net immigration or emigration and no improvements in healthcare that raise average life expectancy.)

You might expect that when the fertility rate falls to 2.1, births and deaths would be in balance, and population growth would stop. This is not the case, at least not immediately. The reason is demographic momentum. A population that has had high fertility in the years before reaching replacement-level fertility will have a much younger age structure than a population with low fertility before crossing the replacement threshold. Consider the two sets of countries in Figure 10.1. For a developed country (with the rectangular "pyramid"), the number of females expected to enter their childbearing years over the next five years (the female cohort ages ten to fifteen, roughly) is almost exactly the same as the number of females expected to exit their childbearing years (the female cohort ages forty-five to fifty, roughly). Therefore the number of childbearing women will remain about the same, and a replacement fertility rate would imply a stable population size. For a developing country, however, the ten- to fifteen-year-old cohort is much larger than the forty-five- to fifty-year-old cohort. Therefore, the number of childbearing women will grow over the next five years. Even if fertility fell to a replacement rate (2.1 children per woman of childbearing age), population would continue to grow because the number of women of childbearing age continues to grow. This is the phenomenon of demographic momentum.

On a worldwide basis, population momentum means that "even if there were a sudden reduction of fertility to the level strictly needed to replace the population, the world population would still increase by more than 2 billion" by the year 2050 (FAO 1996b: Background Paper no. 4).

Dependency ratios. The population pyramids also illustrate the dependency ratios in a population. The dependency ratio is usually defined as the ratio of dependents to working-age adults. Working-age adults are generally identified as those from ages fifteen to sixty-five. The adult dependency ratio is the percentage of the population sixty-five and older divided by the percentage of the population between fifteen and sixty-five; the child dependency ratio is the percentage of the population younger than fifteen divided by the percentage of the population between fifteen and sixty-five.

Dependency ratios can influence overall nutritional status in a population because the young and the elderly are more likely to be food-insecure, since

Table 10.1 How Changing Age Structure of a Population Can Affect Food Requirements

	Present	Future
Number of children (requiring 1,800 calories per capita per day)	4 million	5 million
Number of adults (requiring 2,700 calories per capita per day)	6 million	10 million
Total population	10 million	15 million
Total calorie requirements	23,400 million	36,000 million
Calories per capita per day	2,340	2,400

they rely on others to provide them with food. In a rapidly growing population, the child dependency ratio is far greater than in a slowly growing population. This is the logic behind the "demographic dividend" concept discussed in Chapter 8. But whereas the demographic dividend focuses on the supply side—more working-age people implies greater output per person in the population—the next section focuses on the demand side—more working age people implies greater calorie requirements per person in the population.

Age structure of population in the future. What kind of age structure will we see in the future? The theory of demographic transition described in Chapter 9 predicts that as living conditions improve, life expectancy will increase, followed by declining fertility rates. This implies that in the future there will be a smaller percentage of children and a larger percentage of adults. Future population pyramids will be narrower.

If there are proportionately more adults than children, the need for food will grow faster than the population. The simple example in Table 10.1 illustrates this point. Although population increases by 50 percent, calorie requirements increase by 54 percent because the future population is 66 percent adult rather than the present 60 percent.

Other Demographic Characteristics and Food Requirements

Average per capita food requirements in a population also depend on other characteristics of the people.

Pregnancy

Pregnant and breast-feeding women require higher caloric intake. Two opposing trends exist here. As the base of the population pyramid contracts, we see an increase in the ratio of women of childbearing age to total population. On the other hand, the drop in fertility rates means that each woman of childbearing age is becoming pregnant fewer times during her lifetime. The combined effect is expected to be close to zero for the period 1995–2025. (FAO, WFS Background paper number 4.)

Physical Activity

Anyone who has ever exercised in an attempt to control her weight knows that physical activity burns calories. On a worldwide scale, what is likely to affect average per capita calorie requirements is not "average visits to the gym," but the average physical activity of adults on the job. Farming (especially in developing countries) requires more physical activity than many city jobs. Therefore, as urban populations grow faster than rural populations in the future, we should expect to see a decline in the average activity level. FAO projects that this change will cause a reduction in per capita food requirements of from 1 to 4 percent for the period 1995–2025 (FAO 1996c: Background Paper no. 4).

Height

Good nutrition during infancy and childhood can cause a person to become a taller adult. But taller adults need more calories to maintain their bodily functions. The FAO projections are based on an underlying assumption that food supplies will continue to grow faster than food demand; thus the incidence of undernutrition will decline, and there will be less stunting. This is expected to add 2 percent to energy requirements in developing countries between 1995 and 2025, and to have no substantial effect in the developing world.

Income Growth and per Capita Food Demand

The total effect of demographic changes on food demand is expected to be small or negligible; however, growth of per capita income is likely to have a much bigger effect on food demand. As we saw in Figure 9.4 during the 1960–2014 period, per capita income grew at an annual rate of 1.8 percent for the world as a whole. If income per capita grows at a rate of 1.8 percent per year, at the end of thirty-five years, average income will be higher by 87 percent. As discussed in Chapter 7, estimates show that the income elasticity for food is between 0.1 and 0.3. This means that a 1 percent increase in a person's income will increase the quantity of food demanded by the person by from 0.1 to 0.3 percent. If we use an income elasticity of 0.2, an 87 percent increase in income would be associated with a 17 percent increase in food demand. Using the changes projected in Table 10.2, an income increase of 42 percent combined with a income elasticity of 0.1 would mean an increase in per capita food consumption of 4.1 percent over the thirty-five-year period; an income increase of 181 percent combined with an income elasticity of 0.3 would mean an increase in per capita food consumption of about 54 percent over a thirty-five-year period.

Table 10.2 The Power of Compound Growth

If income per capita grows at an annual rate of:	Then income after thirty-five years will be higher by a factor of:
1%	1.42
2%	2.00
3%	2.81

The most likely scenario is at the low end of this range, for two reasons. First, although average growth of per capita incomes in the 1.8 percent range have been observed since 1960, it may be hard to sustain this high a level for the next thirty-five years. Second, income elasticities decline as income increases; therefore the 0.1 elasticity is probably more realistic than the 0.3 elasticity.

So a good guess about how food demand per capita will grow over the next fifty years is that it will grow by 4–18 percent. Is this a reasonable guess based on historical experience? Growth of this magnitude would mean that (assuming constant prices) the worldwide average intake of calories per capita might grow from 2,903 per day (as of 2014–2016) to a level between 3,019 calories per day (equivalent to the current average diet in Venezuela) and 3,426 calories per day (approximately equivalent to the current average diet in South Korea). For an additional comparison, in the past twenty-five years, worldwide consumption of calories per person grew about 12 percent.

Growth in Population and Growth in Food per Capita: A Multiplicative Effect

Notice that growth in *per capita* food consumption magnifies the impact of growing population. Imagine a country in which 1,000 people consume 2,500 calories per day—total food consumption in the country is 2.5 million calories per day. Now suppose the population grows to 2,000, and the per capita calorie need to 3,000; now total food consumption in the country is 6 million calories per day. The population has grown by 100 percent (from 1,000 to 2,000), but

Table 10.3 Growth in per Capita Food Consumption Magnifies the Effect of Population Growth

If population grows by 30% over the next thirty-five years, and if per capita food demand grows by:	Then total food demand will grow by:
5%	36%
10%	43%
15%	50%
20%	56%

food consumption has grown by 140 percent (from 2.5 to 6 million). Not only are there more mouths to feed, but each mouth is eating more. The practical effect of this is illustrated in Table 10.3. If population grows by 30 percent over the next thirty-five years, and if per capita food demand grows by between 5 and 20 percent, total food demand will grow by between 36 and 56 percent.

Dietary Diversification and Demand for Food

As average incomes increase, people do not simply eat more food; they eat different kinds of food. In particular, they eat more meat and animal products, and they consume fewer calories from cereals. To illustrate this, consider the diets of various countries and country groups shown in Table 10.4.

In 2011, average number of calories consumed per day worldwide was 2,870, with about 500 (18 percent) coming from animal products and the rest from plant sources. But it takes more than one calorie of grain produced and fed as animal feed to produce one calorie of meat. See Box 10.1 for a discussion of estimates of the number of plant-derived calories needed to produce a human-consumed calorie from various animal products. In the calculations in the next paragraph we will assume that it takes six plant calories to produce one animal-product calorie.

In 2003, people in developing countries consumed about 14 percent of their 2,668 calories as animal products. Suppose this percentage rises to 17 percent (approximately the world average today) by the year 2050. Even if caloric intake remained constant at 2,668, this shift to animal products would mean that each person would need 9.4 percent more plant-derived calories. The calculation is as follows: The current developing-country diet is 369 calories from animal sources and 2,299 from plant sources; if six plant-derived calories are needed to produce one animal product calorie, this means the current developing-country diet requires 4,513 plant-derived calories; if calories from animal products rise to 17 percent of 2,668 (453 calories), the future diet would require 4,936 plant-derived calories. This is a 9.4 percent increase in plant-derived

Table 10.4 **Calories per Capita per Day from Animal and Vegetal Sources, Various Countries and Country Groups, 2011–2013**

	Animal Calories	Plant Calories	Total Calories
Brazil	826	2,437	3,263
India	236	2,223	2,459
Nigeria	103	2,597	2,700
China	726	2,382	3,108
United States	995	2,644	3,639
European Union	992	2,424	3,416
Least-developed countries	191	2,144	2,335

Source: FAOSTAT.

**Box 10.1 Plant-Derived Calories Needed to Produce
a Calorie from Animal Products**

In a background paper for the 1996 World Food Summit, the FAO (1996c) published estimates that it takes:

- 11 plant-derived calories to produce 1 calorie of beef or mutton
- 4 plant-derived calories to produce 1 calorie of pork or poultry
- 8 plant-derived calories to produce 1 calorie of milk
- 4 plant-derived calories to produce 1 calorie of eggs

Time Magazine (Usher 1996) cited a conversion rate of 16 to 1 for cattle.

Fitzhugh (1998) argues that these numbers are too high. Animals can eat grass, crop residues, waste, and by-products that are not part of the human diet. He estimates that the correct conversion rate is 2.3–3.4 plant calories for each calorie of animal products.

     If we convert the figures from the FAO's food balance sheet for the world from kilograms to calories, we find that the ratio of calories used in animal feed to calories of animal products eaten by humans is about 2.2 to 1 (see Chapter 20 for further discussion). Although we will use (in the projections in Chapter 10 and Chapter 23) the figure of 6 plant calories for each animal-product calorie in our projections and discussions in the text, it should be noted that this may overstate the impact of dietary diversification.

---

calories. To put it somewhat differently: if diets in developing countries were slightly more diversified (17 percent animal products instead of the current 14 percent)—even with no increase in calories per capita—the effect on food demand would be the same as a 9.4 percent increase in population.

    Consider a different scenario—suppose that by the year 2050, people in developing countries have incorporated meat into their diets to such an extent that their diets resemble diets in developed countries today. In this case, the future developing country diet would be 26 percent animal product calories (694 out of 2,668). Converting this to plant-derived calories, and adding the 1,974 calories consumed directly from plant sources, yields about 6,200 plant-derived calories—a 36 percent increase from the present diet.

    Delgado (2003) projects that per capita consumption between 1997 and 2020 will grow by 2.1 percent per year for meat, and 1.7 percent per year for milk. These growth rates are considerably higher than the scenarios in the preceding two paragraphs. If animal calories grew at this rate, by the year 2020 or 2025 many people in the world would have reached some kind of satiation point where they no longer reacted to increased income by adding more animal calories to their diets. (In the United States, animal calories per capita have been just shy of 1,000 per day for a decade or more.)

The same multiplicative effect described here between population growth and growth in consumption per capita applies more generally to all the effects described in this chapter. To review, using examples from Table 10.3:

• If population grows by 30 percent, and if income increases demand per capita by 15 percent, total demand grows by 50 percent. (The computation is $[1 + 0.30] \times [1 + 0.15] - 1$.)
• If diversification of diets has an additional impact on effective (or plant-equivalent) demand of 10 percent, the total growth in demand is 64 percent. (The computation is $[1 + 0.30] \times [1 + 0.15] \times [1 + 0.10] - 1$.)

In these examples, the numbers were chosen to be "in the reasonable range." They are by no means intended as an exact projection.

Notice the impact of taking income-induced changes in food demand into account. Population grows by 30 percent (in the example), but total food demand grows by 64 percent—double the growth in population. Even though neither of the income effects is large in and of itself—15 percent growth in calories consumed, 10 percent growth due to diet diversification—the cumulative effect is large.

Agricultural Production for Nonfood Uses

It is easy to make a false equivalence between "food" and "agriculture." In fact a growing proportion of agricultural production is used for nonfood purposes. Fiber crops (such as cotton and jute), tobacco, and coffee and tea are grown on a land area about 3.6 percent of total arable land (arable land plus permanent cropland). This percentage has declined slightly from 4.1 percent in the early 1980s (http://faostat.fao.org, hereafter FAOSTAT). Illegal drugs production accounts for about one-half-of-one-percent of total arable land. (United Nations Office of Drug and Crime, 2007). There is no evidence that this percentage is growing.

One non-human-food use that is growing is pet food, spurred by increased pet ownership in China. A 2008 report estimated that worldwide spending on pet food would more than double between 2004 and 2009 (Chaney 2008), and a 2015 report projected moderate growth from 2015 to 2022 (Grand View Research 2015). However, despite this growth, the total impact of pet food demand on total food demand is fairly small: worldwide expenditure on dog food ($70 billion according to Grand View Research) is less than 1 percent of worldwide expenditure for food.

The nonfood use likely to have a substantial impact on food demand during the next decades is biofuels. This trend is expected to continue and to accelerate. In a 2008 report, the USDA (2008a) projected that US ethanol production will increase from 8 billion gallons a year in 2008 to 30 billion gallons a year in 2025. By 2014, ethanol production had reached 14 billion gallons. (USDA 2016). The Organization for Economic Cooperation and Development

(OECD) and the FAO projected that biofuels production in the United States, European Union, Brazil, China, and Canada would more than double during the 2006–2016 period (OECD and FAO 2007). However, recent projections show much slower growth in biofuels. The USDA's estimates are summarized here: "Projected increases in corn-based ethanol over the next 10 years are much smaller than occurred in 2005–2010. This projection reflects declining overall gasoline consumption in the United States. . . . Nonetheless, a strong presence for ethanol in the sector continues, with about 35 percent of total corn use expected to go to ethanol production during the projection period" (Westcott and Trostle 2013).

Based on the numbers in the OECD/FAO report, in 2006 biofuels used crops equivalent to 150 calories per person per day—about 5 percent of food calories consumed worldwide. This number could triple or quadruple by the year 2050. However, as we try to project further into the future, several uncertainties arise. If all energy and transportation technology were to be frozen at current levels, then undoubtedly food-crop-based ethanol use would continue to grow. However, two types of possible technological developments could slow or reverse the growing use of food crops for ethanol. First, the next decades may see development of alternatives to gasoline-ethanol-powered transportation (electric cars, or hydrogen power, for example). Second, extensive research into producing biofuels without using food crops is under way. For example, it is possible to produce ethanol from cellulose derived from non-food plants like switchgrass (US Department of Energy 2007), and this may become a more profitable source of ethanol than ethanol from corn. It is also possible to produce ethanol and biodiesel from tanks of algae (Haag 2007). Either of these options would allow production of biofuels with considerably less impact on the market for food. In the following scenarios, we examine biofuels growth in the range of 0–15 percent. A 15 percent growth in demand would be 420 calories per person per day compared to the 165 calories per capita per day growth projected by the OECD/FAO for the 2006–2016 period.

Scenarios for the Future Demand for Food

In making projections about the future, the word "if" is used frequently. It is useful to construct alternative scenarios to see how much variation results. Table 10.5 shows a number of scenarios about possible growth in demand for food.

Scenario-building allows us to investigate differences of opinion about how things will change. For example, scenario 2 in Table 10.5 differs from scenario 1 only in the population growth number—scenario 1 assumes that population grows about 28 percent between now and 2050 (similar to the UN medium variant, or the US Census Bureau projection); scenario 2 assumes that population grows only 15 percent (similar to the UN's low variant). Because of the magnifying effects of growing demand per capita, this 13 percent dif-

Table 10.5 Various Scenarios for Growth in Demand for Food to 2050 (percentage increases)

Scenario	Effect of Population Growth	Effect of Increasing Income	Effect of Dietary Diversification	Effect of Growth in Biofuels	Total Growth in Demand for Food
1	28	20	10	5	73
2	15	20	10	5	55
3	15	33	12	5	73
4	40	12	5	5	71
5	28	20	10	15	86

ference in population growth translates into a 18 percent difference in total demand growth between scenario 1 and scenario 2.

However, scenarios need to be internally consistent. For example, it is inconsistent to assume that incomes per capita will be stagnant, particularly while a large amount of dietary diversification occurs; dietary diversification is a result of growth in incomes. Because of the link between income and fertility rates (from the theory of demographic transition in Chapter 8), high population growth is likely to be associated with low income growth (and vice versa). Low income growth reduces total calories per capita (the effect of income growth) and reduces the expansion of animal-derived calories (the effect of dietary diversity).

Therefore the requirement of internal consistency carries with it a certain element of "self-correction" of projections. This is illustrated by comparing scenario 1 to scenarios 3 and 4. Scenario 3 has lower population growth, but higher growth in per capita income (3 percent per year, rather than 2 percent per year assumed in scenario 1). Scenario 4 has higher population growth (along the lines of the UN's high variant), but lower per capita income growth (1 percent annual growth). In these scenarios, the higher (or lower) growth in income is exactly offset by the lower (or higher) growth in population, so that in all of scenarios 1, 3, and 4, total food demand grows by about 73 percent. We will return to these scenarios and others in the final chapter.

Finally, scenario 5 shows the potential impact of a policy-induced growth in ethanol demand (as translated into per capita demand for food) of 15 percent. As discussed earlier, this would result from a continuation and intensification of the trends expected over the next ten years. The impact is to shift out total demand for food by an additional 13 percent compared to scenario 1.

11

Issues of Agricultural Land and Water

The preceding few chapters have helped us analyze questions such as: How much food is enough? How many people will need to be fed? How much food will the average person eat? How does the average level and the distribution of income in the world influence the answers to these questions? Now we turn to the supply side. Will there be enough food? How can we increase the supply of food to make food more affordable? Prices of food are not etched in stone and handed down from on high. They are determined in the market day by day and week by week through the interplay of supply-and-demand forces. When the supply of food increases, prices drop, food becomes more affordable, and hunger decreases. In this chapter we begin an examination of the factors that determine food supply.

The Basic Equation of Food Supply

The typical way to analyze the food supply is to focus on crops, and to split up output according to the following simple equation:

$$\text{Total output} = \frac{\text{Output}}{\text{Acre}} \times \text{Number of acres}$$

Typically "output per acre" is referred to by the shorthand term "yield." Of course, one might think that this equation ignores the possibility of getting food from animal products. But, as described in Chapter 10, animal food products require animal feed, and animal feed comes from crops. And only 17 percent of calories worldwide come from meat products. Almost 50 percent come from cereal crops (rice, wheat, maize, etc.). Therefore we will discuss food production primarily from the perspective of crop production.

The equation obviously splits into two factors: land area and yield. In our discussion in Chapters 11 to 14, we will explore four principal influences on current and future agricultural output:

• Quantity of available agricultural resources—land and water.
• Quality of agricultural resources.
• Intensity of input use on the land.
• Technological change.

This chapter deals with the first of these influences. Chapter 12 deals with the interrelationship of agricultural production and environmental quality, Chapter 13 deals with input use, and Chapter 14 discusses technological change.

Available Land

One way to increase food production is to increase the amount of land devoted to agricultural production. Data in Table 11.1 show that agricultural land has increased slowly but steadily. Worldwide, total land in agriculture increased 2.7 percent during the 1960s, 2.1 percent during the 1970s, 4 percent during the 1980s, and 2.6 percent during the 1990s.

The growth in total agricultural land masks some changes of land use within agriculture. As Figure 11.1 shows, total agricultural land use has remained fairly constant since the early 1990s. Total arable land ("arable land" is land on which crops are grown) grew during the 1960s, 1970s, and 1980s, but then declined for the next two decades. This, and the declining amount of land devoted to cereal production, is consistent with the addition of meat and dairy products to the average diet, described in Chapter 10.

Can the rate of increase in agricultural land use continue into the future? An FAO report (Bruinsma 2011) estimates that there are 4.2 billion hectares of "rainfed land with crop potential" in developing countries. Of this, about 1.6 billion hectares are currently used (arable land plus permanent cropland). At first blush, this would appear to be very good news. But some of this potential

Table 11.1 Worldwide Agricultural Land Use, 1961–2011 (billion hectares)

	Agricultural Land	Arable Land	Permanent Pasture
1961	4.458	1.292	3.078
1971	4.577	1.340	3.141
1981	4.652	1.348	3.202
1991	4.841	1.412	3.309
2001	4.953	1.397	3.416
2011	4.920	1.393	3.364

Source: FAOSTAT.

Figure 11.1 Indexes of Land Use, 1961–2013

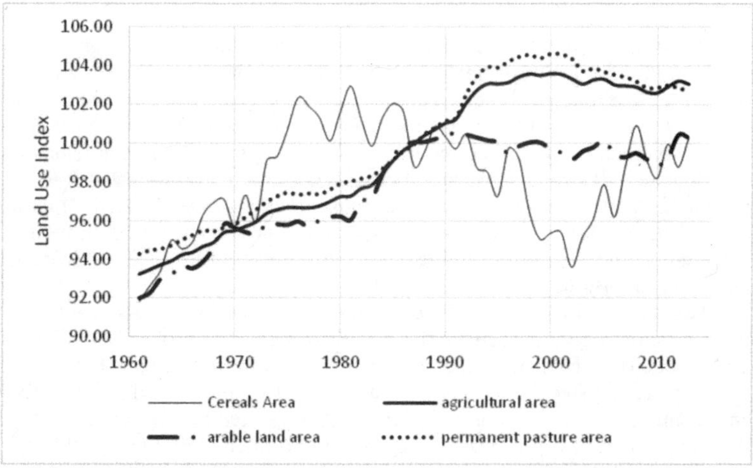

Source: FAOSTAT.

land is hilly, or has poor soil or drainage. Of the 4.2 billion hectares with crop potential, about two-thirds (2.9 billion hectares) is suitable or very suitable (yields more than 60 percent of that achievable on perfect land). Nevertheless, there does appear to be potential to bring new land under cultivation

The potential differs significantly from region to region. In South Asia, the Near East, and North Africa, there is little potential for expansion. In Brazil and the Democratic Republic of Congo (and surrounding African countries), there are large tracts of land that could be brought under agricultural production. (See Grigg 1993: chap. 6 for additional discussion.) Box 11.1 describes a large area of land in Brazil that has only recently begun to be used for agricultural production. A report by the African Development Fund estimates that in the Democratic Republic of Congo, "agricultural land is very vast (80 million [hectares]) but only 10% of the land is being developed at the moment. The hydrographic network . . . offers tremendous water resources that can be mobilized" (2004: para 2.7.3).

The FAO (Conforti 2011) concludes that about 2.9 billion hectares of land are suitable or very suitable for crop production (compared to current arable land use of 1.4 billion hectares). In addition, the FAO projects that arable land use will increase by about 4 percent by the year 2050, with most of the increases coming in Latin America and Africa (and some shrinkage of arable land in industrialized and transitioning countries).

Box 11.1 Expanding Agricultural Land in the Brazilian Cerrado

One place where there is substantial opportunity for adding land to agricultural use is in the Brazilian savannah. About one-quarter of the area of Brazil (200 million hectares) is in an ecological system known as the cerrado. The cerrado has ample rainfall, and the climate in much of the cerrado is warm enough to grow two crops per year. Yet, until the past decade, the cerrado had remained largely underutilized for agricultural production. One study estimated that 137 million hectares of the cerrado are "well suited to large-scale mechanized farming" (Wallis 1997). As of 1990, only 12 million hectares were being used to grow crops and another 35 million hectares were used as pasture (Schnepf, Dohlman, and Bolling 2001).

Two things have held back development of the cerrado: soil quality and transportation capacity. The soil of the cerrado is deep, but has chemical properties that are not conducive to crop growth: soil acidity is high, aluminum content is high, and soil availability of nitrogen and phosphorus is low. But these shortcomings can be overcome. Spreading lime can reduce the acidity of soil. Applying fertilizer can increase nitrogen and phosphorus. And new plant varieties have been developed that can tolerate soils with high aluminum content. Transportation infrastructure that provides a way to ship output from the cerrado to urban or international markets needed to be built.

A measure of how quickly the land of the cerrado was converted to agricultural uses is found in a paper by Trabaquini and colleagues (2012). That paper estimates that 15 percent of the cerrado was used for agricultural production in 1980, increasing to 37 percent by 1990, 51 percent by 2000, and 61 percent by 2010.

The preceding paragraph seems to imply that it is possible to increase the amount of land under cultivation significantly. However, this calculation requires an additional assumption: that no land currently under cultivation is lost to agriculture. There are three reasons to be concerned that land currently used for agricultural production might not be usable for agriculture in the future. First, as population grows, and urban areas expand, some farmland is paved over. The impact of suburban sprawl is obvious in parts of the United States. However, worldwide, urban areas and other human settlements take up only 3 percent of the land mass. Therefore, even significant urbanization will have a small quantitative effect on agriculture worldwide. Second, as we will discuss in more detail in the next chapter, there is concern that global warming may result in expansion of ocean areas and flooding of coastal areas. Third—and this is the factor of most concern to experts—land currently in production may be degraded through soil loss or contamination to such a degree that it can no longer be used to grow crops. This aspect will also be discussed in more detail in the next chapter.

On the other hand, there is undoubtedly some potential for increasing production without increasing yields or acreage. Most significant here is likely to be expansion of double or triple cropping—where a single plot of land is planted with two or three crops sequentially during a year. Double-cropping becomes more feasible if agronomists develop crop varieties that require a shorter growing season. Other new technologies may increase the importance of non-land-based food production—most immediately fisheries and aquaculture, but potentially including hydroponics, food from the sea, and food produced in laboratories.

Taking all of these factors into account, some experts are notably more pessimistic than the FAO regarding the future potential for adding or maintaining land devoted to food production. Kendall and Pimentel cite lack of arable land as "one of the most urgent problems facing humanity . . . [and also] perhaps the most neglected" (1994:205). In another study, Pimentel calculates that nearly one-third of the world's cropland (1.5 billion hectares) has been abandoned during the past four decades because erosion has made it unproductive (Pimentel et al. 1995). Gary Gardner of Worldwatch Institute (1996a) also concludes that there is little room for large-scale expansion of cropland:

> Replacing lost land is likely to be more difficult than many officials think. . . . Optimistic officials often overestimate the potential for expansion by including marginal land, where cultivation may not be sustainable. Indeed, the world's major grain producers have all overexpanded into marginal land in recent years, damaging large areas of land in the process. Many are now pulling back to the land that can be [sustainably] cultivated, with a resulting loss of grain production.

The Importance of Water

Of course, finding new agricultural land is useless unless we also have sufficient water for agricultural production. As Table 11.2 shows, agriculture is a huge user of water, especially in the developing world. The amount of land that is irrigated has grown over time, though the rates of growth have declined since the 1980s (Postel 2003:60). Irrigation is especially important in growing rice. This is evidenced by the fact that irrigated land produces 80 percent of the food in Bangladesh, 75 percent of the food in China in 2009, and over 50 percent in India and Indonesia (FAO 1996a). Worldwide, irrigated land provides about 40 percent of total food. Yields on irrigated land range from 30 to 200 percent higher than on nonirrigated land. Irrigation raises corn yields from 1.7 to 3.9 metric tons per hectare in Latin America and from 1.2 to 3.1 in Africa, and raises wheat yields from 1.8 to 4.1 in Latin America and from 1.4 to 2.4 in North Africa and the Near East; vegetable yields rise from 5.1 to 14.2 in East Asia.

Table 11.2 Water Use by Country Group, 2013

	Low- and Middle-Income Countries (%)	High-Income Countries (%)	World %	World Cubic Kilometers
Agriculture	81	44	71	2,773
Domestic	10	16	12	469
Industry	10	39	18	703
Total	100	100	100	3,906

Source: World Bank 2015a, tab. 3.5.
Note: Percentage columns may not total due to rounding.

Will it be possible to continue increasing irrigation? In the early 1990s, experts were optimistic. The FAO in the mid-1990s wrote: "Half or even two-thirds of future gains in crop production are expected to come from irrigated land" (1996a). A joint study by the World Bank and UNDP (1990) estimated that an additional 110 million hectares of land could be brought under irrigation, producing enough more grain to feed 1.5 to 2 billion people. In 1990 about 260 million hectares were equipped for irrigation, so an additional 110 million hectares would bring us to 370 million. By 2013, that number was 325 million hectares. Bruinsma (2011) projects continued small growth in areas equipped for irrigation as we move to the year 2050. So, looking back at the predictions of the 1990s, it appears that actual irrigation may not expand as fast as those experts believed.

Bruinsma also notes that yields on irrigated land are about 2.4 times yields on nonirrigated land. So as growth in irrigated land keeps pace with, or grows a bit faster than, growth in nonirrigated land, much of the growth in total output does come from irrigated land—about two-thirds of the growth—consistent with the FAO report cited in the preceding paragraph.

However, other experts are more pessimistic about future water availability. Alan Wild concludes, "Shortage of water . . . is probably the biggest biological and physical limitation to agricultural development in developing countries" (2003:217). Sandra Postel (1997) concluded that agriculture cannot increase water use much beyond current levels without causing substantial environmental problems.

Postel noted that water shortages were already appearing as depletion of groundwater. She cited evidence that water tables were falling 20 centimeters a year in India's Punjab. More recent evidence of groundwater problems in this area comes from Rodell, Velicogna, and Famiglietti (2009), who found that groundwater was being removed faster than it was being renewed in the northwestern Indian states of Punjab, Rajasthan, Haryana, and Delhi.

Surface water depletion for irrigation can also be seen in a variety of geographical settings. See Box 11.2 for a discussion of irrigation in China.

Box 11.2 Irrigation in China

The evidence of the impact of irrigation is striking in China, as described by Brown and Halweil (1998). The Yellow River flows through a dry part of China, and farmers draw water out of the river to irrigate their crops. In the years prior to 1972, the Yellow River always had sufficient water flow to reach the sea. Then in 1972, as more and more water was drawn for irrigation, the river ran dry, failing to reach the ocean for fifteen days. Since 1986, not a year has passed in which the Yellow River has not run dry. In the drought year of 1997, the river failed to reach the sea for 227 days. In places like this, irrigation has grown to its limit; irrigation might continue at current rates, but is unlikely to grow any further. In other parts of China, water is used for irrigation at rates that cannot be sustained indefinitely. A study cited by Brown and Halweil found that in many parts of the North China Plain where irrigation water is pumped from below ground, the water table was dropping by 5 feet per year. However, in February 2003, scientists reported discovering a large new aquifer under the Taklamakan desert in northwest China (Goncalves et al. 2013).

Sources: See also US Water News Online 2003.

Other infamous examples of the effects of over-irrigation are found in the decline of the Aral Sea, in the former Soviet Union, and of Lake Chad in central Africa.

Others belittle this talk of water shortages as "doomsaying." Julian Simon of the University of Maryland was one of the most outspoken optimists about future resource availability. He based his optimism on a confidence in human ingenuity:

> Usable water is like other resources, however, in being a product of human labor and ingenuity. People "create" usable water, and there are large opportunities to discover and utilize new sources. Some additional sources are well-known and already in partial use: transport by ship from one country to another, deeper wells, cleaning dirty water, towing icebergs to places where water is needed, and desalination. . . . [In addition,] huge new supplies of groundwater have been found in the Red Sea Province of eastern Sudan, Florida, and elsewhere. (1996: chap. 6)

A survey of African groundwater by the British Geological Survey (2012) lent support to the notion that new water sources could be discovered. The survey team concluded that for much of Africa, small-scale wells with hand pumps could provide water for irrigation. However, they warned that the potential is much lower for high-yielding boreholes such as would be needed to supply larger towns and intensive irrigation.

Efficiency of water use is the most effective way to "create" new water. Water expert Peter Gliek cites the US example: "It is a little-known fact that the United States today uses far less water per person, and less water in total, than we did twenty-five years ago. . . . It's a shocker. People don't believe it, but it's true. This is an indication that things are not the way people think they are. It is not really because we are trying to cut our water use. . . . But we have changed the nature of our economy, and we have become more efficient at doing what we want to do" (quoted in Specter 2006:34)

The FAO makes some small-scale, practical recommendations of ways that water can be used more efficiently, such as water harvesting (collecting runoff and saving it for periods of need) and drip irrigation (delivering irrigation water directly to the roots of plants) (see the FAO's contribution to UNESCO 2006). In addition, agricultural scientists have developed crop varieties that require less water to thrive and have developed chemicals that promote water retention in soil.

As we will see in the next chapter, water use in agriculture is a major source of environmental concern related to agricultural production. Increased irrigation carries the threat of increased soil erosion, increased chemical runoff and resulting water pollution, and increased threat of global warming from paddy-rice production.

Overall, when it comes to soil and water resources, the World Resources Institute gives this "bottom line" assessment:

> At a global level there is little reason to believe that crop production cannot continue to grow significantly over the next several decades. That said, the underlying condition of many of the world's agroecosystems, particularly those in developing countries, is not good. Soil degradation data, while coarse, suggest that erosion and nutrient depletion are undermining the long-term capacity of agricultural systems on well over half of the world's agricultural land. And competition for water will further magnify the issue of resource constraints to food production. Although nutrient inputs, new crop varieties, and new technologies may well offset these declining conditions for the foreseeable future, the challenge of meeting human needs seems destined to grow ever more difficult. (2000:64)

12

Environmental Degradation and Climate Change

The preceding chapter discussed the potential for increasing land and water use for future food production. In this chapter, we explore the issue of the degree and significance of environmental damage. The issue has two faces: environmental quality is an important determinant of agricultural output and agricultural production has a significant impact on the environment. We deal first with the interaction of agricultural production and the local environment (the environment near to the place where the agricultural production takes place). Then we discuss the interaction of agricultural production and the global environment—especially climate change.

Agricultural Production and the Local Environment

Agriculture uses natural resources—soil and water—to produce food. This can lead to deterioration in the quality of the natural resources and the ability of the natural resources to support food production.

Land Degradation

As land quality becomes degraded it loses its potential to support food production. In some cases, land becomes so degraded that it is removed from agricultural production entirely; in other cases, it remains in production but produces less food. Land can become unsuitable for agricultural production in the following ways (UN Population Information Network 1995):

- Soil can disappear from land through erosion.
- Soil can become chemically unsuitable for agricultural production.
- Land can be come physically unsuitable for agricultural production.

Erosion. Wind or water can pick up soil particles from one area and move them. This can harm agricultural production in four ways. The eroded soil may contain nutrients needed for plant development. The remaining soil may be so dense that it is difficult for plant roots to develop. Erosion may reduce the capacity of the soil to retain water needed for plant growth. Finally, erosion may result in uneven terrain that makes cultivation more difficult.

Soil erosion is to a degree caused by agricultural production. Land used for agricultural production may be bare of vegetation for months at a time. The absence of roots to hold the soil in place makes the soil more easily erodible. Plowing the soil in preparation for seeding exposes it to wind and rain and increases the rate of erosion. Irrigation can contribute directly to water erosion.

Chemical characteristics of the soil. Land may become chemically unsuitable for agricultural production for several reasons. The nutrients of the soil may be depleted because of past agricultural production, especially if the same crop is grown year after year. "Salinization" of soil occurs when the salt content of the soil increases to levels unsuitable for agricultural production. Salinization can be caused by irrigating land with water that contains low levels of salts, which are left on the soil when the water evaporates. In some areas, this problem occurs because irrigation depletes the naturally occurring fresh groundwater and causes seawater to intrude into the groundwater system. A third chemical problem with soil is "acidification." This can occur when too much fertilizer of certain types is applied, or when there are drainage problems on certain soils. Finally, other pollutants such as oil or excessive pesticides can reduce the ability of soil to support agricultural production.

Physical characteristics of the land. Agricultural land can also become unsuitable for production because of changes in the physical characteristics of the land. Soil can become less porous through compaction—when heavy machines or animals pack the soil down—or through the action of raindrops that seal the soil. Nonporous soil makes it difficult for seeds to emerge. Waterlogging occurs when water sits in the root zone of plants and thus impedes their development. Waterlogging occurs when drainage is poor, or when a field is over-irrigated.

The Extent and Impact of Land Degradation Worldwide
Over the past twenty-five years, two global efforts have assessed the extent of land degradation. The Global Land Assessment of Degradation (GLASOD) was a comprehensive study of soil quality worldwide, done by the United Nations in 1991 (ISRIC and UNEP 1991). GLASOD estimated that 22 percent of agricultural land worldwide (and 38 percent of cropland) has been subject to one or more of the kinds of degradation described earlier. Of the 2 billion hectares of degraded land, according to this study, 83 percent was degraded by erosion, 12 percent by chemical degradation, and 5 percent by physical degradation. Seventy million hectares are so badly degraded that the damage cannot be repaired.

A more recent study was published by the Food and Agriculture Organization in 2011 (*State of the World's Land and Water Resources for Food and Agriculture,* or SOLAW for short). SOLAW estimating that 29 percent of agricultural land is "prime land"—meaning it can produce yields that are greater than 80 percent of maximum yields achievable; 52 percent is "good land" (40–80 percent of maximum yields); and 19 percent is "marginal land" (less than 40 percent of maximum yields).

How fast is the problem of land degradation growing? The GLASOD results are not directly comparable to the SOLAW results. But the SOLAW report says that soil health is declining throughout both the developed and the developing world in many cropping systems. That report's classification of worldwide land is shown in Table 12.1.

Other studies—Scherr and Yadav 1997 or Pimentel and colleagues 1994, for example—suggest that the rate of degradation is higher (and alarming). However, as we saw in the preceding chapter, agricultural land *has* increased over the decades, despite the existence of degradation. Stanley Wood gives the following assessment of the current state of scientific opinion: "As a global problem, soil loss is not likely to be a major constraint to food security" (quoted in Kaiser 2004:1616).

A related possibility is that land degradation will reduce average yields per hectare. This can occur for two reasons. First, when land becomes so severely degraded that it is no longer capable of supporting agricultural production, new land may be added to agricultural production to take the place of the degraded land. The new land is likely to be of relatively poor quality—otherwise it would already have been in use. Second, when the land is degraded, but remains in agricultural use, yields on that land drop.

There is a lack of agreement among agricultural scientists about the severity of the drop in yields attributable to land degradation. Pimentel and Giampietro (1994) point to evidence that corn yields are about 20 percent lower on severely eroded lands in many parts of the United States. Mitchell, Ingco, and

Table 12.1 Worldwide Status and Trends in Land Degradation

Land Type	Percentage of Total Land
Stable land slightly or moderately degraded	36
High degradation trend or highly degraded	25
Bare areas or water	20
Improving land	10
Moderate degradation trend or moderately degraded	8

Source: FAO 2011: 113.
Note: Percentages may not total due to rounding.

Duncan (1997:54) cite other studies that estimate that soil erosion was responsible for yield declines of 3–4 percent over a hundred years. Scherr and Yadav (1997) report yield losses of 5–15 percent attributable to land degradation. See Crosson (1996a) for a review of the debate.

More recent studies include that by den Biggelaar and colleagues (2004), who estimated that yields grew at a 0.3 percent slower annual rate than would be seen if there were no land degradation, and even this might overestimate the true impact of degradation, since farmers can take steps (choosing different crops, or using more fertilizer, for example) to counteract the degradation (see Kaiser 2004:1616). Other studies have focused on particular geographical areas. For example, Jolejole-Foreman, Baylis, and Lipper (2012) found that in Ethiopia, land degradation has caused the value of agricultural production to be 7 percent below what could have been achieved with no land degradation.

Water Quality

In Chapter 11, we discussed the importance of water in agricultural production, and cited predictions that expanded irrigation will be a substantial source of increased food production in the future. Expanded irrigation requires a supply of usable water. But agricultural production can lead to degradation of water quality.

Irrigation itself is the main culprit. As described in the preceding chapter, irrigation in China and India has caused water tables to drop significantly, by withdrawing water faster than it is replenished. In coastal areas, depletion of groundwater reserves can result in saltwater intrusion into the groundwater system. In some soils, irrigation leeches certain salts from the soil and carries those salts back into the groundwater, contaminating it and making it unsuitable for future irrigation. Irrigation or rainwater runoff can also carry residues from fertilizers and chemical pesticides. This also creates water quality problems. In addition, as noted, irrigation can contribute to land degradation, increasing erosion, waterlogging, salinization, and acidification.

The use of surface water for irrigation also affects the ecology of rivers, lakes, and even oceans. Diversion of water for irrigation has caused the volume of water in the Aral Sea in Uzbekistan to drop by 75 percent since 1960. This huge loss of water changed the chemical composition of the remaining water and resulted in large decline in the fish population. Total fish catch dropped from 50,000 metric tons in 1959 to 5,000 metric tons in 1994 (see the contribution of the United Nations Environment Programme [UNEP] to UNESCO 2006). Even without intensive irrigation, water runoff from agricultural land, carrying residues of agricultural chemicals and animal waste, can damage fishery ecology. In the Chesapeake Bay, oyster populations are now 2 percent of the levels common in the 1950s to the 1970s (Chesapeake Bay Foundation 2008). See Box 11.2 in the preceding chapter for a description of the impact of irrigation on the Yellow River in China.

The SOLAW report cited earlier gives the following summary of the state of water in the world:

> Through the global hydrological cycle, renewable water resources amount to 42,000 km/yr. Of this, about 3900 km3 is withdrawn for human uses from rivers and aquifers: . . . 70 percent is for irrigation. . . . It is estimated that more than 60 percent of all water withdrawals flows back to local hydrological systems by return flows to rivers or groundwater. . . . With the doubling of the global irrigated area over the last 50 years, withdrawals for agriculture have been rising. Globally, total water withdrawals still represent only a small share—about 9 percent of internal renewable water resources but this average masks large geographical discrepancies. (FAO 2011:26)

Table 12.2 shows the geographical areas where water withdrawal puts "substantial pressure" (SOLAW classification) on water resources (more than 20 percent of renewable water resources are withdrawn each year), or where water use is "critical" (more than 40 percent of renewable water resources are withdrawn each year).

Problems Associated with Agricultural Input Use

We have already discussed how agricultural chemical use can lead to land degradation or water pollution. In addition, chemical use can create health problems for farm workers. The manufacture of agricultural chemicals can also create environmental hazards. The 1984 explosion at a chemical plant in Bhopal, India, provided a tragic example of this. The poison gas released by the explosion is used primarily in production of insecticides. Thousands were killed and tens of thousands were seriously injured (Baylor 1996). In laboratory experiments, some pesticides have been shown to affect hormone levels—which could cause cancer, abnormalities in newborns, or reproductive

Table 12.2 **Geographical Areas Where Water Use Is High Compared to Available Resources**

Subcontinental Area	Agricultural Water Use as Percentage of IRWR	Total Freshwater Withdrawal as Percentage of IRWR
Northern Africa	170	201
Central Asia	57	61
South Asia	52	57
Western Asia	47	55
East Asia	13	20

Source: FAO 2011: tab. 1.4.
Note: IRWR = internal renewable water resources.

problems. However, evidence is weak that this effect can be found outside the laboratory (Kamrin n.d.).

As there is increasing use of mechanization and petrochemicals in agriculture, there may be concern that energy use in agriculture will become an environmental problem. However, R. S. Chen (1990) reports that agricultural production accounts for only 3.5 percent of commercial energy use in developed countries and 4.5 percent in developing countries. In developed countries, food processing and distribution uses more energy than food production. A report by the FAO (2000a) reaches similar conclusions: 3–5 percent in rich countries and 4–8 percent in poor countries.

Other Environmental Problems

Water quality is not only a concern when it impinges on food production. People drink water, and reduced water quality can directly harm public health. Of special concern here is the possibility that water becomes contaminated with pesticides—chemicals that are deliberately developed to be toxic. Rachel Carson's book *Silent Spring* (1962) pointed out the impact that agricultural chemicals could have on the environment. This affects not only humans but also birds, fish, and other wildlife.

Another environmental concern associated with agricultural production is the issue of maintaining genetic diversity. Especially with the increasingly widespread use of improved varieties of cereals, there is concern that the genetic material contained in traditional varieties will be lost. For example, in 1949 there were 10,000 wheat varieties in use in China; by the 1970s only 1,000 remained in use. The loss of genetic diversity can make the food supply more susceptible to disease, and may foreclose the option of future technological improvements based on genetic characteristics of the "lost" varieties. In an effort to protect future generations from lost genetic diversity, the Global Crop Diversity Trust has begun the Svalbard Global Seed Vault, which hopes to store and preserve usable seeds for every crop on the planet (Walsh 2008).

Environment and Future Prospects for Agricultural Production

Are these interfaces between the environment and food production likely to create critical constraints on future food production? Some ecologists are very alarmed about this (see Cohen 1996a and 1996b for a review). David Pimentel of Cornell University states that the world's resources can support a high standard of living for fewer than 2 billion (compared to today's actual population of over 6 billion). This pessimistic view of the future is based on the belief that the world has already expanded agricultural production into areas that cannot sustain it and has achieved yields per hectare by using production methods that cannot be continued for very long. Pimentel cites studies that show that agricultural methods that do not use chemical fertilizers will result in cereal yields of between 0.5 metric tons per hectare (in semi-arid regions with no fertilizer) and 2 metric tons per hectare (in humid regions using animal manure for fertilizer) (Pimentel and Giampietro 1994). Compare these amounts to the average current yield of about 3 metric tons per hectare worldwide and over 5 metric tons per hectare in the United States.

Economist Lester Brown is another leading voice raising concern about environmental degradation and food production. In a 2015 interview with the newspaper *The Guardian,* Brown predicted the following:

> We are pushing against the limits of land that can be ploughed and the land available for grazing and there are two areas of the world in which we are in serious trouble now. One is the Sahel region of Africa, from Senegal to Somalia. There is a huge dust bowl forming now that is actually stretching right across the continent and that dust bowl is removing a lot of top soil, so eventually they will be in serious trouble. [The second area is China, where villagers] will be abandoning so much land, both for farming and for grazing, that it will restrict their efforts to expand food production. [The dust bowl of the 1930s in the US] was confined and within a matter of years we had it under control . . . these two areas don't have that capacity. (Brown 2015)

Technology and the Trade-off Between Production and the Environment

If Lester Brown and David Pimentel represent one extreme in the debate about how many people the world can feed, Julian Simon represents the other. He describes the experience of a company called PhytoFarm, which grows vegetables indoors, and estimates that these techniques "could feed a hundred times the world's present population—say 500 billion people—with factory buildings a hundred stories high, on one percent of present farmland" (Simon 1996: chap. 6). By 2008, high energy prices, and the potential to locate indoor agriculture in urban areas and thereby reduce food transportation costs, led to a resurgence of interest in this concept (see Despommier 2010 or the Vertical Farm website, http://www.verticalfarm.com).

Simon's attitude reflects an enormous confidence in the ability of technology to solve problems. Technological progress is all about getting more from less. A good deal of agricultural research in the past decade has been devoted to the problem of maintaining or improving agricultural yields while doing less damage to the environment. For example, new plant varieties are being developed that are naturally resistant to pests and thus require less pesticide use. Tilling and landscaping methods to reduce soil erosion have been widely adopted in parts of the world. "Drip irrigation," which delivers water directly to plant roots, reduces water used in irrigation without causing any reduction in the effectiveness of irrigation. The new technology of aquaculture has made "fish farming" a rapidly growing source of food, as Table 12.3 shows. Nonmarine fish production has increased tenfold since 1980. The huge increase during the 1980s and 1990s reflects in part the introduction of aquaculture. (Table

Table 12.3 Fish Production Worldwide, 1950–2013 (million metric tons)

	Freshwater Fish	Marine Fish	Total Fishery Production
1950	1.515	13.319	14.833
1960	3.068	24.923	27.992
1970	4.763	46.407	51.170
1980	5.903	46.703	52.606
1990	12.523	68.158	80.681
2000	24.513	71.326	95.839
2010	42.763	66.109	108.871
2013	50.577	68.423	119.000

Source: FIGIS 2016.

12.3 also shows a source of environmental concern: natural ocean—or marine—fisheries have increased production to such a degree that they are in danger of being overfished to the extent that the breeding stock will be depleted and the total ocean fish population will begin to fall.)

Another aspect of agricultural research is to develop technology that relaxes the constraints that environment imposes on agricultural output. For example, scientists are working to develop plants that can survive in brackish water. "Researchers have transferred a gene for salt tolerance from an Old World ice plant into three plants lacking salt tolerance . . . all of which then displayed significantly increased capability to grow with their roots exposed to salt. . . . [This] will contribute to the effort to engineer plants with improved ability to withstand adverse growing conditions such as under seawater irrigation" (National Science and Technology Council 1995). Other examples of technological ways to relax the environmental constraint to agricultural production are chemicals that increase the ability of soils to retain moisture, and seed varieties that are more drought-resistant (so the crops can be grown in more arid regions). Box 12.1 describes an effort to reclaim degraded land in China.

Agricultural Production and the Global Environment

Agricultural production also interacts with the environment on a global scale, especially on the issue of climate change. Climate change refers to the phenomenon by which water vapor, carbon dioxide, methane, and other trace gases in the atmosphere trap heat on the earth's surface. As the quantities of these gases (the so-called greenhouse gases) in the atmosphere increase, the amount of heat trapped will increase, causing an increase in the average temperature of the earth and related changes in precipitation and prevailing wind patterns. On these matters there is a high degree of consensus among scientists (see IPCC 2007a).

Box 12.1 Reclaiming Degraded Lands in Southern China

The five southernmost provinces of China have been farmed for over a thousand years, primarily with slash-and-burn techniques that cleared forests but left the soil exposed to severe erosion. The process of land degradation here is described by Parham (2001):

> When vegetation is removed in these regions, the exposed soil . . . reaches temperatures so high that seeds and sprouts are killed. . . . Since new vegetation cannot be established easily, soil organic matter is reduced, and the soil becomes desiccated. . . . Even small decreases in soil organic matter have a pronounced negative effect on the soil's fertility. . . . When the original topsoil is removed by erosion, the surface becomes a mixture of aluminum-rich clays and quartz sand that contain very few minerals useful to plant life. . . . The loss of vegetative cover and soil organic matter leaves the soil subject to damage from intense tropical rainfall. With little organic matter in the soil, clay particles are moved by raindrops and plug soil pores, thus inhibiting water infiltration and increasing runoff and erosion. . . . The finer-grained eroded sediments damage aquatic productivity and bury what were once freshwater and near-shore marine aquatic breeding grounds. The remaining coarser, sandy material of the weathered granite yields soils of low fertility. Stripped of vegetation that would otherwise have absorbed or slowed the flow of water, the water pours rapidly into streams and rivers, cutting deep ravines in the soft, deeply weathered granite.

By the end of the twentieth century, an estimated 45 million hectares (over 20 percent of the agricultural land of southern China) was degraded. Use of commercial fertilizers was unsuccessful in replacing the nutrients lost with eroded soil, because the remaining coarse soil was a poor medium for holding the nutrients provided by the fertilizers.

Recent research suggests that it may be possible to restore most of the degraded lands to agricultural production within two years. One research project planted fast-growing ground cover amid alternating rows of rubber trees and tea bushes. The ground cover shields the soil from the hot sun and reduces evaporation of soil moisture. The roots of the plants help reduce soil erosion, and the plant residue provides organic material to the soil. The rubber trees provide shade for the tea bushes, and the tea bushes help moderate the temperatures near the roots of the rubber trees. Experimental plots indicate that this type of agriculture is profitable and can restore soil quality while reducing water runoff and flooding.

There is some disagreement about the extent to which global warming has already occurred and about the extent to which human activities are responsible for the buildup of greenhouse gases (see Leggett 2007 or Hulme 2009 for a review of the issues).

The Impact of Agriculture on Greenhouse Gas Emissions

Agricultural production is a significant source of greenhouse gas emissions worldwide. In fact, although the industrial revolution (with the widespread burning of coal and oil products) is usually thought of as the beginning of anthropogenic climate change, some (see Ruddiman 2005) point to the advent of agriculture as the first chapter in human-caused global warming.

The three greenhouse gases that are the primary means by which human activity may cause global warming are carbon dioxide, methane, and nitrous oxide. Carbon dioxide comprises nearly 75–80 percent of greenhouse gases, nitrous oxide 15 percent, and methane 6 percent. Agriculture and forestry account for 24 percent of anthropogenic (human-made) greenhouse gas emissions (IPCC 2014). Carbon dioxide emissions come from deforestation in tropical areas when trees are cut down to clear land for agricultural production (FAO 1997a). Agriculture is the primary source of anthropogenic methane and nitrous oxide. The digestive processes of ruminants (animals such as cattle that ferment their plant-based food in a specialized stomach) contributes 37 percent of anthropogenic methane (Steinfeld et al. 2006). Paddy-rice production is responsible for another 13 percent.

The good news about methane emissions from agriculture is it should be relatively easy to reduce those emissions. The FAO (2013) concludes that emissions from livestock production could be reduced by between 18 and 30 percent simply by persuading all producers to adopt the best emissions-producing methods of production. In paddy-rice production, methane forms when manure used as fertilizer decomposes in an oxygen-free environment (under the water in the flooded rice paddies). Methane production from paddy rice will decline as rice farmers use production methods that substitute commercial fertilizer for animal manure, that conserve on water use, and that use improved rice varieties that store more carbon in the rice plants. (See Neue 1993; Lashof and Tirpak 1990; Graham 2002; and Casey 2007.)

Agricultural production is a substantial source of greenhouse gases; if agricultural production grows as fast as food demand, that could add noticeably to the greenhouse gas problem. Furthermore, any realistic program to reduce greenhouse gas emissions must address the agricultural component; and there is an unavoidable tension between raising agricultural output and reducing greenhouse gases. Perhaps this tension can be reduced by technological innovations, but the tension is there.

Expected Impacts on Temperature and Sea Levels

The Intergovernmental Panel on Climate Change (IPCC) is a group of climate scientists who convene to review the current state of knowledge. The most recent report of the group presented predictions of temperatures and sea levels extending to the year 2100 (IPCC 2014). Some of those results are presented

Table 12.4 Past and Future Changes in Surface Temperature and Sea Level

	Past Change, 1880–2012[a]	Future Changes Under Least Severe Scenario Reported, 1986–2002 to 2046–2060	Future Changes Under Most Severe Scenario Reported 1986–2002 to 2046–2060
Change in surface temperature (mean degrees centigrade)	0.85	1.0	2.0
Temperature-increase range of predictions		0.4–1.6	1.4–2.6
Mean increase in sea level (meters)	0.19	0.24	0.30
Sea-level-increase range of predictions		0.17–0.32	0.22–0.38

Source: IPCC 2014.
Note: a. Past change for sea level is for the period 1901–2010.

in Table 12.4, which shows the expected acceleration of rising temperatures and sea levels. The table illustrating the range of uncertainty about the future. The different scenarios show a range of possibilities about how successful the world will be in cutting greenhouse gas emissions. But even within a scenario—that is, assuming a given path of greenhouse gas emissions—there is a range of possible outcomes in temperatures and sea levels.

The Impact of Global Warming on Agricultural Production

Obviously, when the average temperature in an area changes, the agricultural capacity of the area changes—it may become better for some crops and worse for other crops. Global warming is not expected to result in a gradual increase in temperature in every area of the globe. Some areas may become much warmer, some only a little warmer, some possibly colder. And global climate change does not simply mean changes in temperature. It is almost certainly associated with changes in rainfall patterns, making some areas dryer and some wetter. And it also changes the incidence of severe weather, making some areas more prone to hurricanes, tornadoes, and droughts.

As shown in Table 12.4, there are huge uncertainties about future climate change. Will the changes be dramatic, or nearly imperceptible? Even if the *average* global temperature increases significantly, what will that mean for climates in different geographical areas? Because of these uncertainties, there are a wide variety of opinions among scientists about the possible future impacts of global warming on agricultural production. This debate has centered on two questions: Will global warming cause flooding of coastal areas and loss of agricultural land? And what will the impact of climate change be on average crop yields worldwide? (See Box 12.2 for a related debate—200 years old—on the impact of sunspots on wheat prices.)

Box 12.2 Sunspots, Crop Yields, and Wheat Prices

In 1801, British astronomer William Herschel had a theory: sunspots influence wheat prices. Sunspots are vortices of gas on the surface of the sun. Herschel hypothesized that sunspots would result in "copious emission of heat and therefore mild seasons" on earth. Mild seasons would improve crop yields, which would in turn lead to lower crop prices. Herschel reported that the facts supported his theory: during five prolonged periods of low solar activity (few sunspots), wheat prices were higher. The Royal Society ridiculed Herschel's theory as a "grand absurdity." By the 1840s, astronomers had discovered that sunspots followed a cycle peaking every eight to seventeen years, with an average cycle length of about eleven years. In the late 1800s, economist William Jevons suggested that this might be an explanation of business cycles (alternating periods of economic growth and recession).

A paper by Pustilnik and Din (2003) examined the link between wheat prices and sunspot activity and discovered that for all of the ten solar cycles in the 1600s and 1700s, high sunspot activity was associated with low wheat prices. The explanation, say Pustilnik and Din, is somewhat different than the Herschel "mild seasons" theory: in periods of high solar activity, it is more difficult for charged particles from deep space to reach the earth's atmosphere; since these charged particles contribute to cloud formation, skies over England are less cloudy; this reduces threats to wheat production by frost and extended rainfall; better wheat harvests result in lower wheat prices.

See Baliunas 1999 for a report relating this to global warming.

Climate Change and Agricultural Area

If the average temperature of the earth increases, the volume of water in oceans will increase. This is not primarily (as the popular belief has it) because of melting polar ice caps but rather because the volume of water expands as its temperature increases. The data in the most recent IPCC report (2014, the fifth report of the panel) shows that global temperature has increased by 0.85 degrees centigrade since the 1880s and that the average sea level has increased about 0.19 meters (8 inches) during roughly the same period. The report projects that increases in greenhouse gas emissions would likely increase global temperatures by 0.3–4.8 degrees centigrade during the twenty-first century. Under these temperature-increase scenarios, average sea level is expected to rise between 0.26 and 0.82 meters (10–32 inches) by the year 2100. This estimate confirms an earlier projection of Rosenzweig and Hillel (1995) that the sea level is likely to rise from 4 to 20 inches by the middle of the twenty-first century.

Although this could make some areas uninhabitable and increase the threat of flooding for other areas (see Parry, Magalhaes, and Nih 1992; Ibe and Awosika 1991), it is not expected to have a significant impact on the worldwide availability of agricultural land. In the United States, for example, the Federal Emergency Management Agency (FEMA) estimates that a 1-foot increase in sea level would increase the size of the "hundred-year flood plain" by about 20 percent, from 19,500 square miles currently to 23,000 square miles. But this increase is only one-tenth of 1 percent of the entire land mass of the United States. And as the dikes of Holland remind us, human behavior can adapt to, as well as cause, rising sea levels. In addition, Rosenzweig and colleagues (1993) point out that in some areas, global warming may result in new land becoming suitable for agricultural production, because of an extended growing season or changes in rainfall pattern. (Also, the Meteorological Service of Canada [2006] estimates that 10 million hectares of agricultural land in Canada are currently not utilized because of climate constraints— though it notes that soil quality is poor on much of this land.) Overall, these opinions fall in line with Wittwer's: "Although important for localized regions, [cropland loss from rising sea levels] would be relatively insignificant on a worldwide basis" (1995:165–166). Of course, if the rise in sea level were to be much higher than the mentioned IPCC projection, impacts on agriculture would be much greater (Rowley et al. 2007). However, Pimentel's estimates of cropland reductions of 10 to 50 percent are outliers in this debate.

Zhang and Cai (2011), based on the projections in the IPCC's fourth report, concluded that worldwide agricultural land area would decline by a small amount (about 1 percent) by the year 2100 as a result of climate change. However, regional differences can be much larger: arable land area increasing by 37–67 percent in Russia (as areas now too cold for agriculture become suitable) and decreasing by 11–17 percent in Europe.

The risk from higher sea levels is not only that land will be flooded but also that drainage problems will increase, and seawater intrusion into freshwater sources will occur. The IPCC (2007a) lists the most likely impact of rising sea levels on agriculture as the impact on salinization of irrigation water.

Climate Change and Agricultural Yields

Greenhouse gases and climate change can affect crop yields in a variety of ways (Rosenzweig and Hillel 1995).

Increase in atmospheric CO_2. Atmospheric carbon dioxide comprises about 80 percent of the greenhouse gases, and increases the efficiency of photosynthesis and thereby boosts plant growth. Wheat, rice, and soybeans are especially responsive to increased atmospheric CO_2. High CO_2 levels also significantly increase water-use efficiency. This fact may actually increase demand for irrigation water, as farmers discover that irrigation has a larger impact on yields. In addition, high CO_2 levels increase plants' resistance to salinity and drought, and increase nutrient uptake. Finally, noxious weeds are (for the most part) less responsive to CO_2 than are crops (Wittwer 1995).

Higher temperatures. As higher temperatures will on average increase the length of the growing season, agricultural production may become feasible in areas (closer to the North and South Poles) that are currently too cold. Soils in some of these areas (Canada and Russia) are less fertile than other soils; thus, bringing these lands under cultivation could cause a drop in average yield. In addition, some crops (notably rice) show yield declines when the temperature is too high. Finally, increased temperatures make plants mature faster. But plants that mature faster have lower food yields. On the other hand, the faster maturation combined with the longer growing seasons may extend the areas in which double or triple cropping is feasible.

Change in rainfall patterns. As noted earlier, climate change entails not just changes in temperature but also changes in rainfall. As described in Chapter 11, soil moisture is essential to crop growth. Rainfall also can influence soil erosion. The Environmental Protection Agency (EPA) reports predictions that precipitation will increase in areas close to the earth's poles and decrease in tropical regions, by as much as 20 percent.

Extreme meteorological events. Hurricanes, tornados, heavy rainstorms, or droughts disrupt crop production and tend to lower yields. (See Box 12.3 for a discussion of a meteorological event not related to global warming.)

Box 12.3   El Niño and Food Production

Every few years, the surface of the Pacific Ocean becomes warmer. Peruvian fisherman named this phenomenon El Niño ("the boy-child") because it coincided with Christmas (or the coming of the Christ-child). In 1997, the warming was especially large, and this caused worldwide changes in weather patterns. In Washington, D.C., for example, the winter of 1997–1998 was exceptionally mild, with virtually no snowfall. In Los Angeles, rainfall in early 1998 was nearly twice the usual level. The winter also saw March blizzards in the US Midwest, and ice storms in New England that left people without electricity for days. The United States was not the only country to feel the effects of El Niño. South America and East Africa experienced heavier rainfall than usual; parts of South Asia were unusually dry.

Because of this unusual weather, thirty-seven countries faced food emergencies in early 1998. But the problems were limited to certain areas. Worldwide, cereal production for 1997–1998 was slightly above the record levels of 1996–1997. FAO scientist Rene Gommes concludes, "It is important not to minimize risks but also to remember that there have been El Niños without any catastrophes and catastrophes without any El Niños." (FAO 1997c)..

Increase of tropospheric ozone. Ozone (O_3) is created at ground level when human-caused chemicals react with one another. Readers may recall hearing reports of "ozone levels reaching unhealthy levels" in weather reports on hot hazy days. The EPA (2008) reports: "Since ozone levels in the lower atmosphere are shaped by both emissions and temperature, climate change will most likely increase ozone concentrations. Such changes may offset any beneficial yield effects that result from elevated CO_2 levels." According to the USDA's Agricultural Research Service (USDA 2012), "Ground level ozone causes more damage to plants than all other air pollutants combined." The impacts are especially severe for soybeans, where high ozone concentrations can cause yields to decline by 40 percent. (A different process by which human-produced chlorofluorocarbons [CFCs] cause higher concentrations of ozone in the stratosphere (miles above the earth's surface) can also affect yields by increasing ultraviolet radiation levels on the planet. See Wittwer 1995.)

Pests and diseases. Insect pests and crop diseases thrive in higher temperatures. Thus global warming may increase the incidence of pests and disease, and reduce yields.

Rosenzweig and colleagues (1993) estimate that if temperatures increase 2 degrees centigrade, wheat and soybean yields will increase 10–15 percent, and maize and rice yields will increase about 8 percent. However, if temperatures increase 4 degrees centigrade, yields will decline. (According to UNEP [1990], climate models predict an increase of 1.5 to 4.5 degrees centigrade over the next hundred years.) Wittwer (1995) believes that these estimates may underestimate the yield growth from global warming because they ignore some of the possible benefits from increased levels of atmospheric CO_2.

The IPCC (2007b) concludes: "Many studies . . . have confirmed . . . projections [that] indicate potentially large negative impacts in developing regions, but only small changes in developed regions, which causes the globally aggregated impacts on world food production to be small." Consistent with this conclusion, a recent paper by Deschenes and Greenstone (2007) shows that US agriculture is likely to benefit from global warming as yields and profits increase.

As part of the most recent IPCC report effort, an exhaustive study was undertaken of the literature on the impact of climate change on agricultural production (Porter et al. 2014). That study reached the following conclusions:

• Climate change has had an impact on food production in the past. In some areas (especially near the poles), the impact has been positive; in other areas the impact has been negative, and "negative impacts ... have been more common than positive ones." (p. 488).

• The expected impact of climate change on yields, averaged over all the studies reviewed, is about 2 percent per decade.

• Temperature increases of more than 2 degrees centigrade above late-twentieth-century baseline are expected to result in a negative impact on worldwide food production. Crop yields fall dramatically when daytime temperatures exceed 30 degrees centigrade; therefore if worldwide surface temperatures increase by more than 4 degrees centigrade, a much larger impact on crop yields is expected.

• Studies generally confirm the existence of a positive impact of atmospheric CO_2 on crop yields, and a negative impact of surface-level ozone on crop yields.

An important determinant of the impact of climate change on crop yields is the extent to which farmers adapt their production decisions to the new climatic conditions. For example, suppose we are analyzing production in an area where rice is the predominant crop. Suppose further that we conclude that global warming will result in rice yields dropping by 30 percent in this area. A simplistic analysis would conclude that food production would drop by 30 percent in the area. A more sophisticated analysis would recognize the likelihood that many farmers in the area will stop growing rice and will switch to some alternative crop. The actual drop in production may be much less than 30 percent, depending on the alternative crops available and the extent to which farmers change their cropping decisions. The IPCC study described earlier (Porter et al. 2014) concludes that "agronomic adaptation improves yields by the equivalent of 15–18% of current yields," offsetting several declines caused by rising temperatures.

Other prognoses for crop yields are less optimistic. For example, UNEP (1990) reports: "Mid-latitude yields may be reduced by 10–30 percent due to increased summer dryness," though it admits that "higher yields in some areas may compensate for decreases in others." Pimentel reports: "Under the projected warming trend in the United States, farmers can expect a 25 to 100 percent increase in losses due to insects, depending on the crop. . . . US crop losses due to weeds are projected to rise from 5 to 50 percent. . . . In North America, projected changes in temperature, soil moisture, carbon dioxide, and pests associated with global warming are expected to decrease food-crop production by as much as 27 percent" (1993:54–57). However, Pimentel does see some reason for hope. He projects that yields in North Africa may improve 10–30 percent as a result of global warming. The IPCC study (Porter et al. 2014) sees these extremely pessimistic predictions as outliers. However, Porter and colleagues report that 10 percent of the projections for the 2030–2049 period show yield losses of greater than 25 percent compared to late-twentieth century. (At the other end, 10 percent of projections show yield increases of 10 percent or more during this period.)

Finally, it should be noted that if global warming causes agricultural production to shift from one geographical area (say North America) to another (say North Africa), there may be problems establishing the institutions and infrastructure needed to move the food from the producing areas to the consuming areas. "While the overall, global impact of climate change on agricultural production may be small, regional vulnerabilities to food deficits may increase, due to problems of distributing and marketing food to specific regions and groups of people" (Rosenzweig and Hillel 1995).

13

The Potential of Input Intensity

In Chapter 11, we introduced the basic equation of food supply. In Chapters 11 and 12, we discussed one aspect of that equation: the availability of land and water, and the interactions of resource quality and agricultural production. Now we turn to the second part of the equation: yields.

Crop Yields Since 1960

The increase in crop yields in the last half of the twentieth century is one of the great accomplishments of human history. To put the yield growth in context, consider the historical record of wheat yields in Britain shown in Table 13.1. It took 350 years for wheat yields to triple from their 1450 levels; it took 300 years to triple from their 1550 levels; it took 250 years to triple from their 1700 levels; then they nearly tripled again in 50 years. An acre today produces fifteen times as much wheat as it produced 500 years ago.

Table 13.1 Wheat Yields in Britain, c. 1450–2010

Approximate Year	Approximate Yield (kilograms per hectare)
1450	500
1550	600
1600	750
1650	900
1700	1,100
1750	1,300
1800	1,500
1850	1,800
1900	2,100
1950	3,100
2000	7,700
2010	8,600

Sources: Overton 1996:77; Cooke 1967:191, 463; FAOSTAT.

Worldwide, cereal yields have more than doubled since the early 1960s. As shown in Table 13.2, this growth is seen in all three of the most important cereal crops, and in most geographical areas of the world. (A "percentage increase" of more than 100 signals that yields have more than doubled.) Yield growth is lowest for maize and rice in Africa. Yields in Asia have grown faster than worldwide yields in all three crops.

Worldwide cereal yields are illustrated in Figure 13.1, and the consistent growth is demonstrated by the upward trend. Figure 13.2 looks at these data in a slightly different way; it shows growth rates in yields rather than the yields themselves. To eliminate year-to-year fluctuations caused by weather and other temporary conditions, we show average annual growth rate in yields over a seven-year period, rather than for a single year. The dotted trend line in Figure 13.2 is a (second-order) polynomial curve fitted to the data. That trend line suggests that yields are growing (notice that average growth rates are positive at every point), but that growth rates slowed considerably from the 3-plus percentage-point growth rates of the 1960s. Average growth rates fell below 1 percentage point in the period around 2005, but have rebounded over the past few years.

What Makes Yields Increase?

Three things cause yields per acre to increase:

- Productive inputs (labor, fertilizer, machinery, for example) are used more intensively on each acre of land.

Figure 13.1 Worldwide Cereal Yield, 1961–2014

Source: FAOSTAT.

Table 13.2 Yields of Maize, Wheat, and Rice for Various Geographical Areas, 1961 and 2014 (hectograms per hectare)

	Maize			Wheat			Rice		
	1961	2014	Percentage Increase	1961	2014	Percentage Increase	1961	2014	Percentage Increase
World	19,423	55,729	186.92	10,899	32,893	201.80	18,693	45,389	142.81
Africa	10,844	20,985	93.52	6,930	26,343	280.13	15,520	26,923	73.47
North America	39,229	106,845	172.36	13,258	29,942	125.84	38,227	84,473	120.98
South America	13,734	52,462	281.99	11,358	25,627	125.63	18,246	51,828	184.05
Asia	11,827	51,466	335.16	7,486	30,945	313.37	18,585	46,257	148.89

Source: FAOSTAT.

Figure 13.2 Growth Rates of Worldwide Cereal Yield

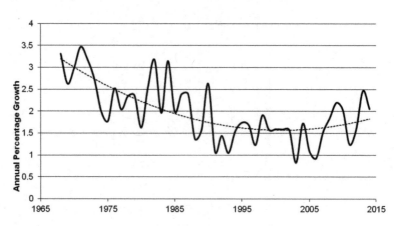

Source: FAOSTAT.

- New technology increases the output obtainable without increasing inputs.
- Farmers increase their efficiency so that less potential output is lost to poor farming practices.

These three ways are illustrated in Figure 13.3, which shows a "production function." The production function shows the maximum quantity of output that is obtainable from any given quantity of input. (To review why production functions are shaped this way, review Box 7.2 from Chapter 7.) Here we will define output as food production per acre, and we will define input as input use per acre, and will illustrate with the example of a farmer growing corn on a plot of land using nothing except his own labor.

An increase in input will move production up along an upward-sloping production function, such as from point B to point C in Figure 13.3. As the farmer puts more and more hours into caring for the field, weeding more frequently or removing insect pests from the plants, more corn plants will survive, the ears will be bigger, and the yield of that plot of land will increase. This source of increasing yields will be discussed in this chapter.

A new technology—broadly defined as new information about how to obtain output from the input—will cause an upward shift in the production function. For any given level of input, a larger output can now be achieved, such as the move from point B to point D in Figure 13.3. Perhaps the farmer is using an improved seed variety that produces bigger ears of corn, or perhaps the farmer has learned that weeding in the first month of growth is especially ef-

Figure 13.3 Different Ways of Increasing Output per Acre

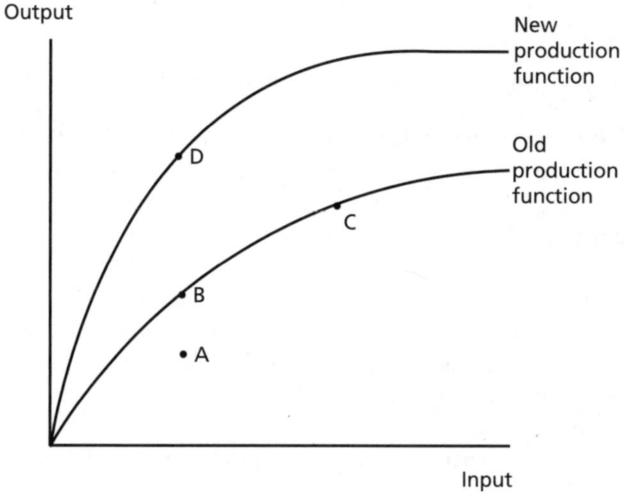

Note: Eliminate inefficiency and move from A to B. Increase input and move from B to C. Advance technology and move from B to D.

fective, so that without increasing the number of hours of weeding, he can increase the effectiveness of weeding, and therefore the crop size. This source of increasing yields will be discussed in Chapter 14.

An improvement in efficiency is illustrated by the move from point A to point B in Figure 13.3. At point A, the farmer was failing to obtain the maximum possible output using the old technology. Perhaps the farmer was stepping on his corn plants as he worked in the field, or perhaps his hours of work were less effective because he was weakened by hunger or sickness. This source of increasing yields will not be discussed in detail here; we discussed in Chapter 5 how undernutrition can contribute to reduced economic productivity; in Chapter 15 we will examine the interaction of undernutrition and health in more detail.

Yields and Input Use: Purchased Inputs

In Chapter 11, we saw that yields on irrigated land can be twice as high as yields on similar nonirrigated land. This is a dramatic example of how yields can be increased by adding more inputs to the land. "Inputs," as economists use the term, refers to things that contribute to production. Water, labor, chemicals, and machinery are all examples of inputs. As a general rule, when we increase the intensity of input use on a plot of land, we increase the output of that plot. Federico (2005) offers an in-depth description of trends of input use over the 1800–2000 period.

Fertilizer

Fertilizer use—especially the application of nitrogen fertilizer—has mushroomed around the world over the past four decades, growing to nearly four times its 1961 level. (See Table 13.3. The FAO revised its method of measuring fertilizer use and the new method goes back only to 2002. The table shows fertilizer use for both the old and new measurement methods.)

At a regional level, several points are worth noting:

• Fertilizer use in developed countries (represented by the United States and Canada as North America in Table 13.3) was already widespread by 1961; therefore growth over the succeeding decades has been much more modest. This is a pattern that applies to purchased inputs in general (see Federico 2005:55–56).
• Fertilizer use expanded enormously in Asia and South America between 1961 and 2002.
• In the most recent decade, the region with fastest growth of fertilizer has been South America—this reflects, in part, the use of fertilizers in the expansion of production in Brazil's cerrado, described in Chapter 11.
• Fertilizer use in Africa grew much more slowly than use in Asia for the period 1961–2002. However, in the past decade, fertilizer use in Africa has grown more rapidly than in Asia, holding the promise that cereal yields in Africa will begin to catch up with the rest of the world.

One way to see the impact of fertilizer is to compare countries based on their fertilizer use and their cereal yields. This comparison shows a clear positive relationship: countries that have low fertilizer use per hectare have relatively low yields. This is shown in Figure 13.4. Many experiments have verified the effectiveness of fertilizer in increasing crop yields. Two of these are described in Box 13.1. Several general conclusions can be drawn from these experiments:

• Fertilizer use can have quite dramatic impact on yields, ranging from 20 percent improvement to over 1,000 percent improvement.
• For low levels of use, increasing fertilizer application increases yield, but at a decreasing rate, giving a yield response curve that has the same general shape as the production function illustrated in Figure 13.3.
• At some point, further increases in fertilizer application actually reduce yields.
• The impact of fertilizer on yields depends on a number of other factors, such as whether the crop is irrigated, the timing of fertilizer applications, and other farming practices used (weeding, types of crop rotation).

Table 13.3 Growth in Fertilizer Use by Continent, 1961–2013 (million metric tons)

	Africa	Asia	South America	North America	World
1961	0.716	3.809	0.558	8.048	31.182
1971	1.850	12.672	1.792	16.460	73.310
1981	3.535	31.657	3.692	21.385	115.147
1991	3.534	58.787	5.141	20.957	134.606
2001	3.946	73.546	9.979	22.089	137.831
2002	4.278	77.116	10.692	21.912	141.282
2002 (new)	4.102	68.891	10.631	22.098	133.500
2013 (new)	5.953	89.452	18.714	24.080	166.594
2002 as multiple of 1961	5.97	20.24	19.15	2.72	4.53
2013 as multiple of 2002	1.45	1.30	1.76	1.09	1.25

Source: For 1961–2002, FAOSTAT fertilizer archives(http://faostat3.fao.org/download/RA/*/E); for 2002–2013, FAOSTAT.

Despite the dramatic growth of fertilizer use, there appears to be potential for additional fertilizer use in many parts of the developing world, especially sub-Saharan Africa. This can be seen by comparing fertilizer use (per hectare of permanent crop and arable land) in a developing country to fertilizer use in a more developed country in the same region. For example, average fertilizer application rates in the Democratic Republic of Congo are about 2 percent of application rates in South Africa; in Nigeria application rates are about 25 percent of application rates in South Africa. The experience in Asia is instructive.

Figure 13.4 Higher Fertilizer Use Increases Crop Yields: Evidence from 160 Countries, 2001

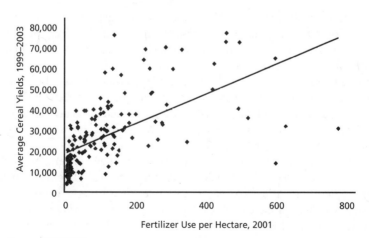

Source: FAOSTAT.

Box 13.1 Fertilizer Increases Crop Yields: Experimental Evidence

The best evidence about the impact of fertilizer on crop yields is not comparisons between different countries' fertilizer rates and yields, or analyses of changing use and yield patterns over time within a country or region. The best evidence is gathered from individual plots on which carefully controlled experiments are conducted holding all variables constant except the uses of fertilizers.

In the mid-1800s, the British Experimental Station in Rothamsted carried out experiments that first demonstrated that applying nitrogen, potassium, and phosphate to crops could increase crop production. In a series of experiments there between 1848 and 1919, average barley yields were 1,210 pounds per acre when grown without fertilizer, and 2,061 pounds per acre when grown with fertilizer; average wheat yields increased from 1,434 pounds per acre to 1,994 pounds per acre when fertilizer was applied (Cooke 1967: 191). The Rothamsted experiments "have often been interpreted as demonstrating that high levels of inputs of inorganic fertilizers . . . can maintain and increase yields for more than a century and a half. While this is true of wheat grown on the soil of the Broadbalk field, it is not always true" (Greenland, Gregory, and Nye 1998:45).

Alan Wild (2003) reports on two fertilizer experiments in Africa. In one experiment in Tanzania, cotton yields were 1,000 kilograms per hectare when grown with compost and phosphate, but no nitrogen. When nitrogen was applied at a rate of 37 kilograms per hectare, yields increased to 1,500 kilograms per hectare; when nitrogen application was increased to 112 kilograms per hectare, yields increased further to 2,000 kilograms per hectare. (Notice how this path of increased input use traces out a curve of the same general shape as that in Figure 13.3.) In a second experiment in Nigeria, fertilized fields had maize yields of 4,369 kilograms per hectare compared to yields of 56 kilograms per hectare in unfertilized fields.

In 1961, application rates in China, India, and Indonesia were 1–3 percent of application rates in Japan. Today, application rates in China are higher than those in Japan, and those in Indonesia and India have risen to 45–60 percent of the Japanese level. If sub-Saharan Africa can follow in the next thirty to forty years the path taken by Asian countries during the past thirty to forty years, fertilizer use in sub-Saharan Africa will grow substantially. (See Box 13.2 for a description of the fertilizer industry in the nineteenth century.)

Table 13.4 shows a projection (by Wood, Henao, and Rosegrant 2004) of future nitrogen fertilizer use for food production under two scenarios—constant and improved efficiency of fertilizer. "Efficiency" of fertilizer use is a measure of the degree to which fertilizer contributes effectively to plant growth. Fertilizer efficiency can increase over time for a variety of reasons: training can help farmers optimize the timing and application rates of fertilizer; farmers can also learn the best combinations of nutrients for a particular

Box 13.2 The Natural Resource Crisis That Wasn't

The development of the worldwide fertilizer industry in the nineteenth century provides an interesting example of a pending natural resource crisis that was averted by luck and new technology.

In the early 1800s, Prussian explorer and scientist Alexander von Humboldt studied the agricultural practices of Incans in Chile and Peru, who used guano—dried bird droppings—to fertilize their crops. Over the millennia, bird deposits had caused some offshore rocks to grow into islands of guano. And word of the effectiveness of this fertilizer had caused an explosion in European demand for South American guano. The guano islands were mined, with blocks of dried guano loaded on ships and sent to fulfill the demand in Europe and North America.

By the 1840s the guano islands were disappearing at such a rate that it was feared that guano supplies would soon run out. The concern was so great it made its way into US president Millard Fillmore's 1850 State of the Union address: "Peruvian guano has become so desirable an article to the agricultural interest of the United States that it is the duty of the government to employ all the means properly in its power for the purpose of causing that article to be imported into the country at a reasonable price. Nothing will be omitted on my part toward accomplishing this desirable end."

Spain sent a naval force to gain control of the vital supplies but was defeated by a combined force from Peru, Chile, Bolivia, and Ecuador. (There is no historical evidence that Spanish protesters marched under banners proclaiming, "No blood for guano.")

But an alternative supply of nitrates was discovered—saltpeter from the Tarapaca desert of Chile. Chileans took advantage of their near monopoly by running up prices in the 1880s and 1890s.

By 1898, Sir William Crookes—president of the British Academy of Sciences—warned that at present rates of extraction, nitrogen fertilizer would disappear within twenty or thirty years: "England and all civilized nations stand in deadly peril," he said. Crookes challenged the scientific community to find an alternative way of producing nitrogen fertilizer.

And within a decade, German chemist Fritz Haber (with later contributions from Carl Bosch) showed how nitrogen can be extracted from the atmosphere (which is 78 percent nitrogen). The Haber-Bosch process is still used in production of chemical fertilizers, and the threat of running short of guano is now a distant memory.

crop/soil combination, and the best crop rotations; "time-release" fertilizer can increase the impact of fertilizer without increasing total quantity of fertilizer; in developed countries, farmers use computerized equipment and global information systems to apply just the right amount of fertilizer to different parts of the same field. (See Ladha 2014.)

According to a the projections in Table 13.4, fertilizer use will grow more rapidly in Africa than in other parts of the world. But even with these in-

Table 13.4 Nitrogen Fertilizer Use: Projections to 2050 (million metric tonnes)

	2002	2013	2020		2050	
			Constant Efficiency	Improved Efficiency	Constant Efficienct	Improved Efficiency
Africa	2.6	3.9	3.8	3.7	5.8	5.5
Asia	44.6	55.9	62.5	51.7	69.4	58.9
North America	12.6	14.9	15.5	14.3	16.1	15.2
Latin America and Caribbean	4.9	8.5	7.7	6.3	8.9	7.5
World	79.2	99.6	111.7	96.2	121.2	106.6

Source: For 2002 and 2013, FAOSTAT; for 2020 and 2050, Wood, Henao, and Rosegrant 2004

creases, fertilizer application rates in Africa will be less than half those in Latin America.

Fertilizer use may be less than the economic optimal rate in the poorest countries because farmers are unable to borrow money and unable to save enough money to buy as much fertilizer as they would like. In addition, states the FAO: "In sub-Saharan Africa, where fertilizer use is still very low, consumption is hampered by high distribution costs, the lack of markets for output, lack of a domestic fertilizer industry and poor yield response, and the high risk of using fertilizer in traditional agricultural settings" (FAO 1996c: Background Paper no. 10). (In Chapter 22, Box 22.1 discusses policies intended to encourage fertilizer use in sub-Saharan Africa.)

Animal Traction

Another important input in agricultural production worldwide is "animal traction"—the use of draft animals to pull equipment or transport goods. Table 13.5 shows an estimate of the relative importance of human power, animal power, and engine power in preparation of land for agricultural production in geographical subregions. In these regions in aggregate (accounting for about half the world's arable land), about 40 percent of land uses human power, 30 percent animal power and 30 percent tractor power. Much of the agricultural land outside these areas is in industrialized countries (the United States, Canada, countries in Europe and Oceania), where tractor power is the dominant energy source.

When a farm shifts from hand tools to draft animals, dramatic changes take place on the farm; if the shift takes place on a large number of farms in a country, it can profoundly affect the country's economy. A draft animal can do the work of three or four adult humans (Stout 1998:76). By using animal traction rather than hand tools, a farmer is able to farm a greater area of land. This increases the self-produced food supply for the farmer's family and increases the likelihood that the farmer will produce a marketable surplus. In addition, use of animal traction may increase crop yields for other reasons: (1) plowing

Table 13.5 **Sources of Power for Land Preparation in Agriculture (percentage of total land)**

	Human Power	Draft Animal Power	Engine Power
Sub-Saharan Africa	65	26	10
East Asia	40	40	20
South Asia	30	30	49
Latin America and Caribbean	25	25	50

Source: Ahmed 2015.

with animals breaks up the soil more deeply and more completely, and thereby aids in plant growth; (2) animal manure is a source of fertilizer for the soil; (3) animal traction allows tasks such as field preparation to be done quickly, therefore within a time window that maximizes yield potential; (4) animal traction can be used during seasonal labor shortages to replace missing workers. In addition, animals provide other benefits to subsistence farmers: milk from cows, goats, and sheep is an additional food source; animal hides and wool are used for clothing and shelter; animal manure is used as fuel for cooking and heating; animal power is used for nonagricultural purposes such as pumping water, or transportation. (See Box 13.3.)

Pingali (1987) conducted a review of twenty-two published studies about the impact of animal traction on agriculture in various parts of the developing world. He found

• Seventeen of the twenty-two studies examined the effect of animal traction on the area farmed. All seventeen found that farmers who used animals had larger farms than nearby farmers who farmed with hand tools.

• Nineteen of the studies examined the effect of animal traction on the use of land to produce crops that could be sold, rather than crops to be consumed by the farm household. Twelve of the nineteen studies found that farmers who used animals devoted more land to market crops.

• Fourteen of the twenty-two studies examined the effect of animal traction on yields. Four of these studies found a positive effect on yields; two found a negative effect; eight found no statistically significant effect.

Box 13.3 Sacred Cows

Why is the cow venerated in India? Wouldn't it be better nutritionally to devote scarce agricultural resources to feeding humans rather than to feeding cows—and, at that, cows that will not even be slaughtered for human food? Anthropologist Marvin Harris (1974) has an intriguing answer to this. Cattle contribute in three important ways to improved life in rural India. First, they are a source of power for crop cultivation: "The shortage of draft animals is a terrible threat that hangs over most of India's peasant families. . . . The main economic function of the zebu cow is to breed male traction animals" (pp. 10–11). Second, cows provide milk: "Even small amounts of milk products can improve the health of people who are forced to subsist on the edge of starvation" (p. 16). Third, cattle produce manure: "India's cattle annually excrete about 700 million tons of recoverable manure. Approximately half of this is used as fertilizer, while most of the remainder is burned to provide heat for cooking. The annual quantity of heat liberated by this dung . . . is the equivalent of . . . 35 million tons of coal. . . . Cow dung has . . . one other major function. Mixed with water and made into a paste, it is used as a household flooring material" (p. 13).

• Sixteen of the studies found that farmers who used animal traction had higher farm incomes than nearby farmers who farmed with hand tools.

Pingali also identifies impediments to the more widespread use of animal traction in the developing world:

• Cattle in sub-Saharan Africa succumb to a disease—trypanosomiasis—spread by the tsetse fly. Trypanosomiasis occurs in thirty-seven sub-Saharan African countries and threatens 50 million head of cattle. About 3 million cattle die from the disease each year, and another 35 million are treated for the disease. (For more information, see FAO's Programme Against African Trypanosomiasis website: FAO n.d.)
• Many farmers in developing countries lack necessary experience and training in care of animals and equipment.
• The initial cost of animals and equipment is high, making animal traction impossible for farmers with limited access to credit.
• Using draft animals makes sense only when the farmer can expand the land under production. In some situations, all available land is being farmed by individuals who cannot or will not transfer the land to another farmer. In other situations, the land is too steep or rocky to be suitable for animal traction.
• Increasing production beyond what is needed for the farmer's family makes sense only if the farmer can sell surplus production. This requires adequate transportation and access to reliable markets for agricultural goods.

Tractors and Machinery

For the poorest farmers of the world, a major turning point may be the move from hand cultivation to animal traction. For a smaller group of slightly less-poor farmers, the replacement of animal traction with mechanized farming equipment represents a major change. Worldwide data on use of tractors and agricultural machinery are shown in Table 13.6.

Table 13.6 Worldwide Use of Tractors and Machinery, 1961–2006 (millions)

	Agricultural Tractors	Combine Harvesters-Threshers
1961	11.257	2.225
1971	16.351	2.640
1981	21.673	3.624
1991	25.100	3.943
2001	26.340	3.805
2006	26.947	3.648

Source: Ahmed 2015.

Poor farmers with limited access to credit may not be able to buy as much machinery (or fertilizer or irrigation equipment) as they would like. But we should be cautious in assuming that production methods that are most efficient in rich countries are also the most efficient methods in poor countries. Agricultural production in the United States tends to be done on large-scale farms using a lot of machinery and relatively little labor. Because the United States is a rich country and a large agricultural exporter, there is a tendency to regard this kind of capital-intensive farming as the "modern" and "efficient" method to which all farmers in all countries should aspire. This type of farming is efficient in the United States because of the relative prices of inputs that prevail there. Labor is relatively scarce in the United States, so labor wages are high. Capital markets are well developed, so farm credit is widely available at relatively low interest rates. Gasoline and equipment prices are also relatively low.

Consider the fact that farm laborers in the United States earn about $15 per hour, while gasoline costs $1.80 per gallon (figures for February 2016). Thirty days of labor costs the same as 2,000 gallons of gas. In some developing countries, thirty days of rural labor costs the same as 30 gallons of gas. Now consider a simple example in which a farmer trying to decide whether to adopt a method of production that uses machinery more intensively—weeding between crop rows with a tractor rather than by hiring people with hoes. The method will allow the farmer to use less hired labor (suppose it would save thirty days of hired labor per year), but will require the farmer to use more gasoline (suppose it would require 500 more gallons of gasoline each year). For a farmer in the United States, adopting the new method is sensible and efficient. The farmer saves enough money (in reduced labor costs) to buy 2,000 gallons of gas, but needs to buy only 500 gallons. For a farmer in a developing country, adopting the new method may not be sensible and may be inefficient. That farmer saves only enough money (in reduced labor costs) to buy 30 gallons of gas, but needs to buy 500 gallons.

Of course, "machinery" does not need to consist of the giant large-scale tractors and equipment we find in the United States. In developing countries, farmers are more likely to use smaller-scale farm machinery, or machinery that relies more on human or animal power.

Country Case Studies of Agricultural Traction

A recent FAO volume (Kienzle, Ashburner, and Sims 2013) collected a number of papers reviewing the status of animal traction in a variety of countries and regions. Those papers give insights into the current status and trends in animal traction. For example, Table 13.7 shows the wide differences between African countries in the extent to which farmers use animal or mechanical power.

China and India, with their rapid rates of economic growth have already followed a trajectory that many African countries might follow over the next

Table 13.7 Primary Sources of Agricultural Power in Selected African Countries

	Percentage of Farms Using:		
	Human Power	Draft Animal Power	Mechanical Power
Botswana	20	40	40
Ghana	50	42	8
Kenya	84	12	4
Mali	17	72	8
Nigeria	90	7	3
Tanzania	80	14	6
Zimbabwe	15	30	55

Source: Kienzle, Ashburner, and Sims 2013: chaps. 2–3.

decades. The past experience in India, with projections out to the year 2050, are shown in Table 13.8. In the fifty years from 1960 to 2010, tractor use increased by a factor of 100, and power-tiller use also increased rapidly. The growth is expected to continue over the next four decades, with mechanical power displacing animal power to a considerable degree. Though not shown in Table 13.8, the percentage of Indian land cultivated by hand power had fallen to less than 20 percent of land by the early 1990s. So the major shift seen in India has been from draught animals to mechanization, with especially high growth in small-scale power tillers.

A similar trend is seen in China, as shown in Table 13.9. Use of large tractors has grown modestly (35 percent from 1980 to 2003), whereas growth in use of small tractors has been enormous (635 percent).

Table 13.8 Agricultural Power Sources in India, 1960–2010 with Projections to 2050

	Number of Draft Animal (millions)	Number of Tractors (thousands)	Number of Power Tillers (thousands)
1960	80.4	37	—
1970	82.6	146	9.5
1980	73.4	531	16
1990	70.9	1,200	31
2000	60.3	2,600	100
2010	50.0	4,000	200
2030	18.0	6,000	400
2050	8.0	7,000	500

Source: Kienzle, Ashburner, and Sims 2013: chap. 5.

Table 13.9 Tractor Use in China, 1980–2003

	Number of Large Tractors	Number of Small Tractors
1980	745	1,874
1985	852	3,824
1990	814	6,981
1995	672	8,646
2000	975	12,643
2003	981	13,777

Source: Kienzle, Ashburner, and Sims 2013: chap. 6.

Population, Labor, and Agricultural Productivity

In Chapter 8, we saw that under any reasonable assumptions population will grow substantially over the next decades. As population grows, there are more people available to work in agricultural production. Of course, it is possible that the future population growth will occur only in the cities. In fact, Mundlak, Larson, and Crego (1996) found that agricultural labor dropped in 40 percent of countries worldwide over the period 1967–1992. However, it appears likely that population growth will lead to increases in average labor per hectare in many parts of the developing world. Table 13.10 shows trends in the agricultural labor force. The number of agricultural workers per unit of agricultural land has increased steadily in Africa, has remained fairly stable in Latin America, and in Asia increased until the early 1990s and has declined since. Asian agriculture, reflecting the generally high population density, uses labor intensively (more than ten times as many workers per hectare in Asia as

Table 13.10 Workers per Hectare of Agricultural Land, Selected Regions, 1961–2005

	Africa	Latin America	Asia	World
1961	0.098	0.065	0.579	0.191
1971	0.114	0.066	0.641	0.207
1981	0.134	0.068	0.713	0.232
1991	0.156	0.064	0.737	0.255
2001	0.182	0.061	0.618	0.267
2005	0.191	0.059	0.637	0.274

Source: FAOSTAT.
Note: Economically active population in agriculture (2004 revision) divided by agricultural land area in hectares.

in Latin America). (Not shown in the table, numbers of workers per hectare are decreasing in the developed world. In the United States there are about 0.007 workers per hectare—the average farm worker tends over 370 acres. Compare that to Asia at 4 acres per worker, or Africa with 13 acres per worker.)

Adding labor to each hectare of land will increase yield as long as there is productive work for the additional workers to do. Economists describe this situation as one where there is a "positive marginal productivity." One can imagine a situation where existing workers are already doing all that is possible and adding another worker to a plot of land causes a decline in production as workers begin to get in each other's way ("negative marginal productivity of labor").

In those areas that are already under cultivation, what is the marginal productivity of labor in agriculture? That is, by how much would the addition or subtraction of one worker change farm production? In the years before World War II, a considerable literature developed that assumed that such a large pool of unemployed and underemployed labor languished in third world agriculture that substantial amounts could be withdrawn for the industrial labor force with no diminution in agricultural production—in other words, that the marginal product of labor in agriculture was very close to zero (Lewis 1954; Fei and Ranis 1964).

Gary Becker (1975) called that thesis into question with a powerful argument that people attach at least some value to their leisure time. If this is the case, then they will not work their fields up to the point that another minute spent farming yields no product at all. They would rather spend those few minutes at leisure.

Still, we see considerable evidence that the marginal product of labor may be low on small subsistence farms in developing countries. A number of studies have shown that yields on small holdings in India (so small that all labor is supplied by the farm family) are significantly higher than yields on large farms where a substantial proportion of the labor force is hired (Berry and Cline 1979). In terms of a production function such as that shown in Figure 13.3, the smaller farms have moved up the production function to a point where output per hectare is larger, but the production function is flatter—so marginal productivity of the input is lower. Stevens and Jabara (1988) find similar results for farms in India, Taiwan, and Brazil: yields decline as farm size increases.

Farmers who hire labor are unwilling to hire so much that the product for the last hour worked by the laborer is less than the cost of hiring him for that hour. But when all labor comes from the family, for those last few hours worked family members may be willing to work for something less than the going wage, because the family will benefit from those last few hours and because they may have no higher-valued use for their time (Mazumdar 1965, 1975; Sen 1964, 1966). All this suggests that the marginal productivity of labor in agriculture is low, and comparisons of wages in agriculture versus nonagricultural activities in the third world support this thesis. The International Labour Organization (ILO 1987) lists the daily wage rate for agricultural activities in the Philippines in 1985 as about 24 pesos per day (just over one US dollar), but the daily rate for nonagricultural activities is about 56 pesos per day, or 2.4 times the agricultural rate. The ILO lists the daily rate for farm labor in India at about half a dollar and shows the manufacturing wage to be over five times that amount. More recent data in Table 13.11 show that this pattern has persisted in recent years.

AIDS and Agricultural Productivity

Chapter 8 discussed the problem of AIDS and the high incidence of HIV infection in some countries in sub-Saharan Africa. HIV infection and AIDS reduce labor productivity in the following ways:

• As people fall ill to AIDS, their capacity for work is reduced.
• The labor of healthy family members is diverted from agricultural production to caretaking.
• Premature deaths of AIDS victims removes a source of expertise and experience from the household.
• Fear of AIDS and its spread may make HIV-infected people unemployable even when they are capable of working.
• Orphaned children receive less education and care than children with living parents; thus these orphans grow up to be less productive as adults.

Several reports verify the effects of AIDS on agricultural production. In Thailand, one-third of rural families affected by AIDS saw their agricultural output drop to less than one-half of earlier levels. A study of Tanzanian households found that a woman married to an AIDS patient spent 60 percent less time

Table 13.11   Ratio of Nonagricultural to Agricultural Wages, Various Countries and Years

	Wage Measure	Men Only, or Both Men and Women	Ratio of Wage for Construction Laborer to Wage for Agricultural Field-Crop Farm Worker
Indonesia, 2006	Per month	Men	1.60
Zambia, 2006	Per month	Men	1.34
Mexico, 2007	Per month	Both	1.38
India, 2000	Per day, minimum	Men	2.38
India, 2000	Per day, maximum	Men	1.00

Source: ILO 2008.

on agricultural activities. A study in Uganda found that two-thirds of households who had lost a family member to AIDS produced less food than before.

Population Growth as a Stimulant to Productivity

A number of thinkers have argued that population growth in and of itself is a stimulant to productivity. One of the writers in this school (Clark 1973) capsulized one of its chief arguments in the title of his article: "More People, More Dynamism." That is, society is better off with a large population than with a small one "as a result of there being more knowledge creators" in a large population (Simon 1986:169). An exploration of the circumstances under which this argument is consistent with economic theory has been done by Kremer (1993).

Critics of this argument note that in today's high-tech world, large numbers of people create little assurance of a high level of knowledge creation. If they did, then India and China, with over a third of the world's population between them, should account for a greater share of the world's technological development than do Germany, France, Great Britain, the United States, and Japan, which collectively account for only 10 percent of the world's population. In the third world, many Einsteins may be undiscovered for want of a proper education.

Ester Boserup, in her book *Population and Technological Change,* argues that population growth creates a kind of crisis situation that stimulates the invention of new technology: "Shrinking supplies of land and other natural resources would provide motivation to invent better means of utilizing scarce resources or to discover substitutes for them" (1981:5). Note that in this "necessity is the mother of invention" argument, it is population growth that drives the creation of technology, and not the creation of technology that expands the capacity of the economy to support more people.

Boserup argues that farming is most intense in the densely settled regions of the world (not that people have tended to gather in those regions of the world where soils are most productive). She argues that, because periods of technological innovation and expanding productivity have usually been accompanied by increases in population, growth of population must have caused the increase in technology and production. Critics of this thesis argue that it is just the other way around: that it is the technological innovation and expanding productivity that have in fact made possible the associated increase in population.

Because productivity is related to income, and income is so closely related to food consumption, those who argue that population growth itself is a stimulant to productivity imply that population growth would help alleviate the world hunger problem, or at the least impose no threat to a solution. This school of thought has to contend with a series of arguments that claim population growth has a detrimental impact on the nutrition of the poor.

Kahkonen and Leathers (1997) suggest an additional reason why increasing population density may be beneficial to agricultural development. If transactions costs—the costs associated with setting up an exchange of goods—decline with the number of transactions, then areas with high population density are more likely to have established markets (or other means of exchange); this in turn gives farmers incentives to produce marketable surplus.

Small-Scale and Subsistence Agriculture

In the flood of numbers in this chapter, it may be easy to overlook one important fact: many of the poorest and most food-insecure people in the world live as subsistence farmers working tiny plots of land to feed themselves. The predominance of small-scale subsistence farming in the developing world was a major theme of the World Bank's 2008 *World Development Report.* It reports, for example, that 85 percent of rural farm households in Nigeria sell less than half their agricultural output on the market, and that in Ghana the number is 76 percent (World Bank 2007:76).

A detailed survey of subsistence and nonsubsistence (or "market-oriented") farmers in Vietnam shows that market-oriented farmers have higher incomes, lower poverty rates, and larger farms; they are more likely to live in a community that has a market or a commercial enterprise; they produce more "high value and industrial crops" (World Bank 2007:74).

A study of farmers in India shows that in the early 1990s, 60 percent of India's farmers had less than 1 hectare of land (accounting for 17 percent of land farmed; tab. 2), and that farms of that size provided no marketable surplus (Singh, Kumar, and Woodhead 2002: tabs. 1–2, 27).

A study of small-scale farmers in Ghana (Aalangdong, Kombiok, and Salifu 1999) gives some insight into the link between yields and undernutrition in subsistence households. Average maize yields (output per unit of land) for the farmers in this study were 0.6–2.7 metric tons per hectare (compared to 7.95 in the United States). A very poor rural Ghanaian, who relied on maize for all of his calories (say 2,400 per day), would need 0.274 metric tons of corn per year to achieve that diet. In other words, he would need 0.1–0.4 hectares of maize (at a yield of 0.6–2.7 metric tons per hour). We can see how a farm of 1–2 hectares might be just barely enough to provide a subsistence diet for a family, and we can see how precariously the family's food security rests on the hope of good weather and freedom from pests and diseases.

The study also reports how much labor was used in farming, and shows how labor needs can also be a constraint on food security. The farmers in this study worked between 1,900 and 4,050 days per hectare. One farmer in the study worked 40.5 hours on a 0.01 hectare experimental plot, and produced 10 kg of maize, or about 32,000 calories. In order to generate 2,400 calories per capita per day, he would need 27 such plots (0.27 hectares), requiring 1,093.5 days of labor per year (nearly three times as many days as there are in a year).

This gives us clear indication of how undernutrition can coexist with subsistence agriculture.

Another farmer in the study was considerably better off. He owned two bullocks and a plow; he obtained a yield of 25 kilograms of maize on his 0.01-hectare experimental plot, and he worked only 19 hours on the plot. (Perhaps the animal manure was used as fertilizer to increase this farmer's yields.) For a 2400-calorie-a-day diet of maize alone, this farmer would need 11 plots (0.11 hectares), or about 200 days of labor.

Partial Productivity Measures

This chapter has focused on yield per unit of land. But this is only one of the possible measures of "input productivity" or "partial productivity"—output per unit of input for a single input (in this case the input "land"). Work by economists Craig, Pardey, and Roseboom (1994, 1997) analyzes differences in partial productivity measures across different countries. Some of their data are shown in Tables 13.12 and 13.13.

Table 13.12 shows two partial productivity measures: the value of agricultural output per hectare and the value of agricultural output per worker. Notice how the numbers here reinforce a concept presented earlier in the section on machinery use: efficient agricultural practices conserve use of the scarcest resource. In densely populated parts of the world (Japan and Asia), returns per hectare are approximately equal to returns to worker; agricultural practices in

Table 13.12 Value of Agricultural Output per Agricultural Worker and per Hectare of Agricultural Land, 1986–1990

	Average Value of Output per Worker ($)	Average Value of Ouput per Hectare ($)
Sub-Saharan Africa	412	123
China	324	300
Asia and Pacific	817	955
Latin America and Caribbean	3,260	239
West Asia and North Africa	2,608	534
Australasia	38,580	216
Western Europe	18,088	1,231
Southern Europe	6,662	652
Eastern Europe	5,324	703
Former Soviet Union	4,432	150
North America	32,948	224
Japan	3,103	2,589
South Africa	3,812	72

Source: Craig, Pardey, and Roseboom 1994.

Table 13.13 Output and Input Use per Hectare, Selected Countries and Regions, 1986–1990

	Output ($ per hectare)	Labor (workers hectare)	Fertilizer (kilograms hectare)	Tractors (HP per hectare)	Animal Traction (HP per hectare)
Japan	2,589	834	373	13,095	4
Western Europe	1,231	70	186	4,222	17
Asia and Pacific	955	1,289	80	173	230
Eastern Europe	703	147	171	1,632	32
Southern Europe	652	118	82	1,955	23
West Asia and North Africa	534	292	63	519	116
China	300	925	48	177	70
Latin America and Caribbean	239	179	21	121	71
North America	224	7	35	629	9
Australasia	216	5	13	188	4
Former Soviet Union	150	34	43	274	11
Sub-Saharan Africa	123	354	2	14	18
South Africa	72	19	8	107	3

Source: Craig, Pardey, and Roseboom 1994.
Note: a. HP = horsepower.

these parts of the world use relatively high amounts of labor on each plot of land in order to extract the most from the scarce resource—land. In parts of the world where population density is low (Australasia and North America), returns per worker are 150 times that of returns per hectare; agricultural practices in these parts of the world use relatively low amounts of labor on each plot of land in order to extract the most from the scarce resource—labor.

Table 13.13 illustrates how increased output per unit of land is associated with more intensive use of other inputs. In this table, the countries and areas have been sorted according to value of output per hectare. The other columns of the table show per hectare use of labor, fertilizer, and horsepower (both mechanized and animal traction). The countries at the top of the list attain high outputs per acre by using a lot of inputs per acre. The countries at the bottom of the list have low output per acre, but also low inputs per acre. (The data shown are input and output per unit of agricultural land. The fertilizer application rates discussed for countries such as China and Japan are fertilizer use per hectare of arable and permanent crop land. This accounts for the difference in numbers presented earlier in the text and the numbers in Table 13.13.)

14

The Potential of
New Technology

The previous chapter shows that yields per hectare can be increased by using productive inputs more intensively on each hectare of land. We now turn to an alternative way of producing higher yields—improved technology. As described at the beginning of Chapter 13, and illustrated in Figure 13.3, technological improvement allows us to gain more output from the same quantity of inputs (or the same output using fewer of the inputs).

The Green Revolution

There can be no doubt that the centuries-long climb in yields reported in Tables 13.1 and 13.2 in the previous chapter is the result of better agricultural techniques: improved knowledge about crop rotations, timing and levels of fertilizer applications, and selective animal breeding. Much of the new knowledge came from trial and error by farmers themselves, but the scientific experiments (such as those reported in Box 13.1 in the previous chapter) also played a role. Since the 1960s, the most highly publicized new technology has been the new seed varieties developed in the so-called green revolution (described in Box 14.1).

The green revolution began with the work of crop scientist Norman Borlaug in Mexico in the 1940s. (For his efforts, Borlaug was awarded the 1970 Nobel Peace Prize.) At that time, wheat yields in Mexico were severely depressed by a fungus disease ("wheat rust") that shrivels the wheat grain. In his search for a rust-resistant variety of wheat, Borlaug collected 8,500 varieties of wheat being grown in different parts of Mexico; two of these 8,500 varieties proved to be rust-resistant. Borlaug and his associates, using tweezers and a magnifying glass, bred these rust-resistant varieties to other high-yielding varieties using the technique of crossing. Year after year, Borlaug experimented with new crosses, searching for varieties that gave higher yields. By 1957, the wheat rust problem in Mexico was solved, and average wheat yield had nearly

Box 14.1 What Is the Green Revolution?

Dana Dalrymple

In October 1944, about a year before the close of World War II, the Rockefeller Foundation brought to Mexico a young plant scientist to join a team of agriculturalists that had recently started work to assist in the agricultural development of that country. In a few months, the new man, Norman Borlaug (who was later to be awarded a Nobel Prize for his work in Mexico), was put in charge of the wheat program. He and his team set out to develop new varieties of wheat that would do better than the local varieties. Disease resistance (e.g., resistance to the fungus causing the disease rust) was particularly important at first. In the mid-1950s increased emphasis was given to increasing yields and within a few years varieties had been developed that could produce much more than the traditional ones.

Encouraged by this success, in the 1960s the Rockefeller Foundation joined with the Ford Foundation to establish two permanent research stations for the development of high-yielding cereals, the International Rice Research Institute (IRRI) in the Philippines and the International Maize and Wheat Improvement Center (CIMMYT) in Mexico. The success of these centers in developing high-yielding varieties led to such enthusiasm for the idea of international agricultural research centers that by the late 1980s, thirteen centers, treating various aspects of improving third world agriculture, had been set up worldwide, and sponsorship had spread to a consortium of donors worldwide including both foundations and government agencies.

The high-yielding varieties of wheat and rice have spread more widely, more quickly, than any other technological innovation in the history of agriculture in the developing countries. First introduced in the mid-1960s, they occupied about half of these countries' total wheat and rice area by 1982–1983 (Dalrymple 1985). Figure A shows the remarkable growth in adoption of high-yielding varieties in South and Southeast Asia.

Figure A

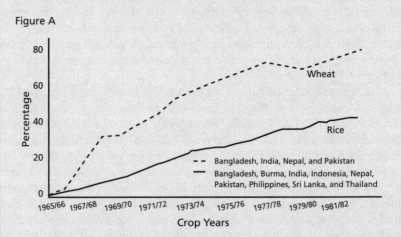

Struck by the remarkable speed with which high-yielding varieties of wheat and rice were being developed for the third world and by their potential to alleviate world hunger, William S. Gaud, who was then administrator of the US Agency for International Development, referred, in a 1968 speech, to the phenomenon of their development and spread as "the green revolution" (Dalrymple 1979:724).

Actually, the green revolution's wheat and rice varieties, also known as high-yielding varieties (HYVs) or modern varieties (MVs), do not do much better than the traditional varieties (they can even do worse) unless they have appropriate amounts of water and fertilizer. In fact, it is largely tolerance of and response to substantial amounts of fertilizer that makes them so successful.

The traditional varieties of wheat and rice were not tolerant of significant amounts of fertilizer. When third world farmers attempted to increase rice or wheat yields by adding fertilizer—especially nitrogen fertilizer—to their fields, their plants would grow so tall that they would fall over. The technical term for this is lodging. What the plant scientists at the international institutes did was to locate plant varieties with genes for shortness and breed these genes into plants that had other characteristics desirable for the third world. The new plants, called semidwarfs, borrowed dwarfism genes from Japan (for wheat) and China (for rice). When used with fertilizer, they grew taller than without the fertilizer, but not excessively so. Thus they were much more resistant to lodging (Figure B).

Plant scientists did not stop merely with the development of nonlodging plants. They bred into their new varieties a host of other characteristics such as disease resistance.

Figure B

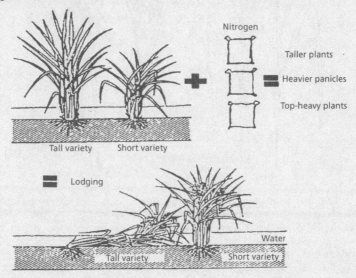

(continues)

Box 14.1 continued

One of the more intriguing changes in plant design that they accomplished involved rearranging the location of the seed cluster on the plant. Traditional rice plants sent their cluster of seeds (the panicle) high into the air. The seeds themselves store energy, but they do not make it. Photosynthesis is concentrated in the leaves. It did not make sense for the seed cluster to shade the highest leaves on the plant, so the scientists bred rice plants whose topmost leaf, the flag leaf, extended well above the panicle, thus taking maximum advantage of the available sunshine (Figure C).

Figure C

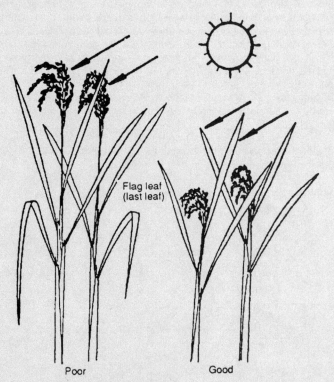

The green revolution, then, is a whole complex of innovations, such as those described above, that combine to make up new plant varieties. The modern plant varieties, when used with a package of appropriate inputs such as fertilizer and water and good management, are dramatically raising crop yields in the third world.

(For more about the green revolution, see Brown 1970; US Department of State 1986a, 1986b; Stackman, Bradfield, and Mangelsdorf 1967.)

doubled from 11 to 20 bushels per acre. In the meantime, Borlaug was working to solve another problem: as yields increased, the heavier grain caused plants to tip over ("lodge," as illustrated in Figure B in Box 14.1). Crossing with "dwarf" varieties of wheat—wheat with shorter and stronger stems— solved this problem. By 1963, Mexican wheat yields had grown to 30 bushels per acre, and experimental plots showed yields of 105 bushels per acre (Paarlberg 1988:102–105).

The shorter and stronger stems of the dwarf varieties meant that the plants could support a heavier crop of grain. The new seed varieties achieved this improved yield in two ways: they were more responsive to fertilizer and they used the photosynthetic energy of the plant more efficiently for grain growth. The traditional seed varieties responded to fertilizer at a rate of 10 kilograms of increased grain output for each kilogram of increased fertilizer use. The new varieties responded at a rate of 25 kilograms of grain for each kilogram of fertilizer. This made use of commercial fertilizers much more attractive for farmers who used the new seed varieties. The old seed varieties allocated about 20 percent of the photosynthetic energy of the plant to grain production and the remaining 80 percent to growth of roots, stems, and leaves. The new seed varieties improved this ratio to about 50:50.

Borlaug's methods were adapted to developing new varieties of other crops, most notably rice for Asia. The International Rice Research Institute (IRRI) has been the leading institutional support for this research. In the early 1960s, average rice yields in Asia were 1–2 metric tons per hectare. By 2002, IRRI could claim in their project report: "The adoption of improved varieties that have a yield potential of 10 tons per hectare is almost complete."

As Table 14.1 shows, adoption of modern varieties has been most widespread for wheat. By the late 1990s, dwarf wheat varieties accounted for about 80 percent of the wheat planted in the developing world. In Asia and Latin America, the figure is about 90 percent, while in sub-Saharan Africa about 50 percent of wheat land is planted in modern varieties. Modern varieties of rice have been widely adopted in Asia. In all crops, adoption in sub-Saharan Africa has lagged behind adoption in other regions.

Criticisms of the Green Revolution

The green revolution is not without its critics. As already described, the new seed varieties encourage farmers to use more fertilizer; the green revolution also brought increased use of irrigation and pesticides. For these reasons, the green revolution has been criticized as potentially damaging to the environment. A second criticism centers on whether the green revolution varieties have crowded out traditional varieties and led to a loss of species diversity.

But perhaps the most widespread criticism of the green revolution is the fear that it might increase inequality of income; indeed, it might make the poor much worse-off in regions where it has been adopted. After all, it has

Table 14.1 Percentage of Land Planted in Modern Crop Varieties, 1970–1998

	1970	1980	1990	1998
Latin America				
Wheat	11	46	83	90
Maize	10	20	30	46
Asia				
Wheat	19	49	74	86
Rice	10	35	55	65
Middle East and North Africa				
Wheat	5	16	38	66
Sub-Saharan Africa				
Wheat	5	22	32	52
Maize	1	4	15	17
Cassava	—	—	2	18

Source: Evenson and Gollin 2003b.

been common for new agricultural technologies to be adopted earlier by the most progressive and prosperous farmers in a region, who are often those with the biggest or best farms, the best education, and the greatest willingness to take a risk by trying something new. Furthermore, a tendency exists for public services to be more available to the big farmers than to the small, for technology to carry with it a labor-saving bias that reduces labor's share of the product, and for technological innovations to be more appropriate to some geographical areas than to others. Would not wealthy landlords use the benefits from green revolution technology as a stepping-stone to increasing the size of their holdings at the expense of small farmers, thus increasing income inequality?

Some of these fears turn out to have been justified, but most have not. Early adopters did tend to be the bigger, better farmers, but this has not prevented smaller farmers, who are often slower to change, from adopting green revolution technology.

Still, the benefits of the green revolution have accrued more to farmers in regions where water, especially irrigation water, is plentiful. Growers of lowland rice (rice that spends much of its early growing days with its stalks standing in a few inches of water) benefit more than growers of upland rice. Wheat and rice farmers, who predominate in tropical regions with 40 inches or more of annual rainfall, benefit more than sorghum and millet farmers, who farm the semi-arid tropics where rainfall is usually less than 40 inches per year.

The high-yielding fine grains (wheat and rice) grown with adequate water are far more responsive to fertilizer than are even the best varieties of the coarse grains (sorghum and millet) grown in the dry regions where irrigation water is scarce to nonexistent. The fertilizer subsidies that third world governments frequently provide to their farmers therefore benefit the fine-grain producers more than the coarse-grain farmers. Thus, the benefits of the green revolution have concentrated mainly in the wetter tropics and especially on the flatter lands where irrigation and water management are easier. This phenomenon may well have increased income inequality between regions.

Nevertheless, within regions "the benefits from adopting modern varieties have been remarkably evenly distributed among farmers differing in size of holding and tenure status." This is the conclusion of a major study commissioned to examine the impact of the international agricultural research centers (Anderson et al. 1985:4).

In a detailed study of the economy of a northern Indian village where modern varieties had been widely adopted, Bliss and Stern found no strong association between size of holding and the intensity of use of inputs associated with the adoption of green revolution technology. In fact, "the adoption of various newer varieties and intensive practices seemed to be particularly associated with the younger educated farmers" (1982:291).

How is it that the benefits could be so evenly distributed among farms of different sizes and farmers of different tenure status? For one thing, the capital requirements of the green revolution are minimal. Unlike hybrid corn, which has done so much to increase corn yields in the United States and Europe, the green revolution fine-grain seeds breed "true" (produce offspring almost identical to the parent plant). Hybrid seed corn must be produced annually under technically demanding conditions on specialized farms and sold to farmers each year. A farmer who planted the grain from his hybrid corn crop as seed would be most disappointed in the yield results. Green revolution rice and wheat, although the result of complicated crosses, are not true hybrids. You can plant a little one year, take the resulting grain as seed for next year's crop, and rapidly and cheaply multiply your seed stock. Thus, a handful of green revolution seed is all you need to begin farming—and it usually does not cost any more than traditional seed.

On the one hand, green revolution varieties do require expenditures on commercial fertilizer. On the other hand, fertilizer, like seed, is almost infinitely divisible, and a farmer need purchase only as much as he needs for his particular plot. Unlike capital investment in a tractor, the capital investment in the green revolution is not "lumpy"—that is, it does not come only in large, indivisible units.

A second reason for the evenly distributed benefits is that the green revolution technology is not laborsaving. To the contrary, it turns out to be labor-using (Hossain 1988b:12; Ranade and Herdt 1978:103; Pinstrup-Andersen and Hazell 1985:11). Much of the third world grain crop is harvested and threshed by hand, and the increased crop yield requires more labor for harvest. More important, though, the fertilizer applied to the crop turns out to stimulate the growth of weeds as well as grain. Farmers are finding it profitable to remove these weeds and, in the third world, weeding a field is labor-intensive (weeds are pulled by hand or chopped with a blade, for example).

Because the poor spend a greater proportion of their income on food than do the rich, the benefits from price drops associated with increased production following the adoption of green revolution technology favor the poor over the rich. Because of the very low overall elasticity of demand for cereals, consumers benefit substantially from the price drop caused by increased production, but farmers as a whole experience a decline in total revenue.

In a study of the social returns to rice research, Evenson and Flores (1978:255) found that in the Philippines, during the period from 1972 to 1975, the annual loss to producers from the adoption of the high-yielding rice varieties was $61 million, while the annual gain to consumers was $142 million, yielding a net annual gain to society of $81 million. Similarly, working with Colombian data, Scobie and Posada (1984) concluded that, during 1970–1974, Colombian rice producers lost $796 million, while consumers benefited by over $1.349 billion, for a net gain to society of $553 million. Furthermore, they concluded that "while the lower 50 percent of Colombian households received about 15 percent of household income, they captured nearly 70 percent of the net benefits of the [rice] research program" (p. 383).

The very fact of adopting high-yielding varieties increases cereal production. Because cereal demand elasticities are well below 1, prices decline by more than 1 percent for every 1 percent increase in quantity supplied. Therefore the increase in cereal production results in a loss of revenue for commercial growers of cereals who sell their entire crop. At the same time, near-subsistence farmers, who grow most of the food needed for their households but sell the surplus production, may actually see an increase in revenue from cereal sales.

Consider a near-subsistence farmer who produces 100 units of grain and consumes 90 of those. The remaining 10 units he sells on the market for $10 a unit—total revenue $100. Now, suppose he sees his neighbors on larger commercial farms practicing green revolution technology and copies them, purchasing some seed and fertilizer and irrigating his crop as usual. Yield on the subsistence farm increases by 10 percent to 110 units, so the farm can maintain home consumption of 90 units and now sell 20 units on the market. Even if price falls by 25 percent to $7.50, the farm revenue increases to $150.

Impact of the Green Revolution on Yields

Whatever one makes of the criticisms of the green revolution, there can be no doubt that it has led to increased yields. How much of the yield increases are attributable to increases in inputs described in the previous section, and how much to new technology? This question is hard to answer because of the nature of the new seed varieties. As we have seen, the new varieties have achieved their higher yields in part by being more responsive to fertilizer; in addition, the new varieties are often more sensitive to drought, and thus have been frequently grown on irrigated land. Therefore, the higher observed yields are the result of a complex interaction between technological improvement and additional levels of inputs.

Several researchers have attempted to unravel this complexity. The Consultative Group on International Agricultural Research (CGIAR 1997) reports that "22 percent of the developing world's [wheat] production increase resulting from higher yields is attributed to the gradual spreading of modern or high yielding varieties." A study of Syrian wheat found the increase in wheat yields (which more than quadrupled from the 1950s to the early 1990s) was due to several factors: new varieties accounted for about 35 percent of the increase; better management and increased fertilizer use accounted for 23 percent each; and irrigation accounted for 19 percent of the increase (CGIAR 1995). Peter Oram (1995), in a paper for the International Food Policy Research Institute (IFPRI), writes: "It is estimated that about 50 percent of the gains in farm yields have resulted from plant breeding and the balance from the application of other improved practices." These suggest that of the average yield growth of 2 percent per year from 1968 to 1997, new technology accounts for between 0.5 and 1 percent per year, and input growth accounts for the remaining 1 to 1.5 percent per year.

Evenson and Gollin (2003a) completed a comprehensive review that is summarized in Table 14.2. For all developing countries, total yield growth was faster in the twenty years between 1961 and 1980 than in the twenty years between 1981 and 2000. In the earlier period, increased input use was responsible for about 80 percent of the yield growth; in the later period, input use and new technology were about equally responsible for yield growth. Yield growth due to new technology was actually higher in the second twenty-year period. The table also shows that sub-Saharan Africa has lagged behind other geographical areas, both in technological change and in growth of input use.

The technological improvements shift out the aggregate supply curve for food and cause food prices to be lower than they would otherwise have been. The CGIAR reports that in developing countries, prices for crops targeted by the CGIAR have dropped more than the prices for non-CGIAR crops. The USDA (1991) estimates that research into improvements in agricultural production methods has reduced the average yearly food bill in the United States by $400 per person. A model by Evenson and Rosegrant (2003) estimates that the development of new crop varieties has kept food prices 18–21 percent lower than they would have otherwise been.

Federico, following a detailed analysis of studies on technical change, concludes that technical change (as measured by "total factor productivity"—see the next section) "accounted for almost all of the production growth in [developed countries], while it accounted for between a third and a half in the [less developed countries]" (2005:81).

Table 14.2 Contributions of Increased Input Use and New Seed Varieties to Yield Growth, 1961–1980 and 1981–2000

	1961–1980			1981–2000		
	Average Annual Yield Growth	Contribution of Increased Input Use	Contribution of New Technology	Average Annual Yield Growth	Contribution of Increased Input Use	Contribution of New Technology
Latin America	1.587	1.124	0.463	2.154	1.382	0.772
Asia	3.120	2.439	0.682	2.087	1.119	0.968
Middle East and North Africa	1.561	1.389	0.173	1.505	0.722	0.783
Sub-Saharan Africa	1.166	1.069	0.097	0.361	-0.110	0.471
All developing countries	2.502	1.979	0.523	1.805	0.948	0.857

Source: Evenson and Gollin 2003b.

A review of more recent literature on the subject by Pingali summarizes the impact of the green revolution as follows: "Estimates suggest that, without the CGIAR and national program crop germplasm improvement efforts, food production in developing countries would have been almost 20% lower (requiring another 20–25 million hectares of land under cultivation worldwide). World food and feed prices would have been 35–65% higher, and average caloric availability would have declined by 11–13%. Overall, these efforts benefited virtually all consumers in the world and the poor relatively more so, because they spend a greater share of their income on food" (2012:12303).

Box 14.2 shows how biological and mechanical innovations contributed to productivity growth in US wheat production.

Box 14.2 Technical Change and Productivity in US Wheat Production

The experience of wheat production in the United States gives some insight into the ways that new production techniques contribute to improved productivity.

During the period 1839–1909, US wheat yields were nearly constant, increasing only 24 percent—from 11.3 bushels per acre to 14.0 bushels per acre—over the seventy-year period. Over the same period, wheat output per hour of labor grew fourfold, from 0.3 bushels per hour worked to 1.3 bushels per hour worked. The prevailing wisdom attributed this productivity improvement to mechanization. New equipment—the mechanical reaper and thresher and the self-binder—allowed a farmer to cultivate more and more acres of wheat. This mechanization impact was strengthened by the westward movement of the US farm population to flat expanses of the Great Plains.

Olmsted and Rhode (2002) challenged this prevailing wisdom. They argued that biological innovation in the form of new seed varieties was an important component of the productivity increase. The contribution of new seed varieties was twofold. First, the westward expansion of wheat production was made possible by the development of wheat varieties that were suited to the agroclimatic conditions of the Great Plains. One expert in wheat production, writing in 1860, opined that with existing wheat varieties, commercial wheat production was viable only in Ohio, Pennsylvania, and New York; however, new varieties of wheat suited to the growing conditions of states farther west led to expansion of commercial wheat production far beyond that limited area. Second, new varieties were introduced to "solve" an increasing number of disease and pest problems that would have caused wheat yields to decline substantially in the absence of the new varieties. In the absence of these biological innovations, Olmsted and Rhode estimate, wheat yields would have fallen from 11.3 bushels per acre to 7.5 bushels per acre (rather than the increase to 14 bushels per acre actually observed in 1909), and that labor productivity would have increased only from 0.3 bushels per hour to 0.8 bushels per hour (rather than the 1.3 bushels per hour actually occurring in 1909).

Total Factor Productivity

One systematic way to quantify the impact of all different kinds of technical change is to calculate *total factor productivity* (TFP). Recall the earlier discussion of partial factor productivity, such as growth in output per unit of land or per unit of labor. When looking at growth in partial factor productivity, it was not readily apparent what part of that growth was attributable to technical change and what part was attributable to growth in use of other inputs. Total factor productivity is calculated by first constructing two indexes: an index of output that is a single number that reflects changes in levels of all outputs, and an index of input use that reflects changes in levels of all inputs (or at least all inputs on which data are available). Total factor productivity is the ratio of these two indexes: outputs divided by inputs. (See Box 14.3 for an example of how index numbers can be constructed.) Therefore (referring again to Figure 13.3 in Chapter 13), an increase in TFP means that output can be increased without increasing input, either because inefficiency has been eliminated (moving from A to B) or because a technological improvement has caused an upward shift in the production function (moving from point B to point D).

Pingali and Heisey (1999) review TFP estimates from fifteen separate studies, covering thirty-two different countries, for a variety of time periods. They report seventy-two total measurements of annual percentage growth in TFP; sixty-six are positive and six negative; seventeen of the estimates are greater than 2 percent per year. To put this in perspective, worldwide production of all cereal crops grew at an annual rate of 2.21 percent from 1961 to 2014; total calories consumed worldwide increased by 2.21 percent per year over approximately the same period.

Federico (2005:77–79) does an even more comprehensive review of TFP studies. He finds more variation in estimates than do Pingali and Heisey, and finds a higher prevalence of negative estimates of average TFP in developing countries. His conclusions:

> 1. Agricultural productivity has grown remarkably in the large majority of countries and periods. Almost 70% of estimates (438 out of 636) are positive; and the average TFP growth for the whole database is 0.58 percent per annum. . . . Out of 175 country/period observations, there are 109 "good performers" [a majority of estimates show positive TFP growth] [and] 53 "poor performers" [a majority of estimates show negative TFP growth]. . . .
> 2. The performance of OECD countries has been quite good. TFP has grown in almost all cases. . . . Furthermore, the growth in TFP has been accelerating in almost all cases. . . .
> 3. The performance of LDCs has been decidedly mixed. . . . The main feature is the large number of "poor performers"—forty-five out of a total of ninety-four LDC countries.

Box 14.3 Index Numbers

An index number is essentially a weighted average of quantities, scaled to reflect the level of that average compared to some base period. Suppose a farm produces wheat and corn. In 2002 the farm produces y^1_{corn} units of corn and y^1_{wheat} units of wheat. In 2003 the farm produces y^2_{corn} units of corn and y^2_{wheat} units of wheat. Let p_{corn} be the price of corn and p_{wheat} be the price of wheat. To construct an index of output, first choose a "base year." This is arbitrary, so we could choose either 2002 or 2003; for this example we will choose 2002. The index number for each year is:

$$\text{Output index year t} = 100 \times \frac{p_{corn}\, y^t_{corn} + p_{wheat}\, y^t_{wheat}}{p_{corn}\, y^{2002}_{corn} + p_{wheat}\, y^{2002}_{wheat}}$$

where t can be 2002 or 2003.

The sample outputs and prices in the following table show how the index is constructed:

Year (t)	Corn Output (y^t_{corn})	Wheat Output (y^t_{wheat})	Corn Price (p_{corn})	Wheat Price (p_{wheat})
2002	125	50	3	5
2003	150	45	3	5

For 2002, the sum of price times quantity is $(125 \times 3) + (50 \times 5) = 375 + 250 = 625$. For 2003, the sum is $(150 \times 3) + (45 \times 5) = 450 + 225 = 675$. The index numbers are therefore:

$$2002: 100 \times \frac{625}{625} = 100$$

$$2003: 100 \times \frac{675}{625} = 108$$

A number of points should be obvious:

- For the base year, the value of the index is 100 by definition.
- If all outputs increased by exactly 10 percent from 2002 to 2003, the index number for 2003 would be 110. If all outputs decrease by exactly 10 percent, the index number would be 90.

(continues)

Box 14.3 continued

- In the example, the increase from 100 to 108 reflects an average of the 20 percent increase in corn production and the 10 percent decrease in wheat production. The weight assigned to the different commodities depends on the price of those commodities.
- This concept is easy to extend to more than two outputs, or more than two years. It can be applied to output of a single farm, or a state, or a nation, or a combination of nations.

If the farm used three inputs—land, seed, and labor—we could construct an index of input use in a similar fashion:

Year (t)	Land Input (x^t_{land})	Seed Input (x^t_{seed})	Labor Input (x^t_{labor})	Land Price (r_{land})	Seed Price (r_{seed})	Labor Price (r_{labor})
2002	2	50	10	30	2	40
2003	2	55	12	30	2	40

For 2002, the sum of price times quantity is $(2 \times 30) + (50 \times 2) + (10 \times 40) = 560$. For 2003, the sum is $(2 \times 30) + (55 \times 2) + (12 \times 40) = 650$. The input index numbers are therefore:

$$2002: 100 \times \frac{560}{560} = 100$$

$$2003: 100 \times \frac{650}{560} = 116$$

Total factor productivity is the ratio of the output index to the input index. The total factor productivity measures are therefore:

$$2002: 100 \times \frac{100}{100} = 100$$

$$2003: 100 \times \frac{108}{116} = 93$$

In this example, even though output increased (as indicated by the increase in the output index from 100 to 108), input use increased faster (as indicated by the increase in the input index from 100 to 116); so total factor productivity declined by 7 percent.

4. . . . . [T]he agricultural sector moved from laggard to leader, at least from a purely statistical point of view.

In a 2003 article, Nin and colleagues used FAO data on 115 countries and country-groups for the period 1965–1994 to estimate TFP separately for crops and animal products. TFP for all countries is estimated at 0.51 percent per year for livestock and 0.63 percent per year for crops. This is one-quarter to one-third of growth rates in worldwide output reported in the preceding paragraph. This is consistent, at the low end, with the discussion in the last section about the extent to which yield growth is attributable to new technology and the extent to which it is attributable to increased input use.

Fuglie and Rada (2015) estimated TFP for 173 countries for ten-year periods from 1961 to 2012. Several points are worth noting:

- Their data show that the rate of technological change is accelerating in the most recent decade.
- Technology remains a significant factor in growing agricultural output, accounting for about two-thirds of output growth in the 2001–2010 period in developing countries. (See Table 14.3.)
- Technological improvement continues to lag in sub-Saharan Africa compared to other parts of the developing world.

Table 14.3 Average Annual Growth in Output, Input, and Total Factor Productivity, 2001–2010

	Growth in Agricultural Output	Growth in Total Factor Productivity	Growth in Input Use
Developed countries	0.59	2.32	−1.73
Transition economies	1.49	1.90	−0.41
Developing countries	3.39	2.20	1.20
Asia	3.40	2.69	0.71
Latin America	3.37	2.67	0.70
Sub-Saharan Africa	3.26	0.99	2.28
World	2.50	1.81	0.70

Source: Fugli and Rada, 2015.

Prospects for Future Yield Growth

Can crop yields continue to grow? And if so, at what rate? The answers to these questions go a long way to determining whether the future food supply will keep pace with demand. We have reviewed the different opinions about the prospects for adding irrigation, fertilizer, and labor to agricultural production. Even the most optimistic projections see input usage growing more slowly than in the past. But what about technology? Can technological advances pick up the slack caused by slower growth in input use? We find optimists and pessimists on this question.

Reasons for Concern

The pessimists have pointed out that growth in yields has been slowing (see Figures 13.1 and 13.2 in Chapter 13). Imagine (say the pessimists) that crop yields are growing according to an S-shaped curve; we have gone through a period of rapidly rising yields, but we are now reaching the top, where yields become flat: "Countries that have doubled or tripled the productivity of their cropland since mid-century are the rule, not the exception. But with many of the world's farmers already using advanced yield-raising technologies, further gains in land productivity will not come easily" (Brown and Kane 1994:132). An IRRI 2002 project report warns: "Yield at the farm level is approaching a plateau."

The rationale for pessimism is twofold: the successful innovation cannot continue at the rate seen in previous decades; resource degradation will make it more and more difficult to maintain or increase agricultural production.

Some pessimism about yields is based on a belief that scientists cannot discover new ways to increase yields. "Rising grain yield per hectare . . . must eventually give way to physical constraints. . . . Yields may now be pushing against various physiological limits such as nutrient absorption capacity or photosynthetic efficiency" (Brown and Kane 1994:138). Thomas Sinclair, a horticulturist at the University of Florida, Gainesville, explained to *Science* magazine: "To grow corn, . . . you have to have leaves, stalks, and roots, so there's got to be mass committed to what you don't harvest. . . . At the beginning of this century, . . . many crops had harvest indexes on the order of 0.25 of their weight in grain, and now many crops are approaching 0.5. . . . Maybe you could go up to 0.6 or 0.65, but beyond that you can't have a viable plant" (quoted in Mann 1997:1042).

Another source of pessimism about yields is concern about whether they are environmentally sustainable. According to this school of thought, the current high yields have been obtained by putting extreme pressure on the natural environment. As discussed in Chapter 13, the environment can stand this pressure for only a short time; yields then naturally begin to decline.

Nevertheless, cereal yields have continued to grow. Figure 13.2 shows a slight rebound in yield growth rates in recent years, and the Fuglie and Rada

TFP estimates discussed earlier also show more rapid technological progress in the most recent decade compared to earlier periods.

A Second Green Revolution:
Research Efforts to Reduce Environmental Degradation

Perhaps in response to these legitimate concerns about the environmental impact of agricultural production, the emphasis of international agricultural research shifted during the 1990s from increasing yields to reducing environmental impact. Some of the new production techniques developed include low-till and no-till cultivation methods that reduce soil erosion, and drip irrigation techniques that improve the efficiency of delivery of irrigation water to the plants.

Not all of the innovations rely on high-tech solutions. One example comes from China, where a fungus was destroying rice fields. Wherever the fungus emerged, windblown spores would spread the fungus from row to row until the entire field was affected. Scientists discovered a low-yielding wild variety of rice that was resistant to the fungus. By alternating rows of the high-yielding but fungus-susceptible rice with rows of the lower-yielding but fungus-resistant rice, scientists were able to halt the spread of the fungus. Spores would be blown from the infected rows to the neighboring resistant rows, which stopped the spread of the fungus. This research simultaneously pursued the objectives of improved yields and reduced stress on the environment, since it found an alternative to chemical fungicide.

Some research into indigenous farming practices also has found ways to increase agricultural production in an environmentally friendly way. For example, some indigenous populations use fish or anthill waste as a source of fertilizer. In the Sudan, planting millet under the acacia albida tree improved millet yield. The tree roots drew nutrients from deep in the soil and the dropping tree leaves transferred those nutrients to the top of the soil. Furthermore, the timing of the leaf growth and decay allowed the millet plants to receive sun and shade at crucial times in the life cycle of the millet plants.

Box 14.4 describes two examples of "low-tech" improvements in agricultural technology.

Reasons for Hope

The change in focus of agricultural research from increasing yields to reducing environmental impact may help explain why yields in experiment stations (the laboratories of crop production) have shown slower rates of growth in recent decades. A related explanation is that international crop research has been underfunded (Pardey and Alston 1995). Alexandratos (1995) argues that the slowdown in yield growth is less a result of technological feasibility and more a result of low farm-level prices. Finally, worldwide average crop yields were brought down during the 1990s by a large drop in yields in the former Soviet

---

Box 14.4 Low-Tech Approaches to Improved Crop Yields

The preceding discussion of the green revolution, and the discussion of genetic engineering later, may give the impression that improved crop yields are solely a product of the efforts of PhD agronomists working in well-equipped laboratories. But some breakthroughs come from low-tech methods (and patience).

The PBS video "Silent Killer" relates the story of an African seed dealer who noticed that some corn stalks bore two corn cobs, rather than the usual one. He saved corn kernels from those "double cobbers" and grew crop after crop until he had a seed variety that would quite reliably produce double-cobber corn stalks.

In recent years it has been shown that rice yields can be increased by 20–100 percent using a set of production methods known as the System of Rice Intensification (SRI). The methods include planting seedlings individually rather in clumps, careful spacing between plants, and aerating soil around the plant roots. The discovery of the correct spacing, for example, requires trial-and-error experimentation, not high-tech methods. (For more information, see the SRI website, http://sri.ciifad.cornell.edu.)

Union, probably a temporary phenomenon. If you accept any of these explanations about the slowdown in yield growth, you may be more optimistic about future growth in yields.

Many analysts have been more optimistic about future yields. In the early 1990s the FAO projected that cereal yields would grow at 1.4 percent per year between 1990 and 2010, compared with a 2.2 percent growth rate between 1970 and 1990; actual cereal yields grew at 1.3 percent between 1990 and 2010 (Alexandratos 1995). A World Bank study (Mitchell et al. 1997) estimated that grain yields would continue to grow at a 1.5–1.7 percent annual rate; actual growth between 1990 and 2014 was 1.3 percent. An IFPRI report (2005) on projected food supply and demand for the year 2020 presented a base scenario in which yields continue to grow at the rate observed in the late 1980s and early 1990s; actual yield growth has fallen slightly from the earlier period. Rejesus, Heisey, and Smale (1999) review a number of studies that project annual growth rates for wheat yields of between 1.4 percent and 1.9 percent for developing countries during the first decades of the new millennium, and slightly lower growth rates for developed countries. A decade and a half into the new millennium, we see that cereal yields have grown by 1.4 percent per year worldwide. Box 14.5 presents some optimistic evaluations by crop scientists.

Box 14.5 Agronomists' Perspectives on Potential for Future Yield Growth

---

A 1998 symposium (Waterlow et al. 1998) heard a number of papers reviewing the scientific literature on specific ways that crop yields could be increased. The tone of the papers was optimistic.

"The rapid rise in yield potential and response to inputs . . . seems unlikely to be maintained beyond the next two decades . . . unless crop growth rates can be enhanced. Although these may . . . be limited by the photosynthetic rate, other process . . . may also have a significant effect. . . . Even in the absence of any further rise in genetic yield potential, crop yields could continue to rise with improvements in climatic adaptation, pest and disease resistance, and agronomic support." (Evans)

"I have no hesitation in stating that . . . plant biotechnology can bring major progress to tropical agriculture." (Van Montagu)

"Before writing this article I approached 10 or more leading exports on photosynthesis research throughout the world. . . . All agreed that the efficiency of photosynthesis in the field is far from the theoretical maximum and is restricted by environmental factors. . . . [Research into ways of] enhancing . . . protective and repair mechanisms [of plants] will help us to approach levels of photosynthetic efficiency observed under optimal/nonstressed conditions." (Barber)

"The possible prize for successful engineering of Rubisco [an enzyme that reduces photorespiration in plants] in the world's major . . . crops—an increase of 20% in the potential yield in temperate regions and of 50% in the tropics—must surely justify increased effort toward this single charge." (Long)

"Metabolic engineering of source-sink relationships is a promising approach to increase . . . genetic yield potential of cereal crops. . . . By combining the expression of several different transgenes . . . a significant increase in . . . crop yields may be achieved." (Choi et al.)

"With the availability of biotechnological tools . . . procedures for breeding genetically diverse parental lines and hybrids can be made more efficient." (Khush, Peng, and Virmani)

Other papers at the symposium discuss research efforts to promote tolerance to salinity and drought (Verma) and resistance to disease (Lamb).

Biotechnology and Genetically Modified Food

One source of optimism about future yield growth are the scientific advances in the field of genetic engineering and biotechnology. In the past two decades, the issue of genetically modified food has become a subject of public debate and discussion. Genetic engineering creates new seed varieties that contain specific genetic characteristics. Genes from one organism can be inserted into the DNA of another organism to create certain characteristics. To date, the most common types of genetic changes are the following:

- Plants are modified so that they contain a bacterium (*Bacillus therogensis,* or Bt) that is a natural pesticide. Thus these plants are protected from pest damage without being sprayed with a commercial chemical pesticide.
- Plants are modified so that they are particularly resistant to certain weed killers. Therefore, the weed killers can be applied more heavily to kill weeds without killing the crop.
- Plants are modified to thrive in adverse conditions: for example, to be more resistant to disease or pests, or to be more tolerant of frost, drought, or saline soil.
- Plants are modified so that the crop has certain nutritional characteristics: for example, a potato that is rich in protein.
- Salmon grown in fish farms have been genetically modified to change their inbred eating habits and increase weight gain.
- Genetically modified microbes can be applied to soil to assist in nitrogen fixation.
- Genetically modified animals may produce more milk, less manure, and use feed more efficiently (CAST 2003).
- Pharmaceutical drugs can be produced in genetically modified plants and animals.

Genetically modified (GM) crops have been adopted by farmers in growing numbers since they were commercially introduced in the mid-1990s. Figure 14.1 shows the growth in worldwide acreage planted to GM crops. In 2014, 180 million hectares of land were planted in GM crops. Slightly less than half of this is in developed countries (almost all of it in the United States, Canada, and Australia), and slightly more than half is in developing countries (led by Brazil, Argentina, and India, which together account for 43 percent of the total GM land). Soybeans, corn, and cotton account for most of the GM land. Table 14.4 shows that more than half of the land planted to soybeans worldwide is planted with GM varieties. It is estimated that 60 percent of the food supply in the United States contains GM products either directly or indirectly, as when GM crops are fed to animals (James 2002).

Adoption of genetically modified varieties is growing faster in developing countries than in developed countries. One explanation for this is found in a 2003 paper by Qaim and Zilberman. They showed that some genetically modified crops that reduce pest damage may be especially effective in boosting yields in developing countries, where farmers are unable to afford commercial pesticides. The study examined cotton yields in India and found that Bt cotton had yields 80 percent higher than non–genetically modified varieties. However, the advantages of Bt to the farmer evaporate if the price of the genetically modified seed is too high. In a study of Bt cotton adoption in Argentina, Qaim and de Janvry (2003) found that the cost of the seed was twice as high as the

Figure 14.1 Land Area Planted with GM Crops Worldwide, 1996–2014

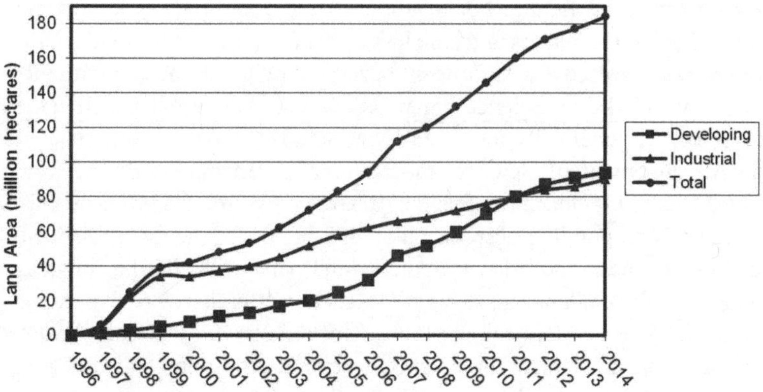

Source: James 2014.

average expenditures on chemical pesticides by farmers who adopted non-GM cotton.

Concerns about GM crops, especially food crops, have been so strong that many countries, especially European countries, have banned their use. During the 2002 famine in southern Africa, some African countries felt pressure to refuse food aid from countries that permitted GM crops, or refused to distribute GM food to their starving citizens. What are the concerns that drive opposition to GM crops?

Three types of concerns have been raised about the impact of genetically modified organisms (GMOs) on human health: "hidden" genes may trigger allergic reactions (see Haslberger 2003); GMOs may weaken immune systems (see Myles 2014, for example); and genetic manipulation may lead to development of diseases that are resistant to antibiotics (see Ho et al. 1998).

Table 14.4 Area Planted in Genetically Modified Crops, 2006

	Million Hectares Planted in GM Crops	GM Area as Percentage of Total Area Planted in That Crop
Soybeans	91	82
Maize	55	30
Cotton	25	68
Canola	9	25

Source: James 2014.

With the passage of time (and GMO foods are now in their twentieth year in the United States) and as the research evidence mounts, human health concerns seem to be fading. For example, Nicolia and colleagues reviewed ten years of scientific papers and concluded, "The scientific research conducted so far has not detected any significant hazards directly connected with the use of GE crops" (2014:1). Science organizations that have published statements on the safety of genetically modified food include the American Association for the Advancement of Science, the National Academy of Sciences, and the World Health Organization. See the (unabashedly pro-GM) website GMOPundit, http://gmopundit.blogspot.co.uk/p/450-published-safety-assessments.html, for links to these and other statements and papers. While this suggests what might be called a "consensus" that GMOs are safe, there are dissenting views on the subject (see Hilbeck et al. 2015 for an example). Human health is not the only concern raised about GMOs: several environmental problems have been associated with GM crops. The biggest of these concerns is the possible development of "superweeds" that are resistant to insects and to commercial herbicides. If the genetic material that makes crops resistant to insects or to herbicides "escapes" into the genetic material of weeds, it may make the weeds difficult or impossible to eradicate. A recent review (Bonny 2016) confirms that the GMO revolution has resulted in glycophosphate becoming the overwhelming herbicide of choice among soybean farmers in the world. And the number of herbicide-resistant weed species has grown considerably since 1990. In addition, the inclusion of the natural insecticide (Bt) gene raises the possibility that nontarget insects could be harmed by the GM crops (see Wolfenbarger and Phifer 2000: tab. 2 for a review).

A third environmental concern is that GM organisms will upset the current ecological balance. For example, herbicide-tolerant crops lead to heavier application of herbicides and more complete elimination of weeds; but animals that feed on those weeds may be adversely affected. Also, genetic modifications might enhance an organism's ability to become an invasive species. GM crops may interbreed with wild relatives, ultimately leading to the extinction of the wild varieties (Wolfenbarger and Phifer 2000). More broadly, the concern that GM organisms may lead to an erosion in species diversity has been discussed, for example in Schaal 2003.

These discussions suggest that there is a degree of uncertainty in the scientific community about the effects of biotechnology. The "precautionary principle" has been proposed to urge policymakers to oppose use of GM organisms until the scientific uncertainty is resolved and the organisms have been proven to be safe. Of course this raises the possibility that unscrupulous or ideological scientists could deliberately create or perpetuate uncertainty in order to achieve their own policy goals.

Not all environmental impacts of GM organisms are negative. Bt crops allow farmers to use less insecticide. Herbicide-resistant crops allow application rates and chemicals that may in the aggregate be less stressful on the environment. GM fish may reduce pressure to overfish wild stocks. The Council on Agricultural Science and Technology (CAST) convened a colloquium of agricultural scientists to discuss the overall environmental impact of GM organisms. They concluded that "biotechnology-derived [crops] . . . are consistent with improved environmental stewardship . . . [and] can provide solutions to environmental . . . problems" (CAST 2002:2).

Some opposition to GM organisms is based on political or ethical arguments rather than on scientific evaluations. Some doubt whether any social benefit can be derived from multinational corporations whose primary motivation is to increase their own profits. "The vast majority of scientific research being undertaken today is driven more by the goal of being first in line at the patent office than that of meeting profound social needs" (Dawkins 2003:39). A related argument is that GM crops put small subsistence farmers at a disadvantage and force farmers to deal with giant corporations on terms of unequal power. Other critics question whether our laws should permit a genetic sequence to be "owned," patented, and sold. Finally, some are uneasy about biotechnology for religious reasons, questioning whether the scientists are "playing God" with their experiments.

Balanced against the health, environmental, and other concerns about biotechnology are the benefits of increased yields. A panel of experts reporting to the World Bank and the Consultative Group for International Agricultural Research in 1997 concluded that GM crops could boost world crop yields by 25 percent. Nigeria's minister of agriculture, writing on the op-ed page of the *Washington Post,* states: "We do not want to be denied this [GM] technology because of a misguided notion that we don't understand the dangers or the future consequences. . . . The harsh reality is that, without the help of agricultural biotechnology, many will not live" (Adamu 2000:A23).

Postproduction Food Losses

Before leaving the subject of food production, we should recognize that food consumption theoretically can be increased *without* increasing food production—if we can reduce losses between the field and the consumer (FAO 1996c: Background Papers nos. 4, 8). These losses are estimated as high as 30 percent (Erlich and Erlich 1991). In developing countries, postharvest food losses have been attributed to pests (Angé 1993), poor facilities for storage and transportation (James and Schofield 1990), and on-farm handling (FAO 1996c: Background Paper No. 8). One might think that postharvest food losses would decline as countries develop economically, because of improvements in roads, credit, and information. However, a study in the United States (Buzby, Wells, and Hyman 2014) estimates that over 30 percent of food is lost in retailing, restaurants, and at-home consumption. So in rich countries there may be less food lost to pests and poor storage facilities but more food is wasted by consumers or thrown away by restaurants.

15

An Important Aside:
The Question of Health

This book is about food supply and demand and undernutrition caused by insufficient food consumption. The next part of the book looks at policies intended to influence food production and consumption. But before turning to those types of policy issues, we need to recognize the ways that health and nutrition interact. Previous chapters have touched on the subject, so some of the discussion here will be a recap. But most of the chapter will deal with medical interventions and policies.

Almost all of the deaths ascribed to undernutrition are in fact caused by diseases whose impacts are intensified in a person whose natural defenses are weakened by undernutrition. So, of course, an obvious way to reduce deaths associated with undernutrition is to improve nutrition. But an alternative way is to reduce the incidence and severity of disease episodes.

The Synergisms Between Nutrition and Health
A healthy person has a good appetite, likely has a good diet, digests their food well, and makes efficient use of it in their body. A well-nourished person can keep their immune system functioning at a high level and is likely to be healthy.

A sick person is likely to lose their appetite, have a poor diet, digest their food poorly, and use some of their nutrients to fight infection. A poorly nourished person suffers a weakened immune system and is susceptible to infections.

Earlier, we discussed deaths caused by undernutrition. Typically, these deaths occur because a person weakened by undernutrition catches an infectious disease, and the weakened body cannot fight off the disease, so the person dies. A well-nourished person could get the same disease and survive it. An undernourished person who avoided the disease likewise would survive. Death is caused by the combination of undernutrition and disease. The impacts of undernutrition can be reduced by improving the general health of the population.

This interrelationship is so important that a definitive review of the literature concluded, "Where both malnutrition and exposure to infection are serious, as they are in most tropical and developing countries, successful control of these conditions depends upon efforts directed equally against both" (Scrimshaw, Taylor, and Gordon 1968:267). (For a more recent review, see Keusch 2003).

We begin by reviewing the mutually reinforcing synergies between malnutrition and disease: disease contributes to malnutrition; malnutrition contributes to disease. The impact of disease on malnutrition was touched on in Chapter 3; the impact of malnutrition on disease was discussed in Chapter 4.

Disease Exacerbates Malnutrition

Disease—especially infectious disease—increases the potential for and severity of malnutrition. Some of the mechanisms for this impact are fairly obvious; others are more obscure.

To understand the impact of disease on undernutrition, and to separate that issue from the problem of food availability, consider how a person might become undernourished even when there is sufficient food available. A sick person might fail to eat because of loss of appetite; the person might eat but the ability of the digestive system to absorb nutrients might be impaired; the food might be excreted too quickly for the digestive system to absorb the nutrients; disease may put extra nutritional demands on the body.

Everyone has experienced a loss of appetite during a feverish bout of flu. But when an infection is left untreated (for example because antibiotics are not available or are too expensive) or if the infection recurs, the loss of appetite can lead to weight loss and undernutrition. Chronic infections and some other diseases cause a more serious condition known as "cachexia," which is characterized by loss of appetite and weight.

Malabsorption—when the digestive system fails to properly digest food and absorb nutrients—can be caused by diseases of the liver, the pancreas, or the intestine. In addition, malabsorption can be a side effect of cardiovascular problems or diabetes. Intestinal parasites compete with the human body for nutrition ingested by the human, and therefore lead to malabsorption (Brasitus 1979).

Another reason that nutrients may not be derived from ingested food is that food is excreted too quickly for the digestive process to work. Gastrointestinal infections can lead to diarrhea or vomiting—so the potential nutrition in food consumed is not actually available to the person.

Diarrhea (or its extreme form, dysentery) is the most common illness affecting nutritional status. An outstanding feature of kwashiorkor, for instance, is the frequency with which it is precipitated by an attack of acute diarrheal disease (Scrimshaw, Taylor, and Gordon 1968:27). Diarrhea particularly affects children under five years old, and fecal matter is a main source of the in-fective material. Food and water are key transmission routes. Children often make their first contact with diarrheal disease organisms through weaning foods (Durand and Pigney 1963). As described in Chapter 3, unsanitary water supplies are also a major cause of diarrheal diseases.

In recent years, epidemiologists have identified environmental enteropathy as a major concern in some developing countries. Environmental enteropathy is a condition resulting from frequent fecal-oral contamination, which can occur in circumstances where toilet facilities are rudimentary and unsanitary, where hand-washing practices are imperfect, and where drinking water is drawn from contaminated sources. The frequent intestinal infections that arise under these conditions cause diarrhea; but they also cause changes in the physical and biological condition of the digestive tract, and these changes result in malabsorption, as described earlier. In 2010, the Bolivian ambassador to the United Nations told that body: "The vast majority of illnesses around the world are caused by fecal matter. 3.5 million people die of waterborne illness each year" (Solon 2010). The WHO and UNICEF (2015) estimate that 2.4 billion people lack improved sanitation facilities. That is almost a third of the world's population. But, on the bright side, 2.1 billion have gained access to improved sanitation since 1990. The biggest remaining problems are in rural areas.

In Chapter 6, we pointed out the anomaly in measures of undernutrition—prevalence of undernutrition is highest in sub-Saharan Africa, but anthropometric measures of childhood undernutrition (percentage of children stunted, or underweight) identify South Asia as the region with the biggest nutrition problems. Environmental enteropathy may be an explanation for this—the potential for fecal-oral contamination is higher in densely populated areas.

Infectious disease can also cause loss of protein in the body. What happens is that protein tissue in the body is used up to fight the infection. To manufacture such disease-fighting materials as interferon, white blood corpuscles, and mucus, the body needs amino acids, which it acquires in part by breaking down previously existing protein—chiefly from the muscles. This borrowing of muscle tissue for fighting infection is one of the reasons we feel so weak following a serious illness. It might seem reasonable to try to keep up the body's supply of protein during an illness by eating more, but the loss of appetite often keeps this from happening. During convalescence, with an appropriate diet, the lost body protein is usually replaced. The problems cited here also mean that diseases (and especially infectious diseases) can exacerbate or cause micronutrient deficiencies, as described in Chapter 3.

An example of the impact of disease on nutritional status is reported in a survey article by Schaible and Kaufmann: "A study in Nigeria found that the severe metabolic demands made during acute measles infection further deteriorated the condition of malnourished children, leading to further weight loss, wasting, and reduced serum levels of essential amino acids" (2007:808).

Malnutrition Exacerbates Disease

Malnutrition often amplifies the impact of disease. Considerable evidence of this was presented in Chapter 5. To review briefly: malnutrition increases the risk of death; but short of death, malnourished people are more likely to get a disease, more likely to suffer from a more severe form of the disease, more likely to suffer complications from a disease. We begin with a few more examples.

Severely undernourished children admitted to a hospital in the Philippines for acute respiratory infection were found to be thirteen times as likely to die from the disease as children whose nutrition was normal (see Figure 15.1).

Malnutrition is almost always synergistic with intestinal diseases caused by worms or protozoa and with any disease caused by bacteria (Scrimshaw, Taylor, and Gordon 1968:263–264). That is, malnutrition aggravates the course of the disease, and the disease, in turn, intensifies the malnutrition.

A wide variety of nutrients have been demonstrated to have an impact on the competency of the body's immune system (Gershwin et al. 1985:2; Phillips and Baetz 1980). Undernutrition increases the duration of infections, especially diarrhea.

Unequivocal evidence shows that the immune response is reduced in severe undernutrition, and some evidence suggests a diminished immune response in moderate undernutrition, particularly in wasted children (Rivera and Martorell 1988). Two examples illustrate the impact of undernutrition on im-

Figure 15.1 Acute Respiratory Infection Mortality by Nutritional Status, Philippine Hospital Cases

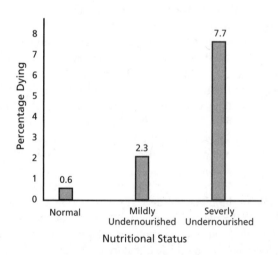

Source: Adapted from Galway et al. 1987:23 using data from Tupasi 1985.

mune response: (1) elderly patients who were given nutritional supplements along with their flu shots had better protection against the flu compared to patients who were given shots without the supplements; and (2) among individuals given a vaccine to protect them from tuberculosis, the effectiveness of the vaccine was positively correlated with nutritional status (Chandra 1988).

Malnutrition interferes with various bodily mechanisms that attempt to block the multiplication or progress of infectious agents. The list of ways it can do this is long, but significant among them are a decrease in the response and activity of white blood corpuscles; a reduction in the production of interferon; a decrease in the integrity of the skin, the mucous membrane, and other tissues that serve to bar the entrance of infection; and interference with normal tissue replacement and repair (Scrimshaw, Taylor, and Gordon 1968:263–264).

The mucous membrane not only provides a physical barrier against the entrance of foreign particles that might cause infection (bacteria, viruses), but provides a chemical barrier as well. Mucus contains a variety of biochemical and immunological disease fighters, one of which is an enzyme called lysozyme, which has the capacity to attack the cell walls of invading bacteria. Colombian children suffering from protein-energy malnutrition were found to be producing reduced levels of lysozyme. In a process called cell-mediated immunity, T-lymphocytes play a key role attacking disease-causing microbes. Children with protein-energy malnutrition are also likely to suffer an atrophied thymus, the organ primarily responsible for the "education" and proliferation of T-lymphocytes, and at the same time to produce fewer of these lymphocytes than expected when their bodies are challenged with invading disease organisms (Sherman 1986).

Not only does malnutrition reduce resistance to infection but it also decreases stamina, which in turn decreases the capacity to cope with life and to perform on the job, making it more difficult to earn money to pay for transportation to healthcare centers, to pay for the services themselves, and to pay for appropriate drugs for combating infection.

Even risks associated with respiratory and heart diseases can be increased by malnutrition. The heart and lungs are muscles, and muscles require protein for proper functioning. As the undernourished body begins to break down the body's proteins in a search for missing nutrients, those muscles are weakened and therefore more susceptible to disease and failure.

Policies to Improve Health

The synergy between disease and undernutrition has been explored in this chapter: malnutrition leads to disease; disease leads to malnutrition. Most of the rest of this book will deal with policies to address undernutrition through improved food production and distribution. But implicitly this is taking undernutrition as the underlying cause, and disease as a symptom. As we have mentioned repeatedly, "deaths from undernutrition" are in fact the result of a confluence of undernutrition and disease. So before we turn to questions of how we might reduce those deaths by reducing undernutrition, let us consider how we might reduce those deaths by reducing the incidence of disease. In the rest of this section, we consider a policy approach that focuses directly on reducing incidence and severity of disease, especially focusing on developing countries.

Policies to Combat the Source of the Disease

For some diseases and conditions, it may be possible to attack the problem at its source. For example, rich countries put a substantial effort into identifying and eradicating bovine spongiform encephalopathy (BSE, or "mad cow" disease), which can cause serious disease in humans who consume the brains of infected cows. Efforts at universal inoculation have resulted in worldwide eradication of smallpox and raised hopes for worldwide eradication of measles, polio, rubella, and other diseases.

Policies to Impede the Spread of the Disease

The spread of infectious diseases can be reduced by interfering with the mechanisms or vectors by which disease moves from one person to another. Use of treated malaria nets keeps malaria-infected mosquitoes from biting people as they sleep. (Hoffman [2009] investigated whether families who were given mosquito nets used those nets differently than did families who purchased the nets.) Where a disease is limited geographically, quarantine or travel restrictions may reduce the spread of the disease. The Ebola outbreak in 2015 spurred a worldwide effort to reduce spread of the disease. An important part of this effort was the tracing of people who had had contact with individuals who contracted Ebola so that those people could also be tested and monitored for the disease (Griender et al. 2015).

Policies to Promote Immunization Against Disease

Vaccination or inoculation exposes an individual to a small dose of a disease-causing agent to induce the development of disease-fighting mechanisms inside the person's body. When the individual is exposed to the disease-causing agent in the real world, they either do not contract the disease or contract a mild episode. As noted earlier, in the case of smallpox, immunization has been so successful that the organism that causes the disease has been made extinct (outside the laboratory).

In 1974, less than 5 percent of children in the developing world were immunized against six common vaccine-preventable childhood killers—measles, tetanus, diphtheria, pertussis, tuberculosis, and polio. Today, that number is more than 80 percent. This enormous increase is due in large part to government policies—in particular the World Health Organization's expanded immunization program. UNICEF estimates that over 9 million lives per year are saved by immunization. However, the work is not finished. About 22 million infants worldwide are not immunized each year (WHO 2014).

Measles-associated diarrhea is more severe and is more likely to lead to death than other diarrheas. One estimate suggests that up to a quarter of diarrheal deaths among preschoolers could be prevented by an effective measles immunization program (Feacham and Koblinsky 1983).

The World Bank in its 1993 *World Development Report* urged public health officials to promote immunization with a new vaccine—for hepatitis B and yellow fever—and recommended that this be combined with supplements of vitamin A and iodine, saying such a combination "would have the highest cost-effectiveness of any health measure available today." Two decades later, research and implementation of this approach are still under way. Newton and colleagues conclude, "Vitamin A supplementation reduces child mortality . . . and the Expanded Program on Immunization offers an ideal opportunity to deliver supplements in developing countries" (2007:1272). McDonald and colleagues (2014) highlight the importance of timing of the vitamin supplementation.

Policies to Promote Clean Drinking Water

In developed countries, governments have been involved in developing and maintaining public systems of clear water for nearly 200 years. Modern engineering principles were applied to waterborne sewage disposal systems in the West during the 1840s.

The WHO and UNICEF (2015) estimate that 663 million people—9 percent of the world's population—do not have access to improved water supplies. About 80 percent of those (530 million) live in rural areas. Improving the local water supply in rural areas can involve something as simple and effective as technical assistance and encouragement for the construction and use of rainwater-gathering vats. Use of such vats provides not only a clean but also a convenient source of household water. When a mother does not have to walk so far to get her household supply of water, she has more time available for other activities, including childcare.

The issue of whether water should be provided by public utilities or by private companies continues to be a subject of heated debate. Box 15.1 relates anecdotal evidence for and against relying on private firms for safe drinking water.

Policies to Require Food Fortification

Micronutrient deficiencies can be reduced or eliminated by government programs that require commonly purchased foods to be fortified with the missing micronutrients. In the twentieth century, public programs promoting the iodization of salt and the fortification of flour with vitamins became routine in the West. (The history of such programs in the United States is outlined in Box 15.2.)

Box 15.1 The Political Economy of Drinking Water: Success and Failure of Private Water Provision

As the need for safe drinking water became a more and more obvious public health problem, developing countries considered how they could finance the capital investments needed to build new water treatment and delivery systems. Many developing countries turned to the World Bank—an international organization that helps finance development projects at preferential terms. During the 1990s the World Bank promoted public-private partnerships in development, and investments in safe drinking water were a natural target for these partnerships.

Rather than relying solely on public financing, a public-private partnership could find private companies willing to make investments in safe water; in return these companies would be granted the concession to sell the water to municipal water consumers. These experiments with water privatization had mixed degrees of success.

One of the cities where privatization succeeded is Manila in the Philippines. (The Manila privatization divided the city into eastern and western sectors; here we discuss the experience in the eastern sector.) In 1997, prior to privatization, the Manila water supply was limited in its reach and unreliable in its performance. Only 49 percent of city residents were hooked up to municipal water, and three-quarters of those with water service had no water in their faucets from time to time.

The Manila government granted a water concession for the eastern part of the city to a consortium made up of private company partners from the Philippines, the United Kingdom, and the United States. This consortium won the concession by promising to deliver water at rates that were much lower than the existing prices.

By 2013, 94 percent of potential customers were hooked up to water, more than doubling the number of people with access to water. Continuity of supply was nearly 100 percent and customer satisfaction had soared past 90 percent.

Critics of privatization point to the high prices charged by the private water company and the high profits earned. Prior to privatization, prices were $8.78 pesos per cubic meter. The company promised low prices ($2.32) in its bid, and in early years, water prices were indeed low, increasing slightly to $2.61 in 1999. But the company sought and received permission from the regulatory agency to raise prices to $14.22 in 2002, to $18.55 in 2005, and to $26.98 in 2008. Low-income customers were permitted to pay prices much lower than these rates.

After losses in the two initial years, the company began earning profits, which rose to about 30 percent of revenues in the 2005–2012 period.

The city of Cochabamba, Bolivia, had a much less positive experience with water privatization. Prior to the privatization experiment, in the mid-1990s, the Cochabamba water supply was a mess. "Service did not improve despite major investment funded by international donors: Water losses remained high, water was supplied only 4 [hours] per day and water quality remained poor. This was a great source of frustration, including for the employees of the international development banks who saw that the investments they financed were not well taken care of. Only about 60% of the population was connected to the network" (Schiffler 2015:18).

One can see from this experience why privatization seemed like an attractive alternative. The public utility approach had apparently failed, with few incentives to control waste and inefficiency and to respond to customer needs.

The government of Cochabamba sought bids from companies that would agree to ensure twenty-four-hour water service and 90 percent access; in return the companies would be permitted to earn 15 percent annual returns on investment. Because of political turmoil and uncertainty about World Bank support, no companies submitted bids, until at the last minute a bid came in from a US company, which later added other partners, including Bolivian companies.

The water system was turned over to private management in 1999, and a rate increase was requested and approved in early 2000, raising water prices by somewhere between 35 and 50 percent.

Popular opinion turned sharply against the private water company—prices were rising and the obvious beneficiary was a company owned by rich foreigners. What is more, the commodity being sold was water, which fell from the sky as rain. Why, the public wondered, should foreigners be enriched by selling to Bolivians their own rain? In early 2000, people took to the streets to protest the water privatization, and a water bill "strike" was call for.

The government responded to the protests by cutting rates and freezing them for most of the rest of 2000. The consortium pursued legal actions against the government for failing to abide by its promises. Ultimately the private company walked away from the arrangement (or by some accounts "was kicked out"). Three years after the aborted privatization, "the water supply remains intermittent, and half the people of Cochabamba remain without tap water" (Schiffler 2015:25).

For more information on water privatization, see Schiffler 2015 and Kapoor 2015.

Direct Treatment of Diseases and Symptoms

We have no problem thinking of high blood pressure as a medical condition that responds to medical treatment. And the 2010 Survey on Global Disease Burden ranks high blood pressure as the number one problem worldwide, measured by decreased life expectancy. But if we look at past surveys, we see that in 1990 the number one health problem worldwide was "childhood underweight"—clearly a nutritional condition. (Even in 2010, childhood underweight was the number one problem in sub-Saharan Africa—see Lim et al. 2012.)

If we think of malnutrition—especially childhood undernutrition—as a medical condition, it focuses our attention on the question: What kind of medical intervention would be effective in treating that disease?

Preventive efforts notwithstanding, people still do get sick, and turn to the health system for treatment. One notable example of a policy effort to treat di-

---

Box 15.2 A Brief History of Food Fortification in the United States

Richard Ahrens

The leading cause of draft deferment in the United States during World War I was the swelling of the thyroid gland called goiter. . . . [B]oys who had the condition could not fit into the tight collars of the military uniforms. In 1923 the Harding Commission, appointed by President Warren Harding, recommended a voluntary program for the iodization of salt to combat goiter. A gentlemen's agreement was worked out between the salt companies and the executive branch of the government that there would be no price difference charged between the iodized and uniodized product.

During Word War II a bill was introduced into Congress that would have made it mandatory that all table salt be iodized, but the bill was defeated in committee when a number of medical doctors testified that there were probably some people in the United States who were sensitive to iodine and who would have skin problems as a result of being unable to obtain iodine-free salt.

Fortification of flour arose at the start of World War II, after President Franklin Roosevelt asked the National Academy of Sciences (NAS) to evaluate the nation's readiness for war. As one of their recommendations, the NAS came up with a proposal to ask flour millers to fortify wheat flour with iron, thiamin, riboflavin, and niacin. The flour fortification program became policy in 1940 . . . and now it is the province of the US Food and Drug Administration.

Source: Richard Ahrens is professor emeritus of nutrition at the University of Maryland.

---

arrhea directly is the effort to subsidize the use of oral rehydration therapy (ORT) to treat the impact of extreme diarrhea. For generations, it was thought that the only way to replace electrolytes lost because of diarrhea was through intravenous injection. Oral replacement using the salts alone simply did not work. In the late 1960s researchers in India and what is now Bangladesh found that merely adding common cane sugar to the missing salts produced a formula that worked by mouth. This simple technology—ORT—was first used to fight cholera (the most virulent form of dysentery) in an epidemic in India in 1971. Since then it has become a third world public health mainstay and has been vigorously promoted by both UNICEF and the WHO. UNICEF (1987:8) has called ORT the cheapest and most effective health intervention that can be implemented in the home to decrease childhood mortality. UNICEF estimates that 1 million deaths per year are prevented by ORT.

Direct "Medical" Interventions to Reduce Undernutrition

Perhaps the most direct "health policies" that address malnutrition are programs deliberately designed to treat patients who are acutely undernourished and near death, and patients who are suffering from (or who have a high probability of suffering from) a particular kind of malnutrition.

For example, an interesting controlled experiment was conducted in Ache province in northern Sumatra, where vitamin A deficiency may well be the most severe in the world. During a one-year period, some preschoolers in Ache were given one capsule containing 200,000 international units of vitamin A every six months. Others were given no vitamin A supplement. The vitamin A supplement was shown to reduce dramatically both the risk of xerophthalmia and the death rate (Sommer et al. 1986; Gopalan 1986). Vitamin A pills such as those used in this experiment can be manufactured for less than 5 cents each. However, the cost of distribution far exceeds the cost of the pills. The presence of an ongoing maternal and child healthcare center permits the cost of a vitamin A supplementation program to be shared among the costs of other health delivery programs.

A similar "prescription" has been introduced to treat calorie deficiency. The group Doctors Without Borders (2008a) has developed a high-calorie food supplement (Ready-to-Use-Food, or RUF, sometimes called Ready-to-Use-Therapeutic-Food, or Plumpynut). This is a paste made from peanuts and milk that comes in airtight foil packets. The packets can be prescribed to individuals who are suffering from acute calorie deficiency. Some research about the use of these RUFs in developing countries was delivered at a 2008 symposium (Doctors Without Borders 2008b).

One glimpse into how calorie malnutrition is dealt with in developed countries can be found in a pamphlet from the United Kingdom's National Health Service (2006). That pamphlet identifies five underlying causes of malnutrition among the elderly—loss of appetite, difficulty eating, inability to absorb food, other disease, and social situation—and recommends actions to deal with each of the underlying causes, including (in some circumstances) the prescription of a high-calorie food supplement.

General Policies to Improve Medical Care

The final issue we consider here is policies to improve general medical care. Questions arise, such as: Should healthcare professionals work for the government or as private entrepreneurs? Should government promote the building and use of small community clinics or large hospitals?

Over the years, the view became widespread that, by and large, it is cheaper to maintain good health than it is to make people well after they get sick. Most common third world illnesses can be successfully treated in the field by paramedical workers using simple equipment and a limited range of medicines. Thus a strong argument develops for placing increased emphasis on preventive medicine carried out by lower-level technicians in clinics close to people's homes, contrasted with curative medicine carried out by highly trained physicians surrounded by a hierarchy of staff in expensive urban hospitals. This idea is coloring many of the current healthcare developments in the third world, which are emphasizing low-cost delivery of health services to the poor. We see "barefoot doctors" in China, "nutrition huts" in the Philippines, and "health huts" in Haiti.

A review of the literature by Filmer, Hammer, and Pritchett found that there was little empirical evidence to back up the prejudice in favor of publicly financed low-cost "primary" healthcare delivery:

> [A] combination of experiences has led to a strong consensus among public health specialists who focus on developing countries. They argue that the existing allocation of health expenditures toward curative care in secondary and tertiary facilities, such as hospitals and clinics to which patients are referred, is inappropriate and that a reorientation of government efforts toward primary health care would bring both health gains and cost savings. . . . Although the images and statistics that motivate primary health care appear compelling, the gains have rarely been demonstrated in practice. . . . Has public spending on health and, more particularly, on primary health care promoted good health? If so, there should be empirical regularities at both the national and local levels. First, given a level of total health expenditures, more spending on primary health care activities and greater access to primary health care services should be associated with lower aggregate mortality. Second, at the local level (household, village) greater access to primary healthcare facilities should reduce mortality. Third, projects that develop primary care facilities should reduce mortality. None of these regularities finds much support in the data. (2000:199–201)

Rather, they find that almost all of the observed differences in healthcare outcomes can be explained by socioeconomic variables, especially income per capita. In other words, people in higher-income per capita settings have better health outcomes than people in lower-income per capita settings, regardless of the level of government spending, or the access to primary healthcare. Descriptions of how healthcare is provided in developing countries are found in Box 15.3.

Development programs that lean toward emphasizing human capital development (which would include primary healthcare and public health programs) not only serve to improve people's productivity, especially at the bottom end of the income distribution, but may also improve health outcomes by raising per capita income. Policies to promote economic growth will be discussed in Chapter 17.

People's Behavior and Effective Healthcare

A lot of the material in this chapter points out the relatively cheap and easy actions that can treat common diseases. "Each year, 7.6 million children under the age of five die from avoidable causes. In countries that suffer the greatest share of these deaths, the most effective interventions are almost all preventive

---

Box 15.3 Healthcare Quality in Developing Countries

Professor Ken Leonard and his colleagues report on their experiences observing how healthcare is delivered in developing countries. Their stories paint a picture of healthcare systems that are very different from the healthcare system of the United States. Below are two stories from their report (Das, Hammer, and Leonard 2008: 94).

"Dr. SM and his wife are the most popular medical care providers in the neighborhood, with more than 200 patients every day. The doctor spends an average of 3.5 minutes with each patient, asks 3.2 questions, and performs an average of 2.5 examinations. Following the diagnosis, the doctor takes two or three different pills, crushes them using a mortar and pestle, and makes small paper packets from the resulting powder, which he gives to Ms. Sundar [the patient] and asks her to take for two or three days. These medicines usually include one antibiotic and one analgesic and anti-inflammatory drug."

"In rural Tanzania, Ms. M brings her nine-month-old to the local health clinic, carrying the child on her back. When she enters, Dr. K (an Assistant Medical Officer with O-level education and four years of medical training) asks her what the problem is. Still standing in front of his desk, she replies that her daughter has a fever. Dr. K fills a prescription for malaria based on this statement, even though he cannot see the child, much less observe her condition. The consultation and medicine are both free and Ms. M leaves the facility with the prescribed medicine. During the exit interview, a nurse on our team notes that the child is suffering from severe pneumonia. The health facility has the medicine to treat both malaria and pneumonia. Dr. K is trained in the diagnosis and treatment for these diseases and saw only 25 patients that day. Yet, but for the intervention of the nurse on our research team, the child would have died."

---

or therapeutic measures that should be within the reach of most households and communities" (World Bank 2015b:146). These measures do not require major investments in infrastructure or government provision of medicine and health services; they are things like breast-feeding, vaccinations, mosquito nets, and oral rehydration therapy.

The country of Libya, along with other oil-rich states in the Middle East, saw exploding economic growth in the 1970s as oil prices tripled, and their status change from low-income to high-income in a matter of years. High income alone was not enough to change health outcomes, because behavior changed more slowly than income. Earlier editions of this book contained this reflection from a researcher writing in the 1970s: "I was long of the opinion that infantile marasmus would be essentially eliminated when social and political change were accomplished such that abject poverty no longer existed. However, . . . experience in Libya, a rich but still developing nation, has caused me to reconsider somewhat this view. . . . [Despite growing prosperity from rising oil prices] in 1977 infantile marasmus in Libya remained a widespread problem. As elsewhere in the developing world, breast-feeding had declined" (Pellet 1977: 54). Nearly four decades later, the challenge of how to promote breast-feeding in developing countries remains a topic of widespread interest and research (Dyson, McCormick, and Renfrew 2006).

What keeps these cheap and easy actions to promote health from being taken? For example, most cases of pneumonia are easily and effectively treated with common antibiotics. But UNICEF (2011) reports that 40 percent of children with suspected pneumonia in the developing world, and 60 percent of such children in sub-Saharan Africa, are never taken to see a healthcare provider who might administer those antibiotics.

The common policy approach has been to ask what government actions can be taken to ensure people have access to healthcare professionals, or to ensure that antibiotics are available. But perhaps the answer lies in the behavior of the sick child and their family. Perhaps what we need is a better understanding of how to motivate and influence that behavior.

The World Bank's 2015 *World Development Report* looked at lessons for development from the field of "behavioral economics," and included a chapter summarizing what researchers have learned about the behavior of sick people in identifying impediments to care. A sampling of these insights is listed below:

• A campaign to encourage use of zinc supplements was successful in Bangladesh because it combined advertising (messages painted on rickshaws), giveaways (plates with a pro-zinc message), community meetings, and entertainment (plays or puppet shows about the benefits of zinc supplements).

• Advertisements to discourage drug use among teens in the United States failed to achieve the desired goal in part because they inadvertently sent the message that drug use was common (and presumably "cool") among teens.

• An effort to promote use of oral rehydration therapy (which, as described earlier, entails drinking a liquid with salt and other nutrients) failed in India. The effort failed because it could not overcome the "mental model" Indian mothers typically had about diarrhea—that diarrhea occurred because the individual had ingested too much fluid and could not be solved by intake of even more fluid.

• People who are willing to adopt a health-improving product or practice when it is free may refuse to adopt if there is even a very small charge. For example, in a Kenyan trial, 60 percent of households adopted water disinfectant when it was free, but fewer than 10 percent adopted when the cost was 15 cents.

• In some cases, people refuse even free health services but can be induced to use them by offering incentives such as cash payments or gifts.

• People do share information and put a high degree of confidence in the experiences of their peers.

Box 15.4 describes a study of how public health objectives (related to reduction of environmental enteropathy, described earlier in the chapter) can be achieved by changing behavior.

Box 15.4 Shaming to Change Health-Related Behavior

As noted earlier in this chapter, the diarrhea-related condition known as environmental enteropathy is a serious disease-related cause of undernutrition. The condition arises from frequent drinking of fecally contaminated water. The condition is found in densely populated areas where residents practice the unhygienic behavior of open defecation rather than using latrines where the excrement can be contained.

Public health officials had long attempted to change this open defecation behavior through information and advertising campaigns, without much success. Economic subsidies for households to construct latrines were also available.

In 2006, a new intervention was tried in the Indian state of Orissa, where (despite the information campaign and latrine subsidies) less than 10 percent of the population had access to safe water and good sanitation. The new intervention was studied by Pattanayak and colleagues (2009).

The campaign "seeks to generate strong emotional responses at the community level that will culminate in a community-wide resolve to end open defecation." The campaign had three parts: first, a "walk of shame"—where community members walked through a neighborhood and directed comments intending to shame individuals observed in open defecation; second, defecation mapping—which identified the places in a village where open defecation was causing water contamination; and third, "core faecal counts" aimed at communicating the extent of the problem caused by open contamination.

To study the impact of this kind of shaming campaign, the authors chose forty villages and applied the shaming campaign in twenty, while the other twenty villages continued with the existing programs of communication and latrine subsidies, but without the shaming campaign. The study found that the new public shaming effort was remarkably successful. In the "control" group of villages (those that did not have the shaming campaign), there was virtually no change in latrine ownership; in the villages that did receive the "treatment" of the shaming campaign, latrine ownership increased from 5 percent of households to over 30 percent of households.

The shaming campaign affected behavior in both poor and nonpoor households. The authors conclude that "the favourable response seen among households above the poverty line suggests that subsidies are not necessary to spur action and that shame alone can be very effective in this population."

See Chapter 17 for a related discussion of how social pressure has been used to encourage family planning.

Part 3

Policy Approaches to Undernutrition

16

Philosophical Approaches to Food Policy

In this part of the book, we consider policies that can be adopted to reduce the degree of worldwide hunger. Before proceeding, we spend a few pages exploring philosophical approaches to the issue. What motivates governments, societies, individuals, or groups of individuals to concern themselves with the issue of undernutrition? How does the motivation influence the policy decisions?

From the Standpoint of a Moral Philosopher

Charity or Concern for the Poor and Hungry

Our first chapter opened with a reference to starving Ethiopian babies—babies with bloated bellies, spindly arms and legs, and bodies too weak to sit up. The device is a standard technique for grabbing the attention of people attuned to Western culture and making them stop to think about the world food problem.

Those who live in the Western world are exposed to repeated appeals to conscience, asking them to join the battle to end hunger. In 1980, the Presidential Commission on World Hunger urged that the United States "make the elimination of hunger the primary focus of its relations with the developing world." Commenting on this in a paper written for a religious audience, Martin McLaughlin of the group Interfaith Action for Economic Justice said that "the moral and humanitarian reasons for such a policy seem self-evident" (1984:3).

A common argument in favor of studying and solving the world hunger problem is the moral dictate that each of us should help individuals who are less fortunate than ourselves. The Pope's statement to the World Food Summit, for example, contains the following:

In the analyses which have accompanied the preparatory work for your meeting, it is recalled that more than 800 million people still suffer from malnutrition and that it is often difficult to find immediate solutions for improving these tragic situations. Nevertheless, we must seek them together so that we will no longer have, side by side, the starving and the wealthy, the very poor and the very rich, those who lack the necessary means and others who lavishly waste them. Such contrasts between poverty and wealth are intolerable for humanity.

It is the task of nations, their leaders, their economic powers and all people of goodwill to seek every opportunity for a more equitable sharing of resources, which are not lacking, and of consumer goods; by this sharing, all will express their sense of brotherhood. It requires "firm and persevering determination to commit oneself to the common good; that is to say, to the good of all and of each individual, because we are all really responsible for all" (Sollicitudo rei socialis, no. 38). This spirit calls for a change of attitude and habits with regard to life-styles and the relationship between resources and goods, as well as for an increased awareness of one's neighbour and his legitimate needs. (Pope John Paul II 1996)

The philosopher Peter Singer approaches the issue from a distinctly nonreligious point of view. He concludes, "I begin with the assumption that suffering from lack of food, shelter, and medical care are bad. . . . My next point is this: if it is within our power to prevent something bad from happening, without thereby sacrificing anything of comparable moral importance, we ought, morally, to do it" (1972:231).

Garrett Hardin (1974) reached a completely opposite conclusion. To Hardin, the most ethical action is staunchly to *refuse* to help the poorest of the poor. His reasoning is this: the planet is like a lifeboat with a limited capacity; the altruistic impulse to save people will overcrowd that lifeboat and thereby doom everyone, even those who could have been saved. Of course, the underlying logic of this requires that the planet's lifeboat actually be full, and the experience since 1974, when Hardin wrote this—with world population increasing more than 60 percent and the number of undernourished people declining—contradicts that assumption.

The arguments described in the past few paragraphs describe the issue of helping the world's undernourished as a matter of religious conviction or personal ethics. The motivation to help comes from within the individual. I may believe that I "owe" compassion to the hungry, but that debt is a product of my beliefs, something generated from within myself. In that regard, it is quite different from the debt I owe to the government as taxes.

Food as a Right
This distinction (between being motivated by personal ethics and being motivated by an obligation to society) is important as we consider a second type of moral argument about why we should be interested in the problem of world

hunger. That is the issue of "food as a right." Some eighty-five countries have endorsed the International Covenant on Economic, Social, and Cultural Rights (adopted by the United Nations General Assembly in 1966), which defined and formalized the right to food as a basic human right. The right to food was widely discussed in preparation for and during the World Food Summit of 1996 (Pinstrup-Andersen, Nygaard, and Ratta 1995; Alston 1997).

If food is a right, then hunger is a violation of that right, and we have a second ethical motivation to be concerned about hunger—the moral requirement that we seek justice and oppose violations of rights. There is a difference between the "charity" motivation (we have an ethical obligation to help the hungry) and the "justice" motivation (food is a right). That difference is illustrated by the following:

• If you accept the view that there is a fundamental right to food, then you are motivated to address the hunger problem even if you do not believe that you have a moral duty to help the poor and hungry. Your motivation here is simply to ensure the protection of that fundamental right.

• If you believe that you have a moral duty to help the poor, then you are motivated to address the hunger problem even if you do not believe that there is a fundamental right to food. Your motivation here is your duty to be charitable.

To illustrate this difference, consider the right to religious freedom. A Christian who embraces the concept of this right could simultaneously believe (1) that people have a right to worship as a Jew or Muslim, and (2) that nobody ought to exercise that right, because those religions deny the divinity of Christ. Or consider the right to free speech. A person might simultaneously believe (1) that people have the right to read pornographic books, and (2) that nobody ought to exercise that right.

The assertion that people have a right to food is in this sense stronger than the assertion that people have a moral responsibility to help the poor and hungry. The latter is an assertion of a principle that will guide the speaker's behavior, and a plea to others to adopt the same principle. The former is an assertion that other people have a responsibility to help the poor and hungry even if those people do not choose to adopt the moral principle that would motivate that behavior. In other words, a coercive element is embedded in the "rights" assertion that is absent from the "moral principle" assertion.

The assertion that food is a right (or that people have a fundamental right to food and other necessities or "basic needs") is highly controversial. Let us consider some of the sources of controversy by means of analogies.

Consider a right that we accept as fundamental in the United States: the right to remain silent, or the right not to incriminate oneself. We accept the existence of that right even when we disapprove of its exercise. For example, if a kidnapper refuses to tell where he has hidden his victim, we may doubly abhor the kidnapper for his silence as well as his violence. But we do not argue that laws should permit police to torture suspects. The widespread acceptance of the right to remain silent sets this issue beyond the reach of political debate. It simplifies decisionmaking; we don't need to consider the pros and cons of any action, we need only to answer the question: Does the action violate the right?

This may explain why activists have pushed to have the right to food accepted as a fundamental right. They may hope to eliminate debate over the costs and benefits of various programs; the existence of the right trumps all other arguments. The FoodFirst Information and Action Network (FIAN 1997) fact sheet "Twelve Misconceptions About the Right to Food" states that "governance is negotiable; rights are not." A panel of constitutional experts supporting the concept of economic rights stated: "Fundamental needs such as social welfare rights should not be at the mercy of changing governmental policies and programmes, but must be defined as entitlements." The intention of advancing the "right to food" concept is to force acceptance of more active government programs to combat world hunger without having to justify those programs economically.

The strongest objection to the concept of food as a right is that unlike traditional civil rights, which require government *not to act* in certain ways, economic rights appear to require the state *to act* in certain ways. Traditional civil or political rights do not require government to act. Consider the right to religious freedom, or the right to worship as one chooses. This right imposes on the state the restriction that it cannot pass laws or take actions that interfere with an individual's right to worship. Suppose you want to attend a Zoroastrian temple for weekly worship; but suppose the nearest such temple is in Chicago, and suppose further that you cannot afford to travel to and from Chicago each week. Does the government have any obligation to buy a weekly plane ticket for you? No, at least not as the right to religious freedom is interpreted in the United States.

Economic rights not only require the government to avoid actions that would interfere with any individual's ability to obtain food; they additionally require the government to take actions to increase the ability of hungry people to obtain food. Legal scholars refer to this as the difference between "positive" and "negative" rights.

The most extreme objections to the concept of economic rights assert that these rights are immoral themselves because they require government to limit the freedom of some members of the society. It is hard to conceive of any effective assertion of economic rights that does not require extensive redistribution of income from rich to poor. If we accept the argument that government limits on freedom are immoral, then any taxation is immoral, since the taxation itself is coercive, restricting individual liberties. But isn't taxation required to guarantee other civil rights? To ensure the right to be free of cruel and unusual punishment, the government must use tax revenue to build new prisons. As long as it is costly to guarantee individuals their civil rights, some element of government coercion through the taxation system is necessary. (See Holmes and Sunstein 1999.)

The word *rights* in the traditional sense refers to entitlements that are in most applications absolute. The US government cannot censor a newspaper, or ban a religion, because those rights are absolute. Of course, it is easy to find examples of ways in which "absolute rights" are not absolute. The right of free speech does not extend to cover the right to yell "Fire!" in a crowded theater. The right of freedom of association (the right to choose whom you associate with) does not mean that an employer has the right to hire individuals of only one race. Absolute rights become limited only when the exercise of the right interferes with another person's exercise of his or her rights. The false yell of "Fire!" interferes with other people's right to congregate safely in a theater. Racial discrimination interferes with employees' rights to be free of discrimination. When one right conflicts with another, as in these cases, it is impossible to guarantee both rights absolutely.

On the one hand, what makes the concept of economic rights so controversial is that economic rights inevitably conflict with other rights, because economic rights require government expenditures. On the other hand, the assertion that food is a right gives those who favor government intervention an important argument to use against libertarians. The civil libertarian argues: "The government cannot take my money (through taxes) to buy food for a poor person because I have a right to control my own property." (Notice how the assertion of a right is used to trump other arguments about whether a policy is a good or bad idea.) The hunger activist can respond: "You have a right to property; but the poor person has a right to food. This is a conflict of rights and the government has an appropriate role in settling that conflict."

Further, because economic rights are in inevitable conflict with rights to property, economic rights can never be absolute. So a right to food does not mean that as long as a single hungry person exists in the world, the United States cannot devote any government expenditures to defense, or student loans, or drug interdiction, or civil rights enforcement. We have competing social goals that must be pursued with limited resources.

Who decides the priorities for these competing social goals? In the United States, conflicts between rights are typically resolved in the court system, not by democratically elected representatives. This raises the additional question of whether we have a fundamental right to control the level of taxation through a political process. If we have no such right, then courts could require higher and higher taxes to ensure economic rights. If there *is* such a right (to a social contract on taxes), then this right must be balanced against economic and other civil rights.

If we maintain the current system of establishing priorities through a political process, we impose a severe limit on economic rights. The process of simultaneously "guaranteeing" economic rights and property rights is really no different than the process of setting policy goals and balancing competing interests.

From the Standpoint of an Economist

The preceding section started as a discussion of moral imperatives, moved on to the notion that the assertion of a right makes economic policy analysis unnecessary, and ended by raising the question: How should we allocate scarce resources to accomplish competing objectives? This question covers familiar ground for economists. Whether the trade-offs are made by courts, legislatures, or administrators, the economic rule for policymaking is *maximize total benefits minus total costs* (see Posner 1986). Much of the remainder of the book will look at policy from the standpoint of an economist; before proceeding, we lay out some of the basic doctrines of economic policy analysis, and critiques of those doctrines.

Perhaps the questions they ask say more about economists than the way they answer those questions. The two questions that identify the asker as an economist are (1) What is the appropriate ("optimal") policy for the society as a whole? (2) How can government best manipulate human greed to achieve its policy objectives?

What Is the Best Policy?

A political scientist wants to know: What do different people or different groups care about? Then: How will those differences in those objectives be resolved? What political processes will be involved in resolving those conflicts? What are the levers of power and who controls those levers?

Economists start at the same place: What do different people want? And in one sense economics is inherently about resolving conflict; after all, the buyer wants to pay a low price and the seller wants to receive a high price. But from the economist's perspective, there is some ideal way of balancing the conflicts. Any decision or choice imposes costs on some people and provides benefits to some people. The economist's ideal (at least in its simplest and purest form) says that the best choice is the one that maximizes the extent to which benefits exceed costs.

Policymaking as a rational process. Economists implicitly view policymaking as a rational, orderly process managed by benevolent, well-informed, rational, analytical policymakers. This view tends to be so ingrained in the economics literature that many professional economists may not have even considered that they have adopted this view. If pushed on the subject, few even among economists would say that this is a realistic view—that policies are actually made according to this idealized process. Nor do economists really propound this as the way policy should be made; certainly it would be nice (in the minds of economists) if policy were made like this, and the policy outcomes are likely to be improved if made this way, but no one can conceive of a practical way of implementing such a process, except perhaps through the dictatorship of an enlightened well-trained economist, and no one is striving to have such a process implemented.

Economists do their analytical work in the hope of tweaking the consciences of the actual policymakers, saying in effect: "Of course you can do whatever you want, but a benevolent, well-informed, rational, analytical policymaker would do the following . . ." The hope here is that actual policymakers who like to think of themselves as benevolent, well informed, and the like, will adopt the recommended policy to avoid the shame of doing otherwise.

This idealized view of the policymaking process is that policy debates are more like scientific inquiries than like forensic debates. The scientific method presumes that truth is discovered through a series of interchanges among scientists who share the same objective—uncovering the truth. In jurisprudence, the truth is presumed to be arrived at through an adversarial contest of advocates. The prosecutor presents the very best case as to why the defendant should be found guilty, and the defense presents the very best case as to why the defendant should be found not guilty; the judge or jury, balancing those two cases, comes to a decision (in most cases) in which one side wins and the other side loses; the defendant is found guilty of the charge or not guilty.

An example of a real-world policy decision. Let us consider a concrete policy example (this is a fictitious example, but it closely resembles a policy decision that might be made in the real world). The government has built a dam and reservoir and every year must decide how much water to release from the reservoir to provide irrigation water for farmers. If the water is left in the reservoir, it will provide a healthy habitat for fish and birds, and be a place where people can enjoy outdoor recreation (hiking, canoeing, sport fishing, and bird watching). Of course, the policymakers can release none, some, or all of the water from the reservoir.

How does an economist look at the issue? We use this example to illustrate a number of important points:

• *Point 1: Every action has costs and benefits.* There are benefits (to farmers) from releasing the water—the farmers will use the water for irrigation that will increase crop yields and therefore increase the farmers' profits. But there are costs (to fish and wildlife and people who value these) associated with releasing the water.

• *Point 2: "Declining marginal benefits" and "increasing marginal costs."* As described in Chapter 7, economists make frequent use of the concepts of "marginal costs" and "marginal benefits." Benefits to farmers increase as the quantity of water released increases—but the benefits increase at a decreasing rate. The costs to the habitat increase as the quantity of water increases—and increase at an increasing rate.

• *Point 3: The economist's ideal decision—where marginal costs equal marginal benefits.* Just as the boy with the berries in Chapter 7 based his decision on equalizing marginal cost and marginal benefit, so too, say economists, should policymakers. To apply this rule to the hypothetical water allocation example here, the ideal water allocation would be to continue to release water until the point is reached where the marginal benefits (the increased value of crops attributable to the last 1,000 gallons released) just equals the marginal costs (the additional value of environmental amenities lost by the last 1,000 gallons released).

• *Point 4: Under certain circumstances, an unfettered free market allocates resources in the optimal way.* One way to reach the optimum is to sell each increment of the water to the highest bidder. If a coalition of hikers, canoeists, conservationists, and environmentalists submits the winning bid, that increment of water stays in the reservoir; if a coalition of farmers submits the winning bid, the water gets released for irrigation. This will result in the optimal allocation of water: each increment of water is allocated to the use (farming or wildlife) in which it has the highest use. If the water were owned by a private owner whose selfish objective was to make as much money as possible, he would accomplish that objective by selling it to the highest bidder, and the water would be allocated in a way that is socially optimal. This is an expression of Adam Smith's "invisible hand," and explains why economists do not think of free competitive markets and private enterprise as inherently bad.

But economists recognize that there can be a number of problems with markets that cause the "market solution" to be different from the social optimum. We turn next to a discussion of some of these problems.

Criticisms and Extensions of the Simple Policymaking Rule

Having laid out the general tenets of how economists define an "optimal policy," we now explore some finer points, including criticisms of the simple rule as just laid out.

Objectivity and Prejudices and the Role of Economics in Policymaking

In the simple example, there is a clear, apparently objective, answer to the question "What is the best policy?" If we provided the preceding example of marginal costs and benefits and asked twenty randomly chosen economists to identify the optimal policy, all twenty would likely come to the same conclusion.

But does this mean that economists never disagree with each other about policy? Clearly, the answer to this question is a vehement no! Economists have prejudices or opinions about policy that influence their evaluations. An economist knows how to undertake an objective analysis, but if that analysis arrives at a conclusion that contradicts their prejudice, they may decide that their prejudice needs to be reexamined, *or* they may decide that there was some mistake in the analysis.

Of course, an easy way to cleave to the economist's dictum ("the optimal choice is where marginal cost equals marginal benefit") and come to a different conclusion about the optimal policy is to dispute the empirical basis of the decision. An economist with an environmentalist prejudice may say: "Release 2000 gallons?! That can't be right; it's much too high. How did my analysis lead me to this conclusion? Oh, I see. The numbers are clearly skewed in a pro-farmer way." We will examine later some of the ways that numbers can be wrong in their basic development. For now, suffice it to say that if we raise our estimate of the value of environmental amenities, then the "optimal" water release decreases. In exactly the same way, an economist with a pro-farmer prejudice may be shocked that the analysis leads to a recommendation of such a small amount (in her or his opinion) of water being released, and may find "mistakes" in the underlying data—"Farmer benefits from water are grossly understated" might be this economist's claim.

On the one hand, this recognition of how economists actually analyze and debate policy undercuts their claim to scientific objectivity. However, this also illustrates a major strength of the economics approach: people on different sides of an issue (people with different prejudices) are forced to think in a careful and orderly way about what their opinions are based on; they are forced to define terms clearly; they are forced to produce and to defend empirical data supporting their position. In a policy debate among economists, sincere conviction and clever phrasing count for little.

Comparability of Costs and Benefits and the Dollar Valuation of Intangibles

You have read the preceding description of how economists think about policy. If you read it uncritically, you may not have noticed that we slipped something by you—we put the costs and benefits in dollar terms so that they could be compared to each other. This is the aspect of economic analysis that is most nettlesome to many thoughtful non-economists. Suppose, at some level of water release from the reservoir in our example, a species of fish that lives only in that reservoir dies off and becomes extinct: How do you put a dollar value on that species? Or suppose that the food produced with the water used for irrigation saves ten people who otherwise would die of undernutrition: How do you put a dollar value on those lives?

For many things, economists measure costs and benefits by prices deter-mined in a competitive market. So, in our example, the value of increased pro-duction from irrigation can be measured using the market price of the crops grown. Even this has a controversial side, as we will discuss in more detail later. But for other goods that are not traded in markets, the problem of valu-ation is trickier. What, for example, is the value of a species of fish that might become extinct under certain policy choices? Economists have developed ways to assign dollar values to these nontraded commodities by conducting surveys that ask, for example, "How much would you be willing to pay to pro-tect this fish from extinction?" or "How much would we have to pay you to compensate you for the loss of this species of fish?"

The underlying assumption that everything can be valued in dollar terms is troubling to many people. For example, there are those who would say to the fish extinction survey question: "It is wrong to take an action that would delib-erately lead to the extinction of a species. In one sense, the value of protecting the species is very high to me; to compensate for the loss of the species you would have to pay me an infinite amount [or some arbitrarily high number]. But I am opposed to the idea that I should be required to pay money to preserve the species; therefore I am not willing to pay anything to preserve the species."

Economist Tyler Cowen recognizes this weakness in the economic ap-proach to policymaking:

> On the negative side, the economic approach considers only a limited range of values, namely those embodied in individual preferences and expressed in terms of willingness to pay. This postulate is self-evident to many econ-omists, but it fails to command wider assent. It wishes to erect "satisfying a preference" as an independent ethical value, but is unwilling to consider any possible competing values, apart from preferences. It is hard to see why non-preference values should not be admitted to a broader decision calculus.
>
> Typically economists retreat to their intuition that satisfying preferences is somehow "real," and that pursuing non-preference values is religious, mystical, or paternalistic. The rest of the world, however, has not found this distinction persuasive. They do not see why satisfying preferences should be a value of special and sole importance, especially when those same prefer-ences may be ill-informed, inconsistent, malicious, or spiteful. The decisions to count all preferences, to use money as the measuring rod, and to weight all market demands equally must themselves rely on external ethical judgments. For that reason, the economist has no a priori means of dismissing non-pref-erence values from the overall policy evaluation. (2006:9).

The issue of putting a dollar value on things is especially troubling when it comes to human life. What is a human life worth? That may seem at first a horribly crass question to ask. But government policy has to deal with that question in many different contexts (the numbers in the examples that follow are entirely made up for the purposes of illustration).

• Requiring every car to have a seatbelt and an air bag will increase car prices by $800 (or $800 million over the 1 million cars sold each year) but will save 20,000 lives in auto accidents. Do the benefits from the law exceed the costs?

• Requiring all cars to drive no faster than 10 miles per hour will reduce gross national product by $1 trillion but will save 5,000 lives in auto accidents. Do the benefits from the law exceed the costs?

• Requiring all vegetables sold to be tested for pesticide residues will cost $50 billion per year but will save fifteen lives. Do the benefits exceed the costs?

Even more difficult are cases where lives are saved by restricting people's liberty, or by forcing them to take actions they believe are wrong—for example, forcing parents to immunize their children when the parents have religious beliefs that prohibit immunization.

Market Prices, Market Allocations of Resources, and the Distribution of Income

The market works, as described earlier, in allocating resources among their various alternative uses. Over the past century, a lot of the labor force in the United States shifted from farm work in the early 1900s to factory work in the mid-1900s to producing services and entertainment by the end of the century. This shift in resource allocation was driven largely by market forces. As profitable opportunities developed in manufacturing, the market directed more resources into factories. As profitable opportunities developed in the health services sector, the market directed more resources into hospitals.

If we take a step back, a troubling question arises: Why did the market direct resources toward the production of a television show or a sporting event rather than toward the production of more food in a world where millions of people are undernourished? If you think of the market as an election in which goods are produced in levels that depend on how many votes they get, the people with more dollars to spend get more votes than the people with fewer dollars to spend. Theoretical economists recognize that the "social optimum" achieved by perfectly competitive markets is an optimum that can be defined for a given distribution of income and that draws no conclusions about what distribution of income is appropriate.

Externalities and the Optimum

There is one set of circumstances that economists recognize as a common reason why competitive markets may not lead to a social optimum: when a decision made in the market by a buyer and a seller has benefits that accrue to or costs that are borne by others. Because these costs and benefits go to people outside the market transaction, they are referred to as "externalities," or "external costs" and "external benefits."

To return to our reservoir-water example, suppose that farmers bought a certain amount of water and it was released out of the reservoir; homeowners along the river between the reservoir and the farmers would get an external benefit from the release: they would be able to swim or boat or fish, and they would get these benefits without paying for them, but the benefits only exist because someone else (the farmers) *did* pay for the water release. In measuring the costs and benefits of water release, the market has taken into account only the private benefits of the farmer (who participates in the market), and not the full social benefits (that would include the benefits to the river users). In a case where there are external benefits, the amount that is bid for the good is lower than its true social value and the market price is "too low" and the quantity provided is "too low" compared to what would be a social optimum.

An external cost might occur if someone who never visited the reservoir enjoyed watching birds that summered in the reservoir and then migrated many miles away to where the birdwatcher lived. Releasing water imposes a cost on this distant birdwatcher that would not be reflected in the bids for water by the reservoir users. In this case the social costs would exceed the private costs.

Economic Incentives and Human Behavior

A second insight of economics is that personal materialistic satisfaction is a strong motivation of human behavior. Of course, if you think about your own behavior, you will be able to identify a lot of other motivations: a sense of honor or a sense of duty, a desire to be liked or admired, and so forth. Some of these motivations are appealed to by advertisers: to get people to buy more of our product, we will run ads to convince people that if they buy our product others will think that they are "cool." But even marketing experts recognize that people respond to materialistic motivations: to get people to buy more of our product, we will lower the price.

In our study of the problem of world hunger and policies to deal with that problem, this insight will enter in at least three ways:

• We will see how economic incentives can be and have been used to achieve policy objectives. For example, policies that make it more expensive to have children have been successful in reducing population growth, and policies that make it more expensive to degrade the environment have been successful in reducing environmental degradation. In this context, we will see that assigning and enforcing property rights is often an integral part of creating economic incentives.

• The production of goods also responds to economic incentives; the more you materially reward people for producing a certain good, the more of that good will be produced. The implication of this is that the distribution of goods influences the quantity of goods available for distribution.

• The third aspect of incentives and human behavior that will be important in our study of the world food problem has to do with the dynamic nature of production. As a commodity or resource becomes more scarce, or as increased demand for the commodity or resource bids its price up, people respond by finding ways to use the resource more efficiently, by finding ways to produce the commodity or make the resource available more cheaply, and by finding alternatives to the commodity or resource.

On the second point, a mistake that non-economists frequently make in discussing policy options is to conceive of the policy problem as one of how to distribute a fixed stock of goods. For example, we noted that there is sufficient food available for human consumption in the world so that every person could consume his or her caloric requirements. Many people when they hear this think, "So the problem is just one of distribution. If people in developed countries just consumed less, the extra food could be used in the developing world, and the undernutrition problem would be solved." The first sentence is true: the problem can be thought of as a distribution problem. But the second sentence is false, or at least grossly misleading.

The amount of food that is available for human consumption depends on the amount of food that farmers worldwide produce. And the amount that farmers produce depends on the economic incentive—the price farmers receive for their output. If people in rich countries made a concerted effort to consume less food—if they spent less money on food and more on items other than food—then the price farmers receive would drop and farmers would produce less food; in the world economy as a whole, resources would move from production of food into production of nonfood items. There would be a positive effect on the undernutrition problem in poor countries, but the effect would be much smaller than imagined by those who think, "If I consume 1,500 fewer calories each day, then that food can be given to people in poor countries, and three people there can each have an extra 500 calories per day."

In order to get this kind of redistribution to work, the rich person would have to continue to buy the food (or at least to pay for its production in some way) and then donate the 1,500 calories per day to the poor people.

The energy crisis of the 1970s provides excellent examples of the human responses to economic incentives. During the 1970s, oil prices shot up dramatically. Many people perceived this as an inevitable result of growing demand for a fixed resource, and therefore predicted that prices would continue to rise. But the high prices for petroleum products caused a number of reactions over time. People began to use the resource more efficiently: auto gas mileage increased, and people began to insulate their homes more effectively. Oil exploration companies discovered new sources of oil and developed ways to pump more of the oil out of the ground. Alternative energy sources—nuclear, solar, and wind power—grew. As a result of these reactions, prices of oil and gas did not continue to rise.

Economics and the World Food Problem

How do these economic insights apply to the problem of worldwide undernutrition? What is the "optimal" nutrition policy? What kinds of government programs can be used to achieve the objective of reducing undernutrition?

Optimal Policy to Reduce Undernutrition

The benefits of reducing undernutrition are obvious: lives saved, health improved, productivity increased. For an individual case, the costs of achieving adequate nutrition are remarkably low. In countries with an average calorie deficit (see Chapter 6, Table 6.5, for a partial list), 250 calories per person per day would erase the deficit. (Though derived in a different way, this is consistent with the FAO estimates of average calorie deficits among people who are undernourished, ranging from about 100 to 500 calories per person per day— see the FAO's 2001 *State of Food Insecurity in the World* report.) Two hundred and fifty calories is about the equivalent of a peanut butter sandwich (two slices of bread and 2 tablespoons of peanut butter is 370 calories). The cost of a peanut butter sandwich is 35 cents. If you put $5,000 in a bank account paying 2 percent annual interest, you could take out 35 cents a day from that account for seventy-five years. Thus, we can conclude that there are a substantial number of people whose lives could be saved at a cost of $5,000. Compare this to an estimated "value of human life" of $150,000 to $360,000 found in a study of Indian manufacturing workers (Simon et al. 1999).

Or, compare this $5,000 figure to the estimated costs of saving a life implicit in policy choices made in the United States, shown in Table 16.1. Saving lives by means of improved nutrition is an incredible bargain. Economic analysis here serves only to raise the question: If the benefit-cost ratio is so favorable, why haven't policymakers leapt to make the investments necessary to substantially eliminate undernutrition?

There are a couple of possible answers. The first has to do with targeting. The preceding calculation assumes that the peanut butter sandwich actually gets eaten by a person who is undernourished. But in reality food donations are sometimes diverted to people who are not undernourished. A report (Strategy Page 2004) on the situation in North Korea states,

> The current food crisis is a result of foreign donors refusing to contribute food for North Korea because the government has not allowed foreigners to observe where the donated food goes. Other witnesses have consistently reported that the donated food goes to the armed forces and is not sent to areas where there has been unrest, or where the government suspects there might be unrest (because a number of locals have fled to China or Russia). . . . New supplies will not arrive for several months. But after that, the food aid could dry up again if the North Korean government does not become more cooperative.

Table 16.1 Dollar Costs per Life Saved of Various Regulations in the United States

Government Action	Cost per Life Saved
Requiring seat belts and air bags in cars	$100,000
Banning flammable sleepwear for children	$1,200,000
Requiring seat belts in rear seats of cars	$3,800,000
Restricting arsenic emissions from glass- manufacturing plants	$40,200,000
Banning asbestos	$329,000,000

Source: Viscusi and Gayer 2002; Viscusi 1993.

It is natural to want to avoid being "conned"—tricked into making chari-table donations to people who do not deserve our charity. From an economic standpoint, however, even if only one in ten of the donations hits its mark, the program would still be more cost effective than any of the policy steps listed in Table 16.1. A more cynical answer is that the people dying from lack of seatbelts or from asbestos are "like us" and therefore it is worth the high cost to save those lives. We can empathize with the people who would die in the absence of the government policy, but we imagine the people dying from un-dernutrition are "not like us"—we cannot imagine being that poor, and there-fore our empathy is low. Subramanian and Cropper (1995) cite other unfunded programs that would save lives at a low cost.

Finally, the $5,000 figure from the preceding example is the cost of saving a single life, without taking into account any impacts on market prices that would occur if the policy were aimed at reducing undernutrition among many of the 800 million suffering from it. As subsequent chapters will explain, a large-scale program would increase food prices and environmental costs asso-ciated with increased food production.

Policy Instruments to Reduce Undernutrition

Economic analysis has a lot more to contribute to the question: What kinds of policy actions can contribute to reduced undernutrition? Most of the rest of the book is devoted to some answers to this question. The supply-demand frame-work helps organize the discussion.

Chapter 7 emphasized the two elements of the food security equation—income and price. For the most part, our policy discussion can be broken down into policies that influence income and policies that influence price.

Policies to raise incomes of the poor. Chapter 17 will discuss policies that raise the incomes of the poor. There are two possibilities: redistributing income from rich to poor, or improving the rate of economic growth.

The main economic rationale for redistributing income from the rich to the poor is the belief in declining marginal utility of income. Previously we discussed the principle that as food consumption increases, unit by unit, declining marginal benefits (or "decreasing marginal utility") accrue from adding an additional unit. Many economists accept the hypothesis that this principle can be extended to cover the consumption of all goods taken together: thus a decreasing marginal utility of income.

A direct implication of this is that a dollar is worth more to a poor person than to a rich person. On the one hand, the idea is that a couple more dollars to a poor person will be spent on necessities—items that are fundamental to life. On the other hand, taking a couple dollars away from a rich person will cause that person to consume fewer frivolous things. The research relating income to happiness (see Chapter 9, Box 9.2) is consistent with this hypothesis. A 10 percent increase in income has the same impact on happiness regardless of the income level, so taking $1,000 from a person making $100,000 (reducing her or his income by 1 percent) and giving the $1,000 to a person making $10,000 (increasing his or her income by 10 percent) will increase the poor person's happiness more than it decreases the rich person's happiness. Therefore, this transfer from rich to poor increases the "common good." This may explain why governments are motivated to adopt programs that have the effect of redistributing wealth from the rich to the poor.

The practical problem is that the "declining marginal utility of income" hypothesis implies that the appropriate policy is a total and complete equality of income distribution. If one person in the country (or the world) earns slightly more than another, then dollars should be taken from the former and given to the latter. Most people reject this policy prescription. That rejection raises questions about whether this is the true explanation for policy concern about the poor and hungry.

There is much literature on the subject of what kinds of policies may promote general economic growth. Our discussion in Chapter 17 will give a general overview. In it we will address the issue of globalization and whether integration into the global economy can be beneficial to growth rates in developing countries.

Policies to reduce the price of food. Chapters 18 through 22 will consider a variety of policies that may cause the price of food to be lower than it otherwise would be. Chapter 18 discusses population control policies. If population growth can be reduced, the demand curve for food will not shift out as fast, food supplies per capita will be higher, and food prices will be lower than they otherwise would have been.

Chapters 19 through 22 consider policies that target food prices more directly. These policies can be thought of in one of two ways. They can distort the social equilibrium and cause a reduction in economic efficiency, or they can correct a distortion and increase economic efficiency.

If the aggregate supply-and-demand curves represent the true social costs and benefits, then policies that alter the equilibrium price are "distortionary"— they reduce economic efficiency. This is illustrated in Figure 16.1, wherein a government policy creates a wedge between the price that consumers pay and the price that farmers receive. Perhaps the program is one that sells food to consumers at below cost, or perhaps the program pays subsidies to farmers, or perhaps the subsidy is paid to firms in the processing or marketing sector. In any case, the price received by farmers is higher than the price paid by consumers (the difference between the price at point A and the price at point D in the figure).

This type of policy achieves the direct objective we are looking for here: quantity increases (from the "market quantity" to the "quantity with the program" in the figure). But the policy reduces economic efficiency. As the quantity produced increases above the market quantity, the cost of producing an additional unit exceeds the value that consumers get from consuming the additional unit. The quantity of this efficiency cost is shown as the shaded triangle in Figure 16.1. Subsidies also have a direct cost paid by the government. This is the amount paid per unit (producer price minus consumer price) times the number of units. This cost is shown as rectangle ABCD in the figure.

But policies that change prices can sometimes be seen as "corrective." For example, we discussed previously the possibility that production or consumption of a good might create external benefits that are not reflected in the market

Figure 16.1 Impact of a Policy That Subsidizes Production or Consumption

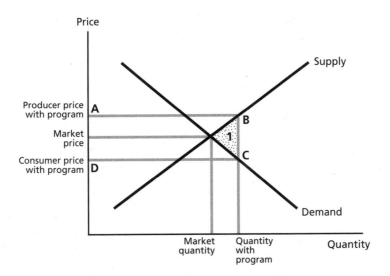

supply-and-demand curves. In this case, the market equilibrium quantity will be lower than the optimum, and a government policy to subsidize consumption or production may correct the situation.

Economist Arnold Harberger (1983) suggested that we all (or at least many of us) suffer when any person in the world (or country or ethnic group or family) suffers from undernutrition or failure to meet basic needs. When a hungry person is fed, a direct benefit goes to that person (which benefit is reflected in the market transaction), but also an indirect benefit goes to us, because we care about human suffering. This indirect benefit is external to the market. Because such a reduction affects our happiness, we would be willing to pay to see the incidence of hunger reduced or eliminated. The reduction of hunger is a good: the more it happens, the better we feel. But there is no market on which we can purchase this good. This is a case of missing markets, or *externalities*. Private action is unlikely to solve this problem. Because we know others also care, we may wait for *them* to take actions to reduce hunger, in which case *we* get the good (reduced world hunger) free of charge. Government action may be justified in creating an artificial market by collecting money from each of us who derives satisfaction from reductions in hunger, and using that money to reduce hunger.

Chapter 21 will examine another kind of corrective action: removing distortive policies that actually *reduce* food output and consumption. Chapter 22 will discuss policies that cause the aggregate supply curve to shift out, increasing output and reducing price. These policies include investments in research and development, where private markets may underinvest. They also include government interventions to correct market failures in the provision of loans to farmers.

17

Raising the Incomes
of the Poor

The world's hungry are hungry because they are poor. They cannot afford enough food to provide their basic needs. Policies to alleviate their poverty fall into two categories: policies that promote general economic growth and policies that redistribute income or wealth from rich to poor.

Economic Growth

There is no doubt that broad-based economic growth is one of the most effective antipoverty programs. Economic growth creates jobs and raises the incomes of the poor. From Chapter 9, Figure 9.1 provides some evidence of the benefits of economic growth. A 2002 paper by Dollar and Kraay concludes

- On average, growth helps the poor as much as the average person in a country, simultaneously, without waiting for a trickle-down.
- When incomes *fall*, poor do not get hurt disproportionately.
- Globalization, and improving rule of law (property rights), improve growth, and the poor share in that growth (more on these issues later).
- Cutting inflation and cutting public spending spur growth, and the poor gain more than the rich from that growth.

A paper by Haddad and Alderman (2000) looked specifically at the relationship of income growth to the prevalence of undernutrition. "Some people argue that the way to meet nutrition targets is to stimulate greater economic growth and higher incomes for poor people. . . . Others, however, argue that income growth is a blunt instrument for reducing malnutrition. . . . What do the data say about how far income growth can take us?" The answer provided by Alderman and Haddad is twofold. One the one hand, "There is a strong and regular relationship of malnutrition to GDP [per capita]. . . . [And] income growth indeed contributed to improved nutritional status." On the other hand, income growth may be a slow and inefficient way of addressing undernutrition: "It would take many years of high growth . . . to reduce the prevalence of underweight children even by 50%. . . . Direct interventions are needed to reduce malnutrition in the short to medium term."

The history of the past five decades frames the debate over what kinds of policies best promote economic growth. A couple things are obvious:

• *Economic growth is possible.* For example, per capita income in Thailand grew from $1,054 in 1970 to $5,210 in 2012 (in constant, or inflation-adjusted, dollars). South Korean incomes grew from $2,662 in 1970 to $22,670 in 2012. Of a comprehensive sample of fifty-eight countries with low incomes in 1970 (per capita incomes of less than $1,800), per capita incomes doubled in thirty-two of them by 2012.

• *Economic growth is not inevitable.* In these fifty-eight low-income countries, per capita incomes declined in ten countries over the 1970–2012 period, and grew by less than 1 percent per year in eleven other countries. Per capita income in the Democratic Republic of Congo fell from $530 in 1970 to $220 in 2012. Per capita income in Zimbabwe fell from $1,457 (above where Thailand was) in 1970 to $680 (about 13 percent of the Thai level) in 2012.

The growth in prosperity of South Korea stands in stark contrast to the lack of growth in North Korea. Another example of two countries with different growth paths is found on the Caribbean island of Hispaniola, which is split into two countries—Haiti on the western end and the Dominican Republic on the eastern end. In 1950, the two countries had virtually identical incomes per capita—about $2,000 per person per year in current dollars. By 2008, incomes in the Dominican Republic had risen to about $9,000, while incomes in Haiti had fallen to below $1,500 (Acemoglu and Robinson 2012).

A large economics literature deals with prerequisites and policies concerning economic growth. See the World Bank website on macroeconomics and growth (World Bank 2016) for a review of the issues and a guide to the literature. If there were a simple strategy that guaranteed economic growth, then we would see growth everywhere (and this would be a very short chapter). But there is no such simple strategy, and economists continue to debate which approaches are most likely to be successful.

Evolution of the Washington Consensus

In the 1980s and earlier, most attention was focused on macroeconomic policy as the main determinant of successful economic growth. In 1990, John Williamson published a paper that laid out the general consensus about what policies Latin American countries should adopt to promote growth. This set of recommendations became known as the Washington Consensus, because it reflected the thinking of economists at the World Bank and the International Monetary Fund (IMF). The Washington Consensus is based on the observation that economic growth comes from three main sources:

- High savings leading to increased capital stock.
- High labor productivity.
- Adoption of new technology.

This translates into three broad sets of policy recommendations:

- Promotion of savings and investment through good macroeconomic policy.
- Promotion of labor productivity through education, health, and antipoverty programs.
- Market orientation to promote appropriate incentives to economic decisionmakers.

Rodrik summarizes the original Washington Consensus as prescribing "a simple and universal list of policy reforms: liberalize trade, privatize public enterprises, deregulate prices, bring down inflation through monetary and fiscal retrenchment," and notes that the consensus evolved to include "deeper institutional reforms: fight corruption, improve courts, enhance public administration, improve regulation" (2008:2). These recommendations were successfully followed by a number of countries, notably the high-growth Asian countries. However, they were not universally successful.

The recognition that "pro-growth policy" should be defined broadly enough to include initiatives to change underlying institutional arrangements led economists to expand their scope of analysis. Easterly and Levine (2002) did an extensive empirical analysis to see whether high rates of economic growth could be explained by (a) geography (climate, access to the sea), (b) institutions (property rights, democracy, individual liberty), or (c) policies (low inflation, openness to international trade, stable exchange rates). Their answer: institutions make the biggest difference. "Good" policies cannot overcome the disadvantage of "bad" institutions. (Easterly and Levine do find an indirect effect of geography on quality of institutions: European colonizers settled in larger numbers in colonies with moderate climates, and these colonizers brought their European institutions with them.) Institutions will be discussed in more detail later.

In 2008, the Commission on Growth and Development, under the leadership of Nobel Prize–winning economist Michael Spence, produced a report enunciating a "new consensus" that each country must discover its own path to economic growth:

The Spence report represents a watershed for development policy—as much for what it says as for what it leaves out. Gone are confident assertions about the virtues of liberalization, deregulation, privatization, and free markets. Gone are the cookie cutter policy recommendations unaffected by contextual differences. . . . Yes, successful economies have many things in common: they all engage in the global economy, maintain macroeconomic stability, stimulate saving and investment, provide market-oriented incentives, and are reasonably well governed. [These] frame the conduct of appropriate economic policies. Saying that context matters does not mean that anything goes. But there is no universal rule-book; different countries achieve these ends differently. . . . The new policy mindset . . . is explicitly diagnostic and focuses on the most significant economic bottlenecks and constraints. Rather than comprehensive reform, it emphasizes . . . narrowly targeted initiatives in order to discover local solutions. (Rodrik 2008:pp. 1–2)

Institutions and Economic Growth

Economist Douglass North gives this definition of institutions: "Institutions are the way we structure human interaction—political, social and economic—and are the incentive framework of a society. They are made up of formal rules (constitutions, laws and regulations), informal constraints (norms, conventions and codes of conduct), and their enforcement characteristics" (2005:A14).

Thinking of "institutions" as defining the incentive framework of a society leads to the following (perhaps obvious) observations. The incentive framework is more likely to lead to success if it:

• Rewards people for success resulting from their effort.
• Punishes people for failure caused by their decisions.
• Encourages people to focus on producing things of economic value rather than expending effort overcoming impediments and quarreling with one another about who should get how much of the things society does produce.

There are at least three interrelated aspects: assignment and enforcement of property rights, regulatory efficiency, and lack of corruption.

Property rights assign ownership of productive assets to individuals and give the owners the legally enforceable right to use those assets as they choose. Economist Hernando de Soto (2000) has been a leading voice about the importance of property rights to economic growth. He notes the following advantages that flow from a system of well-identified and clearly enforceable property rights: (1) the property or assets can be pledged as collateral, thus improving the availability of credit; (2) assets can be divided or consolidated in an efficient way among users, so that (for example) where small farms are more efficient, small farms can evolve by sale or rental of land that breaks up inefficient large farms; (3) assets can be owned and managed by the individual who is best suited; (4) information about asset value is more readily available, allowing investors from far away to evaluate investment opportunities; (5) tying an individual owner to an individual piece of property (especially real estate) makes it easier to identify, locate, and enforce agreements with that person.

De Soto cites numerous examples of problems that arise where property rights are not well developed, or not enforceable. Squatters in developing countries build homes on land they do not own; but the squatters cannot borrow money against the value of those homes, and the squatters have little incentive to improve the quality of the homes, since they could be thrown out at any instant. Tribal chiefs assign farmland to tribal members; but the farmer has little incentive to improve the land, since it may be reassigned next season.

Regulatory inefficiency can contribute to weak property rights. *The Economist* (2001) reports that in the Philippines, it can take thirteen to twenty-five years for a squatter to complete all the legal steps required to obtain ownership of the land on which he lives; in Egypt, it can take six to eleven years for an owner of farmland to obtain legal permission to build a house on that land. Many other examples, and country-by-country indicators of regulatory efficiency, can be found in reports from the Doing Business website of the World Bank (http://www.doingbusiness.org/downloads).

Government bureaucracies can be inefficient, and regulations governing economic transactions can be cumbersome, even when the bureaucrats and regulators are impeccably honest. But the possibility of government corruption adds another layer to the problem of regulatory efficiency, as dishonest regulators may deliberately hold up the regulatory process in order to put pressure on people to "facilitate" the bureaucracy with a bribe or other emolument. The organization Transparency International (http://www.transparency.org) publishes a Corruption Perceptions Index and a Bribe Payers Index that rank countries according to various measures of corruption. Mauro undertakes an empirical analysis of the relationship between corruption and economic growth and concludes that "corruption may have large, adverse effects on economic growth and investment" (1997:93).

One (imperfect) check on government corruption is a healthy democratic process and an adversarial free press. *The Economist* has developed a Democracy Index that ranks countries according to whether they have a competitive multiparty political system, universal suffrage, regularly contested elections, and media access (see Kekic 2007).

One measure of how important institutional arrangements are to economic prosperity comes from Hendricks (2002). He compares output per worker of immigrants to the United States with output per worker of people who remain in the migrants' home countries. Overall, he finds migrating to the US makes workers about four times more productive. About one-third of that improved productivity is attributable to the fact that workers in the United States have better physical capital—better tools and equipment. The other two-thirds is attributable to the fact the institutional environment in the United States is more conducive to productivity.

Globalization and Economic Growth

Since the early 1990s, a vociferous debate has taken place about the desirability of globalization. Though the term may mean different things to different people, it refers generally to a policy of increasing integration of countries in the world economy. For developing countries, a policy that embraced globalization would entail

- Opening borders to trade by reducing impediments to imports and exports, and subjecting these regulations to restrictions imposed by the World Trade Organization (WTO).
- Adopting macroeconomic policies required as conditions for loans from the International Monetary Fund.
- Adopting market-oriented industrial, agricultural, and sectoral policies, as a condition of obtaining IMF loans.
- Reducing restrictions or regulations that discourage foreign investment.
- Adopting labor or environmental policies or both that will attract foreign investment.

As this list makes clear, globalization promotes the same kinds of policies that make up the Washington Consensus. Critics of globalization raise the following objections:

- Policies that attract investment are policies that encourage or permit low wages, poor working conditions, and poor environmental quality.
- Fiscal policies imposed by the IMF require countries to reduce or eliminate health, education, and poverty alleviation programs.
- Policies imposed by the IMF and the WTO are antidemocratic, since these international organizations may countermand decisions made by democratically elected leaders and legislatures.
- There is also a suspicion on the part of globalization critics that the international organizations are controlled by multinational corporations, and that the entire globalization effort is intended to harm ordinary people in order to enrich these corporations.

But has increased globalization been good for economic growth of poor countries, and has it been beneficial to the poorest people in poor countries? Paul Collier and David Dollar (2002) of the World Bank conducted a study in which they divided countries into three groups: in rich countries, income per capita grew at an annual rate of about 2 percent per year; in "more globalized" poor countries—poor countries with a relatively high proportion of international trade to national income—income per capita grew at an annual rate of 5 percent per year; in "less globalized" poor countries, income per capita *declined* at a rate of 1 percent per year.

The comparative experiences of Asia (which experienced dramatic economic growth from the early 1980s to the late 1990s) and Africa (which had stagnant growth over the same period) suggest that integration into the global economy can be good for growth.

Per capita incomes in Southeast Asia and sub-Saharan Africa were nearly identical from 1970 to the mid-1980s. Then per capita income in Southeast Asia shot up, while per capita income in Africa regressed. By 2014, the Asian incomes were about two-and-a-half times higher than those in Africa. Court and Yanagihara (n.d.) provide evidence that this was related to the fact that during the 1980s and 1990s, Asian governments adopted policies that embraced world markets. Exports from Southeast Asian countries grew at over 12 percent per year from 1985 to 1995; exports from sub-Saharan African countries grew at 3 percent over this period. In the mid-1970s, exports were about 30 percent of GNP in both regions; by 1997, exports were over 50 percent of Asian GDP but were still at 30 percent in sub-Saharan Africa. In the early 1970s, foreign direct investment was nearly zero in Malaysia, Indonesia, Ghana, and Kenya. By the late 1990s, it was still nearly zero in the African countries but had grown to $4–6 million a year in the Asian countries.

As described in Chapter 9, many countries in sub-Saharan Africa have grown much more strongly since the turn of the twenty-first century compared to earlier periods. And there is evidence that the strong growth is occurring during a period of growing globalization of African economies. Figure 17.1 shows how foreign direct investment in Africa has grown faster than in Asia since the late 1990s, and especially since 2006. And trade between Africa and the rest of the world also began to grow during the period. In the early 1990s, exports from East Asia and the Pacific were $767 billion per year on average, while exports from sub-Saharan Africa were about 2 percent of that level— $17 billion per year. In the 2010–2014 period, East Asian exports had grown to $5 trillion; sub-Saharan Africa's exports had growth to $270 billion per year—now over 5 percent of the Asian figure.

A paper by MacMillan, Rodrik, and Verduzco-Gallo examines the causes of growth differences in different parts of the world. They note that "large gaps in labor productivity between the traditional and modern parts of the economy are a fundamental reality of developing economies" (2014:11). A major source of economic growth, they argue, is the movement of people from one sector to another. In Asia, the movement has been from the low-productivity sector to the high-productivity sector, and this movement has propelled Asian countries to faster economic growth. In Africa during the 1990s, the movement of population was in the opposite direction—from the high-productivity sector to the low-productivity sector, explaining the relatively low economic growth in

Figure 17.1 Index of Foreign Direct Investment in Developing Countries: Sub-Saharan Africa and Asia, 1990-2014

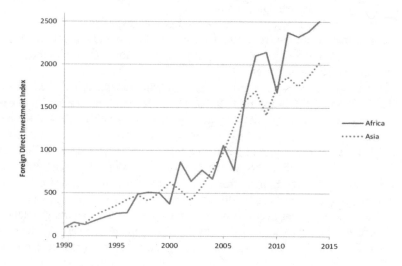

Source: UNCTAD 2011 and 2015: tab. 1.

Africa. However, since 2000, the situation is turning around in Africa, and "structural change"—the movement of people to the high-productivity sector—is behind the recent growth spurts observed on the continent.

Can globalization explain these different patterns of structural change? MacMillan, Rodrik, and Verduzco-Gallo find no general pattern. "All . . . countries in our sample have become more globalized during the time period under consideration. They have phased out . . . quantitative restrictions on imports, slashed tariffs, encouraged direct foreign investment. . . . However it is also clear that [the role of globalization] cannot have been a direct, straightforward one. . . . A common external environment cannot explain such large differences [in structural change]. . . . So whatever contribution globalization has made, it must depend heavily on local circumstances, choices made by domestic policy makers, and domestic growth strategies" (2014:25).

The financial crisis in many Asian economies in the late 1990s reveals some of the weaknesses of the globalization strategy. Nobel Prize–winning economist Joseph Stiglitz (2002) points out that policies imposed by international bodies do not always take into account the special circumstances of each country. Private-sector solutions require the existence of an institutional and cultural infrastructure that may not exist in every case. The best macroeconomic policy is not the same for all countries at all times. The pace of globalization can influence its effectiveness. Stiglitz calls for the globalization process to be reformed so that it can help poor countries grow.

Pranab Bardhan (2006) says that the experiences of three large Asian countries (China, India, and Indonesia) serve as the basis for many pro-globalization arguments because those countries did embrace globalization and poverty rates fell dramatically. But, he argues, in each of those countries there is an alternative explanation for the decline in poverty: China lifted restrictions on rural-to-urban migration, reformed land- and grain-purchasing policies, and built new infrastructure; India saw increased agricultural prosperity from the green revolution; Indonesia adopted successful macroeconomic policies.

But perhaps these kinds of beneficial policies go hand-in-hand with globalization. Economist Anne Harrison (2007) summarizes the results of fifteen country studies as showing that globalization can help the poor, but only if appropriate policies and institutions are in place in the globalizing country. The poor will gain from globalization when the economy encourages mobility from sector to sector and from region to region, and when policies have been put in place to help poor farmers get access to funds for investment. (Chapter 22 of this book covers policies to expand farm production capacity.)

Agricultural Development

In addition to these recommendations for growth, some economists would emphasize the importance of promoting growth in the agricultural sector (DFID 2002). The economies of almost all developing countries are dominated by the agricultural sector. One of the most important stimulants to economic growth and increased employment in these economies is increased agricultural production. This is important not only because increased agricultural production increases farm employment but also because increasing the quantity of food supplied lowers its price.

Food is a wage good (Mellor and Johnston 1984). That is, the cost of food can substantially affect the wage rate. Consider two developing countries that are competing in the international marketplace to sell a labor-intensive product such as shoes. In country A the price of food is high, and in country B it is low. Even though a shoe manufacturer in country B pays lower wages than his competitor in country A, the workers in the shoe factory in country B can live as well as those in country A because they can buy food more cheaply. Low food prices stimulate employment.

As low food prices make possible low wage rates, employment is stimulated not only in the export sector but also in the domestic sector of the economy. Local manufacturers can compete more successfully with importers to manufacture goods. Low food prices reduce the proportion of the household budget that all people, middle- and upper-income people as well as low-income people, must allocate to food, thus release purchasing power for nonfood items. This raises the demand for nonfood goods and services and further increases employment.

Stimulating agricultural production will involve making policy shifts away from the large number of production disincentives now in place and toward production incentives (see Chapter 21). There are other avenues to stimulating increased agricultural production, such as government sponsorship of agricultural research (see Chapter 22) and educational services or improved roads (see Box 17.1).

Box 17.1 Roads in Africa

Western travelers to sub-Saharan Africa are often amazed by the lack of adequately paved roads and highways. For example, a visitor to Zambia in the late 1990s would find that one of the main highways leaving the capital of Lusaka was only one lane in each direction, and those lanes were riddled with potholes, causing average speeds to fall to about 35 kilometers per hour. Experienced drivers would swerve into the wrong lane, or out onto an unpaved shoulder to avoid some of the worst of the potholes. And off of this main highway, "roads" were simply dirt tracks, sometimes made impassable by ditches carved by flooding rains.

The magazine *The Economist* ("The Road to Hell Is Not Paved," 2002) sent a reporter to ride along with a beer truck driver delivering beer to a town 500 kilometers from the brewery. The truck was stopped at police road blocks forty-seven times. Sometimes, the policeman only wanted to check the driver's papers; sometimes, the policeman wanted cash; sometimes, the policeman wanted a beer. Only two-thirds of the truckload of beer arrived at its destination. At one such stop, seven policemen and the three people in the truck spent three and a half hours negotiating the terms of passage (they settled on $12). One policeman, citing a hitherto-unknown law, was challenged by the driver and responded: "Do you have a gun? No. I have a gun, so I know the rules." Along one stretch of road, locked barriers had been erected to stop heavy trucks that tear up the dirt roads when they are wet. But the man with the key was nowhere to be found. When they found the man with the key and opened the barriers, they drove a few more miles and discovered that a bridge was out. All in all, the 313-mile trip took four days.

In 2006–2007, the West African Trade Hub project of USAID (2007) undertook a study of travel conditions between Ouagadougou in Burkina Faso and three other cities (Tema in Ghana, Bamako in Mali, and Lomé in Togo). Truck drivers were outfitted with impeccable credentials and sent to drive the routes. On the worst stretch (417 kilometers in Mali), drivers were stopped nineteen times with a delay of over two and a half hours and paid $105 in bribes. (For comparison, a truck driver on a modern highway without stops could expect to complete the 417-kilometer trip in about four hours.)

An analysis of public investments in India (Fan, Hazell, and Thorat 2000) found that investments in road construction had a greater impact on poverty reduction than any other type of public investment.

Economic Growth and the Reduction of Undernutrition

In Chapter 9, Figure 9.1 showed that the percentage of population that is undernourished declines as a country's income per capita grows. The data on a continental level confirm this relationship. Per capita income growth in East Asia (which includes China) grew at 5.6 percent per year between 1970 and 1990 and 7.5 percent per year between 1990 and 2012 (UNICEF 2013: tab. 7). Growth in South Asia (which includes India) also grew quickly—2 percent per year from 1970 to 1990 and 4.6 percent from 1990 to 2012. In Chapter 6, Table 6.2 shows that during the four decades of rapid growth in per capita incomes, Asia made enormous progress in reducing the incidence of undernutrition:the percentage of people suffering from undernutrition dropped from 41 percent in 1969–1971 to 12.3 percent in 2014–2016. In Latin America, per capita income growth was a little slower (annual income growth of 1.4 percent and 1.7 percent in the two periods), and progress on undernutrition was a little less (20 percent and 5.5 percent undernourished in the two periods). But in Africa, where per capita income growth was much lower (zero growth in per capita income from 1970 to 1990 and 2.1 percent annual growth from 1990 to 2012), the reduction in undernutrition was also much lower (36 percent and 23 percent in the two periods). This reaffirms the preceding conclusion that per capita income growth reaches the poorest of the poor and improves their nutritional status.

While these numbers (or see the discussion of Haddad and Alderman earlier in this chapter) make a compelling case at the national (or macro) level, the evidence from the household (or micro) level raises some interesting questions. Subramanian and Deaton review the state of debate:

> In the recent literature . . . , there is debate on the extent to which nutrition responds to income. For many years, conventional wisdom has held that hunger and malnutrition would be eliminated by economic growth. . . . [S]ome recent studies . . . have argued that the elasticity is close to zero, so that "increases in income will not result in substantial improvements in nutrient intakes" [Behrman and Deolalikar 1987:505]. If this position is accepted, there are important implications for the way economists think about development. In accord with some popular beliefs, economic policies that are good for growth do not imply the elimination of hunger. Indeed, even policies that increase the incomes of the poorest may not improve their nutrition. [This] also creates a chasm between the way economists think about living standards . . . and the way living standards are often characterized by nutritionists and development practitioners, who see development largely in terms of guaranteeing that people have enough to eat. . . . To take but one example, economists think of substitution possibilities as welfare enhancing; if it is possible to substitute across a wide range of foods, consumers are well protected against changes in relative prices. To the nutritionist concerned only with adequate diet, welfare is decreased by voluntary substitution away from approved to disapproved food. (1996: 134–135)

In their study of the Indian village of Maharastra, Subramanian and Deaton found that calories could be purchased quite inexpensively—a 600-calorie-per-day deficit could be eliminated by spending 4 percent of the daily wage—and that even the poorest individuals could afford adequate calories. But instead of focusing solely on increasing calorie intake, households allocate their food expenditures to better-tasting but less nutritious food. "If nutrition is a trap, it is one from which there is a ready escape" (Subramanian and Deaton 1996:135).

Programs That Redistribute Wealth or Income Within a Country

Previously we discussed growth in *average* income per capita as a way of reducing undernutrition. Implicit in this is that increases in average income go hand-in-hand with increases in the incomes of the poor and undernourished; and as mentioned, the research by Dollar and Kraay confirm this interlinkage.

However, another way to address the problem of undernutrition is by focusing specifically on increasing the incomes of the poor and undernourished—regardless of how that affects the average income. There are three ways to accomplish this: (1) we can raise the market incomes of the poor by increasing their labor productivity; (2) we can eliminate structural or market imperfections that allow some members of society to exploit the poor and pay them less than their marginal product is worth; (3) we can institute redistributive policies that add to the market incomes of the poor by taxing or taking away from the market incomes of the rich.

Programs to Increase Human Capital of the Poor

Economic theory tells us that in perfectly functioning competitive markets, a person's wage reflects the person's labor productivity. Viewed from this perspective, the issue of "income inequality" is fundamentally an issue of "productivity inequality."

An individual's potential labor productivity depends on some immutable characteristics of the individual but also is influenced strongly by the person's "human capital"—job skills, capacity to learn new job skills, general knowledge that may be helpful in job performance, good health, and other similar intangibles.

The kinds of government policies and programs that increase human capital among the poor include things like

- Improving education of the poor.
- Providing job training.
- Improving healthcare access, or other programs to improve health (see Chapter 15).

Even programs that improve communication and transportation can be effective indirectly in improving human capital of the poor by providing better access to information, education, and markets.

Of course, undernutrition and poverty are part of a vicious cycle—low incomes cause undernutrition, which causes low productivity and therefore low incomes. So programs intended to improve nutrition of the poor will increase the human capital of the poor and make them more productive.

Programs to Eliminate Structural or Market Imperfections That Exploit the Poor

Economists recognize that the conditions of perfect competition often fail to apply in real-world situations. These "market failures" can lead to situations in which wages, income, and wealth of the poor are kept artificially low. Stiglitz explains: one of the reasons that we see enormous wealth inequality is that "there can be an increase in what might be called "exploitation" rents. . . . [W]e will use the term[s] 'market power' and 'exploitation' interchangeably. The deviations from the competitive benchmark that we are interested in here take on many forms besides that classically associated with imperfect competition in product or labor markets. There can also be exploitation by corporate or other special interests of the public" (2015:23).

Here we look briefly at three types of policy interventions that may reduce, eliminate, or ameliorate the impacts of market imperfections and power imbalances: minimum-wage laws (and related regulations on working conditions), land reform, and government assistance for victims of natural disasters.

Minimum-wage laws are often viewed as an effective way to improve the income of the poor. There is no question that, for those workers covered by minimum-wage legislation and whose wages are higher than they would otherwise be, minimum-wage laws yield a higher standard of living. However, effective minimum-wage legislation, as it raises wages at the bottom end of the scale, motivates entrepreneurs to substitute capital for labor. This drives labor out of the economy covered by minimum wage and increases unemployment in the economy generally (Mincer 1976). In addition, minimum-wage laws are more easily enforced in urban than in rural areas. Therefore, they may not be effective in raising incomes of the rural poor.

A common way of exploiting the poor, especially the agricultural poor, is to keep them "land poor" with land tenure systems that concentrate landownership in the hands of the few. Since 1960 virtually every country in the world has passed land reform laws (de Janvry 1981:385). Land reform can mean many things, but typically it means at least one of the following:

1. *Redistributing the ownership of private or public land in order to change the pattern of land distribution and size of holding.* At one extreme this might mean creating small plots from large blocks of land and allocating these

small plots to the poor. At the other extreme it might mean nationalizing all agricultural land and assigning it to large, state-owned farms.

2. *Changing the rights associated with land.* For instance, tenant farmers or sharecroppers can be made owners of the land they work. Lenders, too, can be prohibited from taking land from smallholders for lack of payment of debt.

Land reform can also consolidate individual fragmented holdings into contiguous blocks of land (World Bank 1975:2–21). This kind of reform is intended to improve productivity, not to redistribute wealth. But in most cases of land reform, the hope is that the twin objectives of accelerated growth and increased equity can be accomplished.

There are two ways in which land reform can promote agricultural productivity. In cases where concentrated landholdings make it difficult to monitor and control production decisions, production per unit of land may be lower on large farms than on small farms. If so, dividing up large landholdings should result in increases in productivity. In addition, farmers with a permanent ownership interest in land have more incentive to make improvements on the land, and to work longer hours than would sharecropping farmers who share the fruits of their labor with an absentee owner (Herring 1983).

Deininger and Squire (1998) showed that rates of national economic growth are higher in countries where land is distributed more equally. Using a similar dataset, Deininger and Olinto (2000) examined the experiences of sixty countries over the period 1966 to 1990. Of the thirty-five countries with Gini coefficients on land distribution of less than 0.72 (remember, a lower Gini means a more equal distribution), twenty-one had growth rates that were higher than average. Of the twenty-five countries with land Gini coefficients higher than 0.72, only six had growth rates higher than average.

However, in some instances, land redistribution has created impediments for economic growth. For example the Communist Revolution in China brought with it an agrarian reform that eliminated private ownership of land in the early 1950s. The move to communal ownership initially spurred agricultural production; but by the late 1950s agricultural production had stagnated (see Chapter 2, Box 2.3, page 14). Ultimately, during the 1980s, as laws were changed to return agricultural land to private ownership, landholdings became more concentrated (Ying 1996).

Other attempts at land reform have produced unforeseen consequences, some of which made the supposed beneficiaries worse off than they might have been without the reform. One of the most pressing goals of the 1962 Algerian land reform was to provide employment for as many workers as possible. Yet it did not take the self-management committees on the newly nationalized large estates long to realize that fewer workers on their farms meant more returns per worker, and an early study of the situation showed that employment on the farms actually decreasing after reform (Foster and Steiner

1964). Pfeifer concluded that the Algerian reform "promoted, rather than curtailed, the class differentiation of agricultural producers into successful commercial farmers and propertyless wage workers" (1985:81).

Likewise an agrarian reform law passed in Peru in 1969 was intended to do something about the skewed landownership in that country, but the main beneficiaries turned out to be the relatively well-off permanent workers. Families living outside the sugar plantations received no benefits at all. Alberts concluded that "the agrarian reform did not accomplish a radical and lasting improvement in the degree of equity within the agricultural sector. The economic policies implemented by the military government were not conducive to agricultural growth nor did they accomplish anything toward reducing the urban-rural income gap" (1983:226).

In the early 1950s, Burma (Myanmar) passed a law requiring agricultural land to be worked by its owners. To keep from losing their lands, absentee owners began working the land themselves, forcing their former tenant farmers off the land. The former tenants usually stayed on as laborers, but they no longer enjoyed some of the benefits that had been theirs as tenants (Walinsky 1962:137, 294).

This same Burmese law made it illegal to foreclose on mortgages on agricultural land when the owners defaulted on their loans. Without land to pledge as collateral, farmers had trouble finding people willing to lend money to them, interest rates rose, and agricultural investment declined (Walinsky 1962:504–505).

In the late 1990s, a major land reform program was instituted in Zimbabwe. In 1997, President Mugabe proposed a plan that would seize 10 million acres of farmland owned by about 1,500 large commercial farmers and redistribute it. The land reform initiative was a response to landownership patterns that were established during colonialism when blacks in Zimbabwe (then called Rhodesia) were legally prohibited from owning some of the best farmland. As a result, "whites made up 2 percent of Zimbabwe's population but own[ed] 70 percent of the nation's best land" (Duke 1998:A27). The land reform has been harshly criticized for the way in which it has been implemented, with extralegal bands of squatters seizing farms, and is a contributing factor to the famine conditions in Zimbabwe in recent years.

De Janvry makes this observation: "With agriculture well advanced on the road to modernization . . . any drastic land redistribution is likely to nullify past technological achievements and imply shortfalls in production, at least in the short run. Where the population is increasingly landless and urbanized, the social cost of higher food prices [because of the inefficiencies resulting from land reform] may be more widespread than the welfare gains of land redistribution" (1981:389).

One final problem associated with land reform, or even the threat of land reform, is the chilling effect it may have on investment in agriculture relative to investment in other productive activities. Landowners who fear that land reform may be in the offing are understandably hesitant to invest heavily in productive improvements for their farms. In this view, land reform is part of a number of anti-agricultural policies collectively referred to as *urban bias,* about which we will have more to say in Chapter 21.

Natural disasters—hurricanes, earthquakes, floods—hit all countries and affect people at all income levels. But the poor have less capacity to avoid and adapt to these disasters when they strike. For this reason a program that guarantees assistance for victims of a natural disaster can have the effect of buoying the incomes of the poor relative to the rich. These issues and many examples are discussed in Seck 2007.

Direct Redistribution Programs

Incomes of the poor and undernourished in developing countries can also be raised by direct policies to redistribute income within the country. Studies of developed countries show a wide degree of variation in the extent of redistribution (see Table 17.1). Based on "market income" (income before redistribution), Poland has much more unequal distribution of income than does Taiwan (Poland's Gini is 50 and Taiwan's is 33). But Poland is much more aggressive than Taiwan in redistributing income. After the impact of redistribution is taken into account, Taiwan has a less equal distribution of income than Poland (Taiwan's Gini is 30 and Poland's is 29).

Table 17.1   Impact of Income Redistribution Programs in Fifteen OECD Countries, 1996–2001

	Gini of Disposable Income After Redistribution	Gini of Market Income Before Redistribution	Reduction of Gini Percentage of Before-Distribution Gini
Taiwan	30	33	9
Switzerland	28	36	22
Finland	25	38	34
Romania	28	38	26
Netherlands	25	39	36
Norway	25	41	39
Canada	30	42	29
Denmark	23	42	45
Czech Republic	26	44	41
Sweden	25	46	46
Australia	32	48	33
Germany	28	48	42
United States	37	48	23
Poland	29	50	42
United Kingdom	34	51	33

Source: Brandolini and Smeeding 2007.

These policy tools of redistribution consist of progressive taxation (taxing the rich at a higher rate than the poor) and cash transfer programs for the poor.

Progressive Taxation

Taxes that take a greater percentage of income or wealth from the rich than they do from the poor are called *progressive*. Progressive taxation is one way of transferring income or wealth from the rich to the poor. In developed countries the income tax is usually designed to be progressive, and the same features can be incorporated into the tax structure of the third world, as they often are.

Taxes that take a greater percentage of income or wealth from the poor than they do from the rich are called *regressive*. Sales taxes have a reputation for being regressive. In the developed world the poor spend a greater proportion of their income compared to the rich, who save a greater proportion of theirs. However, in the third world the poor are not generally as well integrated into the market economy as are the rich. The poor are much more likely to barter and exchange goods and services and to raise some of their own food. In a situation like this, even a sales tax may be progressive.

The work of Tanzi and Zee (2000) on taxation in developing countries allows us to draw the following general lessons:

• Taxes in developing countries are low—about half the level of taxes in developed countries.

• Developing countries use taxes on exports and imports much more heavily than do developed countries. One explanation for this is that taxes in exports and imports are easier to collect (compared to income or consumption taxes) with a small group of customs agents monitoring movements into and out of the main port or ports of the country.

• Many developing countries impose consumption taxes (or value-added taxes).

• There is a wide variation about the extent of progressivity of income taxes in developing countries.

These characteristics imply that, on the whole, developed countries use their tax systems more aggressively to redistribute income than do developing countries.

The method of spending the money in the government tax till can have distributive effects just as surely as does the method of collecting it. A government that taxes some rich people only to provide services to other rich people will do little to reduce undernutrition. Spending public money on programs to increase agricultural production (see Chapters 21 and 22) or on programs that subsidize food consumption (see Chapters 19 and 20) is what we think of as the expenditure side of redistribution through progressive taxation. A mere transfer of purchasing power from the rich to the poor may prove less effective as a way of improving the nutrition of the poor. For example:

> Take a simple case within a developing country, say India. If one rupee of purchasing power is taken away from a person in the top 5 percent of the income distribution, that will cause a reduction, in constant prices, of 0.03 rupee in food-grain consumption. That same rupee provided to a person in the bottom 20 percent of the income distribution will provide increased demand for 0.58 rupee of food grains. The one-to-one equality of financial transfers is matched by a nineteen-to-one inequality in the material transfers. Thus, a marginal redistribution of income is profoundly inflationary in driving up food prices. In this case, what the left hand of society gives to the poor, the right hand of the market takes away. (Mellor 1988:1003)

This is illustrated in Figure 17.2. Taking income from the rich shifts back their demand for food, but by a relatively small amount, since income elasticity of demand for food is low for rich people. Giving income to the poor shifts out their demand for food by a relatively large amount, since their income elasticity of demand for food is large. Therefore, the shift in aggregate demand (combining the demands of rich and poor) shifts out, driving up the equilibrium price. This partially offsets the impact of the income on food consumption of the poor, though the new quantity is still above the old quantity.

Taxing land according to use-value is another way to implement a progressive tax. Through a properly executed land-use survey, farmland can be classified according to its value associated with its use potential. Often, third world taxes on good farming land are so low that large landholders can afford to keep their holdings while farming them inefficiently. By raising taxes and keeping them proportionate to land use–value, farmers who are making poor

**Figure 17.2 Effect of an Income Transfer from the Rich to the Poor
Is Partially Offset by an Increase in Aggregate Demand
and a Resulting Increase in Food Price**

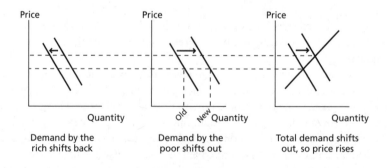

or inefficient use of their land will be forced to sell out to those who would farm the land better. The beauty of this system is that it readjusts resource use by weeding out the bad farmers without uprooting the good farmers, who may be doing a fine job for society.

Cash Transfer Programs

The flip side of progressive taxation (taking from the rich) is cash transfers (giving to the poor). The United Kingdom's Department for International Development (DFID) commissioned a paper (Arnold with Conway and Greenslade 2011) reviewing the academic literature on cash transfer programs throughout the world. That paper points out that cash transfer programs should not be thought of in terms of their immediate short-term impact, but rather as part of a longer-term dynamic process. In this light, cash transfers can be part of a program to increase human capital of the poor, or to redress power imbalances that result from imperfect markets.

Cash transfer programs have been criticized. Some recipients use the cash transferred for "bad things" like drugs or alcohol. There can be corruption in program operations: people who don't qualify, or "shouldn't" qualify, receive benefits. Cash transfers can be used to reward political supporters of a party in power, thereby subverting the democratic process.

But the biggest criticism of cash transfers (or other, noncash transfer programs we will discuss later) is that they cause dependency—people lose their incentive to work harder because higher incomes will be offset by loss of government benefits.

The DFID review of evidence reaches the following conclusions:

• There is little evidence that cash transfers provide a disincentive to effort.
• There is strong evidence that cash transfers improve *access* to health and education services.
• But the evidence is much weaker that cash transfers improve health and education *outcomes*.
• However, "nutrition may be an exception: households receiving transfers spend more on food, resulting in significant gains in children's weight and height in several countries" (Arnold with Conway and Greenslade 2011:ii).

The DFID paper contains a number of examples of the impact of cash transfers on nutrition. Ethiopia adopted three types of programs to help the poor: cash for work, unconditional cash transfers, and food aid. Seventy-five percent of participants in the Ethiopian program consumed more food after receiving the assistance. In Malawi, 75 percent of cash transfers were spent on groceries. In South Africa, boys in families who received child support payments had taller height-for-age at three years compared to boys in similar families who did not receive payments. In Nicaragua, children in a cash transfer program had a reduction in malnutrition 1.7 times the national average reduction due to general economic conditions.

Programs That Redistribute Wealth from Rich Countries to Poor Countries

Economic growth is one sure way to increase the incomes of the poor. But that may also be accomplished by redistribution. Foreign aid, or foreign development assistance, consists of money sent by governments of rich countries to governments (or nongovernmental projects) in poor countries. The purpose of this aid is not to put money directly into the hands of poor people in developing countries but to help finance projects that will promote economic growth. Therefore, although the foreign aid on the surface appears to be a redistribution from rich to poor, it is more closely related to the discussion in the previous section about policies to promote growth.

Table 17.2 shows the largest donors of aid for 2014. Not one country donates more than 1 percent of its wealth to the poor, and the average is 0.28 percent. Table 17.3 shows the largest recipient countries, with Afghanistan, Ethiopia, India, and Pakistan leading the way. In many recent years, the list of

Table 17.2 Foreign Development Assistance by Donor Country, 2014

Amount of Assistance Donated, 2014 ($ millions)		Assistance as a Percentage of Donor GNI	
United States	33,096	Norway	0.95
Germany	16,566	Sweden	0.93
France	10,620	Luxembourg	0.91
United Kingdom	19,306	Denmark	0.81
Japan	9,266	Netherlands	0.81
Netherlands	5,573	Ireland	0.55
Spain	1,877	Austria	0.50
Sweden	6,233	Belgium	0.43
Canada	4,240	Finland	0.39
Italy	4,009	France	0.38
Norway	5,086	Germany	0.37
Australia	4,382	Spain	0.37
Denmark	3,003	Switzerland	0.37
Belgium	2,448	United Kingdom	0.36
Austria	1,235	Australia	0.32
Switzerland	3,522	Canada	0.29
Ireland	816	New Zealand	0.27
Finland	1,635	Portugal	0.22
Greece	247	Italy	0.19
Portugal	430	Japan	0.17
Luxembourg	423	Greece	0.16
New Zealand	506	United States	0.16

Source: OECD, Stat Extracts, online at http://stats.oecd.org.

top recipients includes places like Afghanistan, Iraq, and the Palestinian Authority, illustrating how foreign aid has been used as a tool to achieve foreign policy objectives other than the objective of helping the world's poor.

Table 17.2 shows that foreign aid is a small part of US gross national income. Despite this fact, and the fact that foreign aid makes up less than 1 percent of federal spending, cutting foreign aid is the most popular way of addressing the federal budget deficit, according to opinion polls (see Lowrey 2012). On a per household basis (for 2013), total federal spending was about $26,000, the annual budget deficit was $5,000, and total government spending on foreign aid was $164. So even eliminating foreign aid would do little to reduce the budget deficit or federal spending.

The United States made a commitment, in its Millennium Challenge Grant program, to increase assistance to developing countries and to direct much of the new assistance to the poorest countries of the world. But recipient countries are required to meet certain standards ("challenges") in order to be eligible for this assistance. More information on this is available at the Millennium Challenge Corporation's website (https://www.mcc.gov).

Table 17.3 Largest Recipients of Donor Foreign Development Assistance, All Sources, 2014

	Amount of Assistance Received ($ millions)
Afghanistan	3,908
Ethiopia	1,915
India	1,892
Pakistan	1,762
South Sudan	1,629
Kenya	1,602
Syrian Arab Republic	1,599
Jordan	1,494
Tanzania	1,455
Mozambique	1,425
Bangladesh	1,381
Democratic Republic of Congo	1,166
Myanmar	1,159
Colombia	1,138
Iraq	1,133
Nigeria	1,062
Morocco	1,061
Uganda	1,030
Brazil	910
Ukraine	826
Senegal	800
Zambia	775
Somalia	764
South Africa	735
Turkey	694

Source: OECD, Stat Extracts, online at http://stats.oecd.org.

There are some strong disagreements among economists about whether or not foreign aid can be effective. A good example of how economists disagree—and how those disagreements help to move a policy debate forward—is found in the question of whether foreign aid is a good thing.

Jeffrey Sachs of Columbia University is confident that development assistance can be a practical way to eliminate worldwide poverty. Sachs's optimism is illustrated here:

> Malaria . . . is largely preventable and utterly treatable. There is no excuse for the millions of malaria deaths that will occur this year. . . . Just $2 to $3 per American and other citizens of the rich world would be needed each year to mount an effective fight against malaria. The rich world's actual spending to fight malaria is closer to 20 cents per person per year. . . .
>   [S]imilar steps would change the face of extreme poverty—indeed, put the world on a path to eliminate it in this generation. Yet these steps are not taken. . . . Americans . . . believe, erroneously, that corruption in poor countries blocks effective use of aid, even though dozens of impoverished countries are rather well governed yet still starved of help. (2005b:A17)

Sachs argues that a relatively modest increase in foreign aid could have a huge difference in reducing world poverty.

William Easterly (2006) of New York University is pessimistic about the possibility that development assistance can be effective. He argues that grand plans such as those espoused by Sachs have been tried repeatedly and have never succeeded. "Economic development happens, not through aid, but through the homegrown efforts of entrepreneurs and social and political reformers." Easterly is not opposed to all foreign aid, but he favors small-scale projects with limited objectives. Aid agencies should stop trying to "achieve general economic and political development" and "start . . . fixing the system that fails to get 12-cent medicines to malaria victims." Aid fails, according to Easterly, because of the lack of feedback and accountability. (For more debate between Sachs and Easterly, see Easterly 2005.)

Dambisa Moyo (2009), a Zambian economist trained in the United States, is an outspoken critic of foreign aid to Africa. She lists seven ways that aid hurts recipient countries:

- It fuels corruption.
- It encourages inflation.
- It leaves developing countries with debt burdens they cannot repay.
- It kills off the export sector.
- It induces civil unrest.
- It kills entrepreneurship.
- It disenfranchises African citizens.

A careful reading suggests that the differences appear much greater than they really are. Sachs agrees with Easterly and Moyo that much aid historically has been ineffective, and for the reasons put forward by the critics—Sachs, especially, accepts the view that corruption among recipient countries has been a problem. Sachs points out specific aid efforts that have been effective—measles reduction, or mosquito nets, for example; Easterly and Moyo don't deny this. So the real differences are this: the anti-aid point of view is that, fundamentally, the system has inherent, and unfixable, flaws. The pro-development point of view is that we know how to design and implement effective aid programs, and that if we use this knowledge, aid can be made effective.

The debate over aid is also an interesting illustration of how economists debate an issue, and attempt to marshal data to resolve differences, or at least to identify the actual source of the differences. A 2000 paper by Burnside and Dollar intended to examine Easterly's claims that aid was ineffective because it went to countries with bad policies. So they proceeded like this: First, they identified countries and years where policies were good. Then, considering only those countries and years, they asked whether the amount of aid received by a country was correlated with its GDP growth rate. They found that it was: the fitted curve was upward sloping. Thus they concluded that foreign aid was effective in promoting GDP growth, but only if combined with good domestic policies in the recipient country.

Easterly together with Levine and Roodman (2004) decided to check the analysis using the Burnside and Dollar data, but augmenting this with new data that had become available since Burnside and Dollar had done their analysis. With the new data, the fitted line is *downward* sloping (but not significantly so), suggesting that aid does not promote and may actually retard economic growth.

No doubt this question will be revisited by other analyses using more data as they become available and making other adjustments or improvements. The point here is not that economists ultimately prove what's right but that the debate attempts to identify the sources of disagreement and to test the alternative points of view using data and methods that both sides agree are appropriate.

Nongovernmental Aid to Developing Countries
Nongovernmental aid has been growing much faster than official government-to-government development assistance. This is shown in Table 17.4.

It is natural, when we speak of private aid, to think of famous philanthropists and foundations such as the Bill and Melinda Gates Foundation. But another source of financial flows from rich countries to poor countries is the person-to-person flows from people who have migrated to rich countries and send money back to their family members remaining in poor countries. These flows are known as "remittances," and it is estimated that these kinds of payments

Table 17.4 Private and Public Aid Flows, 2003–2004 and 2014

	2003–2004 ($ billions)	2014 ($ billions)	Percentage Increase
All OECD foreign development assistance	75	137	82
All OECD private aid	63	403	540
US foreign development assistance	18	33	83
US private aid	10	180	1,700

Source: OECD 2015.

Note: For OECD countries as a group, private aid increased from about equal to official aid in 2003–2004 to more than twice official aid in 2014. The increase in private aid from the United States has been even more remarkable, eighteen times higher in 2014 than in 2003–2004. The United States now accounts for nearly half of worldwide private aid.

have grown from about $150 billion in the 2003–2004 period to almost $400 billion in 2014.

In fact, one economist (Tabarrok 2015) calls migration "the greatest anti-poverty program ever." The direct effect is to raise the wage of the person who migrates as that person moves from the low-wage country to the high-wage country. But the use of remittances is another informal flow of funds from the (comparatively rich) migrant to the (comparatively poor) family remaining in the developing country.

18

Population
Policy

One result of [population/resource] projections and their use in public discussion of population policy has been a shift in concern toward future generations. In China, as in most traditional societies, childbearing decisions were shaped by a desire by parents to be looked after in old age. By emphasizing future population/resource relationships in shaping family planning programs, government officials have shifted the focus of childbearing from the well-being of parents to the well-being of children.

—Brown 1983:38–39

A policy that reduces population growth relaxes the upward pressure on price and increases food availability per person. This is illustrated in the supply-demand diagram in Figure 18.1. A successful policy to reduce population growth will result in an aggregate demand curve for food that is closer to the origin (compared to the demand curve that would exist with higher population growth). The resulting equilibrium is at a lower price and a lower quantity than the equilibrium that would exist if population growth stayed high. But although the quantity of food drops, it drops by less than the decline in population; therefore the food availability per person increases.

What Is the Objective of Population Policy?
The usual way of thinking about population policy follows the logic of the preceding paragraph and assumes that the objective of a population policy is to reduce population by reducing fertility. An economic rationale for this kind of population policy goes like this: the cost of having children is not borne solely by the parents; the decision to have children imposes an external cost on society at large. A growing population puts pressure on the natural environment, makes the task of education more difficult, thins out the supply of capital per person, and tends to decrease equity. (For example, one study estimated the external cost due to climate change associated with each

**Figure 18.1 If Population Grows More Slowly,
Food Price Drops and Food Available per Person Increases**

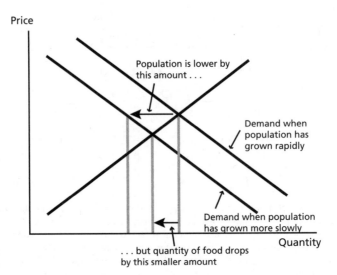

additional birth in developing countries at $300; O'Neill and Wexler 2000.)
As described in Chapter 16, the existence of external costs provides an economic rationale for government to intervene to reduce the number of children. Following this logic, most of this chapter examines policy alternatives
for lowering the fertility rate.

We should note at the outset, however, that, worldwide, fertility rates are
already falling, and in parts of Europe have fallen far below the replacement
rate. Columnist Mark Steyn (2006) argues that population .growth may
strengthen the geostrategic position of a country, and in this way the decision
to have children may actually have external benefits to the society as a whole.
In this case, the government's appropriate population policy would be to increase the fertility rate.

Pro-natalist policies include tax deductions in proportion to the number
of children in the family (common throughout much of the world), unlimited
subsidized maternity leaves sponsored by government or private industry
(again, common throughout the world), and childcare subsidies during the
first several years of a child's life (found only in certain high-income countries, such as Canada, France, and Australia). Box 18.1 explores some high-
income countries that have adopted or are considering pro-natalist population policies.

Box 18.1 Pro-Natalist Population Policies in Industrialized Countries

In many European countries, fertility rates have fallen below the replacement rate, and governments react in different ways.

The mayor of Laviano, Italy, started a program that would pay a woman 10,000 euros (about $15,000) if she would have a baby and rear the child in Laviano (Shorto 2008).

Norway has a program that pays a mother 80 percent of her salary during fifty-four weeks of maternity leave, and subsidizes childcare thereafter (Shorto 2008).

One observer of the Russian situation blames the low fertility rate on the high cost of obstetric healthcare, and notes, "Politicians . . . speak of a demographic crisis in the country. They're saying that Russian women must be forced by any means to have not just one child but two or more" (Kakturskaya 2003).

France has succeed in getting fertility rates to rise. "While falling birthrates threatened to undermine economies and social stability across much of an aging Europe, French fertility rates are increasing. . . . France heavily subsidizes children and families from pregnancy to young adulthood with liberal maternity leaves and part-time work laws for women" (Moore 2006:A1).

Japan instituted a national policy in 2009 to pay a monthly stipend to parents who had children, from birth to the child's fifteenth birthday. The intention was to boost the country's birth rate.

Preconditions for a Successful Policy to Reduce Fertility

Demographers have identified three preconditions for successful policy to reduce population growth: (1) promote a *basic understanding* that fertility decisions are made by parents, (2) give parents an *incentive* to control fertility, and (3) give parents *access* to contraceptive technology to control fertility. In most situations, the first of these preconditions is met without much government effort. However, in some cases there can be widespread misapprehension about the procreative process, or religious attitudes that regard human actions and decisions as secondary or subservient to divine will in causing pregnancy and childbirth. The rest of this section will focus on the second and third of these preconditions—policies that create an incentive for parents to have fewer children, and policies that give parents the ability to have fewer children.

Models of Fertility Decisions

What factors influence parents' decisions about childbearing? Before we can consider what kinds of policies might affect parents' fertility decisions, we need to have a better understanding of how those decisions are made. There are (at least) two models of parental decisionmaking.

The demographer's model emphasizes old-age security. In this model, parents rely on their children for old-age security. The parents make a calculation about how many children surviving to adulthood will be adequate to take care of the parents as they become too old to be economically productive. For example, if a couple decides that they can have a comfortable old age if they have three adult children to rely on, they will have three children if they believe that all three will survive. In a society where child mortality is 50 percent, most parents would have six children in the hope that three survive to adulthood. If child mortality falls to 25 percent, the fertility rate might drop to four children per couple.

Of course, parents' decisions about how many children to have does not adjust immediately as the child mortality rate falls. It takes time for parents to notice the new lower mortality rates, and then to modify the cultural habits inherited from previous generations.

The other model of fertility decisions is an economic model. In this model, parents make decisions about how many children to have based on the costs and benefits of childbearing. For example, in agrarian societies where there is a lot of opportunity to put children to work on the farm, the benefits of having children are relatively large. In suburban areas of the United States, where most children finish high school and go on to (often expensive) universities, costs of childbearing are relatively large.

In Chapter 8 we saw convincing evidence that fertility rates decline as income grows (as economies move into the second stage of demographic transition). See Table 18.1 for more evidence of this relationship. The poorest geographical area (sub-Saharan Africa, with average per capita income of $3,363) has the highest fertility rate (4.4 children per woman of childbearing age). Asia has higher incomes ($7,924) and significantly lower fertility (2.3). In Latin America (income $14,242), fertility rate has fallen to the replacement rate (2.1). And in rich industrialized countries (income $37,658), fertility rates have fallen below replacement rate. (With the policy reactions described in Box 18.1.)

Both the demographic model and the economic model are consistent with the observation that fertility rates decline as incomes grow. The demographic model explains this relationship by pointing out that infant mortality rates improve as incomes rise. The economic model has a more complicated way of explaining the relationship.

As a family's income grows, the *benefits* of having children typically *decline*. As described earlier, there are fewer opportunities for child production, and child contributions to family income are less important in higher-income households. In addition, higher-income countries are more likely to have comprehensive old-age security programs (Social Security in the United States). This reduces the reliance on children for old-age security. In the demographic model, that means a reduction in the target number of surviving children; in

Table 18.1 Population Growth, Birth Rates, and Death Rates for Selected Country Groups, 2014

	GNI per Capita (PPP$)	Population Growth 2004–2014 (percentage)	Total Fertility Rate (births per woman)	Birth Rate (per thousand population)	Death Rate (per thousand population)	Life Expectancy at Birth (years)	Infant Mortality (per thousand live births)
World	14,301	12.2	2.4	19	8	68	36
Less developed countries	9,071	14.3	2.6	20	7	67	39
More developed countries	37,658	3.6	1.7	11	10	79	6
Sub-Saharan Africa	3,363	27.5	4.4	34	11	59	94
Asia	7,924	11.0	2.3	19	7	71	43
Latin America and Caribbean	14,242	12.0	2.1	17	6	75	17

Source: For GNI per capita, UNDP2015: tab. 1 (groups are: developing countries, OECD countries, sub-Saharan African developing countries, Latin American and Caribbean developing countries, and a population-weighted average for the groups East Asia and Pacific developing countries and South Asian developing countries. Remaining population data from US Census, http://www.census.gov/population/international/data/idb/informationGateway.php.

the economic model, that means a reduced benefit of childbearing—the benefit deriving from old-age security.

And as a family's income grows, the *costs* of having children typically *increase*. As already noted, children in higher-income families are more likely to encourage additional education costs. But there are indirect costs to the family of having more children. Parents divert time and attention away from their jobs to rear children (maternity leave and child leave, for example). A higher-paid parent makes a bigger monetary sacrifice for the time away from work. In addition, parents may reduce their long-term earning potential by dropping out of school to have children.

Policies That Give Parents an Incentive to Have Fewer Children

The models of fertility decisions give us insight into the kinds of government or society actions that can cause people to reduce their desired family size. Old-age security programs or programs to reduce child mortality will lead to lower fertility. Programs that increase the costs or reduce the benefits of childbearing will lead to lower fertility. Expressed in different words, economic incentives to reward low fertility and economic disincentives to discourage high fertility can both be used to motivate lower fertility.

One of the more imaginative incentive schemes was set up on three tea estates in India. By law, the tea estates are required to provide substantial maternity and childcare benefits for their workers (tea-pickers are usually women). The benefits include hospitalization and medical care for the mother and infant as well as long-term food, clothing, schooling, and medical care for the child. The tea estates set up a savings account for family planning. Each woman employee of childbearing age is offered a savings account, the proceeds of which are available to her on retirement, and into which the firm will pay the equivalent of one day's wages for each month that she is not pregnant. If a woman becomes pregnant, the company suspends payments for one year. For third and additional pregnancies, the company not only suspends payment for a year, but also reclaims part of its past payments into her account to help pay for its legally mandated maternal and childcare expenses. Women thus have a choice: maternity and childcare benefits for more children, or a better retirement program. Many women are opting for fewer children and more retirement benefits (Brown 1974:169; World Bank 1984:126).

Economic incentives for lower fertility are attractive, but they are expensive. In Bangladesh a program was proposed that would provide a twelve-year bond with a maturity value of around $350 for women of childbearing age who had only two or three children and then underwent sterilization. Attached to the proposal was a scheme whereby couples who signed certificates to delay their first birth for three years after marriage, or who delayed their second and third births for at least five years, would be given $20 on presentation of their certificates after the agreed time, provided they had kept their pledge. It was estimated that to cover the entire population with both schemes would require about 10 percent of the annual government budget (World Bank 1984:126).

Not only are incentive payments for low fertility expensive but they also waste a certain amount of public resources, as people who would have had fewer children despite the program go ahead and claim its benefits. And while economic incentives involve payments provided to delay or limit childbearing, economic disincentives usually involve the withholding of social benefits from those couples who produce more than some targeted number of children.

In the early 1980s a series of economic disincentives to large families was in use in Singapore. The system (which was dropped subsequent to a decline in birth rates) included incentives to have two children but disincentives for more than two. The system was summarized by a Draper Fund report (Salaff and Wong 1983:16) as follows:

- Paid maternity leave for the first two children, but not for third and subsequent children.
- Preference in the choice of primary school given only to the first two children, with highest preference to the two children of a parent who had undergone sterilization before age forty.
- Removal of the large-family priority in the allocation of subsidized housing; only families with three or fewer children were allowed to rent rooms in public housing units.
- Escalating delivery fees in public hospitals for higher-order births, as well as fees for prenatal care (fees remitted if sterilization followed delivery).
- Full tax relief only for the first two children, and none for fourth or subsequent children.

China's one-child policy has had a huge impact on world population growth over the past three and a half decades (see Landman 1983 or Laudermilk 2011 for descriptions). The policy, adopted in 1979, utilized widespread advertising with slogans such as "Have Fewer Children—Lead Better Lives." Parents who agreed to have only one child would receive a "Glory Certificate" that entitled them to a number of economic benefits. Those benefits included priority government medical care, priority admission to government schools, larger accommodations in public housing, bonuses for city workers, or larger private plots for rural peasant workers. The Glory Certificates also provided a certain amount of prestige or social standing.

But the one-child policy was not just a voluntary program fueled by positive incentives to participate. Couples who refused to abide by the one-child policy could be subject to fines as high as a year's salary or loss of housing. There are reports of forced abortions and sterilizations and even infanticide.

The one-child policy had an unintended consequence of radically altering the gender balance of children. Because of a residual cultural desire for male children (traditionally, male children were responsible for the old-age security of the parents), some parents who were pregnant with a female child would abort, and try again for a male child. Currently in China there are about 120 male children born for every 100 female children (compare to the US ratio of 102 boys to 100 girls).

By 2010, fertility rates in China had fallen to about 1.5 children per woman of childbearing age (the one-child policy did not apply to families in some rural areas, and in some ethnic groups). The decline in fertility was caused by a combination of China's rapid economic growth and its one-child policy. In 2015, China announced that the one-child policy would end, to be replaced by a two-child policy (see Hesketh, Zhou, and Wang 2015).

Governments have also tried to influence fertility decisions by policies designed to make parents "feel better about themselves" for having fewer children. In effect these efforts work by creating a nonmaterialistic cost (loss of this good feeling) to having more children. The advertising and issuing of Glory Certificates (which a family could hang in their living rooms) are examples from China.

India has long promoted a vigorous advertising campaign to encourage the small family, with government-sponsored advertisements appearing on billboards, in buses, at movie theaters, in magazines and newspapers, and on radio and television. (India's total fertility rate in 1986 was 4.4. By 2000 it had fallen to 3.1, and by 2015 to 2.5.)

Some countries have tried leveraging intense community pressure on couples of childbearing age to limit their family size. In this context the "cost" of having too many children is the loss of prestige and social standing. Examples of such efforts in Indonesia and China are described briefly in Box 18.2.

Policies That Give Parents the Ability to Have Fewer Children

The preceding section dealt with policies intended to make parents want to have smaller families. But how can they achieve their objective? This section deals with contraceptive policies.

Use of contraceptives among married women of childbearing age varies widely in the third world, from less than 10 percent in sub-Saharan Africa to around 40 percent in Latin America to as high as 70 percent or more in China and Singapore (World Bank 1984:128). Controlled experiments conducted in Mexico, India, Bangladesh, South Korea, and the Philippines have all demonstrated that the provision of family-planning advice, technology, and materials significantly reduces fertility. The strong (negative) correlation between percentage of women using modern contraception and the fertility rate is shown in McDevitt 2004 (tab. 46, p. 60).

Box 18.2 Community Pressures to Lower Fertility

Rodolfo A. Bulatao

Pressures can be exerted by the community, or by major sections of it, to promote lowered fertility. Two cases will illustrate group pressures: banjars in Bali and production teams in China.

Banjars—traditional units of local self-government, which serve as centers for mutual aid and cooperative work—consist of all the male household heads in a hamlet or subvillage. The form is centuries old. The traditional head of a banjar is democratically elected but has no official standing. Instead, the banjar also has a second, official head, who may be appointed and may have charge of more than one banjar (Hull 1978).

Banjar meetings may be held every month (or thirty-five days), usually with perfect attendance (there is a system of fines for absence or lateness), and typically discuss development of the community and religious affairs (Astawa 1979).

Since 1974 these meetings have also included discussion of the family-planning status of each family. Each member is asked what he and his wife are doing about family planning. A register is kept, and a color-coded map of the community indicating eligible couples and their contraceptive status is prominently displayed in the banjar hall (Meier 1979).

The decline in marital fertility in Bali of about 30 percent in less than a decade has been dramatic enough to be labeled a "demographic miracle" (Hull et al. 1977). How much of the change has been due to the community pressures exerted through the 3,700 banjars is a difficult and probably unanswerable question. Other elements of the Balinese situation, such as acute pressures on the land, the penetration of modern influences (through such means as consumer goods, communication, and transportation systems, and Western-style schooling and tourism), and cultural factors such as the relative independence of young couples—which may facilitate contraceptive decisions—may encourage the decline in fertility. Furthermore, the effective logistical system of the family-planning program and creative uses of native art forms to communicate family-planning messages, and a stable, supportive government, may be influential.

Production teams in China, which are usually the effective unit in rural areas for production and income sharing, consist of thirty to forty households in a small village, within which kinship ties may be strong. Production teams assume important responsibility for the fertility of their members. As part of the national wan xi shao campaign (named for the reproductive norms of later marriage, longer birth spacing, and fewer births), the production teams were responsible for deciding which couples could have births, in line with the reproductive norms and with team quotas set from above (Chen and Kols 1982). The team birth-planning leadership group (the leaders all being local residents) might call all eligible couples to a meeting, at which their individual birth plans could be scrutinized and allocations made. Under the one-child campaign, which replaced the wan xi shao campaign in 1979, community birth planning

continues

Box 18.2 continued

still takes place, although allocation of birth quotas follows different norms. As couples become familiar with the system, the time-consuming meeting to adjust birth plans may be dispensed with, and the leaders may simply notify couples of their decisions. Adherence is in theory voluntary, resting on persuasion and education. Such elements as adult study groups and visits from birth-planning delegations maintain the peer pressure (Chen 1981).

As with the Balinese banjars, it is not possible to determine the specific impact of the social pressures exerted through production teams, which are only one element in the Chinese population program.

Source: Bulatao 1984a.

In a thirty-one-country study, Bongaarts (1982) looked at determinants of fertility decline as it proceeds from rates well above six to rates close to two children per woman. The difference in total fertility was almost five children. He found that, in the countries studied, higher age at marriage reduced total fertility by 1.4 children. Increased use of contraception reduced fertility by 4.5 children. Greater use of induced abortion accounted for a reduction of 0.5 children, for a total reduction of 6.4 children. Reduced breast-feeding, of course, works the other way around, and accounted for an increase in fertility of about 1.5 children. Data for selected individual countries are also shown in Table 18.2 (in the bottom row of the table, these data are expressed as percentage contribution to reduction in fertility decline).

McDevitt (2004) has a comprehensive review of information about contraceptive use in developing countries. In most third world countries, a substantial gap exists between women who would like to limit their fertility and their access to modern contraceptive methods (see Table 18.3). However, the information from McDevitt for the late 1990s shows considerable improvement over similar information from the early 1980s published by Galway and colleagues (1987). McDevitt shows that fertility levels and contraceptive use are strongly (negatively) correlated across countries. Countries with fertility rates of six births per woman have contraceptive use rates of 10 percent or less for the most part, while countries with fertility rates of three births per woman have contraceptive use rates in the 45–60 percent range. Simmons and Lapham (1987) note that the impact of contraception use on fertility varies with programmatic and environmental factors. For instance, the availability of multiple public and private channels for the delivery of services increases the effectiveness of national programs. A recent contraceptive effort in Rwanda is described in Box 18.3.

Table 18.2 Accounting for Fertility Decline in Selected Developing Countries

	Total Fertility Rate (births per woman)			Percentage of Fertility Reduction by Contributing Factor				
	Initial	Final	Decline	Older Age at Marriage	Reduced Breast-Feeding	Greater Use of Contraception	Greater Use of Abortion	All Other Factors
India (1972–1978)	5.6	5.2	0.5	41	–58	114	–	3
Indonesia (1970–1980)	5.5	4.6	0.9	41	–77	134	–	2
Korea (1960–1970)	6.1	4.0	2.2	50	–38	53	30	4
Thailand (1968–1978)	6.1	3.4	2.7	11	–17	86	16	4
Composite of thirty-one countries (long-term)	> 6.0	< 3.0	5.0	28	–29	90	10	1

Source: Sources: For composite of thirty-one countries, Bongaarts 1982; for all other data, Bulatao 1984b:38.

Notes: n/a = not available. The composite data of thirty-one countries account for the decline in total fertility typical of countries that started their fertility decline with rates around six births per woman (the predecline phase of fertility rates) and ended with rates below three children per woman (the postdecline countries); the difference between pre- and postdecline rates among these countries amounts to almost five children. Some figures will not total due to rounding.

Table 18.3 Unmet Need for Contraceptives in Selected Countries

	Percentage of Women Without Contraception Who Want . . .		
	No More Children	Fewer Future Children	Total
Haiti	23	17	40
Yemen	21	18	39
Ethiopia	14	21	35
Uganda	14	20	34
Pakistan	17	11	28
Philippines	12	8	20
Nigeria	5	13	18
India	8	8	16
Indonesia	5	4	9
Brazil	5	2	7

Source: McDevitt 2004: fig. 54.

Policies That Work in Multiple Ways to Reduce Fertility

Two kinds of policies make progress on all avenues toward reduced fertility: policies that produce economic growth, and policies that encourage the empowerment of women.

We have already seen some of the ways that economic growth (and higher incomes per capita) can influence population growth by increasing the desire for smaller families. But higher incomes and economic growth make contraception more affordable. Economic growth and education go hand-in-hand, making people more aware of contraception and other healthcare needs. Finally, higher incomes mean that parents are less dependent on children for old-age security.

Policies described by the catchphrase "empowering women" work to reduce fertility in a variety of ways. First, as women feel that society and culture give them greater permission to participate in childbearing decisions, the costs to women of childbearing and child-rearing are more fully taken into account. Second, as women become better educated, they become more aware of birth control techniques. Third, as women become better educated, their value as workers increases; thus they see higher costs of foregone earnings or production as they devote time and attention to childbearing and child-rearing. Fourth, as women become more socially accepted in the labor market, their value as workers increases. Fifth, better education of women is likely to lead to reduced infant and child mortality rates, so that fewer births are necessary to achieve the desired number of surviving children. Sixth, better-educated women are more likely to want a good education for their children. This re-

---

Box 18.3 Norplant Distribution in Rwanda

Rwanda's fertility rate (6.1 children per woman) is among the world's highest. Its population doubled between the mid-1980s and 2008 and is projected by the US Census Bureau to double again by 2038. In early 2007, Rwandan president Paul Kagama sat down with a *New York Times* reporter (Kinzer 2007) to discuss his plan for a national population control program.

Family-planning counseling will be required for every patient at a hospital or health center, regardless of their ailment. Free Norplant devices will be provided to all women of childbearing age. Norplant is a small device that is implanted under the skin and releases contraceptive hormones. It is an effective contraceptive for up to five years after implantation. The cost of the project is being underwritten by donations from the US government.

---

duces children's availability to the labor force and therefore reduces the economic benefits and raises the costs of having children.

The education of women is particularly significant in reducing fertility. Educated women are more likely to postpone marriage in order to enter the work force, more likely to delay having children in order to remain in the work force, and more likely to know about and use contraception than are uneducated women (Anonymous 1988).

The Complementarity of Fertility Reduction Policies

Fertility reduction policies often complement each other. For instance, providing subsidized family-planning services not only makes the technology available for reducing fertility but also sends a message to the community that the government supports the idea of fertility regulation. Joel Cohen (1996b) recommends, as part of any population control policy, "doing everything at once."

However, fertility reduction policies are often also complementary with other programs that help to reduce undernutrition. For instance, successful promotion of prolonged breast-feeding not only reduces fertility but also improves childhood nutrition and health. Persuading couples to marry later in life not only reduces fertility but also, because women remain in the work force longer as a result, raises per capita income, improving nutrition. Increasing the educational level of women not only decreases fertility but also increases their future productivity and undoubtedly improves the quality of the childcare they deliver. Cohen (1996b) quotes economist Robert Cassen as saying, "Virtually everything that needs doing from a population point of view needs doing anyway."

Demographer John Bongaarts (1994:773–774), writing on the eve of a worldwide conference on population, recommended the following steps to reduce population growth:

1. Reduce unwanted pregnancies by improving contraceptive education and availability. . . .
2. Reduce the demand for large families by investing in education and reducing infant and child mortality.
3. Address population momentum by increasing the age of marriage and lengthening intervals between births.

19

Subsidizing Consumption

There is no greater scam in India at this time than the so-called food subsidy. Under the cover of "food security," the Government is keeping millions of tonnes of food out of reach of poor people.

—*Dreze 2001*

In this chapter we survey policies aimed explicitly at lowering the food prices paid by consumers. To many, this is the most obvious and straightforward approach to the problem of undernutrition: give food (or sell it at subsidized prices) to the hungry. Here we will describe the mechanisms of subsidy that have been tried and some of the problems that have arisen.

Rationale for Explicit Food Subsidies

There are a number of reasons why food consumption subsidies have been so popular. Historically, developed countries have generally followed farm production policies that have led to burdensome agricultural surpluses. Furthermore, large numbers of people are hungry now and it is tempting for policymakers to feed people today rather than to sponsor programs, such as enhanced agricultural production research, that may take months or years to produce obvious benefits. And donors of famine relief are more charitable when their donations are directed to the most needy.

There are other reasons for the popularity of food consumption subsidies. By and large, rich people prefer to give hungry people food rather than cash (see the discussion of "basic needs" in Chapter 16). Further, particular groups of rich people derive benefits from food distribution programs: these groups include food processors; farmers, who see the demand for their products increase; owners of storage and transport facilities; and even the private voluntary agencies such as CARE and Catholic Relief Services that assist in distributing surplus food.

In developing countries, political leaders are interested in creating or continuing such programs. The groups most likely to influence political power are the military, civil servants, urban labor, and industrial interests. All of these groups are happy to be the recipients of cheap food, and political leaders are generally happy to curry favor among them, even at the expense of the country's rural sector (Hopkins 1988).

Proof of the political popularity of food price subsidies can be found in the morning newspaper. In 1996, the IMF pressured Jordan to cut food price subsidies. Bread prices doubled, and angry demonstrators demanded that the prime minister be removed from office (Reuters 1996). In Zimbabwe, an economic crisis led the government to increase prices for food staples by 30 percent in 2000. Riots began in the capital city of Harare, and 160 people were arrested (Shaw 2000). In 2007, high corn prices—and high tortilla prices—caused riots in Mexico (Watts 2007).

We begin by reviewing the experiences of a number of food distribution programs in various countries. When a food subsidy lowers prices to the general population, the costs of the program soar. Various reactions to these high costs have been tried—reducing the size of the subsidy (which increases consumer prices), or limiting the scope of the program to certain individuals, which requires complex bureaucratic mechanisms.

Food Subsidies in Asia

Sri Lanka

During World War II, when rice supplies were limited, the government of Sri Lanka (then called Ceylon) instituted a program under which rice was sold at a subsidized price, but the quantity to each consumer was rationed (Edirisinghe and Poleman 1983).

In 1953, the costs of the rice program became too high, and price increases of nearly 300 percent were announced. A massive protest stopped the price increases and forced the resignation of the prime minister. From 1954 to 1966, Sri Lankans could buy rice at prices substantially below the world market price, but, through rationing, access was restricted to 4 pounds per week (equivalent to about 1,000 calories per person per day) (Edirisinghe 1987:12–13). In 1966, the basic weekly ration was cut in half, but issued at no charge. Two things were significant here: first, because government did not need to purchase as much rice overseas, substantial foreign exchange savings accrued; and second, there were no food riots.

In 1978, the ration system was targeted to the lower end of the income range through a "means" test (recipients had to prove their need). A year and a half later, food stamps were substituted for the ration cards. Food stamps carry a fixed rupee value; therefore their purchasing power declines with inflation, resulting in an automatic reduction of the inflation-adjusted costs of the food subsidy with no further government action. In 1985, targeting was restricted further, so that only the poorest quarter of the population were eligible for food stamps (Sahn and Edirisinghe 1993). The policy reforms succeeded in reducing government costs: food subsidies amounted to 23 percent of government expenditures in 1970, 19 percent in 1978, and 4 percent in 1984.

Bangladesh

Bangaldeshi food subsidies began during World War II. By the 1980s the program had evolved into a complex plan that included a variety of programs including rural food rationing, food-for-work, public purchases and sales to stabilize prices, and government control of imports. The International Food Policy Research Institute (IFPRI) began an evaluation of the rural food rationing program. This program provided limited amounts of low-cost food to all rural households. IFPRI concluded that the program was poorly targeted— 70 percent of the subsidized food went to households who did not need government assistance. IFPRI recommended that the money would be better spent on a food-for-education program that provided subsidized food to poor households who agreed to send their children to school. (For more information on food subsidies in Bangladesh, see Ahmed and Goletti 1997.)

India

The Indian food subsidy program (the subject of this chapter's epigraph) is intended to operate by using government funds to purchase food grains and selling the grain through government shops (at a loss) to qualified low-income individuals. In practice, however, the program bought more food than it sold, with government-owned stocks rising, stored food rotting, huge administrative costs, and prices rising. According to Dreze: "Ordinary households . . . benefit very little from this 'subsidy.' . . . What they gain on one side from subsidized food . . . pales in comparison to what they lose as a result of having to pay higher food prices on the market. . . . [E]ven [poor] households see little advantage in purchasing food from ration shops . . . because the price differential is too small to compensate for the quality differential" (2001). So who gains from the program? Lakshmi reports the details of how corrupt dealers take advantage of the system:

> [T]he poorest people of India receive ration cards that they can use to buy wheat from government run "ration shops" at very low prices. But in the village of Kelwara, ration shopkeepers turned card holders away, saying the shops had received no wheat supplies from the government. In fact, the ration shops had received government wheat, but had sold it at higher market prices to people who did not qualify for ration cards. The shop keepers covered their tracks by keeping a fraudulent set of books that showed sales to ration card holders, when in fact those sales had not occurred. (2004:A17)

Philippines

A 1983–1984 experiment in the Philippines provides a case study of costs and benefits from a real-world, subsidized food ration scheme. The experiment was set up so that all households in seven villages, known for a high incidence of undernutrition and poverty, were provided subsidized food. These villages were matched with seven control villages. The program did increase food consumption among the target villages. Although distribution of the extra food within the household favored adults, preschool children also consumed more and showed improvements in their nutritional status. If only weight gains among the undernourished were counted as benefits, the cost of adding 1 kilogram to the weight of an undernourished preschooler was estimated at $101 per year. (Edirisinghe [1987:70], in his study of food subsidies in Sri Lanka, found that discrimination against younger family members diminished when the more productive members of the household had at least 80 percent of their energy requirements met.)

The researchers in the Philippine experiment estimated that the cost-effectiveness of the program compared favorably with other programs. Costs were kept low through careful targeting, the cooperation of the local bureaucratic structure in administering the program, and by using existing retail outlets instead of a parallel, government-operated marketing system (Garcia and Pinstrup-Andersen 1987:9, 78–79).

A 2014 paper by Mehta and Jha reviewed the literature on pilferage from food distribution programs and found that such pilferage was widespread. Some of the results they found in the literature are summarized in Table 19.1. They looked specifically at evidence from the Philippines and concluded that nearly half of the food bought by the government and intended for sale to poor consumers at subsidized prices was stolen, rather than actually sold at the low prices as intended.

Table 19.1 Estimates of Pilferage from Food Distribution Programs, 1988–2011

	Commodity	Percent Pilfered
Pakistan, 1988	Wheat	69
India, 1992	Food grain	35+
Bangladesh, 2005	Food grain	10–65
Indonesia, 2006	Rice	18+
India, 2011	Food grain	37–54

Source: Mehta and Jha 2014.

Food Subsidies in Africa

Egypt

The Egyptian government has a history of intervening in the food-marketing system that dates back to biblical times when Joseph, interpreting the Pharaoh's dream, recommended storing grain during seven fat years to prepare for the seven lean years that he prophesied were to come (Genesis 41). Since the mid-1970s, the Egyptian government has taken on a substantial burden of public expenditures for food subsidies, with the share of the government expenditures for this purpose running as high as 17 percent (Alderman and von Braun 1984:12).

Additional costs of the Egyptian food subsidy have been borne by North American and European governments, which have provided substantial quantities of food at below-market prices. Indeed, the availability of such programs may be one of the reasons that Egyptians embarked on such an ambitious marketwide food subsidy.

As of the late 1980s, the Egyptian government was handling the major share of the sales of bread, flour, pulses, sugar, tea, and cooking oil in the country, making these commodities available to householders at prices significantly below world prices. Farm-gate prices (prices the farmer receives at the farm gate, before paying transportation costs to market) deviated less from world prices than did retail prices (see Table 19.2), but both sets of prices demonstrated a priority goal of Egyptian policy: cheap food for all.

The policy was widely credited with keeping the Egyptian rate of undernutrition low. Average calorie consumption exceeded requirements even among the poorest 12 percent of the population as a whole (USDA 1984:9), although significant numbers of urban households in the lowest-income quartile were found to be calorie-deficient (Alderman and von Braun 1984).

Table 19.2 Farm-Gate and Retail Price of Selected Agricultural Commodities, Egypt, 1982

	Price as Percentage of World Price	
	Farm-Gate	Retail
Beans	75.4	49.0
Cotton	27.2	41.3
Rice	26.6	17.7
Sugar	46.0	27.3
Wheat	64.5	36.8

Source: Rountree 1985.

Despite the apparent success of the Egyptian food subsidy, it has been criticized as inefficient. Sources of inefficiency include

• *Waste.* With bread as cheap as it is in Egypt, farmers purchase significant quantities of it for livestock feed. The resources spent processing the wheat into bread are a deadweight loss to society when the bread is fed to livestock.

• *Underinvestment in industry.* The more foreign exchange that is spent on a food subsidy, the less is available for industrial investment. One study estimated that a 10 percent increase in available foreign exchange would increase industrial investment by 6 percent and industrial output by 4 percent (Scobie 1983). High rates of government spending on imported food could adversely affect industrial employment among the poor.

• *Consumption inefficiencies.* Because of the depressed price of wheat, Egyptians eat more wheat than they would if they were paying the world price. A loss to Egyptian society associated with this overconsumption results, because government pays more for the last tons of wheat it bought at world market prices than Egyptian citizens would have been willing to pay for them. The amount of this cost above worth is represented by triangle 1 of Figure 19.1, which illustrates the case where the government uses subsidies to keep both the consumer price and the producer price below equilibrium, and makes up the difference in quantity demanded minus quantity supplied with (donated) imports from abroad.

Maize Subsidies in Southern Africa

Maize is the staple food crop in many countries of southern Africa. For example, in Zambia, maize makes up about two-thirds of the calories consumed. During the 1980s, countries in the region experimented with government monopolies in the marketing of maize. Farmers could only sell to the government and consumers could only buy from the government. By operating these monopolies at a loss, the government effectively subsidized both consumption and production, as illustrated in Figure 19.2.

(Notice the difference between Figure 19.1 and Figure 19.2. Figure 19.1 describes a policy that sets domestic price lower than the world price, but domestic consumers and producers face the same low price. The quantity consumed at this price is higher than the quantity produced; this difference must be made up with imports. Figure 19.2 describes a policy that allows the price that farmers receive to be higher than the price that consumers pay. But the quantity consumed is equal to the quantity produced.)

However, the costs of these subsidy programs were enormous (Mwanaumo, Preckel, and Farris 1994). For example, in 1990 in Zambia the cost of the maize subsidy program accounted for over 10 percent of the total government budget. The food subsidy programs contributed to overall govern-

Figure 19.1 Cost Above Worth and Producer's Surplus Lost Due to a Marketwide Explicit Subsidy

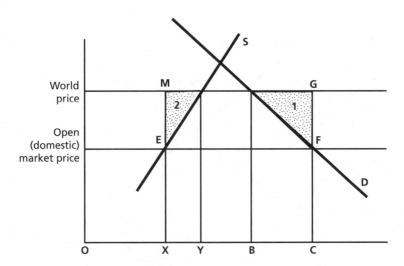

Note: Cost above worth – Suppose that D represents the demand curve for wheat and that OC represents the amount of wheat consumed, given the domestic and market price. If quantity BC is imported, then the area of triangle 1 is the loss to society, since government paid more for this wheat than it was worth to consumers.

Producer's surplus lost – Now suppose that S represents the supply curve for wheat, assuming no concessionary sales were available. Quantity OX represents wheat produced in Egypt given a depressed, domestic market price. Quantity XY represents wheat imported that could have been produced locally had the local price of wheat been equal to the world price. The area of triangle 2 is the loss to the Egyptian farmer, because it is a producer's surplus he could capture were he getting the world price, but which he now misses out on. Notice that the consumer would not care whether he paid the world price to the farmer or to a foreigner. But the Egyptian farmer cares, because he can produce that quantity of wheat with fewer resources than can the foreigner. And the economy cares, too, because triangle 2 is a loss to the Egyptian economy.

ment budget deficits (the Zambian government ran a deficit equal to 20 percent of its expenditures in 1986). As the countries sought help to finance these budget deficits, the International Monetary Fund made eliminating the subsidies and privatizing the parastatals a condition of the loan. Between 1990 and 1996—before and after the elimination of the maize subsidy program—the percentage of population suffering from undernutrition declined in three of the four countries involved, and increased slightly in Zambia. Jayne and colleagues (1995) conclude

> Consumer subsidies on refined maize meal in [the four countries] have not necessarily promoted food security, because they have entrenched a rela-

**Figure 19.2 Impact of a Government Subsidy on Consumption:
Lower Consumer Price, Higher Producer Price, Higher Quantity Consumed**

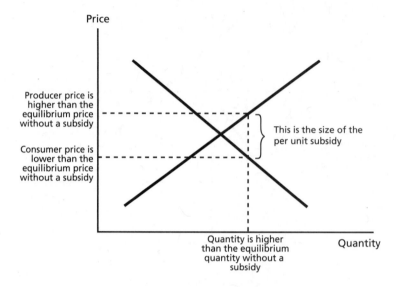

tively high-cost marketing system and impeded the development of lower-cost channels from developing. The negative effects of eliminating subsidies . . . have been partially or wholly compensated by relaxing controls on private grain trade, which has raised consumers' access to less expensive whole maize meal distributed through the emerging informal markets. A 53 percent rise in the price of refined meal in Kenya (due to subsidy removal) has been estimated to raise household expenditures by less than 1 percent of total income for low income groups, due to the widespread availability of cheaper whole meal.

Zimbabwe

In 1996, Zimbabwe's food distribution program was being cited as a good example of how to help the poor improve their nutritional status (Jayne et al. 1996). The changes that were admired at that time were

1. The elimination of a policy under which the government had a central role in maize marketing. That policy

    a. required maize farmers to sell their output to the government, and
    b. sold the maize at subsidized prices to privately owned, large-scale, relatively high-tech "roller mills" that produced highly refined maize meal.

2. This elimination allowed the emergence of small-scale relatively low-tech "hammer mills" that produced more coarsely milled maize, but at much lower cost.

3. Therefore, the elimination of the government subsidy did not hurt poor consumers because they now had the option of low-cost hammer-milled maize meal to replace the subsidized refined maize meal.

4. The subsidy elimination saved the government significant costs of a program that had provided a lot of benefits to the relatively high-income consumers of refined maize meal. Therefore, the change reflected a move from a "nontargeted" subsidy to a system that provided the new option of coarsely milled maize meal—a product consumed mostly by low-income consumers.

But in 2001—in part because of a regional drought, and in part because of government land redistribution policies that discouraged domestic production—food shortages became widespread and food price increases led to riots in the capital city (see Shaw 2000). The government reinstituted central control over the maize market. The new program did not solve the food shortage problem (Mudimu 2003).

By 2005, the government-run maize distribution program had become a corrupting force in the country's politics. As reported by Timberg:

> Hundreds of bags of cornmeal were stacked in front of a bar. . . . The officials first held a rally. . . . The next day, as hundreds of people from surrounding villages gathered to collect the 110-pound bags they had ordered and paid for months before, ruling party officials announced that only their supporters were eligible. When the names of opposition voters were called, they were simply handed back their money, according to several people who were turned away. The leftover bags went on sale hours later for twice the price. (2005:A1)

Next, the government tried to restore economic growth by pumping vast sums of currency into the economy; the subsequent massive inflation then inspired Zimbabwean president Robert Mugabe to impose economy-wide price caps, with predictable results:

> [N]ot even an unchallenged autocrat can repeal the laws of supply and demand. One month after Mr. Mugabe decreed just that, commanding merchants nationwide to counter 10,000-percent-a-year hyperinflation by slashing prices in half and more, Zimbabwe's economy is at a halt. Bread, sugar and cornmeal, staples of every Zimbabwean's diet, have vanished, seized by mobs who denuded stores like locusts in wheat fields. Meat is virtually nonexistent, even for members of the middle class who have money to buy it on the black market. . . . Zimbabwe's vast underclass, the majority of its 10 or 11 million people, has long been unable to afford most food, so the rural poor survive on whatever they can grow. Urban and rural poor alike stay afloat with food and money sent by the two million or more Zimbabweans who

have fled abroad. . . . Mr. Mugabe has cast the price cuts as a strike not against hyperinflation, but against profiteering businesses that he says are part of a Western conspiracy to reimpose colonial rule. . . . The government took over the nation's slaughterhouses in early July after meat disappeared, [but] the takeover . . . seems ineffectual: this week, butchers killed and dressed 32 cows for the entire city. Farmers are unwilling to sell their cows at a loss. (Wines 2007 A1)

The stark failure of government food policies is illustrated with this story:

Less than ten miles from Zimbabwean President Robert Mugabe's mansion in Harare—the largest private residence on the African continent—Cleophus Masxigora digs for mice. On a good day, he told me, he can find 100 to 200. To capture the vermin, he burns brush to immobilize them, then kills them with several thumps of a shovel. This practice has become so widespread in Zimbabwe that . . . state-run television has broadcast warnings against citizens setting brush fires. Masxigora began hunting mice to support (and feed) his wife and three children soon after Mugabe began confiscating thousands of productive, white-owned farms in 2000, a policy that has since led to mass starvation. (Kirchick 2007)

Food Subsidies in Latin America

Brazil

During the period 1966–1982, the government of Brazil attempted to achieve self-sufficiency in wheat production and at the same time provide cheap wheat to its consumers. As part of its attempt to achieve these goals, the government became the sole seller and buyer of both domestically produced and imported wheat. The prices of wheat and wheat products were rigidly controlled throughout the economy. Farmers were encouraged to increase wheat production through a price support subsidy, and millers were provided with wheat at a price substantially below that paid to the producer, with the government making up the difference out of the general tax till.

In their study of the Brazilian wheat policy, Calegar and Schuh (1988) determined that 86 percent of the subsidy went to consumers. This means only 14 percent of subsidy costs went to administration or were lost through slippages such as manipulations by the millers. Even so, only 19 percent of the total subsidy went to the true target group, the low-income consumers. Furthermore, gains in consumer welfare were slightly biased toward the high-income population groups (they bought more bread per capita than did the low-income groups). Calegar and Schuh conclude that the marketwide wheat consumption subsidy was not an effective policy for redistributing income and suggest that a preferred policy would be to target the food subsidy specifically at low-income groups.

In 2003, Brazil adopted a national plan aimed at zero hunger (Fome Zero in Portuguese). As part of this effort, the city of Belo Horizonte (about 300 miles north of Rio) adopted an aggressive set of programs designed to improve food availability to the poor (see World Future Council 2013 for a description). The Belo Horizonte food security program is frequently cited as a successful program and a model for other cities. The program uses a variety of approaches, including

- Providing free market space to commercial green-grocers if they agree to sell a list of products at fixed low prices.
- Organizing farmers' markets at no cost to small-scale farmers.
- Public restaurants open to all at subsidized prices, located in low-income neighborhoods.
- Free school meal programs.
- Food banks that distribute free food through churches and other social institutions.
- Cards given to qualified poor consumers that allow them to buy specific items at below-market prices.

As a result of the program, child mortality in the first twelve years of life has been reduced by 60 percent, and prevalence of undernutrition among children under age five has been reduced by 75 percent.

Venezuela

Like President Mugabe in Zimbabwe, President Hugo Chávez of Venezuela adopted a policy of price controls, while continuing to rely on the private sector to distribute food. The results were exactly as predicted by economic theory: by setting the controlled price below the market equilibrium price, the government created a situation in which quantity demanded was larger than quantity supplied, and shortages developed. Rather than using market price to "ration"—to allocate food among the citizens of Venezuela—this system ended up using long lines to allocate the food to those first in line. In addition, people in the private sector began to devote considerable effort to figuring out how to "game" the system—how to use the price control program to make more money. Some people decided to break the law and buy and sell on a black market at prices higher than the price control program allowed. Others, betting on the possibility that the perception of food shortages would force the government to raise the prices, decided to hold on to food stocks ("hoarding" food in the eyes of government regulators) until after the expected price increases went into effect. This behavior further exacerbated the food shortages.

The situation in 2007 is described by Pearson:

The state runs a nationwide network of subsidized food stores, but in recent months some items have become increasingly hard to find. . . . "They say there are no shortages, but I'm not finding anything in the stores," grumbled Ana Diaz, a 70-year-old housewife. . . . "There's a problem somewhere, and it needs to be fixed."

Gonzalo Asuaje, president of the meat processors association . . . , said that costs and demand have surged but in four years the government has barely raised the price of beef, which now stands at $1.82 per pound. Simply getting beef to retailers now costs $2.41 per pound without including any markup, he said. "They want to sell it at the same price the cattle breeder gets for his cow," he said. "It's impossible." (2007)

Targeted Subsidies

Two common problems appear in these descriptions: subsidies are expensive because they are not well targeted toward those in need, and subsidies are inefficient because of corruption or mismanagement. There is not much to say beyond the obvious about how to eliminate corruption and mismanagement. But there are a number of ways to target subsidies toward those who are food-insecure.

The Sri Lankan program (as it had evolved by the 1980s) illustrates one approach: target subsidies by requiring recipients to prove that they are undernourished, or poor. A study of the Philippines advised a two-step procedure for targeting: (1) identify target villages with high concentrations of underweight preschoolers; (2) within the selected villages, identify households containing preschoolers whose anthropometric measurements indicated high risk for undernutrition (Garcia and Pinstrup-Andersen 1987:78). In other cases, a maximum income or wealth level is established, and individuals must fall below that level to participate in the subsidy. It is difficult to enforce these targets. For example, the Sri Lankan program in 1978 restricted participation to households with annual incomes below 3,600 rupees (about $240). A survey of household income indicated that only 7.1 percent of the population lived in households below this eligible income level. Yet almost half the population managed to qualify for the program (World Bank 1986:93).

Self-Targeting

The easiest way to target a food subsidy is to subsidize foods with negative income elasticities of demand: the inferior goods, to use the economists' jargon introduced in Chapter 7. Inferior foods vary from culture to culture but are typically starchy staples such as cassava, yams, maize, sorghum, or millet. As income increases, people usually eat less of these foods.

The government of Bangladesh experimented with this idea in one area by subsidizing sorghum consumption, but the experiment, although supposedly successful, was not implemented countrywide (Karim, Majid, and Levinson 1984; Ahmed 1988:226).

The review cited earlier (Jayne et al. 1995) of maize meal subsidies in four countries in southern Africa concluded that a distinction should be made between programs that subsidized refined maize meal and programs that subsidized whole maize meal. As Table 19.3 shows, a majority of households in the poorest 20 percent of the income distribution in Kenya consume whole maize meal, a less expensive type of meal produced by small hammer mills. The richest households in the income distribution predominantly consume refined maize meal produced by large-scale roller mills.

Direct Distribution

Affluent countries are familiar with direct food distribution programs carried out through school lunch programs or by soup kitchens set up in low-income urban areas. In the third world, direct distribution of food is more likely to take the form of supplemental feeding programs targeted at the groups most vulnerable to undernutrition: pregnant and lactating women, infants, and preschoolers. Despite the popularity of such programs, the results have been disappointing (Kennedy and Knudsen 1985).

Beaton and Ghassemi (1982) found that in the eight supervised feeding programs and thirteen take-home food programs for which they had data, the net increase in food intake by the target recipients ranged from 45 to 70 percent of the food distributed, with one program showing a net effect of only 10 to 15 percent. Some of the reasons for these disappointing results are discussed in Box 19.1.

Rationing

A subsidized food-rationing system allows a consumer who holds a ration card to purchase a specific amount of some food or foods in a given time at a price lower than the market value. A subsidized food-rationing system requires either that the government set up a marketing system of its own (India's food ra-

Table 19.3 Targeting Food Subsidies for Maize Meal in Kenya

	Percentage of Households in This Income Group Consuming . . .	
	Refined Maize Meal	Whole Maize Meal
Poorest 20 percent	38	59
20th–40th percentile	53	44
40th–60th percentile	74	25
60th–80th percentile	76	22
Richest 20 percent	80	18

Source: Jayne et al. 1995.

Box 19.1 Supplementary Feeding

Eileen T. Kennedy and Per Pinstrup-Andersen

Supplementary feeding programs distribute foods through noncommercial channels to pregnant and lactating women, infants, and preschoolers. These programs are the most common form of nutrition intervention in developing countries.

There are three common forms of delivery: (1) on-site feeding, (2) take-home feeding, and (3) nutrition rehabilitation centers (NRCs). NRCs include both residential facilities and programs in which children are cared for during the day but return home at night.

Data from more than 200 supplementary feeding projects indicate that many supplementary feeding programs have had a significant and positive effect on prenatal and child participants (Anderson et al. 1981; Beaton and Ghassemi 1982). Despite the significant, positive effect, however, the benefits are usually small. Increments in birth weights attributed to the supplementary feeding programs are typically in the range of 40–60 grams. Similarly, the increases in growth seen in preschoolers, although significant, are small.

Several reasons are given for these small but significant effects. First, it appears that only a part of the food given is actually consumed by the target population. "Leakages" occur when the food is shared by nontarget family members or when the food is substituted for other food that normally would be consumed. Other factors, such as the timing of supplementation, duration of participation, nutritional status of recipients, and related services available, all influence the effectiveness of supplemental feeding.

Timing of supplement. Pregnancy and the period from six months to three years of age are the most nutritionally vulnerable times. Studies indicate that it is the last trimester of pregnancy that is the most critical for supplementation. Preschoolers below the age of three are also at special risk. Inappropriate weaning practices, delayed introduction of solid foods, food taboos, and infection all contribute to a higher prevalence of second- and third-degree malnutrition in this group.

Duration. For prenatal women, there appears to be a minimum participation of 13–15 weeks needed to produce significant changes in birth weight. For infants and children, the minimum level of participation needed to affect growth depends heavily on the type of delivery system used.

Nutritional status of participants. Children with second- or third-degree malnutrition exhibit greater benefits from supplemental feeding than do marginally undernourished children. The same is true for pregnant women.

Other services. Inadequate intake of food is only one of several factors that contribute to undernutrition. Undernutrition and infection often occur simultaneously. It is not surprising, therefore, that the most successful supplementation activities have been those with strong ties to primary healthcare programs.

Source: Kennedy et al. 1983:35–40

tion shops), or that the government set up a system for reimbursing commercial retail outlets for the discounts that they give for the rationed food (food stamps, described later). In either case, the government must employ auditors to monitor the system to minimize cheating. For example, as described earlier, operators of food ration shops in India diverted food supplies from their stores and sold them at higher prices in public markets.

Although the Philippine program described earlier was targeted at rural villages, it has been found that nationwide subsidized ration schemes generally show an urban bias. For instance, the subsidized wheat ration system in use in Pakistan was found to contribute about 11 percent of household income for urban households with incomes below the median. Rural households gained less than 1 percent of their income from the system. The reasons for the difference are that rural households are less likely to participate in the program, smaller quantities of rationed food are available there, and wheat is not sold in many rural areas (Rogers 1988c:247).

Food Stamps

Food stamps are somewhat different from ration coupons for purchasing subsidized food. Food stamps have a face value that can be used in any food store to purchase food at the market value. In addition, people are often required to purchase their food stamps. Since a food stamp plan does not require government to set up a parallel marketing system for the subsidized food, the system may be cheaper than rationing.

The first food stamp plan ever was introduced in the United States just before World War II, but it is the 1961 revision of the plan that economists like to talk about. In this version, eligible families received stamps with a cash value depending on household needs for food. They paid varying amounts for the stamps depending on their income level. This arrangement made it possible to vary the food-linked income transfer according to need and therefore extend the limited government food welfare expenditures to a broader segment of the population.

In his study of the food stamp program in Sri Lanka, Edirisinghe (1987:55) found that the caloric intake response to an additional rupee from food stamps was exactly the same as from an additional rupee of income. Because of decreasing income elasticity of demand as income rises, the cost of providing 100 additional calories through food stamps increases as income increases. Despite this finding, food stamp programs will probably continue simply because they are more acceptable politically than straight cash transfers.

Food-for-Work

Adding the requirement that recipients of food aid work in exchange for the food-linked income transfer is an interesting twist. Food-for-work has the potential to increase the productivity of the region in which it is applied and, at the same time, provide productive activities for recipients who would otherwise be unemployed or underemployed (Mellor 1984:104). Food-for-work projects typically improve rural infrastructure through building farm-to-market roads, constructing irrigation canals, and so forth. They have also been used in improving squatter settlements or in erecting community buildings (Jackson and Eade 1982:24).

During the early 1980s a food-for-work project in the Rift Valley of Kenya employed low-income farmers on local public works projects, particularly for erosion control and water-harvesting devices. The project had two positive economic outcomes: a good deal of farmland was improved and its access to irrigation water enhanced, and the participating farmers used some of their food-linked income transfers for capital investments on their farms and thus increased their own productivity. In fact, during the second year of the program the farmers devoted fewer hours to food-for-work activities, apparently in part because of a greater need to tend their own farms (Bezuneh, Deaton, and Norton 1988).

This success story is heartwarming, yet at the same time it introduces one of the problems with food-for-work: the benefits often go mainly to those who possess land. Typically, the recipients of food-for-work programs are not landowners but the landless unemployed and underemployed. If their projects improve the productivity of land owned by others, the inequality of asset distribution in the area could increase. In one food-for-work tree-planting project in Ethiopia, the workers became so resentful that their work was enhancing the private property of already powerful landed people that they planted all the trees upside down (Maxwell 1978a:40).

Another problem stems from the growing number of food-for-work laborers who are women. The extra time they put into food-for-work programs may detract from the quantity and quality of care that they give their children. Typically they leave their infants and preschoolers to be cared for by older siblings (Kennedy et al. 1983:28).

Cash Transfers Compared to Food Distribution Programs

A recent paper (Gentilini 2016) reviewed the results of ten studies that asked the question: "Is cash aid or food aid more effective in increasing food consumption?" These studies were experimental or quasi-experimental—meaning that the recipients were divided into two groups, with one group receiving cash aid and the other group food aid. (When group assignment is done by researchers randomly, a study is experimental; when individuals are assigned based on circumstances—for example, food aid given to individuals who are too isolated from markets to benefit from cash transfers—a study is quasi-experimental.)

Gentilini summarizes the lessons from these studies as follows: "The reviewed evidence shows that . . . both modalities work. When compared to control groups, cash and food transfers (and vouchers when considered) bolstered improvements in a range of indicators such as food consumption, income, dietary diversity, poverty, and malnutrition. . . . We observe a mild tendency of cash transfers to be more effective than food in enhancing food consumption (in five studies out of seven), while food seems to outperform cash in increasing household caloric intake (in four evaluations out of six)" (Gentilini 2016:22). Table 19.4 shows a sample of the results reviewed.

Box 19.2 describes a policy experiment in Ecuador to determine what kind of food distribution is the most effective.

Food Aid from Rich Countries to Poor Countries

Explicit food subsidization is an expensive way of improving nutritional status. This is especially true of food aid—subsidized food sold (or given away) by food-exporting countries (e.g., the United States, Canada, and Europe). The evolution of food aid practices over the years is a good illustration of how economic analysis has had a real-world impact on policy.

Food aid in the United States (the Food for Peace Program, or Public Law [PL] 480) began in 1954 as a way to reduce government-held stocks of commodities that the government acquired as part of its price support operations. As part of the political compromises involved in getting the program through Congress, the food aid legislation required that the food donated to poor countries be grown in the United States and be shipped on US-flagged vessels (which have considerably higher costs than foreign-flagged vessels). In addition, just as money, foreign aid (discussed in Chapter 17) was used to pursue foreign policy objectives other than helping the world's poor; food aid was often given to countries to persuade them to support US interests, rather than on the basis of how much undernutrition there was.

These compromises led to a food aid program that was widely criticized as inefficient in its impact on undernutrition and harmful to farmers in the recipient countries. For example, an Oxfam-commissioned report (Jackson and

Table 19.4 Effectiveness of Cash Transfers in Reducing Undernutrition

	Change in per Capita Calorie Consumption Under Cash Transfers
Bangladesh	4.9% reduction
Sri Lanka	1.5% reduction
Yemen	4.0% increase
Mexico	4.8% increase
Ecuador	10.0% increase

Source: Gentilini 2016.

Box 19.2 A Policy Experiment in Ecuador

As we have noted several times in this book, economists face the general problem of not being able to run "controlled" experiments. Unlike (say) plant scientists, who can measure the impact of fertilizer by growing two plots that are identical in every way except for fertilizer application rate, economists and policymakers have generally been reluctant to "treat" one group and leave others to serve as a "control" group.

However, in recent years, economists have become more and more willing to create artificial experiments in order to gain information that will generate widespread improvements. One example of this comes from Ecuador in 2011.

A number of poor households in Ecuador were randomly assigned to receive assistance in one of three forms: some households received cash that could be spent on food or nonfood items; some households received vouchers that could be exchanged in food markets for a list of nutritionally approved foods; some households received fixed quantities of food items (for example, 24 kilograms of rice per month, 8 cans of sardines, etc.). All three of the interventions had a value of $40 per month per household. Because households were randomly assigned to the subsidy group, the groups were very similar in terms of income, household size and composition, and the like.

The study team then evaluated the comparative effectiveness of the three forms of assistance, according to three effectiveness measures: per capita food consumption, per capita caloric intake, and dietary diversity. The authors of the study describe their conclusions as follows:

> We find that all three treatment arms significantly improve the quantity and quality of food consumed. . . . While food transfers increase food consumption, the increase is concentrated mainly on the food items that make up the food transfer. Vouchers also increase food consumption but are used on more varied food items such as vegetables, eggs, and milk and dairy. The difference in food consumption between cash and vouchers is a little more subtle, and most likely due to the limits placed on vouchers towards nutritious food. . . . Especially for policy makers, an important component of our analysis is related to costs and the cost-effectiveness of implementing the different transfer modalities. We find that . . . food is the least cost-effective means of improving food consumption and dietary diversity outcomes. However, the direct comparison of cash versus vouchers is not as straightforward and ultimately depends on the specific objectives of policy makers. If the objective is to increase the value of food consumption, then there is not a difference between cash or food vouchers. However, if the objective is to increase dietary diversity or caloric intake, then vouchers are more cost-effective than cash.

Source: Hidrobo et al. 2014

Eade 1982) found that the cost of the sea-freight to the US food aid program came to 53 percent of the value of the food. As an extreme example, the sea-freight plus within-country costs of the US food aid program in Guatemala ran to 89 percent of the original cost of the food. If the donated food was purchased in a developed country and sent to a third world country, the effect was to raise farm prices in the donor country and lower prices in the recipient country. The program thus acted as an incentive to agriculture in the developed country but as a disincentive to agriculture in the third world country. (See Box 2.4 for an example of this critique of food aid.)

An IFPRI evaluation (Hoddinott, Cohen, and Bos 2003) of food aid drew these conclusions:

- In recent years, the magnitude of food aid to the developing countries has declined, to about one-third the level of three decades prior.
- A higher percentage of food aid is now going to the poorest countries (rather than recipient countries chosen for their geopolitical significance); but food aid per capita has declined in all country groups.
- Food aid is higher in countries with low per capita incomes, civil conflicts, and natural disasters.

The IFPRI report recommends that food aid can be a useful tool in cushioning the effects of natural disasters, or human conflicts, but should not be relied upon as a permanent source of food in poor countries. The quantities of food aid shipments since 1990 are shown in Table 19.5. These figures confirm that the decline noted by the IFPRI evaluation has continued over the past decade.

What is more, there has been a considerable movement to ameliorate the price disincentive effect by using food aid funds to purchase food locally. Lentz and Barrett (2014) state:

Table 19.5 Quantity of Food Aid from All Donors, 1990–2015 (metric tons)

	Cereals	Noncereals	Total
1990	11,428,772	1,093,413	12,522,185
1995	7,886,134	1,207,347	9,093,481
2000	8,987,699	1,266,926	10,254,625
2005	5,844,927	1,030,734	6,875,661
2010	3,882,970	768,702	4,651,672
2015	663,649	251,701	915,350

Source: FAOSTAT.

Table 19.6 Leading Recipients of Food Aid, 2015 (metric tons)

	Food Aid
Syrian Arab Republic	253,774
Yemen	155,171
Kenya	57,166
Ethiopia	39,658
Somalia	35,849
North Korea	34,148
Democratic Republic of Congo	33,384
Chad	27,229
Tanzania	26,150
Niger	25,821
South Sudan	20,504
Gaza Strip (Palestine)	15,282

Source: FAOSTAT.

Globally, over the past decade, international food assistance has been radically reinvented by most donor countries. . . . The Canadians, Europeans, and other donors now procure little or no food from within their own borders. Instead, they provide cash and vouchers, and increasingly rely on local and regional procurement (LRP) whereby food aid commodities are acquired in recipient or neighboring countries rather than being shipped from the donor country. In 1994–95, 13% of all global food aid (by value) was LRP; by 2010, that number had increased to 67%. The United States has been far slower to embrace new forms of food assistance, becoming increasingly isolated and now almost the sole provider of old-fashioned, transoceanic food aid, responsible for 89 percent of global deliveries in 2011.

A final step toward reforming the international food aid system has been to use the World Food Programme (WFP) of the United Nations as the central organizing and decisionmaking body for food donations. As a result, food aid is now targeted quite carefully at the places where localized severe food shortages exist. The top recipients of food aid in 2015 are shown in Table 19.6. The countries on the list are all countries with famine conditions and extreme poverty (North Korea, Democratic Republic of Congo), civil strife (Syria, Sudan, Yemen, Gaza, Somalia), or refugee crises (Kenya, Ethiopia, Tanzania, Chad, Niger) resulting from wars in neighboring countries.

20

It's All About Distribution (Isn't It?)

In Chapter 8, we saw that the world food supply is sufficient to allow every person in the world to consume an adequate number of calories. It seems logical to ask, therefore: "So, it's really all about distribution, right?" Serious students of the world food problem draw similar conclusions: "Enough food is available to provide at least 4.3 pounds of food per person per day worldwide. The problem, therefore, is not of production but clearly of access and distribution" (Mittal 2002:304). The purpose of this chapter is to take seriously this line of argument, and to demonstrate that this conclusion is grossly misleading.

There Is Sufficient Food, But . . .

Let us begin by reviewing the numbers. The worldwide requirements for food are about 2,350 calories per person per day. This reflects an average of requirements that are smaller for children (and the elderly) than for adults, and are smaller for women than for men (as shown in Chapter 3, Table 3.1). Currently, food supply is about 2,850 calories per person per day. The "average food surplus"—the difference between average supply and average requirement—is about 500 calories per person per day.

A more detailed exploration of the FAO's food balance sheets suggests several ways that the average food surplus might be considered to be even larger. Another 1,100 calories or more per (human) capita per day are fed to animals, but animal products provide the average human with only about 500 calories per day. That reflects an additional 600 calories per person that could be obtained without increasing food production. And food is lost in waste and processing too.

Diet for a Small Planet:
Redistribution Through Voluntary Restraint

These calories "lost" in feeding animals have led some to conclude that voluntary changes in diet in developed countries might succeed in reducing or eliminating hunger in the developing world. The Hearts and Minds website (2016) on "socially responsible food" states, for example, that "if the USA reduced meat consumption by 10 percent, we would free more than 12 million tons of grain a year—enough to feed 60 million starving people."

We can analyze the assertion as follows. Table 20.1 shows calories per day, per capita, and in total for the United States and for the world in 2011. This provides a basis for understanding the Hearts and Minds claim just quoted. First, assume that the United States reduces all calories from animal products (not just meat, but also dairy, eggs, and fish) by 10 percent. The reduction is about 100 calories per day per person, or 31 billion calories per day for the country as a whole, or 11 trillion calories per year.

The Hearts and Minds calculation continues along these lines. To feed 60 million people (1,750 calories per day) we would need about 38 trillion calories a year (104 billion calories a day). A metric ton of grain has about 3.2 million calories, so 12 million metric tons of grain would provide the 38 trillion calories per year, the quantity needed to feed 60 million people.

Implicitly then, the Hearts and Minds calculation uses a feed-to-meat ratio of about 3.4 to 1 (37 trillion plant calories a year to produce 11 trillion animal calories a year). This number is larger than the feed–to–animal products ratio in the preceding (1,100 to 500 = 2.2 to 1), but there are two other fundamental, but less obvious, flaws in the reasoning:

• First, the world food supply is not a fixed quantity. If it were a fixed quantity, when less food is consumed by one group (say meat eaters in the

Table 20.1 Food Consumption Patterns in the United States and the World, 2011

	United States (population 314,912,000)		World (population 6,887,310,000)	
	Per Capita	Total (billions)	Per Capita	Total (billions)
Calories per day	3,639	1,146	2,868	19,753
Calories per day from animal products	995	313	507	3,492
Calories per day from plant products	2,644	833	2,362	16,268

Source: FAOSTAT food balance sheets.

United States), that difference is available to the other group (say undernourished people in developing countries). But food supply is not a fixed quantity. Farmers produce food because consumers buy it. If one group of consumers were to reduce their food demand, prices would drop, and other consumers would increase their consumption, partially offsetting the drop in food consumption in the first group, but producers also would react to lower prices by producing less food.

• Second, the increase in grain available is not automatically allocated to the world's hungry but rather is spread out among all people in the world.

Figure 20.1 illustrates the impact of a small backward shift in aggregate demand for calories for animal products in the United States. What is the relative size of these effects? Imagine that US consumers reduce their calories from animal products by 10 percent (by 31 billion calories per day, or 11 trillion per year) at the current price levels. This is 0.9 percent of world demand for animal calories. Assuming an elasticity of demand of –0.5, and an elasticity of supply of 0.6, to close the gap of 0.9 percent of quantity supplied, price will drop by 0.8 percent. Quantity of animal products demanded in the rest of the world will increase by about 14 billion calories per day (from 3,491 billion to 3,505 billion), quantity demanded in the United States will drop by about 30

Figure 20.1 Impact of a Reduction in per Capita Demand for Food in the United States on Consumption in the Rest of the World

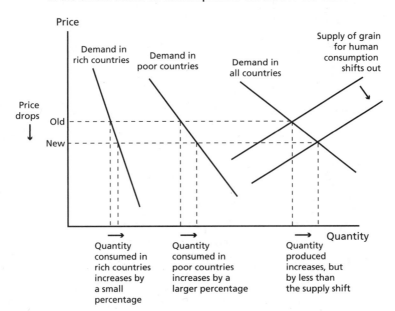

billion calories per day (the 10 percent decline is eroded slightly by the price decline), and quantity supplied will drop by about 17 billion calories per day (6 trillion calories per year).

This net drop of 17 billion calories per day in production of animal products will shift the supply of grain to the right by 38–60 billion calories per day (or 14–22 trillion calories per year). This is about half of the 38 trillion calories projected by Hearts and Minds. (Recall the difference between the FAO's food balance sheets and the Hearts and Minds assertion about whether the proper conversion rate is 2.2 or 3.5 calories of grain for each calorie of animal products.)

If there were some way to direct this "freed-up grain" into the hands of the most hungry, it is sufficient to feed 20–35 million people a diet of 1,750 calories per day. But the market mechanism for allocating goods relies on price. As a gap appears between aggregate quantity available and aggregate quantity demanded, the price will fall; producers will cut their production and consumers will increase their consumption, as shown in Figure 20.2.

The 38–60 billion calories per day of grain added to the market is 0.23–0.37 percent (less than 1 percent) of the total calories from plant (nonanimal)

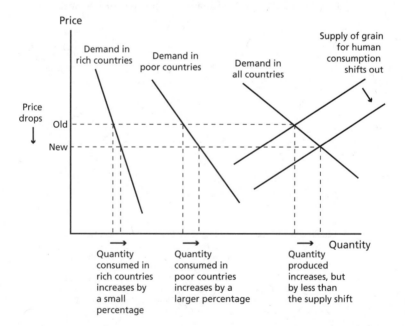

Figure 20.2 Impact of an Increase in Proportion of Grain
Produced for Human Rather Than Animal Food

products. In the calculations that follow, we assume that the elasticity of supply for plant calories is 0.4, and that the elasticity of demand for plant calories is –0.15 in developed countries and –0.35 in developing countries. As an additional 0.23–0.37 percent of plant calories are made available for human consumption, the price will drop by 0.33–0.52 percent. Applying the –0.35 demand elasticity, consumption in developing countries will increase by 0.116–0.184 percent. Applying this percentage change to the 2,339 calories per capita per day in developing countries (see Table 20.2) gives us 2.7–4.3 calories per day. In other words, the net effect of the diet change in the United States is to provide each resident of the developing world with 3–4 additional calories per day.

To review the logic by which the 38 trillion calories per year (or 1,750 calories per day for 60 million starving people) projected by Hearts and Minds has shrunk to 3–4 calories per day:

• The direct impact of a reduced meat consumption by some people is partially offset by increased meat consumption by others, responding to a lower meat price. If changes in diet create a direct reduction of about 11 trillion calories per year in animal products, about half of this is offset, so the net impact is to reduce animal calories consumed by about 6 trillion calories.

• The calories of feed "freed up" for each calorie of animal products may be 2.4 rather than 3.5, so the approximately 6 trillion animal calories per year converts to about 14 trillion calories of feed.

• The direct impact of an increase in available plant calories drives down the price and is partially offset by reduction in supply of plant calories that would otherwise have been available. Of the 14 trillion calories per year of animal feed newly available for human consumption, about 55 percent of this is offset, so the net impact is to increase plant calories consumed by humans by about 6 trillion calories.

Table 20.2 Food Consumption Patterns in Developed and Developing Countries, 2011

	Developed Countries (population 1,244,950,000)		Developing Countries (population 5,602,909)	
	Per Capita	Total (billions)	Per Capita	Total (billions)
Calories per day	3,371	4,197	2,759	15,456
Calories per day from animal products	908	1,130	419	2,349
Calories per day from plant products	2,464	3,067	2,339	13,108

Source: FAOSTAT food balance sheets.

• Some of this increase in plant calories takes place in developed countries: of the 6 trillion increase in calories, about 5.5 trillion occurs in the developing world.

• Within the developing world, consumption increases among the adequately nourished as well as the undernourished. Dividing the 5.5 trillion calories among the 5.6 billion people in the developing world yields about 1,000 additional calories per person *per year,* or 3 calories per day.

This demonstrates that voluntary restraint in the developed world will do little to improve the world undernutrition problem. Complete elimination of animal products from the diets of all people in the developing world would increase calories per person per day in the developing world by 120–180. This would make substantial inroads into the undernutrition problem, but would not eliminate undernutrition. The FAO's estimates of "depth" of undernutrition list many countries in which the average calorie deficiency among the undernourished exceeds 200 calories per day.

Policy Approaches

Of course, those who argue that we can solve the world food problem through redistribution are not restricting themselves to purely voluntary measures. What kinds of programs would be a part of a redistribution solution?

• "Overconsumption" in developed countries must be reduced.
• Overall production must be maintained at current (or close to current) levels.
• "Underconsumption" in developing countries must be reversed, and the increased consumption must be targeted to those who are undernourished.

Reducing overconsumption is conceptually quite simple, but impossible in practical, political terms. Food consumption will drop in response to a tax on income, or a sales tax on food. But huge taxes would be needed to achieve a substantial drop in consumption. In the United States, a reduction in average daily calories consumed from the current level of 3,750 to 3,000 (still a little above calories produced per person worldwide) is a 20 percent drop, too large to apply standard elasticity calculations. However, we can make some inferences about the size of the taxes needed by looking at the historical experience in the United States. The US populace last had an average consumption of 3,000 calories per capita per day in 1968. In 1968, real (inflation-adjusted) disposable income per person was $17,266, less than half of the current income. Food prices have risen more slowly than prices in general since 1968. Therefore a sales tax on food of about 4 percent, combined with an income surtax of about 45 percent, would be needed to return the United States to the consumption patterns of the late 1960s.

The second policy objective of the "redistribution solution" requires that while consumption in developed countries is reduced, overall production remains unchanged. Of course, the tax revenues collected under the programs to reduce overconsumption may well provide government revenues to operate such a program. (Undoubtedly, an income tax surcharge of the size projected here [45 percent] would have substantial incentive effects. Those are ignored here.) A program of government purchases of food could be used to bridge the gap between current levels of production and the reduced levels of consumption attained by the taxes. Assuming that the government purchased 20 percent of farm marketings (current value about $240 billion), the program would cost the US government about $50 billion (about 2.5 times the cost of current farm subsidy programs).

The third part of the "redistribution solution" would be donations of the food purchased by the developed-country governments to countries with undernourished people. The US foreign aid budget is currently about $25 billion, and less than half of this goes to low-income countries. Thus, the kind of food distribution envisioned here would mean not only a huge change in the scope of foreign assistance (increasing it by a factor of five), but also a radical change in the targeting of foreign assistance.

A fourth part of the "redistribution solution" would be a set of programs to ensure that the food donated by the developed countries actually reaches the undernourished people in the recipient countries. Here again, it is not difficult to conceive of programs to target the undernourished; but it may be problematic to get these programs adopted and implemented administratively.

Of course, the kinds of policies considered here are policies that would be adopted within a market-oriented system. Two alternatives to a market-oriented economic system might be considered: central planned production and consumption, and household food self-sufficiency or subsistence agriculture. Both of these alternatives have been tried (or are being tried), neither with notable success in eliminating undernutrition.

Why Does This Matter?

The main conclusion that we draw from the previous section is that a policy to solve the world's food problem solely through redistribution is politically infeasible. Huge taxes to reduce food consumption and huge increases in government expenditures for foreign assistance are not realistic policy proposals. But does it matter?

A sage once said: "In policy debates, never let the obvious go unstated." The reason that it is worthwhile to examine the "redistribution solution" argument seriously is that the conclusions drawn from the argument may actually impede progress toward solving the world food problem. The "dangerous" conclusions are

- Protection of natural resources can be achieved by cutting back on (or at least halting the growth of) food production.
- It is unnecessary to develop and adopt new technology to increase food production.

The first of these conclusions is illustrated by a quote from Rosset, Collins, and Lappe (2000): "Where dominant technology destroys the very basis for future production, by degrading the soil and generating pest and weed problems, it becomes increasingly difficult and costly to sustain yields. Under these . . . conditions, mountains of additional food could not eliminate hunger. The alternative is to create a viable and productive small farm agriculture using the principles of agroecology."

The second of these conclusions is also illustrated by Rosset, Collins, and Lappe: "We must be skeptical when Monsanto, DuPont, Novartis and other . . . companies tell us that genetic engineering will boost crop yields and feed the hungry. . . . [A] second Green Revolution they promise is no more likely to end hunger than the first." Or consider the article "Myth Seven: Biotechnology Will Solve the Problems of Industrial Agriculture" by Kimbrell (2002:62), in which he concludes, "If biotech corporations really wanted to feed the hungry, they would encourage land reform, which puts farmers back on the land, and push for wealth redistribution, which would allow the poor to buy food."

Underlying these conclusions is a deep-seated suspicion of technology: technology causes problems; it does not solve problems. And if agricultural production cannot be increased substantially without new technology, it is reassuring to believe that increased production is not necessary to solve the world food problem.

A clearer view of what kinds of policy changes would make up a "redistribution solution" suggests that improved technology must be a part of the solution to the world food problem. The enormous improvement in the world food situation in the past five decades (the percentage of people suffering from undernutrition in the developing world has dropped from 35 percent in the early 1960s to less than 20 percent today) is undoubtedly attributable in large part to new technology. In addition to boosting yields, new technology (low-impact tillage, drip irrigation, integrated pest management) can also reduce the impact of food production on resource degradation. Perhaps technology alone will not solve the world food problem, but increased production will be an integral part of any solution.

Finally, we should emphasize that although redistribution alone is unlikely to solve the world food problem, food distribution programs that target the poor and hungry are an absolutely critical part of any strategy to reduce undernutrition. We say in Chapter 16 that providing adequate nutrition to the average undernourished person requires a very small investment—the average hungry person is a peanut butter sandwich a day away from adequate nutrition.

The lack of political will in developed countries and in the world community to undertake the necessary investments can be explained in large part by the belief that the efforts will not in fact put food into the mouths of the needy but will instead enrich the already well-fed who have learned how to use the programs to their own advantage.

21

Raising Prices
Paid to Farmers

The most important class conflict in the poor countries of the world today is not between labor and capital. Nor is it between foreign and national interests. It is between the rural classes and the urban classes.

—*Lipton 1977:13*

As we have seen in Chapter 20, increasing production is almost certainly a necessary part of any solution to the world food problem. This conclusion is buttressed further by the findings in Table 21.1. This table shows data for eighty-three countries that had a prevalence of undernutrition of 26 percent or more in the 1969–1971 period; thus the countries shown are all countries with serious undernutrition problems at that time. The countries are split into three groups according to how fast cereal yields grew in the country between 1969–1971 and 2003–2005. Low yield growth is defined as growth of less than 20 percent; high yield growth is defined as growth of greater than 70 percent; and medium yield growth is between 20 percent and 70 percent. In 1969–1971, prevalence of undernutrition was similar in the three groups. But in the 2003–2005 period, the prevalence of undernutrition had declined sharply in the high-yield group; it had declined modestly in the medium-yield group; and prevalence of undernutrition had actually increased in the low-yield group. This suggests that increasing agricultural yields and output may be an important component in any effort to reduce undernutrition.

What kinds of policies will encourage increased agricultural production? Figure 21.1 illustrates two different ways of increasing the quantity of food produced. In this chapter we focus on the left-hand side of Figure 21.1. What kinds of policies can increase *prices received* by farmers? Here we consider two general approaches: increasing farm prices through subsidies and increasing farm prices through removal of programs that impose an implicit tax on farm output. Over the years, many countries have tried many types of programs designed to help domestic farmers.

351

Table 21.1 Yield Growth and the Prevalence of Undernutrition, 1969–2005

	Percentage Growth in Cereal Yields Between 1969–1971 and 2003–2005	Number of Countries	Average Percentage of Population Undernourished in 1969–1971	Average Percentage of Population Undernourished in 2003–2005
Low-yield growth	< 20	30	37.0	40.3
Medium-yield growth	20–70	24	30.6	21.8
High-yield growth	> 70	43	39.1	13.9

Source: Calculated from FAOSTAT data.

Direct Subsidies: Farm Subsidies That Increase Prices

We saw an example of a direct subsidy in Chapter 19 (Figure 19.2). Although the discussion there was couched in terms of a subsidy on consumption, we saw that the per unit subsidy created a wedge between the price consumers paid and the price farmers received. Direct price subsidies to farmers have exactly the same effect: the price farmers receive is the price paid by consumers plus the subsidy amount, so the program has the impact of increasing quantity, reducing consumer price paid, and increasing producer price received.

Historically, many agricultural subsidies have been administered as "target price–deficiency payment" programs. Under these programs the government announces the target price that it will guarantee for farmers. Then, once the crop is produced and sold at the market price, the government makes a payment to farmers (a "deficiency payment") that makes up the difference be-

Figure 21.1 Difference Between an Increase in Quantity Supplied and an Increase (or Outward Shift) in the Supply Curve

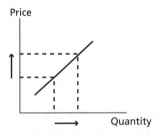 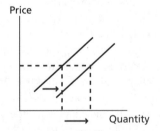

An increase in prices causes an increase in quantity supplied, moving along a stable supply curve

An outward shift in the supply curve causes an increase in quantity supplied, at a constant price

tween the market price (the price paid by consumers) and the target price (the price received by farmers).

These types of farm subsidies are simple to describe and to illustrate with a supply-demand diagram. However, putting the subsidies into practice can require considerable effort and expense. The United States has used a target price–deficiency payment program known as the loan-deficiency payment program. The program works like this:

• Congress sets a support price level in law. (For our example, the corn [maize] support price is $1.95 per bushel.)

• A farmer grows a crop and puts the harvested crop into storage at a government-licensed storage facility. The storage facility gives the farmer a receipt that serves as verification of the size of the farmer's crop for this year. (For our example, the farmer harvests 10,000 bushels of corn.)

• The farmer takes the receipt to the local office of the US Department of Agriculture and registers their crop as being eligible for farm subsidy payments.

• The farmer can remove the crop at any time from storage and sell it on the market at the prevailing price.

• The USDA announces a price every day for every county (the so-called posted county price). Because there are not actual sales of every commodity in every county on every day, these posted county prices are calculated from prices on major commodity exchanges (such as the Chicago Board of Trade) using a formula that adjusts for transportation costs to the specific county.

• Any time that the thirty-day average of the posted county price for the farmer is less than the support price, the farmer can go to the local USDA office and claim a deficiency payment. (For example, if the posted county price [thirty-day average] was $1.50 per bushel on a particular day, the farmer could claim a deficiency payment equal to the support price [$1.95] minus the "market" price [$1.50] times the crop size [10,000 bushels] = $4,500.)

• If the market price is at or above the support price, no subsidy payment is made.

This example shows how the loan-deficiency payment program is illustrated by the supply diagram in Figure 19.2: farmers receive a high price ($1.95); consumers pay a low price ($1.50); the quantity produced equals the quantity consumed (10,000 bushels).

The loan-deficiency payment example also illustrates some of the administrative challenges that need to be overcome. Each farmer's output needs to be verified and recorded. The local market price needs to be measured or calculated. And records must be kept showing whether and when the farmer has claimed the subsidy payment.

Of course, there are different ways to administer a target price–deficiency payment program. As described in Chapter 19, countries such as Zambia have used a program where the government is the sole buyer and seller of a commodity—paying farmers a high price and charging buyers a low price. But regardless of the method of administration, these programs can be expensive to administer and an inefficient way to help farmers and consumers. In addition, these types of programs may fail to provide farmers with incentives to produce high-quality output. (See Box 21.1 for an example.)

Another method commonly used to keep farm prices high is a price support and purchase program. These programs set a support price level and then promise to buy from farmers at that price; the market price can never fall below the support price because farmers always have the option of selling to the government at that price. Box 21.2 describes how this kind of program

---

Box 21.1 Removing Farm Subsidies in Iraq

Under the regime of Saddam Hussein, agriculture in Iraq was dominated by government bureaucracy. The government provided seeds, fertilizer, chemicals, and machinery to farmers at below-market prices. It leased land to farmers at concessionary rates. It bought all wheat and barley produced at a fixed price, regardless of quality. Then government flour mills distributed flour free to consumers.

When the Hussein government fell, the US-led occupation authority was in charge. It discovered that some of the grain produced by Iraqi farmers was of such low quality that it threatened to gum up the flour-milling equipment. To avoid angering the Iraqi farmers, the occupation authority continued to buy grain as under the old regime. But it fed much of the crop to cattle, and destroyed some by burning. Wheat was imported from the United States and Australia to provide flour for Iraqi consumers.

One Iraqi official told a Washington Post reporter that he blamed the subsidy system: "People were making so much money that the incentive to work harder, to increase production—it wasn't there," said Salam Iskender, the new head of the agriculture section for the Wasit [provincial] governorate. . . . As a result, the yield in some regions plummeted from one ton of wheat per [unit of land] to a third of that and, particularly in the last two years, a large percentage of the crop came up 'black,' meaning that it couldn't be eaten" (Cha 2004:A1).

Western advisers to the provisional authority were certain that a more market-oriented approach would succeed in increasing output by 20 percent, and that the upcoming crop year would see an end to government provision of inputs (though the output price subsidy would remain, and even increase). Iraqi farmers were not so sure: "We are afraid of the free economy. We don't understand it. If we grow crops, who will help us and who will buy it?" asked one; "We are like a child which stage by stage needs to grow up. . . . We need time," said another (Cha 2004:A1).

works in India. A basic problem with support price and government purchase programs is that the excess stocks build up in government warehouses. These can be gotten rid of by selling them at below-market prices to domestic consumers, or by selling them to foreign buyers with an export subsidy, or by destroying them. In other instances, the government attempts to minimize surplus stocks by imposing limits on farm production. Of course, selling surplus production abroad or limiting production does not reduce domestic undernutrition.

When people hear the term "farm subsidies" they typically think of a program such as that described here—the government paying a per unit subsidy that augments the market price. And these subsidies do increase farm output. But (as described in more detail later) considerable controversy has arisen over the existence of such subsidies in rich countries, because the expanded production puts downward pressure on world commodity prices and in this way harms farmers (and reduces farm production) in developing countries. The United States and the European Union have moved their farm subsidy efforts away from programs such as those described here and toward other methods of providing assistance to farmers—methods that (it is believed and hoped) will have less impact on farm prices and farm output, and therefore less impact on world markets. Those methods include programs that increase

---

Box 21.2 Farm Subsidies in India

India has an extensive program of farm price subsidy programs, described in Landes 2004. In order to encourage self-sufficiency in wheat and rice, India supports the farm price of those two commodities. The support price is calculated as the amount a farmer would need to cover the full cost of production. Calculating support prices in this way has protected Indian farmers from the pressure of competition; as a result, crop yields and agricultural productivity remain low in India compared to other countries.

The grain purchased by the government at the support price goes into the ration-shop distribution program described in Chapter 19. Since the late 1990s, support prices have engendered surpluses that were larger than could be absorbed by the ration-shop system, and government-held stocks soared. As a practical matter, market grain prices are determined by government decisions about how much grain to release from storage, rather than by the underlying supply-and-demand conditions. In order to reduce some of the government-held stocks, the Indian government began selling grain at a loss to foreign buyers for export.

As India's urban population becomes richer, there is growing demand for a broader range of food. But the agricultural support program encourages farmers to keep their land planted in wheat and rice, so consumers look to purchase imported food while Indian-grown wheat and rice sit unbought in government storehouses.

farmer incomes, but not by increasing farm prices, and programs that provide assistance to farmers during periods of low incomes.

Lump-Sum Payments, or Income Subsidies

During the 1990s the United States adopted a program that sent farmers a subsidy check simply because they owned (or rented) farmland. The amount of the check varied with the quantity of land (and with the kinds of crops that had been grown on the land in the past), but the money amount was not influenced in any way by the current crop decisions of the farmer. Suppose a farmer owned land that had been used to grow 100 acres of corn and yielded 100 bushels per acre at some (specified) period in the past (during the 1980s or 1990s). That farmer would receive (in 2006) a corn direct payment of $2,380. If the farmer only grew corn on 50 of those acres and used the other 50 for pasture, the payment was unchanged at $2,380. If the farmer grew no corn at all but used their land for other crops, the payment was unchanged at $2,380. If the farmer increased their yield to 150 bushels an acre or reduced it to 75 bushels an acre, the payment was unchanged at $2,380. Because the payment was not influenced by current decisions, it can be called a lump-sum payment.

Lump-sum payments would not (in a simple economic theoretical model) have any impact on farm output. Of course, one can imagine circumstances in which these kinds of payments could make a difference in aggregate output. Perhaps some farmers who were considering a different occupation would remain farmers because of the lump-sum payment. Perhaps some farmers would use the subsidy payments to buy new machinery or make other improvements that they would not have been able to afford without the lump-sum subsidy program. Perhaps some farmers would increase their output in anticipation of a future date in which a new program bases the size of subsidy payments on output in 2006.

Programs That Make Payments During Hard Times

In a farm bill in 2014, the United States eliminated the direct subsidy program. In that legislation, farm subsidies now take the form of payments to farmers that are triggered by low prices or low revenues. In that respect, the farm subsidy programs bear a strong resemblance to "disaster payments" or to insurance, where indemnity payments are triggered by the occurrence of some negative event. And in fact over the years, USDA expenditures on domestic farmers have shifted dramatically toward subsidizing farmer purchases of crop insurance.

These kinds of government programs have two kinds of effects on farm output. First, by reducing or eliminating the possibility of low farm prices, the programs cause an increase in average or expected price, and therefore shift up a fixed supply curve (as shown in the left-side diagram in Figure 21.1). Second, by reducing the overall risk faced by farmers, the programs may cause (risk-averse) farmers to be willing to produce more at any given level of expected price. This, in effect, shifts the supply curve down and to the right (as illustrated in the right-side diagram in Figure 21.1).

Policies to encourage use of crop insurance in developing countries have received increasing attention over the past decade (see Miranda and Farrin 2012 for an example).

Agricultural Subsidies and the World Trade Organization

As part of the World Trade Organization negotiations to reduce impediments to freer international trade, countries have been negotiating reductions in their agricultural subsidies. In these negotiations, an important distinction has emerged about the difference between "distortionary" versus "nondistortionary" subsidies.

Distortionary subsidies are subsidies that work through the price mechanism and give a farmer a subsidy *per unit of production*. This means that the more the farmer produces, the larger the subsidy received. Because of this, the subsidy program influences or "distorts" farmer decisions (farmers move up the supply curve as shown in the left-hand diagram of Figure 21.1). In the context of international trade, a program that encourages increased production domestically interferes with free trade because it reduces the market for imports, or because it creates additional exports that must compete with other countries. The deficiency payments described earlier are an example of a distortionary subsidy. Under WTO rules, distortionary subsidies are limited in size, and future negotiations are likely to limit them still further.

However, under WTO rules there are few restrictions on nondistortionary subsidies. Nondistortionary subsidies are subsidies that do not work through the price mechanism and therefore are not tied to the quantity produced by a farmer. As described earlier in the discussion about lump-sum subsidies, if we send every farmer a check for $1,000, this does not change a farmer's decision about what crops to plant or how much to produce. During the past two decades, agricultural subsidies in the United States and Europe have evolved to a considerable extent from distortionary to nondistortionary subsidies. US policymakers have argued that since the subsidy does not influence the farmer's decisions about what and how much to produce, they should be regarded as nondistortionary and are not limited by WTO agreements. See Box 21.3 for a description of the WTO cotton subsidy dispute.

The World Bank's 2008 *World Development Report* (World Bank 2007) devoted a chapter to the current status of agricultural subsidies. That report confirms that subsidies by rich countries do cause lower world prices, but this impact is fairly small. Additional findings of the report are the following:

• Consistent with their commitments under the Uruguay Round agreement (discussed later), developed countries have reduced overall agricultural subsi-

---

Box 21.3 The Cotton Subsidy Dispute Between Brazil and the United States

In 2002, Brazil complained to the World Trade Organization that the cotton subsidy program used by the United States was a violation of US commitments under international agreements. At the beginning of the consideration of this complaint, the United States thought that all of its subsidies were protected by a "peace clause" provision permitting preexisting programs as long as the United States abided by overall commitments. But Brazil argued (and the WTO agreed) that the United States had broken its commitments to cut overall subsidies; the difference of opinion centered around the question of whether direct payments should be included in the group of subsidies that had to be limited. The WTO agreed with Brazil that direct subsidies should be included; therefore the US had failed to make required limitations; therefore the "peace clause" provided no protection.

Brazil was able therefore to pursue its specific complaints, remedies to which included US programs to assist companies that exported cotton, and "price-contingent" subsidy payments to cotton farmers (payments whose existence and size depends on the level of the cotton price). The WTO agreed that these policies suppressed the world cotton price, and thereby harmed Brazil and Brazilian cotton farmers.

The 2014 farm bill in the United States contained a radical revision of the cotton subsidy program, including elimination of the cotton-specific export subsidies and price-contingent subsidies. Brazil and the United States entered into a new agreement in 2014 given that the issues had been resolved in a mutually acceptable way.

---

dies by about 20 percent between 1986 and 2005, and have reduced distortionary subsidies by about 35 percent. In many developing countries, government programs that interfere in agricultural markets are being modified or eliminated, and the more market-oriented policies have often improved agricultural productivity.

• Although barriers to agricultural trade have been reduced over the past decade and a half, remaining barriers impose an efficiency cost of $67–200 billion worldwide, with $20–60 billion of that cost being borne by developing countries. There are considerable differences among developing countries as to the extent to which their economies are harmed by trade restrictions; the cost is less than 1 percent of GDP for developing countries as a group, but for some countries (Vietnam, Thailand), the cost is in the 3–5 percent range.

• Most of the welfare costs cited here are from restrictions on trade, not from distortions caused by domestic agricultural subsidies. "Developed country agricultural policies cost developing countries about $17 billion per year—a cost equivalent to about five times the current levels of overseas development assistance to agriculture" (World Bank 2007:103).

• A further reduction in trade distortions is likely to increase prices in world markets, especially for cotton, oilseeds, dairy products, and cereals. "Because many of the poorest countries spend a large part of their incomes on cereal imports, they may incur an overall welfare loss despite gains from price increases in non-food commodities such as cotton" (World Bank 2007:106).

• Further reductions in trade distortions are projected to increase agricultural output in Latin America and reduce agricultural output in developed countries. Poverty would decline in most, but not all, countries.

What is more, some economists have noted that many poor countries benefit from low prices because they are net *importers* of food. Others concede this point but argue that the benefit of low prices accrues to (relatively wealthy) urban consumers and imposes hardship on the (relatively poor) rural agricultural producers. (See *The Economist* 2005 for more details on these points.

The last agreement under the General Agreement on Tariffs and Trade (GATT) was the Uruguay Round agreement, which established the WTO and formalized the restrictions on domestic agricultural subsidies. In 2001, a new round of negotiations was announced—the Doha Round. However, negotiators have been unable to reach an agreement in the subsequent decade and a half. The main source of disagreement is that outlined previously: developed countries want greater access to the developing world than the developing countries are willing to grant; developing countries want greater cuts in agricultural subsidies than the developed countries are willing to make (Lester 2016).

Urban Bias

Another way to increase farm prices is to remove policies that have the effect of depressing prices. In Chapter 19 (Figure 19.1), we illustrated a policy that reduced both producer and consumer prices in a country by increasing imports. During the twentieth century, many developing countries adopted policies that reduced food prices in the economy as a whole—both the prices paid by consumers and the prices received by farmers.

As pointed out in Box 21.4, one of the surprising anomalies of the world food problem is that developed countries (where agriculture is already highly productive and food supplies are abundant) have generally stimulated farm production by engaging in agricultural policies that result in high farm prices, whereas developing countries (where agricultural production is often marginal and food supplies are scarce) frequently have discouraged farm production by engaging in agricultural policies that result in low farm prices. No doubt, low food prices are politically attractive, because they are an easy way to transfer income to the urban poor. But the impact on the rural poor, many of whom are food *producers,* should not be overlooked.

The degree to which general economic prosperity and quality of life in rural areas have lagged behind those of city dwellers is illustrated in a paper by Sahn and Stifel (2002), which found that in sub-Saharan Africa, rural measures were worse than urban measures in the following categories:

- Asset poverty: twelve out of twelve countries.
- School enrollment: ten out of ten countries.
- Infant mortality: nineteen out of twenty-four countries.
- Stunting (undernutrition): fourteen out of fourteen countries.
- Body mass index (undernutrition): seven out of seven countries.

Box 21.4 Urban Bias and Agriculture

Michael Lipton's 1977 book *Why Poor People Stay Poor: Urban Bias in World Development* laid out a compelling case that the most important "class struggle" in developing countries was the competition between the rural population and the urban population for control of the policymaking apparatus. The urban class, he argued, was winning this competition because they had overwhelming advantages: lower poverty, better education, better capacity to organize and communicate.

The result is that urban-dominated ruling classes directed resources toward low-return projects that helped city dwellers rather than rural investments that had much higher payoffs. "Scarce investment, instead of going into water-pumps to grow rice, is wasted on urban super-highways. Scarce human skills design and administer not village wells and agricultural extension services, but world boxing championships" (p. 13).

Not only is urban bias inefficient, it is inequitable. The people who benefit most from government programs in developing countries are the comparatively rich urbanites, rather than the rural poor. Lipton concludes: "A shift of resources to the rural sector and within it to the efficient rural poor . . . is often, perhaps usually, the overriding developmental task" (p. 18).

Anandarup Ray (1986) pointed out that in the 1970s and 1980s, this urban bias could also be seen in agricultural pricing policies of developing countries. Whereas rich countries such as the United States, Canada, Europe, and Japan heavily subsidize their agricultural sectors, "developing countries tend to tax agriculture—even those low-income countries that depend critically on agriculture for their economic growth. Some pay their producers no more than half the world price for grains and then spend scarce foreign exchange to import food. Many subsidize consumption to help the poor, but end up reducing the incomes of farmers who are much poorer than many of the urban consumers who benefit from the subsidies" (p. 2).

The Mechanisms of Urban Bias

There are six kinds of policies that have led to these disparities between rural and urban dwellers: (1) taxes on agricultural commodities and land; (2) marketing boards and administered prices; (3) exchange rate policies that favor urban consumers over rural producers; (4) rural isolation because of poor roads, infrastructure, and market information systems; (5) corruption and legal institutions; (6) restrictions on movement of goods.

As discussed in Chapter 17, developing countries have relied more heavily on taxing exports (and to a lesser extent on taxing land) as a way of collecting revenue for government operations. Argentina provides a good historical example.

From 1940 to 1972 the government of Argentina generally maintained a policy to keep agricultural prices low relative to the prices of nonagricultural goods. This was accomplished through a variety of measures that, in general, added up to a high tax on agricultural exports and a tariff on nonagricultural imports. This resulted in an implicit tax on agriculture that is estimated to have amounted to 50 percent of total agricultural output during the period. Among the consequences of this policy were that employment in agriculture declined, agriculture lost resources to nonagriculture, and agricultural productivity grew more slowly. In fact, per capita agricultural production in the 1970s was less than it was before World War II (Cavallo and Mundlak 1982:13–14).

During the months of soaring food prices in 2008, Argentina renewed its interest in taxing food exports. Such taxes would discourage exports, keep more domestic production in the country, and keep food prices from rising so drastically. Farmers objected vociferously. Argentine president Christina Kirchner (and her husband, former president Nestor Kirchner) denounced the farmers as unpatriotic, saying farm profits from high prices should "belong to all Argentines" (see Barrionuevo 2008).

Some developing countries have passed laws requiring that agricultural output be sold through a government agency. In these cases, prices are set administratively, rather than through interactions of private buyers and sellers in a market, and the government can keep farm prices low directly (without imposing an explicit tax). Chapter 19 reviewed programs in southern African countries under which the government acted as the sole buyer and seller. That discussion (Figure 19.2) envisions a situation in which net losses to the government agency are used to subsidize both farmers and consumers. However, the government agency could operate at a profit (generating funds for other government operations) by setting farm prices below the equilibrium price and consumer prices above the equilibrium price (and at a quantity below the market equilibrium quantity).

One example of this source of urban bias is from Tanzania in the 1970s and 1980s. During this period, the Tanzanian government controlled most aspects of agricultural marketing; government-controlled farm prices were reduced between 1970 and 1984 so that the average of official producer prices declined 46 percent. Rising export taxes and the costs of the government marketing program reduced the farmers' share of the final sales value of export crops to 41 percent in 1980. Output of some export crops (cashews, cotton, and pyrethrum) fell drastically in the 1970s. By 1984 the tonnage of export crops moving through the government marketing boards was 30 percent less than it had been in 1970 (World Bank 1986:74–75). The implicit tax on agriculture was a substantial disincentive to agricultural production.

For countries that export agricultural goods and import nonagricultural goods, an overvalued exchange rate can have the same impact as an import tax: foreign buyers find the agricultural exports more expensive (hurting rural farmers) and domestic buyers find the nonagricultural imports less expensive (helping urban consumers) (Schuh 1988).

Bale (1985:24) studied five developing countries from the point of view of the impact of overvalued domestic currency on agricultural production. He found that the currencies were overvalued by between 25 and 45 percent. Bautista (1987) found a similar result for the Philippines.

Cleaver (1985) studied thirty-one countries in sub-Saharan Africa and found that in countries that were reducing the amount of currency overvaluation, agricultural production was growing much faster than it did in other countries in the sample.

"Rural isolation"—conditions that make it costly or impossible to move goods and people between rural and urban areas—also depress farm prices. Consider a situation in which local village price for a commodity is $1, and city price is $1.50. If it costs 60 cents to transport the commodity, the farmer will sell locally—the $1 there is higher than the 90 cents the farmer would receive ($1.50 minus 60 cents) from city sales after paying for transport. But improvement of roads or other transportation infrastructure that reduced transport costs to (say) 30 cents would allow the farmer to sell in the city and net $1.20 after transport costs. This aspect of urban bias is discussed in Chapter 17 (Box 17.1) and will be raised again in the next chapter.

Another aspect of rural isolation is that it can allow corruption to flourish in rural areas without the scrutiny of outsiders who otherwise might be able and willing to put a stop to it. The *New York Times* (Weiner 2000) reported a situation in the Mexican village of El Mameyal—a village so poor that it had no running water, no plumbing, no schools, only a single store, and just one street. A gang of criminals, with the cooperation of corrupt local officials and police, began seizing the land of peasants and cutting timber from the land, and the peasants were powerless to stop it. "One villager complained, 'there has been no investigation, no justice, no consequences—there has been nothing.'"

Finally, in some cases countries have imposed restrictions on sales and movement of food, with the result that farmers lose access to markets where prices are higher. The purpose of these programs is to protect consumers from high prices, or large swings in prices. For example, in Tanzania in the 1990s a law was passed requiring that food must be sold in the same province where it was grown. The intention was to stop the export of food from areas where the food was needed. But the effect was to keep farmers from obtaining high prices during periods of food shortage. During the quick run-up of world food prices during 2008, China and India instituted export restrictions to insulate their domestic consumers from these high prices (see *The Economist* 2008). These actions succeed in keeping consumer prices low, but they also keep farm prices low, and this is a disincentive to production.

An End to Urban Bias?

A five-volume World Bank study (Krueger, Schiff, and Valdés 1991) confirmed the policy bias against agriculture in great detail. A synopsis of the findings of that study are found in a 1995 article by Schiff and Valdés, who concluded that (for the eighteen countries in their study), agricultural prices, compared to nonagricultural prices, were 43 percent lower than they would have been in the absence of policies biased against the rural sector.

In the years since that study, a growing body of evidence has accumulated that developing countries are turning away from urban bias. Some of this evidence is summarized and discussed in the World Bank's 2008 *World Development Report* (World Bank 2007) and includes:

• The extent of currency overvaluation in developing countries fell from 140 percent in the 1960s to 80 percent in the 1970s and 1980s to about 9 percent in the early 1990s.

• Direct and indirect taxation of agriculture in sub-Saharan African countries declined from 28 percent in 1980–1984 to 10 percent in 2000–2004. Of eleven countries studied, agricultural tax rates fell in nine.

• The tax rate on agricultural export goods in developing countries declined from 46 percent in 1980–1984 to 19 percent in 2000–2004.

• In agriculturally based developing countries, the net tax on sugar and rice has been eliminated and has been substantially reduced for maize and wheat.

• "Both China and India have reduced their anti-agricultural bias substantially over the past three decades, not only directly but also indirectly via cuts to manufacturing protection" ((p. 102).

A paper by Jensen and Robinson also finds a reduction in the degree of urban bias:

Empirical studies from the 1980s . . . supported the view that policies in many developing countries imparted a major incentive bias against agriculture. Eliminating this bias was one of the goals of policy reform strategies, including structural adjustment programs, supported by the World Bank and others; and many countries undertook such reforms in the 1990s. . . . [Our] analysis indicates that, in the 1990s, the economywide system of indirect taxes, including tariffs and export taxes, significantly discriminated against agriculture in only one country, was largely neutral in five, provided a moderate subsidy to agriculture in four, and strongly favored agriculture in five. (2002)

In an article reviewing the literature on agricultural policies in developing countries, Binswanger and Deininger (1997) explore the conditions under which policy reforms are likely to be initiated. They observe that "a fiscal crisis is usually necessary for initiating reform"—the efficiency costs of the urban bias must become high enough to have an impact on the government budgeting process. They argue that the sustainability of the reform effort depends on (1) whether people who benefit from the reform are organized into groups who can exercise some political clout, (2) whether the central bank and ministry of finance have the will and power to maintain budgetary discipline, (3) whether the reform effort is encouraged by international credit and advice, and (4) whether policy analysts can support the reforms without succumbing to political pressures. It appears that the reform process is well under way in developing countries.

A search of recent literature finds continued interest in the issue of urban bias (e.g., Demont 2013; Gupta 2015). As well, China has an ongoing research effort examining the urban-rural income gap (see *China Daily* 2012 for an example).

Policymakers seem to have absorbed the lessons of urban bias when it comes to policies that keep agricultural prices depressed. However, for most of the developing world, rural incomes, health indicators, and nutritional status remain below urban levels. The political forces that made urban bias an attractive strategy in the 1960s and 1970s may well propel policymakers to consider a return to that strategy, or to some of the policies described here.

22

Increasing
Food Supply

While the most important reasons for inadequate agricultural output are difficult to ascertain, T. W. Schultz, in the first Elmhurst Memorial Lecture to the International Association of Agricultural Economists, left no doubt as to his ranking of the causes. He stated that the level of agricultural production depends not so much on technical considerations, but in large measure, "on what governments do to agriculture."

—Bale and Lutz 1981:8

In the preceding chapter (Figure 21.1), we noted the distinction between increasing the supply of food and increasing the quantity of food supplied. An increase in the supply of food—or as economists call it, an outward shift in supply curve—occurs when farmers are willing to produce more food at the same price, or are willing to produce the same amount of food at a lower price. This is the type of change that would permit the quantity of food to increase while the equilibrium price of food declines (see Figure 22.1). What would make a farmer willing to produce more at the same price, or produce the same amount at a lower price? A reduction in the farmer's costs of production. And how can we reduce food production costs? By reducing prices farmers pay for inputs, by encouraging investment, by developing new technologies that increase farm productivity, and by maintaining or improving the quality of resources.

Subsidies for Purchased Inputs
The most direct and obvious policy mechanism to reduce production costs is to subsidize the prices farmers pay for inputs. The government can do this by compensating farmers for each unit of inputs purchased, by subsidizing the production of inputs, or by producing or distributing the inputs themselves. In this section, we will briefly explore programs that subsidize fertilizer, mechanization, and irrigation.

**Figure 22.1 Effect of Reduced Costs or
Improved Technology on the Supply Curve**

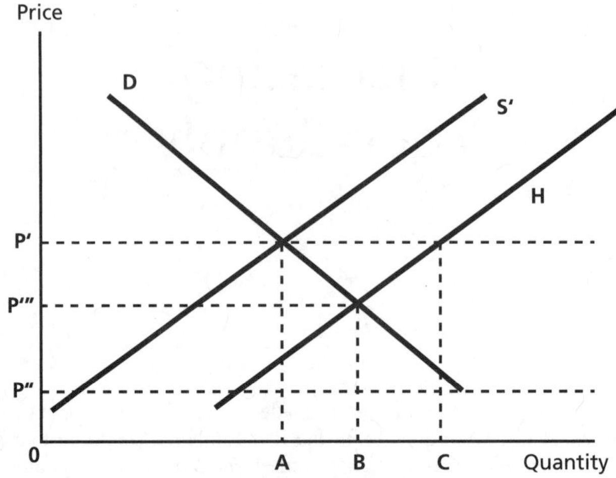

Note: When the supply curve shifts from S' to S", farmers are willing to furnish to the market:
(1) an increased quantity (OC rather than OA) at the same, old price (P'); (2) the same, old quantity
(OA) at a new price (P"); or (3) some other combination of quantity and price—for instance, the
quantity and price represented by point H in the figure.

Fertilizer

In Chapter 13, we saw how fertilizer use could have a big impact on agricultural yields and output. Developing countries have used a variety of policy instruments to encourage fertilizer use.

Fertilizer subsidies have been common. During the 1980s, for example, urea sold at 56 percent below cost in Sri Lanka and at 60 percent below cost in Gambia. Arguments favoring subsidies to fertilizer include encouraging learning by doing, overcoming risk aversion and credit constraints, helping poor farmers, offsetting disincentives caused by taxing or pricing policies, and maintaining soil fertility (World Bank 1986:95).

But as government bureaucracies have played a bigger and bigger role in fertilizer pricing and availability, problems have arisen. As fertilizer use increases, scarcities develop when government-subsidized distribution fails to keep up with demand. Government involvement in production, importation, and distribution of fertilizer inhibits the development of a private distribution system. Furthermore, fertilizer subsidies are expensive, and the high government costs make them an attractive target for cuts during times of budget austerity; this can mean tremendous year-to-year price fluctuations. But the biggest inefficiency caused by a fertilizer subsidy program is that it encourages farmers to use more fertilizer than is economically or socially optimal.

Some of these problems are illustrated by the experience of fertilizer subsidies in India, described in the article by Anand:

> In an effort to boost food production, win farmer votes and encourage the domestic fertilizer industry, the government has increased its subsidy of urea over the years, and now pays about half of the domestic industry's cost of production. . . . Farmers pay so little for [urea] that in some areas they use many times the amount recommended by scientists, throwing off the chemistry of the soil. . . . Like humans, plants need balanced diets to thrive. Too much urea oversaturates plants with nitrogen without replenishing other nutrients that are vitally important, including phosphorus, potassium, sulfur, magnesium and calcium. The government has subsidized other fertilizers besides urea. In budget crunches, subsidies on those fertilizers have been reduced or cut, but urea's subsidy has survived. That's because urea manufacturers form a powerful lobby, and farmers are most heavily reliant on this fertilizer, making it a political hot potato to raise the price. As the soil's fertility has declined, farmers under pressure to increase output have spread even more urea on their land. (2010)

For a description of experiences in sub-Saharan Africa, see Box 22.1.

Fertilizer subsidies in Malawi have had a more positive experience. Lipton reports that Malawian fertilizer subsidies were "almost certainly responsible for three years of substantially expanded maize production, mostly by small holders" (2011:54–55). Ricker-Gilbert and Jayne (2011) found that Malawian fertilizer subsidies did raise crop yields, but did not have any long-term impact on household income or asset wealth. The Malawian program was deliberately designed to utilize, rather than replace, the private fertilizer distribution system.

Duflo, Kremer, and Robinson (2004) describe an experiment designed to give insight into what kinds of subsidy programs would be most effective. They randomly assigned farmers in Kenya into two groups and gave fertilizer to one group; fertilizer was extremely effective in raising yields and profits, but once the fertilizer was no longer available for free, farmers stopped using it. Apparently the farmers were unable to plan and save enough to buy fertilizer during planting, even though they knew it was a good, profitable investment. Duflo and colleagues found that if farmers were given the chance to "prepay" for fertilizer in the following year at harvest time, when the farmers had cash on hand from sales of the current crop, the farmers did buy fertilizer under those circumstances.

Mechanization

Many developing countries have pursued a mix of policies to promote adoption of tractors and other machinery, such as low tariffs on imported machin-

Box 22.1 Impact of Eliminating Fertilizer Subsidies in Sub-Saharan Africa

During the 1970s and 1980s, many sub-Saharan African countries began government programs to distribute fertilizer at below-market prices. In the 1990s, responding to pressure from international organizations, these programs were eliminated. The hope was that getting governments out of the fertilizer distribution business would create a vacuum that would be filled by more-efficient privately owned companies.

The early indications of the impact of this policy reform are mildly disappointing. For example in Ethiopia, eliminating the subsidy was estimated to cause an increase in fertilizer prices by 21–39 percent. Derneke, Said, and Jayne (1997) examined fifty-one farms that differed in geography and crop choice; they found that with the subsidy, fertilizer use was profitable in forty-two of these cases. However, without the subsidy (assuming no increased efficiency of delivery), fertilizer use would be profitable in only twenty of the fifty-one cases. If cost efficiencies could be realized in the fertilizer delivery system, fertilizer use would be profitable in twenty-eight of the fifty-one cases.

A general review by Reardon and colleagues concluded:

African fertilizer use is the lowest in the world and has even decreased over the past decade and a half, i.e., over the same period in which fertilizer and seed subsidies and cheap input financial services programs have been reduced or eliminated. . . . Case study evidence points to a connection between the reduction in fertilizer use and these rising input prices. . . . Moreover, there is growing evidence that private fertilizer and seed merchants have responded much less than was expected to the liberalization of input markets enacted through elimination of fertilizer and seed parastatals. . . . Fertilizer markets in African are plagued by a series of fundamental problems such as risk, seasonal demand, high transport costs, underdeveloped financial services markets, and cash constrained farmers. Small markets add to the problem by limiting economies of scale. . . . Moreover, economies of scale in fertilizer production make domestic production inefficient in most African economies, so domestic fertilizer prices are sensitive to macro trade and exchange rate policies, and to volatile international fertilizer prices. While fertilizer subsidies and domestic fertilizer production schemes have generally proved ineffective in Africa, it appears clear that private market conditions in rural Africa cannot presently support necessary fertilizer deliveries, so some role for government is inevitable in the short-to-medium term. Given the considerable costs of delivering fertilizer to farmers on time and the restricted physical availability of fertilizer to most farmers, investment in improved private marketing infrastructure seems one of the most promising roles for the state. (1999: 381–382).

ery, and preferential tax treatment for machinery investments. Brazil, for instance, has allowed a deduction for farm machinery of six times the value of the machine in the first year of operation. Other farm investments are treated less favorably, and labor costs enjoy no preferential tax treatment at all (World Bank 1986:97). Also, as mentioned in Chapter 21, overvalued exchange rates make imports—including imported farm machinery—cheaper.

The desirability of machinery subsidies has been questioned on several points. First, the benefits of machinery subsidies typically go to large and wealthy farms. Second, mechanization does not necessarily increase yields. Binswanger, in a careful review of the studies concerning the impact of "tractorization" on yields in South Asia, found that the surveys failed "to provide evidence that tractors are responsible for substantial increases in intensity, yields, timeliness, and gross returns on farms in India, Pakistan, and Nepal" (1978:73). It seems that, by and large, an acre of land tilled by animal power does not yield less than an acre of land tilled by a tractor (Campbell 1984:47).

In addition, there is no obvious market failure problem justifying these kinds of subsidies. When machinery is profitable, farmers will buy it and society will benefit from it. Money spent subsidizing agricultural mechanization is money not available for other programs that could be at least as productive and that do not reduce labor demand as much as does the subsidized machinery (Binswanger 1987:1).

Irrigation

Publicly sponsored irrigation systems date back some 6,000 years, to when vast irrigation works were developed for the flood plain of the Tigris and Euphrates Rivers in Mesopotamia. In modern times, huge dams thrown across major rivers throughout the world (the Nile, the Indus, and the Colorado, for example) have furnished low-cost irrigation water to millions of farmers. Cost-benefit analysis has shown substantial gains to society from such projects, which usually are promoted for their multiplicity of benefits—flood control, electricity generation, and irrigation water for agriculture.

There is a natural government role in managing water resources: it is difficult or impossible to assign ownership to a flowing river, or an underground reservoir of indeterminate size; it is difficult or impossible to make sure that only people who pay for the water use it. Therefore public works projects are undertaken to build dams and canals.

But the allocation of water from public water projects is a thorny problem: Should every user pay the same price, or should farmers pay lower prices than urban users? Should every user be allocated the same quantity (or the same quantity per unit of farmland), or should farmers with particular land quality or management skills who can use the water most productively be given relatively more water? Should water be auctioned off to the highest bidder, or sold at a flat rate? If sold at a flat rate, should that rate be set at or below or above the level that would cover the costs of building and maintaining the water project?

In many countries, governments "subsidize" irrigation water—they sell water to farmers at prices that are lower than costs, or lower than other nonagricultural users are willing to pay. In Egypt, irrigation water is free. In the Philippines, during 1980–1981, the subsidy amounted to 90 percent of the marginal cost (Bale 1985:17). In Sacramento, California, farmers pay between $2 and $19 per acre foot, while urban and suburban customers pay $1,275 per acre foot (California Department of Water Resources 2005).

Once the dam is built, it may be illogical to charge even the marginal costs of water delivery to the farmer if (1) the water supply is so abundant that no allocation problem exists, or (2) monitoring may be more expensive than the marginal value of the water. In most other situations, economic efficiency would be improved through charging farmers the full cost of irrigation water or the value of water in its highest alternative use.

Policies to Encourage Investment

Investment, or actions that improve the quality of the capital stock, also can shift the supply curve down and to the right. To pick a rudimentary agricultural example: a farmer with a well-sharpened scythe can harvest more hay than a farmer with a dull scythe; but a farmer who owns their own scythe and knows they will use it day after day is more likely to keep it well sharpened than will a farm worker who is handed a different scythe each day. The act of keeping the scythe well sharpened is an "investment"—it is a use of effort to increase future output rather at the expense of increasing current output. Policies that will encourage investment are of two types: policies that encourage the desire to invest, and policies that encourage the ability to invest.

Policies to Encourage the Desire to Invest

Property rights and institutions. The earlier discussions of the importance of land titling, and the problems of assigning ownership rights to water, illustrate the importance that ownership has for encouraging investment. Recall the discussion in Chapter 17 on the importance of institutions to economic growth. A farmer is more likely to want to make investments in their farm when they know they will reap the benefits of the improved productivity brought on by that investment. That means the farmer wants to have confidence in their right to use the improved asset in the future (ownership or long-term enforceable contracts); they want to have confidence that the legal system will enforce their ownership or contractual rights; they want to have confidence that the political system is stable and democratic—that their ownership rights won't be taken away by a change in political leadership; they want to have confidence that the legal and political system is not corrupt.

Subsidizing farm-to-market roads and rural infrastructure. As discussed in Chapter 21 in the context of urban bias, building a new road into a region that formerly was reached only by human or animal transport can have an important impact on that region's economy. Because it dramatically reduces the cost of transporting farm products out of the region, it raises the farm-gate price of what farmers sell to country marketing agents who buy and transport food to the city. And because it simultaneously reduces the cost of transporting materials into the region, it reduces the cost of purchased farm inputs such as fertilizer. Higher farm-gate prices and lower input costs increase farm income, stimulate greater farm production, increase the demand for farm labor, and raise local wages.

In a study of the impact of new roads on forty-six Philippine rural communities, Santos-Villanueva (1966) found a decrease in transportation costs of from 17 to 60 percent per kilometer and a substantial increase in the amount of agricultural products sold off the farm (see Table 22.1).

In a study of sixteen villages in rural Bangladesh, it was found that villages with a good infrastructure, including good all-weather, hard-surfaced roads, used 92 percent more fertilizer per hectare than villages with poor infrastructure. They used 4 percent more labor per hectare, and they paid their agricultural laborers 12 percent more per day than did villages with poor infrastructure (Ahmed and Hossain 1990).

In addition, higher local wage rates reduce the pressure for out-migration. In other words, good roads help keep people home. Good roads encourage private entrepreneurs to start bus services, often with very small vehicles ranging from large three-wheeled motorcycles to minibuses, and thus make it possible for rural people who live within reasonable commuting distances to work in town but continue to live at home. Good roads enable employment outside the home neighborhood.

Table 22.1 Average Percentage Increase in Sales Volume of Selected Farm Products After Construction of a Nearby Road from Farm to Market, Philippines

	Percentage Increase
Corn	104
Chicken	69
Swine	47
Coconuts	30
Rice	24
Bananas	12

Source: Santos-Villanueva 1966.

As roads reduce the cost of transportation to and from the countryside, the annual fluctuation in the price of food is reduced. Remote communities find it cheaper to export food in good crop years and to import food in poor crop years, thus reducing price swings between the bad and the good harvests. Reducing these price swings reduces the probability that low-income families will face undernutrition during the years of bad harvest.

As a good road network reduces the cost of transporting agricultural commodities around the country, increased agricultural specialization by region can take place. For instance, perishable fruits and vegetables can be grown farther from urban markets than previously, making possible a higher-valued use of land far from market and reducing the income disparity between remote areas and the major cities.

The same sorts of advantages that accrue with new roads into a formerly remote territory apply to improvements in old roads. Putting a hard surface on a dirt road, or mending potholes on a worn-out, older, all-weather road, creates benefits similar, albeit less dramatic, to those from putting in a new road.

In addition to roads, the parts of rural infrastructure that probably have the most bearing on agricultural production are the electrical system, the communications network, and the marketing system. Rural electrification makes possible the powering of a host of time-saving and production-enhancing devices. Small irrigation pumps and power tools are efficiently driven by electricity. This also makes communications easier in the countryside, for example by making a modern telephone switching system possible. Access to a telephone (even if there is only one per village) can save lives in a medical emergency. But efficient communications are also important in marketing farm products as well as in gaining access to purchased farm inputs. Mobile phone availability has skyrocketed in much of the developing world. In 2004, African mobile phone subscriptions per person were about 0.1; ten years later that number had increased to 0.8 (since many relatively rich households have two or more subscriptions, this does not measure availability per household, however) (*The Economist* 2013a).

An important function of a marketing system is to reflect back to producers the wants and preferences of consumers. As economic development brings changes in food demand patterns, a good marketing system will efficiently transmit this information to farmers, who can then reallocate their resources to take advantage of the new production opportunities.

And as the sophistication of agricultural production increases with the adoption of new technology and improved management, a good marketing system for agricultural inputs will reflect farmers' preferences back to the farm suppliers. Bureaucratic, government-sponsored fertilizer distribution schemes usually supply only a limited choice of plant nutrient mixes. But if allowed to function in an appropriate institutional framework, a private-enterprise marketing system will make available a wide variety of fertilizers, allowing farmers to choose the most efficient ones for a particular situation.

Government support can supply radio stations and newspapers to pass along price information of interest to farmers. This is especially important for small farmers who, because of lack of information about market prices, might otherwise be at a disadvantage in comparison with the larger farmers who can afford to get such information on their own.

Government-sponsored terminal markets, where buyers can assemble farm products from the countryside and distribute them to retailers in the city, can increase the efficiency of the marketing system. Increasing the efficiency of the marketing system lowers prices to consumers and increases prices to producers, thus improving nutrition and stimulating increases in production. Appropriate government subsidies are important to an efficiently functioning agricultural marketing system (see Box 22.2).

Box 22.2 Public Goods and Public Investment

Public investments are usually made because of a failure of the market to provide certain public goods. A small public park, a downtown sidewalk, national defense, and free public education are examples of public goods. Public goods have two critical properties: it is costly or impossible to exclude individuals from enjoying the benefits from them, and it is undesirable to exclude individuals from enjoying the benefits from them, since such enjoyment does not detract from that of others (Stiglitz 1986:119). But generally there is much reluctance to produce a public good, because once produced, it is available to all. The producer cannot sell it and capture his or her costs .

The distinction between a private good and a public good may be fuzzy. For instance, we can think of expenditure on the education of our children as a private good, since the children benefit directly; but education also has aspects of a public good, because educated children will be more productive later on in life than uneducated children. The fact that education provides benefits (external benefits) to people other than the students themselves helps explain why governments are involved in paying for public schools.

Likewise, when a consortium of governments pays a public agricultural experiment station for research to develop high-yielding varieties of rice, we may want to call it a public investment. All rice farmers can benefit from the new rice varieties, and of course the public benefits from the lower market price of rice after the higher-yielding rice varieties are put into use. We could also call the rice research and the resulting high-yielding varieties a public good. So it is with many other public expenditures for enhancing agricultural production, such as research on irrigation machinery or agricultural extension programs—they are pitched at the farm sector but they benefit the public.

Price stabilization. When farmers make decisions about whether to invest in projects that will improve their long-term productivity, they base their decisions on beliefs about future prices. Economists have found evidence that farmers are *risk-averse*—other things being equal, they would prefer a sure thing or a low-risk investment to a high-risk investment. When output prices are highly variable and unpredictable, farm investments are riskier, and farmers are less likely to make these investments. For this reason (as described in Chapter 21), some governments have instituted policies to stabilize prices of agricultural commodities (Newbery and Stiglitz 1981).

Governments have used four general types of policies to achieve more stable prices:

1. The most direct policy is that of *administered prices,* under which the government sets prices, either by administrative fiat or by acting as the sole buyer of the commodity. The difficulty with this type of policy is that the government frequently knows even less than farmers about likely future price levels. Therefore, the prices established by the government do not reflect underlying supply-and-demand conditions. Black markets emerge and either the programs are ineffective or they become an enormous drain on the government treasury.

2. A second method is a *buffer stock* program under which the government buys the commodity when supplies are plentiful and prices are relatively low, and sells the commodity when supplies are tight and prices are relatively high. The government storage acts to even out prices over time. In theory, this program should put a ceiling and a floor on agricultural prices: when prices threaten to drop below the floor, the government buys the commodity and bids the price back up; when prices threaten to shoot through the ceiling, the government sells the commodity and brings prices back down. In practice, governments have not been particularly adept at establishing the correct range of prices. In addition, the subsidized government storage tends to discourage storage in the private sector.

3. A *buffer fund* accomplishes much the same thing as a buffer stock program, but does so without the government actually buying and selling the commodity. Under a buffer fund, governments tax sales of the commodity in periods when prices are high (and thereby reduce the price received by farmers), and subsidize sales in periods when prices are low (effectively increasing the farm price). Buffer funds require extensive bookkeeping to verify which farmer sold what quantity at what price.

4. Finally, governments can encourage the development of private market institutions, such as *forward contracting* and *futures markets,* to stabilize prices. These mechanisms allow farmers to lock in a price at the beginning of a growing season, at least for a major proportion of their crop. These types of contracts work well in theory, but farmers have been reluctant to adopt them in the United States and other developed countries.

Chapter 21's review of farm subsidy mechanisms mentioned the trend toward programs that provide a "safety net" for farm incomes. These kinds of programs also have an element of stabilization (of incomes, rather than prices) that may encourage investment by risk-averse farmers.

Policies to Facilitate the Ability to Invest

A farmer who *wants* to invest also has to have the *ability* to invest. For most assets—buildings, breeding stock, machinery, irrigation equipment—the acquisition, improvement, or maintenance requires cash. Unlike major corporations that can raise money by issuing stock or selling bonds, small farmers either have to save the money themselves or borrow the money. Therefore, policies that facilitate borrowing are policies that lead to increased agricultural investment.

Credit subsidies. A number of developing-country governments have experimented with programs that directly subsidize credit. These programs were seen as a way to spur agricultural productivity, to transfer income to the poor, and to compensate low-income farmers for their losses attributable to urban bias (Adams et al. 1984). However, experience has shown that subsidized credit is not an effective instrument for transferring income to the poor. Furthermore, subsidized credit may have harmful side effects on financial institutions and other segments of the economy, particularly the poor.

There are two common ways in which governments have provided low-interest loans. One is directly through a government bank or quasi-government bank that loans the money to preferred borrowers at below-market interest rates. For instance, in Jamaica during the 1970s, the parastatal development bank supplied loans at less than half the interest rate changed by commercial banks.

The other common way of providing low-interest loans is for the government to require commercial banks to supply a given amount of money to preferred borrowers at below-market rates. In Nigeria during the 1980s, for example, banks were required to make 8 percent of their loans to the agricultural sector at approximately half the going commercial interest rate (Bale 1985:17). Beginning in 1965 in Brazil, the law required commercial banks to lend at least 50 percent of their demand deposits to farmers at 17 percent interest per year—less than the inflation rate at that time of 20 to 40 percent per year. In 1971 the mandated rural interest rate was lowered to 15 percent, even though high rates of inflation continued (Sicat 1983:381).

When the government bears the cost of the credit subsidy, the funds spent are not available for other government programs—more agricultural research, better rural roads, or improved educational services. When the cost of the credit subsidy is pushed onto the commercial banking system, by forcing banks to make low-interest loans to a preferred set of borrowers, other, non-preferred borrowers end up paying the cost in the form of higher interest rates or reduced loan availability. In practice, credit subsidies have often become an instrument of urban bias: small farmers and landless laborers rarely benefit from these programs (González-Vega 1983:371).

Other initiatives to encourage credit. The government can take other initiatives to facilitate the availability of credit. A government-operated or privately owned credit information system (such as the credit-scoring companies in the United States) give lenders a source of information about a potential borrower's credit history, job history, income sources, and the like. By making this information available at a low cost, such a system reduces risks of lending.

Government can also influence the ability of a borrower to pledge collateral for a loan. Collateral is an asset that the borrower promises to turn over to the lender in the event that the borrower is unable to make required repayments. For example, in the United States, car loans are secured (or "collateralized") by the cars themselves; if a borrower fails to make their car payments, their car will be repossessed by the lender. Collateral serves several important functions: it provides something of value to the lender even if the loan is not repaid, the threat of losing the collateral provides an incentive for the borrower to make repayments, and the possibility of losing collateral may discourage certain poor-risk borrowers from taking out a loan in the first place.

As mentioned earlier in this chapter, creating transferable ownership rights to land allows land to be pledged as collateral and thus improves the functioning of credit markets. A government-operated "collateral registry" allows a lender to see whether a certain asset has been pledged as collateral on any other loans. Government policies can also influence the ease with which collateral claims can be adjudicated and enforced.

Microcredit: an alternative to subsidized credit. During the 1970s and 1980s, economists began to piece together an alternative to subsidized credit. Muhammad Yunus, an economist from Bangladesh, observed that very small loans could make a huge difference to very poor households. He began to work on a method of providing small-scale loans to these households. Initially, Yunus himself provided the funding. But for the idea to work on a larger scale in impoverished rural areas, there would have to be a local source of loanable funds. Dale Adams (1983) found that the average rural household in five Asian countries *did* have positive savings, and that this savings increased when interest rates rose.

Yunus's plan is now known as "microcredit" and is widely seen as a promising way to make credit available to small farmers (see Boxes 22.3 and 22.4 for examples of how microcredit works). Yunus founded the Grameen Bank of Bangladesh, which promoted the concept of making small loans to

---

Box 22.3 Microcredit in Practice

An actual example of microcredit illustrates how it works. A farmer in the Philippines wanted to borrow $52 to buy two piglets. He planned to feed the piglets with table scraps and spoiled food from the family table, so there would be little cost other than the initial investment. He was able to convince his fellow microcredit group members that this was a reasonable investment, and they knew that the farmer had a reputation for honesty and hard work. The farmer received the loan and promised to repay $2.30 a week for twenty-six weeks (a total repayment of about $60). At the end of six months, the farmer was able to sell the fattened pigs for over $200. The money he repaid plus interest was available to finance projects by other group members.

---

poor families who put up no other collateral than joining and meeting regularly with a support group. The sense of obligation of the borrower to the group was a sufficiently strong incentive so that members did, in fact, pay back their loans (Hossain 1988a:25–26).

The use of small community groups to funnel credit to rural lenders has a number of advantages. The group members know the reputations of the borrowers—who is industrious, who is lazy, who is honest—and can take that into account in making loan decisions. The group members have similar backgrounds and experiences and so are able to analyze the likelihood that a project will succeed in generating income sufficient to repay the loan. The group members can fairly easily determine whether difficulty in repaying is due to a borrower's bad luck or is due to the borrower's poor performance. Finally, borrowers want to repay the loans in order to preserve their social standing in the community. (See Box 22.4.)

One estimate (Global Development Research Center 2003) says that there were at that time about 13 million borrowers from microcredit lenders, with an average loan size of about $500. Repayment rates are reported to be above 95 percent.

Boudreaux and Cowen say that in many respects, microcredit in practice fails to live up to its promise: "Microcredit is mostly a good thing. Very often it helps keep borrowers from even greater catastrophes, but only rarely does it enable them to climb out of poverty" (2008:28). But interest rates are high (often as high as 50–100 percent annually). And many loans are for consumption (a doctor visit, school fees) rather than for investment.

Foreign Investment in Agricultural Land

The preceding discussion treats the world as one in which some farmers have access to land, but limited access to funds for investing, and explores policies

---

Box 22.4 Rural Microfinance in Morocco

In Morocco the microfinance organization Al Amana had been active in urban areas and decided to expand into the countryside. In cooperation with some economists from the United States, they identified eighty-one pairs of rural villages where each village in the pair was similar to the other, in population, income, and so forth. One of the villages in each pair was chosen to receive microcredit services immediately, while the other, "matched" village would receive the same services, but two years later. This allowed the policy analysts to measure how microcredit changed the lives of those in the early-adopting villages compared to the people in the later-adopting villages.

During the first two years, 17 percent of households took out a loan from Al Amana. The average loan size was about $1,300 (GDP per capita in Morocco at this time was about $6,900). The loans were to be repaid in weekly or monthly installments over a period of three to eighteen months. The average interest rate charged on loans was about 15 percent.

Most of the loans were "group liability" loans that worked as follows. A group of three or four members voluntarily agreed to mutually guarantee the loan repayments for all members of a group. This mutual responsibility takes the place of collateral for the loan. When a valuable asset (a house, land, etc.) is pledged as collateral, the fear of losing the asset creates an incentive for the borrower to work hard to make sure the loan can be repaid. The fear of losing the respect and friendship of the other members of the group provides a similar kind of incentive.

The microcredit program appears to have had positive impacts on the villages. About 33 percent of households in microcredit villages had taken out loans, compared to 25 percent in villages without the microcredit program. Households with microcredit loans increased their animal holdings, sales, consumption, and profits.

For more details, see Indicators of Poverty Action 2014 or Crepon et al. 2015.

---

to increase access to funds. But a different solution exists: find individuals with access to funds for investing, but limited access to land, and create policies that encourage those individuals to buy up the land.

There has been an upsurge in foreign investment in agricultural land, especially in land in sub-Saharan Africa. There is considerable controversy about the different measures of the extent of foreign investment in agricultural land (see Arezki, Deininger, and Selod 2015 for a discussion of different data sources). But a few facts are indisputable. One of these is that the extent of foreign investment in land is increasing. *The Economist* reports that a 2011 estimate of 80 million hectares "is far higher than a previous one, . . . which last year said that foreign investors had expressed interest in 57 million hectares. It is higher still than one by the International Food Policy Research Institute

(IFPRI) which put the figure in a 2009 study at 15m-20m hectares." But, *The Economist* notes, "it would be wrong to . . . conclude that land deals have grown fourfold. Since most are secret, knowing what to count is difficult, and the figures refer to different periods" (2011).

Table 22.2 illustrates the growth in land investment. It also shows a second indisputable fact: sub-Saharan Africa is the region in which foreign land investment is most prominent. Where does the foreign land investment come from? Again the data are incomplete, but the evidence points to the oil states of the Middle East and China as the biggest investors in sub-Saharan African land (*The Economist* 2009).

Policies to Promote Technological Improvement

Promoting Agricultural Research
Technological change is one of the primary driving forces behind increasing production. Improved technology (e.g., a higher-yielding variety of rice) can increase the productivity of every item of the set of resources that a farmer uses—land, labor, management, and capital. Yet the agricultural researcher intent on developing new technology for agriculture faces an extraordinarily intricate range of scientific challenges. One analysis of technological change (Lele, Kinsey, and Obeya 1989:42) listed the following areas as important to researchers in improved crop varieties in third world agriculture:

- Yield potential and responsiveness to available chemical fertilizers and pesticides.
- Adaptation to the growing period and drought tolerance.
- Disease and pest resistance.
- Improvements in quality, palatability, and consumer acceptance.
- Storage, transport, and other handling qualities (including processing) with available technology.

Table 22.2 Agricultural Cropland Owned by Foreign Investors, by Region, Compared to Total Arable Land, 2008 and 2011 (million hectares)

	Cropland Owned by Foreigners		Total Arable Land
	2008	2011	
Africa	23	51	221
Asia	25	20	564
Latin America and Caribbean	5	9	164
All developing countries	54	80	940

Source: For 2008, Arezki et al. 2015; for 2011, *The Economist* 2015.

• Changes in labor requirements in production and processing in relation to the available mechanical technology, in view of other requirements for household labor and incentives for labor use.
• Compatibility with other social, cultural, and economic norms.

Not only is the range of challenge complex, but the disciplines brought to bear on agricultural research are varied. Advancing agricultural technology involves research in biology, chemistry, and engineering, as well as in the social sciences, which are crucial to the appropriate integration of the new technology into the production system.

Despite the challenging nature of agricultural research, the payoff has been nothing short of spectacular. As described in Chapter 14, agricultural research has been instrumental in dramatic increases in crop yields per acre as well as in livestock productivity. And when the costs of agricultural research are compared to the benefits to society, agricultural research turns out to be a real bargain.

In Table 22.3, studies of payoffs to research done at agricultural experiment stations around the world are listed. The last column, highest annual rate of return, is of particular interest. The rate of return represents the average earning power of the resources used in a project during the project period. For an agricultural research project, this is the equivalent of the interest rate you would have to get from a savings account to receive the same return on your savings as the public gets from the agricultural research project.

In one of the earliest studies of this kind, returns to research on hybrid corn (maize) in the United States were calculated by economist Zvi Griliches

Table 22.3 Studies on Rates of Return to Agricultural Research

Commodity	Number of Studies	Lowest Annual Rate of Return Found (%)	Highest Annual Rate of Return Found (%)	Average Annual Rate of Return over All Studies (%)
Multicommodity	436	−1	1,219	80
All agriculture	342	−1	1,219	76
Crops and livestock	80	17	562	106
Unspecified	14	16	69	42
Field crops	916	−100	1,720	74
Maize	170	−100	1,720	135
Wheat	155	−48	290	50
Rice	81	11	466	75
Livestock	233	2.5	5,645	121
Tree crops	108	1.4	1,736	88
All studies	1,772	−100	5,645	81

Source: For 1961–2002, FAOSTAT fertilizer archives(http://faostat3.fao.org/download /RA/*/E); for 2002–2013, FAOSTAT.

(1958) (the corn-breeding research was carried out by many scientists). The rate of return to hybrid corn research in the United States is calculated to be 35 to 40 percent. That means for every dollar the US public paid for agricultural research on hybrid corn until 1955, it collected from 35 to 40 cents every year in benefits (mostly through lower prices for corn). It would be hard to find another set of investments that pay off as well as agricultural research. Swindale (1997) cites an example of research in sub-Saharan Africa into methods of controlling an insect pest—the cassava mealybug. The research cost $27 million, but the benefits from the research exceeded $4 billion.

If agricultural research has such a spectacular payoff, why don't farmers themselves pay for it? The two reasons why it is not appropriate to ask farmers to pay are (1) most farmers have far too small an operation to sponsor and benefit from agricultural research, and (2) because price drops relatively sharply as output rises (that is, the elasticity of demand for most farm products is less than 1), the majority of the benefits from agricultural research go to consumers. Farmers generally lose revenue when the new technology is widely adopted because they see their farm-gate prices fall faster than they can increase production.

Long-term data from the United States, with a history of public sponsorship of agricultural research dating back to the 1870s, is illustrative:

> The decline in the real price of food has been dramatic. Available data for the period 1888 to 1891 indicate that consumers spent an average of about 40 percent of their income for food. From 1930 to 1960, the food expenditure proportion of consumer incomes ranged from 20 to 24 percent. In the seventies, the proportion of total disposable personal income spent for food dropped to a range of 1–17 percent. By the mid-eighties, that proportion for the average family had dropped to …15 percent. (Lee and Taylor 1986:20–21).

And today families spend less than 10 percent of their income on food (http://www.ers.usda.gov/data-products/chart-gallery/detail.aspx?chartId=40094&ref=collection&embed=True&widgetId=39734).

But why, if rates of return to research investment are so high, don't private companies undertake the research and sell the results to farmers? The answer is that it is often hard for the firm or person who develops a new technology through research to charge others for the use of that new technology. For example, suppose a scientist spends many months and millions of dollars to research the optimal spacing for rice seedlings—should they be planted six inches apart, or 4 inches, or 8 inches? And suppose the scientist learns that 5 inches spacing is what achieves maximum yield. Once the scientist releases the results, anyone can begin to plant their seedlings five inches apart, whether or not they pay the scientist for undertaking the research. So the scientist undertakes the fixed costs of the research but gets little or no return because it is so easy to share the results of that research. In a similar fashion, a researcher who develops a new wheat seed variety might sell the new seed to a few farmers, but in subsequent years, those farmers can simply save a few thousand grains of wheat from their crop and sell those grains as seed to other farmers. Here too, the researcher who incurs the cost of research fails to gain the returns from sales of the seed.

This means that even though the benefits to society from research are high, the private benefits to a researcher may be much lower. Therefore, the private market tends to underinvest in research. As Table 22.4 shows, private investment is small compared to public investment.

One policy to encourage private investment is patent protections. If a researcher acquires a patent for an innovation, the researcher can sue for damages any person who attempts to sell a copy of the innovation. Patent laws protect mechanical and chemical innovations more effectively than biological innovations. For this reason, some agroindustrial firms have been able to sponsor research in farm machinery or agricultural chemicals and capture the benefits from that research. Hybrid seeds are protectable by patents and, because they do not breed "true," farmers must purchase new supplies each year. So after government-sponsored research led the way, hybrid seed companies set up their own research and are developing their own varieties.

But by and large, biological innovations in agriculture have to be paid for by government. Thus, animal breeding, animal nutrition, plant breeding, plant pathology, entomology, agronomy, soil science, and so on are government-sponsored (Judd, Boyce, and Evenson 1987:7).

As Table 22.5 shows, developed countries spend a greater part of their national income on research than do developing countries. Some countries are too small or too poor to sponsor agricultural research. Their funds are best spent on adaptive agricultural research—finding out which of the innovations discovered elsewhere are most adaptable to their own situations. The agricultural stations of the Consultative Group on International Agricultural Research are helping to fill in the research gap felt by the smaller countries. Twelve in-

Table 22.4 Estimated Public and Private Investment in Agricultural Research and Development, 1995

	Investment ($ millions)			Percentage Private
	Public	Private	Total	
Developing countries	11,770	609	12,379	5
Developed countries	21,567	10,962	32,530	33.7

Source: Pardy and Beintema 2001.

Table 22.5 Public Expenditures on Agricultural Research and Development as Percentage of Agricultural GDP, 1976 and 1996

	1976	1996
Developing countries	0.5	0.6
Developed countries	1.5	2.6

Source: Pardy and Beintema 2001.

ternational agricultural research stations belonged to this group and were sponsored by a variety of sources. The group includes the International Rice Research Institute in the Philippines and the International Maize and Wheat Improvement Center in Mexico, as well as a number of other centers whose activities range from plant and animal breeding to food policy.

Low-income rural householders could benefit from research on hardy but efficient scavenging animals. High-yielding, disease-resistant breeds of chickens, ducks, goats, pigs, cattle, bees, or fish that can utilize garbage or other food that may be locally available but unfit for human consumption would be of considerable benefit to the third world's poor.

Africa poses a particular challenge to agricultural research. Its soils are more diverse, its climate more varied, its pest and disease hazards more pronounced, and its farming systems more complex than those of monsoon Asia, where the green revolution has been such a success (Lele and Goldsmith 1989; Lipton and Longhurst 1990). African agriculture is characterized by *mixed cropping* (more than one crop at a time is grown in a field), which occupies over 90 percent of the cropped area in most countries on the continent.

A special challenge for the agricultural research community working in Africa is to intensify agricultural production within this complex farm management system while maintaining its flexibility and its proven sustainability (Dommen 1988). One production innovation that holds promise for sustainability in the semiarid tropics that cover so much of Africa is *agroforestry,* a system of strip-cropping rows of trees between narrow strips of crops. The trees help conserve water, provide a ready source of organic matter, and reduce erosion. Another example of an effective agricultural research project in Africa is described in Box 22.5.

Policies to encourage development of new technology include not only direct government sponsorship of research but also laws and regulations that encourage private research and development. The FAO's 2004 *State of Food and Agriculture* report (p. 88) concludes

Countries and the international community need to:

• establish transparent, predictable science-based regulatory procedures and harmonize regulatory procedures, where appropriate, at regional or global levels;

Box 22.5 Cassava Research
───────────

In parts of western Africa, cassava—a starchy root crop—is a significant source of calories. From the mid-1980s to the mid-1990s, the International Institute of Tropical Agriculture funded research to develop new varieties. As described in the FAO's 2000 *State of Food Insecurity in the World* report: "These new varieties yielded up to 55 tonnes per hectare, compared with about 10 tonnes per hectare from traditional varieties; matured early; were highly resistant to disease; . . . developed a broad leaf canopy, thus optimizing both weed control and yield potential; had compact root shapes, facilitating harvest" (p. 21).

News about the new varieties spread rapidly, and farmers switched more and more land into cassava production. In Ghana, cassava area nearly doubled between 1983 and 1998. In Nigeria, it nearly tripled. In Ghana, yields increased from 7 metric tons per hectare in 1988 to 12 metric tons per hectare in 1997. Cassava research is one of the factors explaining Ghana's astonishing progress in reducing the prevalence of undernutrition—in 1980 over 60 percent of its population was undernourished; by 1997 the percentage had dropped to 10 percent.

In addition to Ghana and Nigeria, other areas in western and central Africa are suitable for growing cassava, and the new varieties may help address the undernutrition problem in those areas as well.

- establish appropriate intellectual property rights (IPR) protections to
- ensure that developers can earn an adequate return on investment;
- strengthen national plant-breeding programmes and seed systems; and
- promote the development of efficient agricultural input and output markets and reduce trade barriers on agricultural technologies.

Subsidizing Technology Diffusion and Adoption

Profitable technology will spread from farmer to farmer by itself. But the rate of adoption can be accelerated by government-sponsored educational programs. (See Feder, Just, and Zilberman 1985 for a review of the literature on this.) Such programs are often called *extension* services because they were originally conceived to extend the knowledge developed in the US land-grant college system directly to the farmer. Programs that provide education and advice to farmers are now in place in most countries having a significant agricultural economy.

A classic study of Iowa's farmers illustrates the typical growth curve of knowledge that an agricultural community experiences as its farmers gradually become aware of a new technology, then try it out, and finally adopt it as part of their regular farming activities. In this case, a new chemical for weed control called 2,4–D had come on the market. It took approximately eleven years between the time only a few farmers (4 percent) had even heard of it and the time all of them were using it. Notice in Figure 22.2 how awareness precedes trial, which precedes adoption. In 1949, for instance, about midway through the process, 74 percent of the farmers were aware of the existence of the new weedicide, but only 40 percent had adopted it. By 1955 all farmers in the area were using it. Without the vigorous extension program carried on by Iowa State University, the new technology undoubtedly still would have spread, but whether it would have spread as fast is open to question. It is the charge of the extension service to accelerate the adoption of new technology, whether it be new agricultural chemicals, better plant and animal varieties, or better farm management practices.

Accelerating the spread of technology begins with government sponsorship of agricultural training institutions—places where technicians learn the skills necessary for providing assistance and up-to-date information about agriculture to farmers in the field: plant and animal sciences, and farm management and finance, for example. Not only do government-sponsored farm advisers need to know agricultural technology, but rural banks need farm appraisers, and rural tax collectors need to know about the economics of farming. Sponsoring the training of these technicians provides an important subsidy to agricultural production. The success of an agricultural extension service depends not only on the quality of training that farm advisers get at their local agricultural colleges but also, and perhaps more importantly, on the

Figure 22.2 Cumulative Percentage of Farm Operators at the Awareness, Trial, and Adoption Stages for 2,4–D Weed Spray, Iowa, 1944–1955

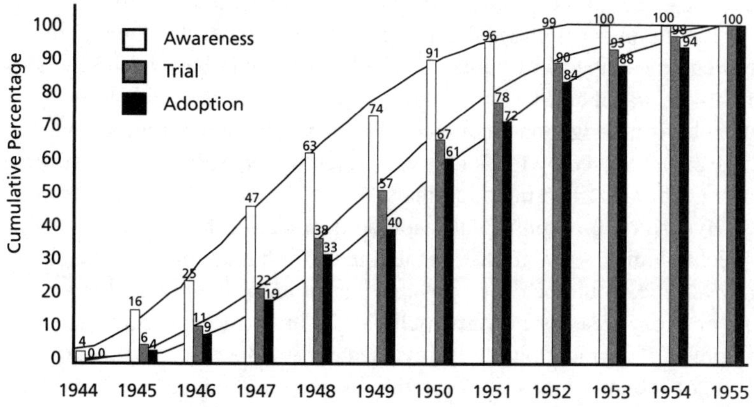

Source: Adapted from Beal and Rogers 1960:8.

quality of the technology they have to extend. Building an array of extension agents without providing them with a set of technologies appropriate to the region where they are working does not endear them to farmers and weakens the future effectiveness of their organizations.

Policies to Promote Sustainable Farming Methods and Environmental Protection

When we look at a supply-demand diagram like Figure 22.1, we are inclined to see it as representing the supply and demand conditions for the current growing season. But with a little imagination, we can see the two different supply curves as representing alternative futures. If quality of land and water resources becomes seriously degraded, the agricultural supply curve will be low; but if resource quality is high, the agricultural supply curve will be high—at any given price level, farmers will produce a higher quantity.

Policies to reduce environmental damage fall into two categories. Some policies are aimed at limiting consumption and production of goods that cause environmental damage (Sagoff 1997). A second approach to environmental policy involves requiring or encouraging technology that limits or reverses environmental damage: some new technology reduces the environmental impact of production; some new technology reduces the impact of environmental damage on humans; some new technology reverses or "remediates" past environmental damage.

Methods of limiting consumption include direct rationing and taxes on consumption. For example, one policy proposed to reduce carbon emissions is a tax on miles driven. A tax on meat and animal products might also be aimed at reducing meat consumption and therefore greenhouse gas emissions associated with animal agriculture. A general tax on food (recall the discussion in Chapter 20 about how to reduce food consumption in rich countries) could have the effect of reducing soil degradation and water depletion.

Technological solutions can be found related to all of the environmental problems described in Chapter 12. Soil erosion can be reduced by adopting low-till or no-till cultivation methods. Water use in crop production can be reduced by drip irrigation techniques. Methane emissions from animal agriculture can be reduced by feed additives (Machmüller, Soliva, and Kreuzer 2003) or by genetic engineering of animals.

Even after environmental resource degradation has occurred, there may be technological ways to reduce the impact on human life. For example, new crop varieties could be developed that permit crops to grow and thrive in salty soil, or in dry areas, or in warmer climates. Furthermore, in some cases the environmental degradation can be reversed or remediated. Box 22.6 gives an example of research into soil restoration by growing the macuna bean. Desalinization technology has been used in the Middle East to replace depleted groundwater resources. Methane from animal production has been captured in barns, stored, and then burned as an energy source.

Box 22.6 Research That Improves Soil Quality

Not all technological discoveries come out of government-funded laboratories with sophisticated equipment. Decades ago, the United Fruit Company began growing mucuna beans to provide cheap feed for mules on its banana plantations in Guatemala and Honduras. Local farmers noticed that the soil in fields where mucuna beans had grown was richer than the soil in other fields.

With more systematic study (much of it funded by private aid groups) the advantages of this magic bean became better understood. When planted in land recently cleared and burned, it grows amazingly fast, reducing soil erosion that can occur on bare land. If the beans are left to rot on the soil, they create a natural fertilizer that makes use of commercial fertilizer unnecessary. Maize and mucuna can be grown together in fields, with mucuna replenishing the soil nutrients used by the maize. The dense mucuna plants also suppress weeds and reduce or eliminate the need for commercial herbicides. Yields of maize double or triple. The mucuna can even be used to "create soil" (organic compost) on rocky hillsides.

Source: Pettifer 2001.

The policy challenges here are those mentioned earlier in this chapter in different contexts: How can farmers be persuaded to make investments that reduce environmental problems? Do farmers have the financial wherewithal to make these investments? What policies can promote research into and development of technologies that are environmental beneficial?

And the policy solutions are generally those discussed earlier in this chapter. Well-defined and enforced property rights give a landowner the incentive to maintain the quality of the soil. Similarly, the government will have a natural role in defining and enforcing patent rights to encourage private research and in direct financing of basic research. It is more difficult, perhaps impossible, to define and enforce property rights to water, and to the atmosphere.

Meinzen-Dick and Rosegrant (2001) review some policy choices to increase water availability and encourage water conservation. New technology—low-cost desalination or methods of long-distance transport—could increase water availability; and policies definitely have a role in promoting research and development of new technology. Pricing and water markets are widely discussed theoretical solutions: if water is costly to buy, consumers have an incentive to conserve; if water can be sold for profit, water owners have an incentive to develop and preserve the quality and sustainability of water resources. However, Meinzen-Dick and Rosegrant warn that this solution may be better in theory than in practice. Measuring use and billing can be difficult, as can defining and enforcing ownership rights. Among their recommendations: "Education, social marketing, and public awareness campaigns to change behavior deserve much greater attention" (2001). For other broad reviews of agricultural water policies, see Boggess, Lacewell, and Zilberman 1993; Rosegrant, Scheleyer, and Yadav 1995; and Sampath 1992.

Policies to control greenhouse gas emissions give additional insight into efficient policy design. Consider a program to achieve a target reduction in carbon emissions from electricity-generation plants. All plants have access to the same kinds of technology, but not all plants are exactly the same. Some plants can make relatively large reductions in carbon emissions without incurring much additional costs; other plants find it very costly to cut emissions. If a government adopts a "command and control" approach, it might require every plant to make the same amount (or the same percentage) of carbon reduction, and this would be a relatively high-cost way of achieving a given carbon reduction goal. The "cap and trade" approach would allow different plants to make different reductions. Under this plan, all plants would receive an allowable limit for emissions. Those that could reduce carbon emissions cheaply could emit less than their allowed limit and sell the remainder to a high-cost-reduction plant. The plants where cutting emissions is costly can buy up the permits from other plants and do less actual cutting of emissions. In aggregate the same cut in emissions is achieved, but at a lower cost to the industry.

Finally, we note the argument, advanced most famously in a memo by economist Larry Summers (1991), then at the World Bank, that environmental standards appropriate for rich countries may be more stringent than the appropriate standards for poor countries.

Multifaceted Approach:
Adopting Many Approaches Simultaneously

In Chapter 17, we discussed the debate among economists about the efficacy of aid, and identified Jeffrey Sachs as a leading proponent of the view that foreign aid could be effective in promoting economic growth in poor countries. Sachs received funding from some major donors to run a demonstration project known as the Millennium Villages project.

Sachs and his team chose a number of villages in sub-Saharan Africa, and provided intensive interventions that include many of the things listed in this chapter. Farmers received free or heavily subsidized fertilizer. A mobile "bank" allowed farmers to save money and earn interest. Education programs communicated information about best production techniques and seed varieties.

The Millennium Village project has claimed some successes (see its website, http://millenniumvillages.org). However, the program has been criticized as being quite expensive. For example, a typical Millennium Village endeavor budgets $120 per person per year, but large households and outside augmentation of funds mean that this can translate into $4,500 per household per year (for one Ghanaian village). And it has been argued that many of the villages are in countries that have seen general improvements in income and health, making it difficult to analyze the impact of the Millennium Village project in isolation from the general improvements. (See Tollefson 2015 for a report on the controversies. See Bump et al. 2012 for a specific criticism.)

A similar multifaceted program (the Graduation Program) was undertaken on a more limited basis over a wider geographical area. "Selected beneficiaries are then given a productive asset that they choose from a list, training and support for the asset they have chosen, as well as general life skills coaching, weekly consumption support for some fixed period, and typically access to savings accounts and health information or services" (Banerjee et al. 2015). That program had the analytical advantage of randomly assigning households either to be program participants or to be in a nonrecipient "control" group.

Analysis indicates that the households that received the aid had better outcomes than the control group in all ten of the quality-of-life indicators targeted by the program: higher consumption, higher food security, and better health among them (Banerjee et al. 2015).

Part 4

Alternative Scenarios

23

The Future of World Food Supply and Demand

> And I beheld a black horse; and he that sat on him had a pair of balances in his hand. And I heard a voice . . . say, A measure of wheat for a penny, and three measures of barley for a penny. . . . And power was given unto them over the fourth part of the earth, to kill with the sword, and with hunger, and with death, and with the beast of the earth.
>
> —*Revelation 6:5–8*

Famine is one of the Four Horsemen of the Apocalypse. And when our visions of the future take an apocalyptic turn, the specter of widespread hunger is likely to appear. What does the future hold? Will the progress of the past decades continue? Or are we on the brink of a slide into catastrophe? Having boldly asked these questions, we less boldly reply, "It all depends . . ." This chapter will briefly review schools of thought about the future of the world food problem and will present a framework for building scenarios about the future.

There are several points on which there is universal agreement. Of course, any prediction is likely to be wrong in certain fundamental ways. But the four Ps identified in Chapter 1—population, prosperity, pollution, and productivity—are almost certain to be the major factors shaping the future. Growth in population and in per capita income will determine, to a considerable extent, demand for food. Growth in yields per hectare and limitations imposed by environmental quality will determine, to a considerable extent, supply of food. The interplay of these factors will ultimately be reflected in the fifth P—the price of food. If demand grows more rapidly than supply, food prices will increase and (if prices increase faster than incomes) hunger will become more widespread. If supply grows more rapidly than demand, food prices will drop. The sixth P—policy—is the means by which humankind can hope to influence the future.

Two Views of the Future

It is tempting to characterize people's views about the future of world food supply and demand as "optimistic" or "pessimistic" (in fact, at several points in this book, such characterizations are made; also see McCalla 1998). But a more accurate division might be between the *establishment* view and the *antiestablishment* view. The establishment view is reflected in reports by the FAO (Alexandratos 1995), the World Bank (Mitchell, Ingco, and Duncan 1997), the International Food Price Research Institute (Pinstrup-Andersen, Pandya-Lorch, and Rosegrant 1998, and other IFPRI 2020 Policy Briefs, such as IFPRI 2005), and the USDA (2008b or Westcott and Hansen 2016). These reports embrace a common vision of the future in which world agricultural production continues to grow (with slight growth in agricultural area and yield growth in the 1 to 1.5 percent per year range), world population continues to grow but ever more slowly than the current 1.064 percent rate, and income per capita continues to grow. Implicit in their vision is an assumption that there will be no catastrophic changes in environmental conditions.

The antiestablishment view is reflected in the works cited in Chapters 12–14 by David Pimentel of Cornell University and by Lester Brown and his colleagues at the Worldwatch Institute. See Gilland (2002) for a careful exposition of this view, which puts a much greater emphasis on the possibility of environmental catastrophe. The types of catastrophe that could occur include losses of agricultural land due to erosion or degradation, reductions in availability of usable water for agriculture due to over-irrigation, and climate change that could (in the worst cases projected by scientists) cause significant loss of land to rising sea levels, and significant yield reductions from changing climate patterns. The antiestablishment view is also notably less confident about the possibility of a "technological fix" for these future catastrophes if they do occur. As described in Chapters 13 and 14, this lack of confidence is based on the slowing of yield growth, and the belief that we are unlikely to see any significant breakthroughs in basic science that would provide a foundation for a new spurt of growth in yields.

Past predictions of global food shortages have been wrong in large part because they underestimated the ability of technological progress to increase food output. The establishment view has confidence that the institutions and processes that generated yield growth in the past will continue to generate yield growth in the future. The antiestablishment view sees the yield growth of the past five decades as a onetime stroke of good fortune that is unlikely to be repeated.

Both the establishment view and the antiestablishment view accept the premise that human actions—especially government policies—can influence the future state of the world. The establishment view is more sympathetic to incrementalism—small changes in policies to ensure the world continues to make progress. The antiestablishment view is that major sweeping changes—

especially in environmental and population policies—must be made to accommodate and ameliorate future problems.

The antiestablishment view tends to see current prosperity—and the fact that "only" 10.9 percent of the world's population is currently undernourished—as coming at the expense of future generations. In effect, proponents of this view argue, we are "eating the seed"—satisfying our current hunger by guaranteeing even more severe and widespread problems in the future. The appropriate response, therefore, is a radical reduction in current levels of consumption of food and nonfood alike. At the extreme, it is argued, accomplishing this radical reduction in consumption may require a similarly radical restructuring of economic and political systems. The establishment view does not accept the vision of inherent conflict between present and future generations: Current prosperity will not cause future poverty; future generations will be on average at least as prosperous as we are today. This attitude leads to a broad endorsement of existing institutions. This is not quite the same thing as saying the establishment view endorses a "business as usual" policy. Rather, the kinds of policies endorsed by the establishment view—market-oriented pricing, increased government funding of research and development, appropriate institutions and macroeconomic policies to promote general economic growth, for example—tend to be policies that can be pursued within the existing political and institutional framework.

Predicting the Future: Principles for Scenario Building

Looking at different scenarios for the future allows us to see how intelligent, well-informed people can arrive at such different views about the future. In this chapter, we present a few alternative scenarios. The main purpose is not to prove that one or the other of these scenarios is "correct" but rather to provide a template from which readers can construct their own scenarios.

These scenarios make projections thirty-five years into the future. This is further than many projections, but those projections are intended for policymakers, who recognize that today's projections will be replaced by a new set within a few years. The 2050 endpoint was chosen to give readers a view of world food supply and demand during much of their lifetimes.

All scenarios are based on assumptions about annual rates of growth: growth in population, growth in per capita income, growth in area harvested, and growth in yields per hectare. The rates of growth assumed are *average* rates for the entire thirty-five-year period. Growth may be higher than average for some years, and lower than average for others. As laid out at the end of Chapter 10, projections about world food demand are based on assumptions about growth in population, growth in income per capita, and growth in biofuels. As suggested at the beginning of Chapter 11, projections about world food supply are based on assumptions about growth in agricultural land area and growth in yields.

In developing the scenarios in this chapter, we use sets of assumptions that are internally consistent. The complexity of interconnections among the factors has been illustrated throughout the book. Agricultural productivity, together with the concomitant prosperity in the farm sector, contributes to economy-wide prosperity and growth in per capita income. Higher per capita income is associated with better healthcare and sanitation, and therefore lower infant mortality; this in turn leads to reduced fertility and ultimately lower population growth rates. Environmental catastrophes, should they occur, are likely to be associated with lower per capita incomes, and therefore higher income elasticities of demand for food.

An "Establishment View" Scenario

At the end of Chapter 10 (Table 10.5), we presented some sample scenarios for growth in total food demand. There we saw a number of different assumptions that were consistent with a growth of demand of between 55 and 86 percent over the next thirty-five years. Here, we revisit this set of scenarios and assumptions and expand them to include the supply side. The basic demand-side assumption is that demand will increase by 73 percent by the year 2050. This serves as the demand-side assumption in scenario E (for "establishment") in Table 23.1. Scenario E also includes assumptions about the supply side. The basic establishment assumptions are reviewed below.

Population and income. As we saw in Table 10.5, demand growth of about 73 percent is consistent with annual population growth of 0.73 percent and annual growth of per capita income of 2 percent (scenario 1 of Table 10.5) To put these figures in perspective, the USDA's ten-year projection (Westcott and Hansen 2016) assumes world population growth of 1 percent per year and per capita income growth of 2.1 percent per year. We also construct scenarios with total demand growth of 86 percent (if biofuels demand grows faster, for example) and with total demand growth of 55 percent.

Table 23.1 Outcome of Various Scenarios to Address Food Supply and Demand, 2050

	Percentage Growth Between 2015 and 2050				
Scenario	Demand Growth	Land Growth	Yield Growth	Supply Growth	Price Increase
E	73	3	55	60	10
E-1	55	3	55	60	-4
E-2	86	3	55	60	19
E-3	73	3	32	36	30
AE	71	-15	7	-9	82
AE-1	71	0	32	32	32
AE-2	86	-15	7	-9	93

Increase in agricultural land. Chapter 11 discusses the potential for increasing agricultural land. Here we assume that land in agriculture increases by 1 percent per decade (not per year), or 3 percent total between now and 2050. To put this in perspective, worldwide agricultural land grew by 11 percent in the forty years between 1961 and 2001, but as noted in Chapter 11, that growth has slowed significantly in recent years.

Increases in agricultural yields. As mentioned, the establishment view projects increases of from 1.0 to 1.5 percent per year in yields. The graphs in Chapter 14 show that this range is consistent with historical trends and experience. Here we take the midpoint of that range (1.25 percent per year) as our assumption. Under this assumption, yields grow to 155 percent of current levels by 2050. To put our assumptions in perspective, the USDA's projections for the next ten years assume that US yields will grow at a little over 1 percent for wheat, about 1 percent for corn, and under 1 percent for rice and soybeans (Westcott and Hansen 2016).

Total increase in supply. Under these assumptions, total food supply (at constant prices) would increase to 160 percent (1.03×1.55) of current levels.

Effect on price. If food demand grows to 173 percent of current levels while supply grows to 160 percent of current levels, we see upward pressure on prices. Assuming a demand elasticity of 0.3 and a supply elasticity of 0.5, food price would increase by about 10 percent from current levels. (Recall that our underlying assumption of per capita income growth is 2 percent per year, so average income will double by 2050. Therefore, even though food prices are projected to increase, food will be more affordable for the average person in 2050.)

Extent of undernutrition. Of course, we cannot estimate what happens to the extent of undernutrition with any precision by using only these worldwide aggregate numbers. But ample evidence shows that the extent of undernutrition will decline substantially under this scenario. The projected calories per capita per day will increase from the current 2,900 to 3,335 (about the level in the developed world in the year 2000). In addition, as just noted, while the price of food (in this scenario) is a little higher in the year 2050, average income per capita has more than doubled. This should lead to a substantial reduction in the extent of undernutrition.

In fact, this is the prediction of the establishment view in published projections. For example, the FAO (Conforti 2011) projects that the number of undernourished in developing countries will decline by 50 percent by the year 2050, and that the percentage of developing world population who are undernourished will decline to 3.9 percent. The International Food Policy Research

Institute projects that by 2050, under the "business as usual" policy scenario, maize prices will rise slightly by the year 2050.

"Sensitivity Analysis": What Happens If We Change Assumptions?

The base scenario permits us to modify assumptions one at a time and see how sensitive the results are to changes in the assumptions.

Scenario E-1: lower demand growth. Scenario E-1 assumes that demand only grows by 55 percent by 2050. This is consistent with slower population growth (such as in the UN's low variant) or slower income growth (1 percent per year, rather than 2 percent per year). If we hold all other assumptions constant, this would mean supply growing much faster than demand, and food price decreases (about a 4 percent decline by 2050). Although the supply curve shifts out by 60 percent, the price decline causes a movement along the supply curve of 2 percent (based on a 0.5 supply elasticity). Thus the total increase in quantity of food supplied is about 57 percent. As in the base scenario E, income grows and prices decline, so calories per capita increase and prevalence of undernutrition declines.

Scenario E-2: higher demand growth. If biofuels demand grows much more than expected in the base scenario, total demand growth could be 86 percent rather than 73 percent. If we again maintain the supply-side assumptions of base scenario E (3 percent land growth and yield growth of 1.25 percent per year), demand growth outstrips supply growth and prices increase by about 19 percent. Even in this scenario, the price increase is smaller than the income growth. The undernutrition picture improves, though by less than under scenarios E and E-1.

Scenario E-3: lower yield growth. If average yield growth is 0.8 percent per year, rather than 1.25 percent in the base scenario E, yields by 2050 will have increased by 30 percent above current levels. Food supply increases much less rapidly than food demand (73 percent increase in this scenario); therefore prices rise substantially, although, again, less rapidly than the increase in incomes. Per capita calorie intake increases modestly.

An "Antiestablishment View" Scenario

A scenario that is consistent with the antiestablishment view (scenario AE for "antiestablishment" in Table 23.1) is likely to reflect the following assumptions.

Population and income. The antiestablishment view is more pessimistic about income growth, so we use a 1 percent per year growth rate. The antiestablishment view does not take a strong stand on population projections; but we assume higher population growth to be consistent (according to the theory of demographic transition) with our assumption of lower income growth.

Total shift in demand. Given these assumptions—see scenario 4 in Table 10.5—total demand for food in 2050 will be 71 percent higher than current demand.

Increase in agricultural land. As noted in Chapter 10, the antiestablishment view believes there may be declines in agricultural land due to degradation and a rise in sea level from global warming. In this scenario, we assume that agricultural area decreases by 15 percent by 2050.

Increases in agricultural yields. The antiestablishment view is doubtful that historical rates of growth can be continued. It may be reasonable (from the standpoint of this view) to assume that yields do not increase at all, or even that they decline as irrigation and land quality decline. Here we assume that yields do continue to grow, but at only a 0.2 percent rate. Under this assumption, yields in 2050 are 7 percent higher than current yields.

Total increase in supply. Under these assumptions, total food supply (at constant prices) would decrease to 91 percent (0.85×1.07) of current levels.

Effect on price. If demand grows by 71 percent and supply declines by 9 percent, price must increase. Using the 0.3 demand elasticity and 0.5 supply elasticity, this 80 percent difference between quantity demanded and quantity supplied at current prices means that the price must rise by 82 percent to return supply and demand to equilibrium—that is, food prices almost double by the year 2050 under this scenario.

Extent of undernutrition. The antiestablishment conclusion is that the extent of undernutrition increases substantially. The decline in average purchasing power supports this conclusion—average incomes increase by about 42 percent while prices double. Additional evidence of food shortage is found in the fact that population is projected to increase by 40 percent while food production also increases by about 40 percent. (Although the supply curve declines under this scenario, we see an increase in quantity supplied in response to the much higher prices. See the appendix to this chapter for details.) Calories per capita per day decline from the current 2,900 to about 2,850. This is the level of calories per capita per day that prevailed in about 2010, when 13 percent of the developing world suffered from undernutrition. So this "pessimistic" scenario means that the decades-long reduction in prevalence of undernutrition comes to an end, and begins to show signs of regression.

Alternative Antiestablishment Scenarios

Scenario AE-1: higher yield growth and less land degradation. Suppose things are not quite as bad as projected under scenario AE. Suppose that the quantity of agricultural land does not decline but stays constant at current levels. And suppose that yield growth is not 0.2 percent per year but is 0.8 percent per year. Under these assumptions (and maintaining the demand-side assumptions of scenario AE) supply grows by 32 percent, more than under scenario AE but still less than the demand growth of 71 percent. Prices increase about 32 percent, a little less than per capita income growth. Calories per capita per day increase slightly, and the prevalence of undernutrition remains at close to current levels.

Scenario AE-2: higher biofuels demand. Suppose we start with the basic AE scenario but add in an assumption of increased biofuels demand (as in scenario 5 of Table 10.5) so that total demand shifts out by 86 percent. In this case prices increase by 93 percent, compared to income growth of about 50 percent. Under these assumptions, the prevalence of undernutrition is even worse than it was under scenario AE.

* * *

The reader is invited to create other alternative scenarios. Again, we stress the importance of consistency. For example, if we construct a high-income-growth scenario, we may want to include an assumption of higher yield growth. Economy-wide prosperity is likely to be linked to increased agricultural productivity: if the economy is prosperous, more money can be invested in agricultural productivity; in developing countries where agriculture is a large sector of the economy, agricultural productivity is a prerequisite for high rates of economic growth.

Other projections for the future can be found in Westcott and Hansen 2016 (the USDA's projection), Conforti 2011 (the FAO's projection), and Nelson et al. 2010 (IFPRI's projection). The USDA's projection is for only a ten-year period, and details of that have been mentioned previously. The FAO projects that by 2050, food consumption will exceed 3,000 calories per capita per day worldwide. IFPRI projects that food prices will increase but by less than the increase in average income. These are broadly consistent with our establishment-view scenarios.

Policies

Scenarios such as those presented here may be useful in evaluating the likely impacts of various policies. Policy action or inaction will influence the future course of events and the severity of the worldwide hunger problem. Experts do not agree on all details about what constitutes a "best policy," nor do they agree on the likely impacts of any policy option. However, it seems clear that policy initiatives should focus on the following objectives:

• *Invest in improved agricultural productivity.* Direct government investment in agricultural research and extension, and improved access to rural credit and markets, will play an important role.
• *Encourage economic growth among the poorest.* Appropriate macroeconomic policies, reliance on competitive markets, and investment in human capital are likely to be important elements of this policy.

These two basic policy objectives have impacts on other basic elements of the world food problem. Income growth creates incentives that lead to reductions in fertility and population growth. Agricultural research not only discovers new ways to increase yields but also discovers ways to preserve quality of natural resources. Some initiatives—such as improving institutional arrangements to enforce property rights—can contribute to both of these basic policy objectives.

Appendix: Mathematics Used in Making Projections

Using Growth Rates to Project the Future

To understand the calculations behind the scenarios presented in this chapter, it is necessary to know some elementary mathematics of growth. A simple example explains the basic point. Suppose a city starts the year with a population of 100,000, and suppose the population grows by 10 percent during the year. At the end of the year (year 1), the city's population will be 110,000. We get this by multiplying the population at the beginning of the year (100,000) by 1 plus the annual growth rate (10 percent or 0.10):

110,000 = 100,000 × (1 + 0.10)
end-of-year value = beginning-of-year value times 1 plus growth rate

To conserve verbiage, we assign symbols to these words, with V_1 being the value at the end of year 1, V_0 being the value at the beginning of year 1 (or at the end of year 0), and r being the growth rate:

$$V_1 = V_0 (1 + r) \tag{1}$$

Now suppose the population grows by 10 percent for the second year. We can use equation (1) to calculate the population at the end of year 2. The population at the end of year 2 will be:

110,000 × (1 + 0.10) = 121,000

Notice that we can also write this as:

$(100,000 \times [1 + 0.10]) \times (1 + 0.10) = 121,000$

Similarly, at the end of year 3 (if growth continues at 10 percent), the population would be:

$([100,000 \times (1 + 0.10)] \times [1 + 0.10]) \times (1 + 0.10) = 121,000 \times (1 + 0.10)$
$= 133,100$

The preceding two calculations show us a pattern:

$V_1 = V_0 (1 + r)^1$
$V_2 = V_0 (1 + r)^2$
$V_3 = V_0 (1 + r)^3$

Thus the general rule used to calculate values at the end of T periods is:

$$V_T = V_0 (1 + r)^T \qquad\qquad (2)$$

To return to the content of this chapter, and see how equation (2) is applied, look at the assumption about yield growth in scenario E. Yield is assumed to grow at an average rate of 1.25 percent (or 0.0125) over the thirty-five year period between 2016 and 2050. Applying equation (2) gives us:

$$V_{2050} = V_{2008} (1+.0125)^{35} = V_0 \times 1.545$$

Rounding 1.545 to 1.55, this means that yield in 2050 is 155 percent of current levels or 55 percent higher than yield in 2008. This information is entered in Table 23.1 as 55 percent in the yield column of scenario E.

Calculating the Total Impact When Two Multiplicative Factors Are Growing

Total supply is land times yield. In our scenarios, both of these factors (land and yield) change. As explained in Chapter 10, when this happens, growth rate for total supply is calculated as follows. Using scenario E as an example, if land grows by 3 percent and if yield grows by 55 percent over the period, growth in total supply is calculated as:

$(1 + 0.03) \times (1 + 0.55) = 1.60$

Total supply in 2050 is 1.60 times (or 160 percent of) supply at the beginning of the period; or supply has increased by 60 percent.

Calculating the Price Change

The changes in demand and supply in our scenarios assume constant prices—we are projecting the degree to which demand and supply curves shift in the future. (Those with more training in economics will notice that our demand factors—population and income—are traditional demand shifters in economic theory; however, our supply factors—area and yield—are not consistent with theoretical economics of supply. We analyze growth in supply using these supply factors because they make the supply side of the equation easier to understand.) If demand grows faster than supply, equilibrium price will increase from current levels. If supply grows faster than demand, equilibrium price will decrease.

How do we calculate the size of the price change? Scenario E illustrates the calculation. Supply is projected to grow by 60 percent and demand is projected to grow by 73 percent. Thus, at constant prices, quantity demanded would exceed quantity supplied. To see that a 10 percent increase in price brings us back to an equilibrium where quantity supplied equals quantity demanded, do the following calculations. The starting position is out of equilibrium where quantity demanded is at 173 and quantity supplied is at 160. A 10 percent increase in price generates an increase in quantity supplied of 5 percent (since supply elasticity is assumed to be 0.5), or $160 \times 1.05 = 168$. A 10 percent increase in price generates a 3 percent decrease in quantity demanded (since demand elasticity is assumed to be –0.3), or $173 \times (1 - 0.03) = 168$. Quantity demanded is equal to quantity supplied and equilibrium has been restored.

References

Aalangdong, O. I., J. M. Kombiok, and A. Z. Salifu. 1999. Assessment of non-burning and organic manuring practices. *ILEIA Newsletter.* Wagingen, Netherlands: Centre for Information on Low External Input and Sustainable Agriculture, September 1999.

Abbot, Patrick. 2003. Ireland's great famine, 1845–1849. http://www.irelandstory.com/past/famine.

Acemoglu, D., and J. Robinson. 2012. Why is Haiti so poor? *Why Nations Fail,* April 3, 2012. http://whynationsfail.com/blog/2012/4/3/why-is-haiti-so-poor.html?utm _source=dlvr.it&utm_medium=twitter.

Adams, Dale W. 1983. Mobilizing household savings through rural financial markets. In *Rural financial markets in developing countries: Their use and abuse,* ed. J. D. Von Pischke et al., 399–407. Baltimore: Johns Hopkins University Press.

Adams, Dale W., et al., eds. 1984. *Undermining rural development with cheap credit.* Boulder: Westview.

Adamu, H. 2000. We'll feed our people as we see fit. *Washington Post,* September 11.

Adelman, I., and C. T. Morris. 1973. *Economic growth and social equity in developing countries.* Stanford: Stanford University Press.

African Development Fund. 2004. *Democratic Republic of Congo: Agricultural and rural sector rehabilitation support project appraisal report.* Abidjan. http://www.afdb.org.

Ahluwalia, Montek S. 1976a. Income distribution and development: Some stylized facts. *American Economic Review* 66 (May):128–135.

———. 1976b. Inequality, poverty, and development. *Journal of Development Economics* 3 (September):307–342.

Ahluwalia, Montek S., N. Carter, and H. Chenery. 1979. Growth and poverty in developing countries. In *Structural change and development policy,* ed. H. Chenery, 456-496. Oxford: Oxford University Press. Also available in *Journal of Development Economics* 6 (September):299–341.

Ahmed, A. 2015. Agricultural mechanization. Background paper for the Feeding Africa Conference, UN Economic Commission for Africa, Dakar, October 21–23. http://www.afdb.org.

Ahmed, R., and F. Goletti. 1997. Food policy reform in Bangladesh. In *1997 annual report of the International Food Policy Research Institute.* Washington, DC.

Ahmed, Raisuddin. 1988. Structure, costs, and benefits of food subsidies in Bangladesh. In *Food subsidies in developing countries,* ed. Per Pinstrup-Andersen, 219–228. Baltimore: Johns Hopkins University Press.

Ahmed, Raisuddin, and Mahabub Hossain. 1990. *Developmental impact of rural infrastructures: Bangladesh.* Research Report no. 83. Washington, DC: International Food Policy Research Institute.

Alberts, Tom. 1983. *Agrarian reform and rural poverty: A case study of Peru.* Boulder: Westview.

Alderman, H., J. Hoddinott, and B. Kinsey. 2003. Long-term consequences of early childhood malnutrition. Paper presented to the International Conference on Chronic Poverty and Development Policy, Oxford University, April 7–9. http://oep.oxfordjournals.org/content/58/3/450.abstract.

Alderman, H., and K. Lindert. 1998. The potential and limitations of self-targeted food subsidies. *World Bank Research Observer* 13, no. 2:213–229.

Alderman, Harold. 1986. *The effect of food price and income changes on the acquisition of food by low-income households.* Washington, DC: International Food Policy Research Institute.

Alderman, Harold, and Joachim von Braun. 1984. *The effects of the Egyptian food ration and subsidy system on income distribution and consumption.* Research Report no. 45. Washington, DC: International Food Policy Research Institute.

Alexandratos, N., ed. 1995. *World agriculture: Towards 2010—An FAO study.* London: Wiley.

Alston, J., et al. 2000. *A meta-analysis of rates of return to agricultural R&D: Ex pede herculem.* Research Report no. 113. Washington, DC: International Food Policy Research Institute.

Alston, Philip. 1997. Recognition of the right to food. World Food Summit fact sheet. Rome: United Nations and Food and Agriculture Organization. http://www.fao.org.

Anand, G. 2010. Green revolution in India wilts as subsidies backfire. *Wall Street Journal,* February 22.

Anderson, J. R., and J. A. Roumasset. 1985. Microeconomics of food insecurity: The stochastic side of poverty. Unpublished paper available through the University of Hawaii, Manoa, Department of Economics.

Anderson, Jock, et al. 1985. *International agricultural research centers: A study of achievements and potential—summary.* Washington, DC: World Bank, Consultative Group on International Agricultural Research.

Anderson, Mary Ann, et al. 1981. *Nutrition intervention in developing countries.* Study 1: *Supplementary feeding.* Cambridge, MA: Oelgeschlager, Gunn, and Hain.

Angé, A. L. 1993. *Trends of plant nutrient management in developing countries.* Rome: Food and Agriculture Organization.

Angel, J. Lawrence. 1975. Paleoecology, paleodemography, and health. In *Population, ecology, and social evolution,* ed. S. Polgar, 167–190. The Hague: Mouton.

———. 1984. Health as a crucial factor in the changes from hunting to developed farming in the Eastern Mediterranean. In *Paleopathology at the origins of agriculture,* ed. M. N. Cohen and G. J. Armelagos, 51–73. New York: Academic Press.

Anonymous. 1974. How hunger kills. *Time,* November 11.

———. 1988. Women and development: Education and fertility. *Finance and Development* 43 (September).

Applebaum, Anne. 2008. When China starved. *Washington Post,* August 12. http://www.washingtonpost.com/wp-dyn/content/article/2008/08/11/AR2008081102015.html?sub=AR.

Arezki, R., K. Deininger, and H. Selod. 2015. What drives the global "land rush"? *World Bank Economic Review* 29, no. 2:207–233. http://www.washingtonpost .com/wp-dyn/content/article/2008/08/11/AR2008081102015.html?sub=AR.

Arnold, C., with T. Conway and M. Greenslade. 2011. *DFID cash transfers evidence paper.* London: Department for International Development.

Askari, Hossein, and John T. Cummings. 1976. *Agricultural supply response: A survey of the econometric evidence.* New York: Praeger.

Associated Press. 2000. UN: Nutrition improving in North Korea. November 4.

Astawa, I. B. 1979. Using the local community: Bali, Indonesia. In *Birth control: An international assessment,* ed. M. Potts and P. Bhiwandiowala, 55–70. Baltimore: University Park Press.

Baden, John. 2003. Move over culture war: Here's the aquaculture war. Tech Central Station, August 29. http://www.ideasinactiontv.com.

Bale, Malcolm D. 1984. Opening of the discussion on plenary paper 5. In *Proceedings of the fourth congress of the E.A.A.E.: Agricultural markets and prices. European Review of Agricultural Economics* 12:82–83.

———. 1985. *Agricultural trade and food policy: The experience of five developing countries.* Staff Working Paper no. 724. Washington, DC: World Bank.

Bale, Malcolm D., and Ernst Lutz. 1981. Price distortions in agriculture and their effects: An international comparison. *American Journal of Agricultural Economics* 63 (February):8–22.

Baliunas, Sallie. 1999. Why so hot? Don't blame man, blame the sun. *Wall Street Journal,* August 5. http://www.wsj.com/articles/SB933817169586278804.

Banerjee, A., and E. Duflo. 2007. The economic lives of the poor. *Journal of Economic Perspectives* 21, no. 1:141–167. https://www.aeaweb.org.

Banerjee, A., et al. 2015. A multifaceted program causes lasting progress for the very poor: Evidence from six countries. *Science* 348 (May). http://science .sciencemag.org/content/348/6236/1260799.

Bardhan, P. 2006. Does globalization help or hurt the world's poor. *Scientific American,* April.

Barrionuevo, A. 2008. Argentina export tax sets off political furor. *New York Times,* July 5.

Bautista, Romeo M. 1987. *Production incentives in Philippine agriculture: Effects of trade and exchange rate policies.* Research Report no. 59. Washington, DC: International Food Policy Research Institute.

Baylor, K. 1996. Biochemical studies on the toxicity of isocyanates. Abstract from a PhD thesis submitted to University College Cork, Ireland, May.

Beal, George M., and Everett M. Rogers. 1960. *The adoption of two farm practices in a central Iowa community.* Special Report no. 26. Ames: Iowa State University, Agricultural and Home Economics Experiment Station.

Bearak, B. 2003. Why people still starve. *New York Times Sunday Magazine,* August 10.

Beaton, George H., and Hossein Ghassemi. 1982. Supplementary feeding programs for young children in developing countries. *American Journal of Clinical Nutrition* 35 (April):864–916.

Becker, Gary. 1975. *Human capital.* New York: Columbia University Press.

Behrman, J., and A. Deolalikar. 1987. Will developing country nutrition improve with income? A case study for rural south India. *Journal of Political Economy* 95:108–138.

Bennett, M.K. 1941. International contrasts in food consumption. *Geographical Review* 31: 365–374.

Berg, Alan. 1973. *The nutrition factor: Its role in national development.* Washington, DC: Brookings Institution.

Berry, A. R., and W. R. Cline. 1979. *Agrarian structure and productivity in developing countries.* Baltimore: Johns Hopkins University Press.

Bettany, G. T. 1890. Introduction. Essay published with the 1890 Ward edition of *Essay on population* by T. R. Malthus.

Bezuneh, Mesfin, Brady J. Deaton, and George W. Norton. 1988. Food aid impacts in rural Kenya. *American Journal of Agricultural Economics* 70 (February):181–191.

Bhargava, Alok. 1996. *Econometric analysis of psychometric data: A model for Kenyan schools.* Washington, DC: World Bank.

Bilger, Burkhard. 2004. The height gap. *New Yorker,* April 5.

Binswanger, Hans. 1978. *The economics of tractors in South Asia: An analytical review.* New York: Agricultural Development Council; and Hyderabad, India: International Crops Research Institute for the Semi-Arid Tropics.

Binswanger, Hans, and Klaus Deininger. 1997. Explaining agricultural and agrarian policies in developing countries. *Journal of Economic Literature* 35 (December):1958–2005.

Binswanger, Hans, et al. 1987. *Agricultural mechanization: Issues and options.* Washington, DC: World Bank.

Black, S. E., P. Devereaux, and K. Salvanes. 2007. From the cradle to the labor market? The effect of birth weight on adult outcomes. *Quarterly Journal of Economics* 122, no. 1:409–439.

Bleichrodt, Nico, and Marise P. H. Born. 1994. A meta-analysis of research on iodine and its relationship to cognitive development. In *The damaged brain of iodine deficiency: Cognitive, behavioral, neuromotor, educative aspects,* ed. John Stanbury, 195-200. Port Washington, NY: Cognizant Communication.

Bliss, C. J., and N. Y. Stern. 1982. *Palanpur: The economy of an Indian village.* Oxford: Clarendon.

Blow, L., A. Leicester, and Z. Smith. 2003. London's congestion charge. London: Institute for Fiscal Studies, Briefing Note no. 31. http://www.ifs.org .uk/consume/bn31.pdf.

Boediono. 1978. Elastisitas permintaan untuk berbagai barang di Indonesia; Penerapan metode Frisch. *Ekonomi dan Keuangan Indonesia* 26 (September): 362.

Boggess, W., R. Lacewell, and D. Zilberman. 1993. Economics of water use in agriculture. In *Agricultural and environmental resource economics,* ed. G. Carlson, D. Zilberman, and J. Miranowski, 319–392. Oxford: Oxford University Press.

Bongaarts, John. 1982. The fertility-inhibiting effects of the intermediate fertility variables. *Studies in Family Planning* 13:179–189.

———. 1994. Population policy options in the developing world. *Science* 263 (February):771–776.

Bonny, S. 2016. Genetically modified herbicide-tolerant crops, weeds, and herbicides: Overview and impact. *Environmental Management* 57, no. 1:31–48.

Boserup, Ester. 1981. *Population and technological change: A study of long-term trends.* Chicago: University of Chicago Press.

Boudreaux, K., and T. Cowen. 2008. The micromagic of microcredit. *Wilson Quarterly* (Winter): 27–31.

Bouis, Howarth E., and Lawrence Haddad. 1992. Are estimates of calorie-income elasticities too high? *Journal of Development Economics* 39:333–364.

Bowles, S., and H. Gintis. 2002. The inheritance of inequality. University of Massachusetts working paper. http://www.umass.edu/preferen/gintis/intergen.pdf.

Brandolini, A., and T. Smeeding. 2007. Inequality patterns in Western-type democracies: Cross-country differences and time changes. Luxembourg Income Study, Working Paper no. 458. http://hdl.handle.net/10419/95393.

Brasitus, T. 1979. Parasites and malabsorption. *American Journal of Medicine* 67, no. 6:1058–1065.

Briscoe, J. 1979. The qualitative effect of infection of the use of food by young children in poor countries. *American Journal of Clinical Nutrition* 32 (March):648–676.

British Geological Survey. 2012. Quantitative groundwater maps for Africa. http://www.bgs.ac.uk/research/groundwater/international/africangroundwater /maps.html.

Brooker, S., P. J. Hotez, and D. Bundy. 2008. Hookworm-related anaemia among pregnant women: A systematic review. *PLoS: Neglected Tropical Diseases* 2, no. 9:e291. http://www.plosntds.org/article/info%3Adoi%2F10.1371%2Fjournal.pntd .0000291.

Brown, Lester R. 1970. *Seeds of change: The green revolution and development in the 1970s.* New York: Praeger.

———. 1974. *In the human interest: A strategy to stabilize world population.* New York: Norton.

———. 1983. *Population policies for a new economic era.* Paper no. 53. Washington, DC: Worldwatch.

———. 1988. *The changing world food prospect: The nineties and beyond.* Paper no. 85. Washington, DC: Worldwatch.

———. 2015. Interview with Suzanne Goldenberg of *The Guardian.* February 24. http://www.theguardian.com/environment/2015/feb/25/lester-brown-vast-dust -bowls-threaten-tens-of-millions-with-hunger.

Brown, Lester, and B. Halweil. 1998. China's water shortage could shake world food security. *World Watch* (July–August):11–12.

Brown, Lester, and Hal Kane. 1994. *Full house: Reassessing the earth's population carrying capacity.* Washington, DC: Worldwatch.

Brown, Lynn. 1997. The potential impact of AIDS on population and economic growth rates. 2020 Brief no. 43. Washington, DC: International Food Policy Research Institute. http://ageconsearch.umn.edu/bitstream/16334/1/br43.pdf.

Brueckner, M., E. Norris, and M. Gradstein. 2015. National income and its distribution. *Journal of Economic Growth* 20:149–175.

Bruinsma, J. 2011. The resources outlook: By how much do land, water, and crop yields need to increase by 2050? In *Looking ahead in world food and agriculture: Perspectives to 2050,* ed. P. Conforti, 233–278. Rome: Food and Agriculture Organization.

Bulatao, Rodolfo A. 1984a. Fertility control at the community level: A review of research and community programs. In *Rural development and human fertility,* ed. W. Schutjer and C. Stokes, 269–290. New York: Macmillan.

———. 1984b. *Reducing fertility in developing countries: A review of determinants and policy servers.* Staff Working Paper no. 680, Population and Development Series no. 5. Washington, DC: World Bank.

Bumb, Balu L., and Carlos A. Baanante. 1996. World trends in fertilizer use and projections to 2020. 2020 Brief no. 38. Washington, DC: International Food Policy Research Institute.

Bump, J. B., M. A. Clemens, G. Demombynes, and L. Haddad. 2012. Concerns about Millennium Villages project report. *Lancet* 379 (May).

Burnside, Craig, and David Dollar. 2000. Aid, policies, and growth. *American Economic Review* 90, no. 4:847–868.

Buzby, J., H. Wells, and J. Hyman. 2014. *The estimated amount, value, and calories of postharvest food losses at the retail and consumer levels in the United States.* Washington, DC: USDA, ERS, Economic Information Bulletin Number 121, February. http://www.ers.usda.gov/media/1282296/eib121.pdf.

Calegar, Geraldo M., and G. Edward Schuh. 1988. *The Brazilian wheat policy: Its costs, benefits, and effects on food consumption.* Research Report no. 66. Washington, DC: International Food Policy Research Institute.

California Department of Water Resources. 2005. *California water plan, 2005.* Vol. 4. Sacramento. http://www.waterplan.water.ca.gov/previous/cwpu2005/index.cfm.

Campbell, Joseph K. 1984. Machines and food production. In *World food issues,* ed. Matthew Drosdoff, 47–50. Ithaca, NY: Cornell University College of Agriculture.

Carson, R. 1962. *Silent Spring.* New York: Houghton Mifflin.

Case, A., and C. Paxson. 2008. Stature and status: Height, ability, and labor market outcomes. *Journal of Political Economy* 116, no. 3:499–532.

Casey, M. 2007. Experts target rice as climate culprit. *Boston Globe,* May 1. http://www.boston.com/news/world/asia/articles/2007/05/01/experts_target_rice_as_climate_culprit?mode=PF.

CAST (Council on Agricultural Science and Technology). 2002. Comparative environmental impacts of biotechnology-derived and traditional soybean, corn, and cotton crops. Washington, DC http://www.cast-science.org.

———. 2003. *Biotechnology in animal agriculture.* Washington, DC.

Caulfield, L., M. de Onis, M. Blossner, and R. Black. 2004b. Undernutrition as an underlying cause of child deaths associated with diarrhea, pneumonia, malaria, and measles. *American Journal of Clinical Nutrition* 80:193–198. http://www.ajcn.org/content/80/1/193.full.pdf+html.

Caulfield, L., S. Richard, and R. Black. 2004a. Undernutrition as an underlying cause of malaria morbidity, and mortality in children less than five years old. *American Journal of Tropical Medical Hygiene* 71 (2004):55–63.

Cavallo, Domingo, and Yair Mundlak. 1982. *Agriculture and economic growth in an open economy: The case of Argentina.* Research Report no. 36. Washington, DC: International Food Policy Research Institute.

CDC (Centers for Disease Control). 2002. Investigation of human health affects associated with potential exposure to genetically modified corn. Atlanta. http://www.cdc.gov/nceh/ehhe/Cry9CReport/pdfs/cry9creport.pdf.

CGIAR (Consultative Group on International Agricultural Research). 1995. Wheat is doing well in Syria. *CGIAR Newsletter* (October). Washington, DC: World Bank. http://www.worldbank.org/html/cgiar/newsletter/Oct95/3syria.htm.

———. 1997. *25 years of food and agriculture improvement in developing countries.* Washington, DC: World Bank. http://www.worldbank.org/html/cgiar/25years/25cover.html.

Cha, A. 2004. Iraqis face tough transition to market-based agriculture. *Washington Post,* January 22.

Chakraborty, R., K. Bose, and S. Bisai. 2009. Mid-upper arm circumference as a measure of nutritional status among adult Bengalee male slum dwellers of Kolkata, India: Relationship with self reported morbidity. *Anthropologischer Anzeiger* 67, no. 2:129–137.

Champakam, S., S. C. Srikantia, and C. Gopalan. 1968. Kwashiorkor and mental development. *American Journal of Clinical Nutrition* 21 (August):844–852.

Chandra, R. K. 1979. Nutritional deficiency and susceptibility to infection. *Bulletin of the World Health Organization* 57, no. 2:167–177.

———. 1980. Immunocompetence in undernutrition and overnutrition. *Nutrition Review* 39:225–231.

————. 1988. Nutritional regulation of immunity: An introduction. In *Nutrition and immunology,* ed. Ranjit Chandra, 1–7. New York: Alan R. Liss.

Chaney, J. 2008. As Chinese wealth rises, pets take a higher place. *International Herald Tribune,* March 17. http://www.nytimes.com/2008/03/17/business/worldbusiness /17iht-pet.4.11191511.html?_r=0.

Chavez, Adolfo, and Celia Martinez. 1982. Growing up in a developing community: A bio-ecological study of the development of children from poor peasant families in Mexico. Mexico: Instituto Nacional de la Nutricion.

Chen, P. C. 1981. China's birth planning program. In *National research council committee on population and demography: Research on the population in China, proceedings of a workshop,* 78–90. Washington, DC: National Academy Press.

Chen, P. C., and A. Kols. 1982. Population and birth planning in the People's Republic of China. *Population Reports* series J, no. 25 (January–February), vol. 10, no. 1:577–618.

Chen, R. S. 1990. Global agriculture, environment, and hunger: Past, present, and future links. *Environmental Impact Assessment Review* 10, no. 4:335–358.

Chen, Y., and L. Zhou. 2007. The long-term health and economic consequences of the 1959–1961 famine in China. *Journal of Health Economics* 26, no. 4:659–681. http://www.sciencedirect.com/science/article/pii/S016762960600141X.

Chenery, Hollis, Sherman Robinson, and Moshe Syrquin. 1986. *Industrialization and growth: A comparative study.* New York: Oxford University Press.

Chesapeake Bay Foundation. 2008. Save the bay: Animals. http://www.cbf.org/how -we-save-the-bay.

Chhibber, Ajay. 1988. Raising agricultural output: Price and nonprice factors. *Finance and Development* (June):44–47.

China Daily. 2012. Urban rural income gap gets bigger: Report. August 14. http:// europe.chinadaily.com.cn/china/2012–08/14/content_15676198.htm.

Chotard, S., J. Mason, N. Oliphant, S. Mebrahtu, and P. Hailey. 2010. Fluctuations in wasting in vulnerable child populations in the Greater Horn of Africa. *Food and Nutrition Bulletin* 31, supp. 3:209S–233S.

CIMMYT (Centro Internacional de Mejoramiento de Maize y Trigo). 1989. *Towards the 21st century: CIMMYT's strategy.* Mexico City.

————. 2003. *Innovation for development: Annual report 2002–2003.* Mexico City. http://www.cimmyt.org/english/docs/ann_report/recent/pdf/ar03_Reducing.pdf.

Clark, Colin G. 1973. More people, more dynamism. *CERES* (November–December). Rome: Food and Agriculture Organization.

Cleaver, Kevin M. 1985. *The impact of price and exchange rate policies on agriculture in sub-Saharan Africa.* Staff Working Paper no. 728. Washington, DC: World Bank.

Cogill, B. 2003. *Anthropometric indicators measurement guide, 2003 revision.* Washington, DC: Food and Nutrition Technical Assistance (FANTA).

Cohen, Joel. 1996a. *How many can the earth support?* New York: Norton.

————. 1996b. Maximum occupancy. *American Demographics,* February.

Cohen, Mark N. 1984. An introduction to the symposium. In *Paleopathology at the origins of agriculture,* ed. Mark Cohen and George Armelagos, 1–11. New York: Academic Press.

Cohen, Mark N., and George Armelagos, eds. 1984. *Paleopathology at the origins of agriculture.* New York: Academic Press.

Coleman-Jensen, A., M. Rabbitt, C. Gregory, and A. Singh. 2015. *Household food security in the U.S. in 2014.* Economic Research Report no. 194. Washington, DC: US Department of Agriculture, September 2015.

Collier, P., 2008. *The bottom billion: Why the poorest countries are failing and what can be done about it.* New York: Oxford University Press.

Collier, P., and D. Dollar. 2002. *Globalization, growth, and poverty: Building an inclusive world economy.* Oxford: Oxford University Press and World Bank.

Conforti, P., ed. 2011. *Looking ahead in world food and agriculture: Perspectives to 2050.* Rome: Food and Agriculture Organization.

Cooke, G. W. 1967. *The control of soil fertility.* London: Crosby Lockwood.

Cornelsen, L., R. Green, R. Turner, A. D. Dangour, B. Shankar, M. Mazzocchi, and R. D. Smith. 2015. What happens to patterns of food consumption when food prices change? Evidence from a systematic review and meta-analysis of food price elasticities globally. *Health Economics* 24:1548–1559.

Correia, I., and D. Waitzberg. 2003. The impact of malnutrition on morbidity, mortality, length of hospital stay, and costs evaluated through a multivariate model analysis. *Clinical Nutrition* 22, no. 3:235–239.

Costa, D. L., and R. H. Steckel. 1997. Longer-term trends in health,welfare, and economic growth in the United States. In *Health and welfare during industrialization,* eds., R. Steckel and R. Floud. Chicago: University of Chicago Press.

Court, J., and T. Yanagihara. N.d. Asia and Africa into the global economy. http://www.unu.edu/HQ/academic/Pg_area4/August-intro.html.

Cowell, F. A. 1977. *Measuring inequality: Techniques for the social sciences.* New York: Wiley.

Cowen, T. 2006. *Good and plenty: The Creative successes of American arts funding.* Princeton: Princeton University Press.

Cox, W. M., and R. Alm. 2008. You are what you spend. *New York Times,* February 10.

Craig, B. J., P. Pardey, and J. Roseboom. 1994. International agricultural productivity patterns. Working Paper no. 94-1. St. Paul: Center for International Food and Agricultural Policy, University of Minnesota. http://ageconsearch.umn.edu/handle /14470.

———. 1997. International productivity patterns: Accounting for input quality, infrastructure, and research. *American Journal of Agricultural Economics* 79, no. 4 (November):1064–1076.

Crepon, B., F. Devoto, E. Duflo, and W. Pariente. 2015. Estimating the impact of microcredit on those who take it up: Evidence from a randomized experiment in Morocco. *American Economic Journal: Applied Economics* 7, no. 1:123–150.

Crosson, Pierre. 1996a. Resource degradation? *Perspectives on the Long-Term Global Food Situation* (Summer). http://www.fas.org/food/issue2.html http://www.fas.org /food/issue2.html.

———. 1996b. Who will feed China? *Perspectives on the Long-Term Global Food Situation* 2 (Spring). http://www.fas.org/food/issue2.html.

Daberkow, S., K. Isherwood, J. Poulisse, and H. Vroomen. 1999. Fertilizer requirements in 2015 and 2030. Presentation at the IFA Agricultural Conference, Barcelona.

Dagum, Camilo. 1987. Gini ratio. In *The new Palgrave: A dictionary of economics,* vol. 2, ed. John Eatwell et al., 529–532. New York: Stockton.

Dalrymple, Dana G. 1979. The adoption of high-yielding grain varieties in developing countries. *Agricultural History* 53 (October):704–726.

———. 1985. The development and adoption of high-yielding varieties of wheat and rice in developing countries. *American Journal of Agricultural Economics* 67 (December):1067–1073.

Dao, James. 2003. US to resume food aid to North Korea after 2-month halt. *New York Times,* February 25.

Das, J., J. Hammer, and K. Leonard. 2008. The quality of medical advice in low-income countries. *Journal of Economic Perspectives* 22, no. 2:93–114.

Davies, Daniel. 2005. Sen on famines and democracy. *Crooked Timber,* January 6. http://crookedtimber.org/2005/01/06/sen-on-famines-and-democracy.

Davis, M. 2001. *Late Victorian holocausts: El Niño famines and the making of the third world.* London: Verso.

Dawkins, K. 2003. *Gene wars: The politics of biotechnology.* New York: Seven Stories.

de Janvry, Alain. 1981. The role of land reform in economic development: Policies and politics. *American Journal of Agricultural Economics* 63:384–392.

de Janvry, Alain,. N. Key, and E. Sadoulet. 1997. *Agricultural and rural development policy in Latin America: New directions and new challenges.* Rome: Food and Agriculture Organization. http://www.fao.org/docrep/W7441E/w7441e00.htm#Contents.

de Soto, H. 2000. *The mystery of capital: Why capitalism triumphs in the West and fails everywhere else.* New York: Basic.

de Zoysa, Isabelle, et al., 1985. *Focus on diarrhoea.* London: Ross Institute, London School of Hygiene and Tropical Medicine.

Deaton, Angus, and John Muellbauer. 1980. *Economics and consumer behavior.* Cambridge: Cambridge University Press.

Deininger, K., and P. Olinto. 2000. *Asset distribution, inequality, and growth.* Working Paper no. 2375. Washington, DC: World Bank.

Deininger, Klaus, and Lyn Squire. 1997. Economic growth and income inequality: Re-examining the links. *Finance and Development* (March):38–41.

———. 1998. New ways of looking at old issues: Inequality and growth. *Journal of Development Economics* 52, no. 2:259–287.

Delgado, C. 2003. Rising consumption of meat and milk in developing countries has created a new food revolution. *Journal of Nutrition* 133:3907S–3910S.

Deltas, G. 2003. The small-sample bias of the Gini coefficient: Results and implications for empirical research. *Review of Eonomics and Statistics* 85(1): 226-234.

Demick, B. 2009. The good cook. *New Yorker.* November 2, 2009.

Demont, M. 2013. Reversing urban bias in African rice markets. *Global Food Security* 2:172–181.

den Biggelaar, C., L. Rattan, K. Wiebe, H. Eswaran, V. Breneman, and P. Reich. 2004. The global impact of soil erosion on productivity II: Effect on crop yields and production over time. *Advances in Agronomy* 81:49–95.

Derneke, M., A. Said, and T. Jayne. 1997. *Relationships between fertilizer use and grain sector performance.* Working Paper no. 5. Addis Ababa: Grain Market Research Project, Ministry of Economic Development and Cooperation.

Deschenes, O., and M. Greenstone. 2007. The economic impacts of climate change: Evidence from agricultural output and random fluctuations in weather. *American Economic Review* 97, no. 1 (March):354–385.

Despommier, D. 2010. *The vertical farm: Feeding the world in the 21st century.* New York: St. Martin's.

Detsky, A., et al. 1987. What is subjective global assessment of nutritional status? *Journal of Parenteral and Enteral Nutrition* 11, no. 1:8–13.

Dever, James R. 1983. Determinants of nutritional status in a North Indian village: An economic analysis. Master's thesis, University of Maryland.

DFID (Department for International Development). 2002. Better livelihoods for poor people: The role of agriculture. Glasgow. http://www.tradeobservatory.org/library/uploadedfiles/Better_Livelihoods_for_Poor_People_The_Role_of.htm.

Diamond, J. 1987. The worst mistake in the history of the human race. *Discover Magazine,* May. http://www.scribd.com/doc/2100251/Jared-Diamond-The-Worst-Mistake-in-the-History-of-the-Human-Race.

Dickens, Charles. 1958. *A tale of two cities.* London: Oxford University Press.

Dikotter, Frank. 2010. *Mao's great famine.* New York: Walker.

Dixon, Robyn. 2008. White farmer's ordeal in Zimbabwe. *Los Angeles Times,* August 7. http://www.latimes.com/news/nationworld/world/la-fg-farmer7-2008aug07,0,1115417.story.

Doctors Without Borders. 2008a. Malnutrition. http://www.doctorswithoutborders.org/our-work/medical-issues/malnutrition.

———. 2008b. Starved for attention: The neglected crisis of childhood malnutrition, a symposium. September 11, New York. http://www.doctorswithoutborders.org/support-us/events/starved-attention-neglected-crisis-childhood-malnutrition.

Dollar, D., and A. Kraay. 2002. Growth is good for the poor. *Journal of Economic Growth* 7, no. 3:195–225.

Dolot, Miron. 1985. *Execution by hunger: The hidden holocaust.* New York: Norton.

Dommen, Arthur J. 1988. *Innovation in African agriculture.* Boulder: Westview.

Donnelly, James. 2001. *The great Irish potato famine.* Phoenix Mill, Gloucestershire, UK: Sutton.

Dray, T. 2015. N.d. Number of dogs and cats in households worldwide. http://pets.thenest.com/number-dogs-cats-households-worldwide-8973.html.

Dreze, Jean. 2001. Starving the poor. *The Hindu,* March 18, p. 12.

Dreze, Jean, and Amartya Sen. 1989. *Hunger and public action.* Oxford: Oxford University Press.

———, eds. 1990. *The political economy of hunger.* 3 vols. Oxford: Oxford University Press.

Duflo, E., M. Kremer, and J. Robinson. 2004. *Understanding technology adoption: Fertilizer in Western Kenya, preliminary results from field experiments.* Unpublished manuscript, Massachusetts Institute of Technology.

Duke, Lynne. 1998. Land reform plan divides Zimbabweans. *Washington Post,* February 15.

Durand, C. H., and J. P. Pigney. 1963. Revue de 410 cas de diarrhees aqueuses infectieuses chez le nourisson et l'enfant de moins de deux ans, traites pendant quatre ans dan les meme service hospitalier. *Annals of Pediatrics* 39:1386.

Dyson, L., M. McCormick, and M. J. Renfrew. 2006. Interventions for promoting the initiation of breastfeeding. *Evidence Based Child Health: A Cochrane Review Journal* 1, no. 2:592–616.

Easterlin, R. A. 1973. Does money buy happiness? *Public Interest* 30:3–10.

———. 1974. Does economic growth improve the human lot? Some empirical evidence. In *Nations and households in economic growth: Essays in honor of Moses Abramowitz,* ed. P. A. David and M. W. Reder. New York: Academic Press.

Easterly, W. 2005. Review of Sach's *The end of poverty. Washington Post Book World,* March 27.

———. 2006. Why doesn't aid work? *Cato Unbound,* April 3. Washington, DC: Cato Institute.

Easterly, W., and R. Levine. 2002. Tropics, germs, and crops: How endowments influence economic development. *Journal of Monetary Economics* 50, no. 1 (January):3–39.

Easterly, William, R. Levine, and D. Roodman. 2004. New data, new doubts: A comment on Burnside and Dollar's 'Aid, policies, and growth' (2000). *American Economic Review* 94, no. 3:774–780.

Ecker, O., C. Breisinger, and K. Kauw. 2012. Growth is good, but is not enough to improve nutrition. In *Reshaping agriculture for nutrition and health,* ed. S. Fan and R. Pandy-Lorch, 47–54. Washington, DC: International Food Policy Research Institute.

The Economist. 2001. No title. March 29.

————. 2002. The road to hell is not paved. December 19.

————. 2005. Punch up over handouts. March 2.

————. 2006. How to make China even richer. March 23.

————. 2007 The end of cheap food? Dec 6.

————. 2008. Cereal offenders. March 27.

————. 2009. Outsourcing's third wave. May 23.

————. 2011. When others are grabbing their land. May 5. http://www .economist.com/node/18648855.

————. 2013a. Doing it my way. March 2.

————. 2013b. Famine mortality. May 13. http://www.economist.com/blogs/graphic detail/2013/05/daily-chart-10.

————. 2015. The twilight of the resource curse? January 10.

Economist Intelligence Unit. 2014. *Global Food Security Index 2014: An annual measure of the state of global food security.* http://foodsecurityindex.eiu.com /Home/DownloadResource?fileName=EIU%20Global%20Food%20Security%20 Index%20%202014%20Findings%20%26%20Methodology.pdf.

Edirisinghe, Neville. 1987. *The food stamp scheme in Sri Lanka: Costs, benefits, and options for modification.* Washington, DC: International Food Policy Research Institute.

Edirisinghe, Neville, and Thomas T. Poleman. 1983. *Behavioral thresholds as indicators of perceived dietary adequacy or inadequacy.* International Agricultural Economics Study no. 17 (July). Ithaca: Cornell University Press.

EPA (Environmental Protection Agency). 2008. *Climate change: Agriculture and food supply.* Washington, DC. http://www.epa.gov.

Erickson, J. D. 2002. Folic acid and prevention of spina bifida and anencephaly. *Morbidity and Mortality Weekly Report,* September 13. http://www.cdc.gov/mmwr /preview/mmwrhtml/rr5113a1.htm.

Erlich, P., and A. Erlich. 1991. *Healing the planet.* Reading, MA: Addison-Wesley.

Evenson, Robert E. 1981. Benefits and obstacles to appropriate agricultural technology. *Annals of the American Academy of Political and Social Science* 458:54–67.

Evenson, R. E., and P. M. Flores. 1978. Social returns to rice research. In *Economic consequences of the new rice technology,* ed. R. Barker and Y. Hayami, 243–265. Los Banos, Philippines: International Rice Research Institute.

Evenson, R., and D. Gollin, eds. 2003a. Assessing the impact of the green revolution, 1960 to 2000. *Science* 300 (May):758–762.

————. 2003b. *Crop variety improvement and its effect on productivity: The impact of international research.* Wallingford, UK: CAB International.

Evenson, R., and M. Rosegrant. 2003. The economic consequences of crop genetic improvement programs. In *Crop variety improvement and its effect on productivity: The impact of international research,* ed. R. Evenson and D. Gollin, 473–497. Wallingford, UK: CAB International.

Ewen, S., and A. Pusztai. 1999. Effects of diets containing genetically modified potatoes expressing Galanthus nivalis lectin on rat small intestine. *Lancet* 354.

Falconer, J. 1990. Hungry season food from forests, unasylva 41. http://www.fao.org.

Family Health International. 1996. Research confirms LAM's effectiveness. *Network* 17 no. 1, Fall.

Fan, S., P. Hazell, and S. Thorat. 2000. Government spending, growth, and poverty in rural India. *American Journal of Agricultural Economics* 82, no. 4:1038–1051.

FAO (Food and Agriculture Organization). 1996a. Fact sheet on water and food security. Rome. http://www.fao.org/wfs/fs/e/WatIrr-e.htm.

———. 1996b. *Sixth world food survey.* Rome.

———. 1996c. World Food Summit (WFS) technical background papers, nos. 1–15. Rome. http://www.fao.org/wfs.

———. 1997a. Contribution of greenhouse gases to global warming. Factfile. http://www.fao.org/News/FACTFILE/FF9715-E.htm.

———. 1997b. *Famine Early Warning System (FEWS) special report: Hungry season in the Sahel.* FEWS Special Report no. 97-5. Rome. http://www.fews.org/fb970825/fb97sr5.html#Hungry.

———. 1997c. Southern Africa plans ahead as report warns of possible El Niño effect. FAO News release 28 November 1997. http://www.fao.org.

———. 2000a. *The energy and agriculture nexus.* Working Paper no. 4. Rome. http://www.fao.org/docrep/003/x8054e/x8054e00.htm.

———. 2000b. *World agriculture: Towards 2015/2030.* Rome. http://www.fao.org.

———. 2004. *State of food and agriculture, 2004.* Rome.

———. 2006. *World agriculture: Towards 2030/2050.* Rome.

———. 2011. *The state of the world's land and water resources for food and agriculture: Managing systems at risk.* Rome.

———. 2013. *Tackling climate change through livestock: A global assessment of emissions and mitigation opportunities.* Rome.

———. 2015a. *How to feed the world in 2050.* Rome. http://www.fao.org/fileadmin/templates/wsfs/docs/expert_paper/How_to_Feed_the_World_in_2050.pdf.

———. 2015b. Republic of South Sudan situation update. July 22. http://www.fao.org/fileadmin/user_upload/emergencies/docs/FAO_SS_Situation-Update_July2015.pdf.

———. N.d. Programme against African trypanosomiasis. http://www.fao.org/ag/againfo/programmes/en/paat/home.html.

———. Various years. *State of food insecurity in the world.* http://www.fao.org/SOF/sofi/index_en.htmhttp://www.fao.org/SOF/sofi/index_en.htm.

———. Various years. *World food situation.* http://www.fao.org/worldfoodsituation/foodpricesindex/en.

FAOSTAT. various years. Statistics. http://www.fao.org.

———. Various years. Food balance sheets. http://www.fao.org.

Feacham, R. G., and M. A. Koblinsky. 1983. Interventions for the control of diarrhoeal diseases among young children: Measles immunization. *Bulletin of the World Health Organization* 61, no. 4:641–652.

Feder, G., R. Just, and D. Zilberman. 1985. Adoption of agricultural innovations in developing countries: A survey. *Economic Development and Cultural Change* 33:255–294.

Federico, G. 2005. *Feeding the world: An Economic history of agriculture, 1800–2000.* Princeton: Princeton University Press.

Fei, John C. H., and Gustav Ranis. 1964. *Development of the labor surplus economy: Theory and policy.* New Haven: Yale University Press.

FEMA (Federal Emergency Management Agency). 1991. *Projected impact of sea-level rise on the national flood insurance program.* Report to Congress. Washington, DC.

FEWS (Famine Early Warning System). 1997. *Hungry season in the Sahel.* Special Report no. 97-5. Rome: Food and Agriculture Organization. http://www.fews.org/fb970825/fb97sr5.html#Hungry.

————. 2015. Food security outlook for Zimbabwe, July 2015 to December 2015. http://www.fews.net/southern-africa/zimbabwe/food-security-outlook/july-2015.

FIAN (FoodFirst Information and Action Network). 1997. Twelve misconceptions about the right to food. http://www.eldis.org.

Fields, G. S. 2002. *Distribution and development: A new look at the developing world.* Cambridge: Massachusetts Institute of Technology Press.

FIGIS (Fisheries Global Information System). 2016. http://www.fao.org/fishery /topic/18043/en accessed February 2016.

Filmer, D., J. S. Hammer, and L. H. Pritchett. 2000. Weak links in the chain: A Diagnosis of health policy in poor countries. *World Bank Research Observer* 15, no. 2:199–224. http://wbro.oxfordjournals.org/content/15/2/199.short.

Fitzhugh, H. 1998. Competition between livestock and mankind for nutrients: Let ruminants eat grass. In *Feeding a world population of more than eight billion people: A challenge to science,* ed. J. C. Waterlow et al., 223–231. Oxford: Oxford University Press.

Fogel, Robert W. 1994. Economic growth, population theory, and physiology: The bearing of long-term processes on the making of economic policy. *American Economic Review* 84, no. 3 (June):369–395.

————. 2004. *The Escape from hunger and premature death, 1700–2100.* Cambridge: Cambridge University Press.

Foster, Phillips, and Herbert Steiner. 1964. *The structure of Algerian socialized agriculture.* Agricultural Experimental Station MP no. 527. College Park: University of Maryland.

Fuglie, K., and N. Rada. 2013. Growth in global agricultural productivity: An update. *Amber Waves,* November. http://www.ers.usda.gov/amber-waves/2013-november /growth-in-global-agricultural-productivity-an-update.aspx#.VtjPd_krJcs.

————. 2015. International agricultural productivity data. Washington, DC: US Department of Agriculture. http://www.ers.usda.gov/data-products/international -agricultural-productivity.aspx.

Gabbert, S., and H. P. Weikard. 2001. How widespread is undernourishment? A critique of measurement methods and new empirical methods. *Food Policy* 26, no. 3:209–228.

Galler, Janina R. 1986. Malnutrition: A neglected cause of learning failure. *Journal of Postgraduate Medicine* 80 (October):225–230.

Galway, Katrina, et al. 1987. *Child survival: Risks and the road to health.* Columbia, MD: Westinghouse Institute for Resource Development, Demographic Data for Development Project.

Garcia, Marito, and Per Pinstrup-Andersen. 1987. *The pilot food price subsidy scheme in the Philippines: Its impact on income, food consumption, and nutritional status.* Research Report no. 61. Washington, DC: International Food Policy Research Institute.

Gentilini, U. 2016. *The revival of the "cash versus food" debate: New evidence for an old quandary?* Policy Research Working Paper no. 7584. Washington, DC: World Bank. http://www-wds.worldbank.org/external/default/WDSContentServer /WDSP/IB/2016/02/29/090224b0841bfc5f/1_0/Rendered/PDF/The0revival0of0or 0an0old0quandary00.pdf.

Gershwin, M. Eric, et al. 1985. *Nutrition and immunity.* New York: Academic Press.

Gifford, R. C. 1992. *Agricultural engineering in development: Mechanization strategy formulation.* Vol. 1, *Concepts and principles.* Agricultural Services Bulletin no. 99/1. Rome: Food and Agriculture Organization.

Gilland, B. 2002. World population and food supply: Can food production keep pact with population growth in the next half century? *Food Policy* 27:47–63.

Gillis, J. 2003. Debate grows over biotech food; Efforts to ease famine in Africa hurt by US, European dispute. *Washington Post,* November 30.

Glauber, J. 2008a. Statement before the Joint Economic Committee on Recent Developments in Food Prices, May 1. Washington, DC: US Department of Agriculture. http://www.usda.gov/oce/newsroom/archives/testimony/2008/GlauberSenate0612 08.pdf.

Glewwe, Paul, Hanan Jacoby, and Elizabeth King. 1996. *An economic model of nutrition and learning: Evidence from longitudinal data.* Washington, DC: World Bank.

Global Development Research Center. 2003. Microfacts: Data snapshots on microfinance. http://www.gdrc.org/icm/data/d-snapshot.html.

Godwin, William. 1793. Political justice. In *A reprint of the essay "Property,"* ed. H. S. Salt. London: Allen and Unwin, 1949.

Gomez, M., C. Barrett, T. Raney, P. Pinstrup-Andersen, J. Meerman, A. Croppenstedt, B. Carisma, and B. Thompson. 2013. Post–green revolution food systems and the triple burden of malnutrition. *Food Policy* 42:129–138.

Goncalves, J., J. Petersen, P. Deschamps, B. Hamelin, and O. Baba-Sy. 2013. Quantifying the modern recharge of the "fossil" Sahara. *Geophysical Research Letters* 40, no. 11:2673–2678.

González-Vega, Claudio. 1983. Arguments for interest rate reform. In *Rural financial markets in developing countries: Their use and abuse,* ed. J. D. von Pischke et al., 365–372. Baltimore: Johns Hopkins University Press.

Gopalan, C. 1970. Some recent studies in the nutrition research laboratories: Hyderabad. *Journal of Clinical Nutrition* (January):35–53.

———. 1986. Vitamin A deficiency and child mortality. *Nutrition Foundation of India Bulletin* 7, no. 3:3–6.

Graham, S. 2002. Rice paddy methane emissions depend on crops' success. *Scientific American,* August. http://www.sciam.com/article.cfm?articleID=00005E42-5440 -1D61-90FB809EC5880000.

Grand View Research. 2015. Pet food market analysis by product and forecasts to 2022. October. http://www.grandviewresearch.com/industry-analysis/pet-food -industry.

Grantham-McGregor, S., L. Fernald, and K. Sethuraman. 1999a. Effects of health and nutrition on cognitive and behavioural development in children in the first 3 years of life. Part 1: Low birthweight, breastfeeding, and protein-energy malnutrition. *Food and Nutrition Bulletin* 20:53–75.

———. 1999b. Effects of health and nutrition on cognitive and behavioural development in children in the first 3 years of life. Part 2: Infections and micronutrient deficiencies: iodine, iron, and zinc. *Food and Nutrition Bulletin* 20:76–99.

Gray, Cheryl W. 1982. *Food consumption parameters for Brazil and their application to food policy.* Research Report no. 32. Washington, DC: International Food Policy Research Institute.

Greenland, D. J., P. J. Gregory, and P. H. Nye. 1998. Land resources and constraints to crop production. In *Feeding a world population of more than eight billion people: A challenge to science,* ed. J. C. Waterlow et al., 39–56. Oxford: Oxford University Press.

Griender, A. K. Angelo, A. McCollum, K. Mirkovic, R. Arthur, and F. Angulo. 2015. Addressing contact tracing challenges: Critical to halting Ebola virus disease transmission. *International Journal of Infectious Diseases* 41:53–65.

Grigg, D. 1993. *The world food problem.* 2nd ed. Cambridge: Blackwell.

Griliches, Zvi. 1958. Research costs and social returns: Hybrid corn and related innovations. *Journal of Political Economy* 66:419–431.

Gupta, A. 2015. Growth scuttlers: Urban bias, poor subsidiarity. *DNA Syndicated Opinion and Viewpoint,* February 22. http://dnasyndication.com/dna/dna_english

_news_and_features/Growth-scuttlers_-Urban-bias-poor-subsidiarity /DNAHM81842.

Gupta, Arun, and Jon E. Rohide. 1993. Economic value of breast-feeding in India. *Economic and Political Weekly* 28, no. 26:1390.

Haag, A. L. 2007. Pond powered biofuels: Turning algae into America's new energy. *Popular Mechanics,* March. http://www.popularmechanics.com/science/energy /a1533/4213775.

Haddad, L., and H. Alderman. 2000. Eradicating malnutrition: Income growth or nutrition programs? In *IFPRI Annual Report 2000.* Washington, DC: International Food Policy Research Institute. http://www.ifpri.org/publication/eradicating -malnutrition-income-growth-or-nutrition-programs.

Haggard, S., and M. Noland. 2007. *Famine in North Korea: Markets, aid, and reform.* New York: Columbia University Press.

Haile, M., M. Kalkuhl, and J. von Braun. 2014. Agricultural supply response to international food prices and price volatility: A cross-country panel analysis. Paper prepared for the European Association of Agricultural Economists.

Harberger, Arnold. 1983. Basic needs versus distributional weights in social cost-benefit analysis. *Economic Development and Cultural Change* 32, no. 3:455–474.

Hardin, G. 1974. Lifeboat ethics: The case against helping the poor. *Psychology Today,* September.

Harris, M. 1974. *Cows, pigs, wars, and witches: The riddles of culture.* New York: Vintage.

———. 1977. *Cannibals and kings: The origin of cultures.* New York: Random.

Harrison, A., ed. 2007. *Globalization and poverty.* Chicago: University of Chicago Press.

Hartini, T., A. Winkvist, L. Lindholm, H. Stenlund, V. Persson, D. Nurdiati, and A. Surjono. 2003. Nutrient intake and iron status of urban poor and rural poor without access to rice fields are affected by the emerging economic crisis: The case of pregnant Indonesian women. *European Journal of Clinical Nutrition* 57:654–666.

Hartzell, M. 2013. Maps: China's uneven economic development. http://matthartzell .blogspot.com/2013/09/chinas-economic-disparityin-maps.html.

Haslberger, A. G. 2003. GM food: The risk assessment of immune hypersensitivity reactions covers more than allergenicity. *Food, Agriculture, and Environment* 1:42–45. http://www.biotech-info.net/hypersensitivity.html.

Haub, Carl. 1987. Understanding population projections. *Population Bulletin* 42, no. 4:3–42.

Haupt, A., and T. Kane. 2004. *Population handbook.* 5th ed. Washington, DC: Population Reference Bureau.

Hayward, S. 2006. *Index of leading environmental indicators.* Washington, DC: American Enterprise Institute.

Headey, D. 2012. Turning economic growth into nutrition-sensitive growth. In *Reshaping agriculture for nutrition and health,* ed. S. Fan and R. Pandy-Lorch, 39–47. Washington, DC: International Food Policy Research Institute.

Hearts and Minds. 2016. Socially responsible food. http://www.change.net /articles/foodiss.htm.

Heilbroner, Robert L. 1953. *The worldly philosophers.* New York: Simon and Schuster.

Heisey, P., and G. W. Norton. 2007. Fertilizer and other chemicals. In *Handbook of agricultural economics,* vol. 3, ed. R. Evenson and P. Pingali, 2747–2786. Amsterdam: Elsevier.

Hendricks, L. 2002. How important is human capital for development? Evidence from immigrant earnings. *American Economic Review* 92, no. 1:198–219.

Herbert, Sandra. 1971. Darwin, Malthus, and selection. *Journal of History of Biology* 4:209–217.

Herdt, Robert W. 1970. A disaggregate approach to aggregate supply. *American Journal of Agricultural Economics* 52:512–520.

Herman, M. O., R. Kelly, and R. Nash. 2011. Not a game: Speculation vs. food security. *Oxfam Issues Briefing,* October 3. http://www.oxfam.org/sites/www.oxfam.org/files/ib-speculation-vs-food-security-031011-en.pdf.

Herring, Ronald J. 1983. *Land to the tiller: The political economy of agrarian reform in South Asia.* New Haven: Yale University Press.

Hesketh, T., X. Zhou, and Y. Wang. 2015. The end of the one-child policy: Lasting implications for China. *Journal of the American Medical Association (JAMA)* 314, no. 24:2619–2620.

Hicks, L. E., R. A. Langham, and J. Takenaka. 1992. Cognitive and social measures following early nutritional supplementation: A sibling study. *American Journal of Public Health* 72:1110–1118.

Hidrobo, M., J. Hoddinott, A. Peterman, A. Margolies, and V. Moreira. 2014. Cash, food, or vouchers? Evidence from a randomized experiment in northern Ecuador. *Journal of Development Economics* 107:144–156.

Hilbeck, A., et al. 2015. No scientific consensus on GMO safety. *Environmental Sciences Europe* 27, no. 4:1–6.

Ho, M., T. Traavik, O. Olsvik, B. Tappeser, C. V. Howard, C. von Weizsacker, and G. C. McGavin. 1998. Gene technology and gene ecology of infectious diseases. *Microbial Ecology in Health and Disease* 10:33–59.

Ho, T. J. 1984. *Economic status and nutrition in East Java.* Washington, DC: World Bank.

Hochman, G., D. Rajagopal, G. Timilsina, and D. Zilberman. 2014. Quantifying the causes of the global food commodity price crisis. *Biomass and Bioenergy* 68:106–114.

Hoddinott, J., M. Cohen, and M. Bos. 2003. *Redefining the role of food aid.* Washington, DC: International Food Policy Research Institute.

Hoddinott, J., and S. Horton. 2015. Stunting as a Sustainable Development Goal. In *Nutrition and the post-2015 development agenda.* New York: United Nations Standing Committee on Nutrition.

Hoffman, V. 2009. Demand, retention, and intra-household allocation of free and purchased mosquito nets. *American Economic Review* 99, no. 2:236–241.

Holick, M. F. 2004. Vitamin D: Importance in the prevention of cancers, type 1 diabetes, heart disease, and osteoporosis. *American Journal of Clinical Nutrition* 79, no. 3 (March):362–371. http://www.ajcn.org/cgi/content/full/79/3/362.

Holmes, S., and C. Sunstein. 1999. *The cost of rights: Why liberty depends on taxes.* New York: Norton.

Hopkins, Raymond F. 1988. Political calculations in subsidizing food. In *Food subsidies in developing countries,* ed. Per Pinstrup-Andersen, 107–125. Baltimore: Johns Hopkins University Press.

Hossain, Mahabub. 1988a. *Credit for alleviation of rural poverty: The Grameen Bank in Bangladesh.* Research Report no. 65. Washington, DC: International Food Policy Research Institute.

———. 1988b. *Nature and impact of the Green Revolution in Bangladesh.* Research report no. 67. Washington, DC: International Food Policy Research Institute.

Houser, D., B. Sands, and E. Xiao. 2009. Three parts natural, seven parts man-made: Bayesian analysis of China's Great Leap Forward demographic disaster. *Journal of Economic Behavior and Organization* 69:148–159.

Huang, Kuo W. 1985. *US demand for food: A complete system of price and income effects.* Technical Bulletin no. 1714. Washington, DC: US Department of Agriculture.

Hughes, V. 2013. The big fat truth. *Nature* 497:428–430.

Hull, T. H. 1978. Where credit is due: Policy implications of the recent rapid fertility decline in Bali. Paper presented at the annual meeting of the Population Association of America, Atlanta.

Hull, T. H., et al. 1977. Indonesia's family planning story: Success and challenge. *Population Bulletin* 32, no. 6.

Hulme, M. 2009. *Why we disagree about climate change: Understanding controversy, inaction, and opportunity.* Cambridge: Cambridge University Press.

Humphrey, J. H. 2009. Child undernutrition, tropical enteropathy, toilets, and handwashing. *Lancet* 374 (September):1032–1035.

Ibe, A. C., and L. F. Awosika. 1991. Sea level rise impact on African coastal zones. In *A change in the weather: African perspectives on climate change,* ed. S. H. Omide and C. Juma, 105–112. Nairobi: African Centre for Technology Studies.

IFPRI (International Food Policy Research Institute). 2005. *New risks and opportunities for food security: Scenario analyses for 2015 and 2050.* 2020 Brief no. 73. Washington, DC.

———. 2008. High food prices: The what, who, and how of proposed policy actions. IFPRI policy brief, May 2008. Washington, DC.

IHME (Institute for Health Metrics and Evaluation). GBD database. Seattle: University of Washington. http://www.healthdata.org/search-gbd-data?s=starvation.

ILO (International Labour Organization). 1987. *Yearbook of Labor Statistics 1987.* Geneva.

Indicators of Poverty Action. 2014. Impact of rural microcredit in Morocco. http://www.poverty-action.org/study/impact-rural-microcredit-morocco.

IPCC (Intergovernmental Panel on Climate Change). 2007a. *Climate Change 2007 Synthesis Report. Contribution of Working Groups I, II and III to the Fourth Assessment Report of the Intergovernmental Panel on Climate Change,* Geneva. https://www.ipcc.ch/publications_and_data/publications_ipcc_fourth _assessment_report_synthesis_report.htm (accessed February 2016).

———. 2007b. *Report of Working Group II on climate change impacts, adaptation and vulnerability.* Geneva. http://www.ipcc-wg2.org/index.html.

———. 2014. *Climate change 2014: Synthesis report.* Geneva.

IRRI (International Rice Research Institute). 2002. Project summary and highlights: Project 3—Genetic enhancement for yield, grain quality, and stress resistance. Manila. http://www.irri.org/science/progsum/pdfs/dgreport2002/project%203 .pdf.

Irwin, S. H. 2013. Commodity index investment and food prices: Does the "masters hypothesis" explain recent price spikes? *Agricultural Economics* 44:29–41.

ISRIC (International Soil Reference and Information Centre) and UNEP (United Nations Environment Programme). 1991. World map of the status of human-induced soil degradation. In *Global assessment of soil degradation,* 2nd ed., by L. R. Oldeman, R. T. A. Hakkeling, and W. G. Sombroek. UNEP, Niarobi and ISRIC Wageningen.

Jackson, R., A. Ramsay, C. Christensen, S. Beaton, D. Hall, and I. Ramshaw. 2001. Expression of mouse interleukin-4 by a recombinant ectromelia virus suppresses cytolytic lymphocyte responses and overcomes genetic resistance to mousepox. *Journal of Virology* 75:1205–1210.

Jackson, Tony, with Deborah Eade. 1982. *Against the grain: The dilemma of project food aid.* Oxford: Oxfam.

James, Clive. 2002. *Preview: Status of commercialized transgenic crops: 2002.* Brief no. 27. Ithaca, NY: International Service for the Acquisition of Agri-biotech Applications.

———. 2014. *ISAAA report on global state of biotech/GM crops.* http://www .isaaa.org/resources/publications/briefs/49/pptslides/pdf/B49-Slides-English.pdf.

James, W. P. T., and E. C. Schofield. 1990. *Human energy requirements: A manual for planners and nutritionists.* Oxford: Oxford University Press.

Jaumotte, F., S. Lall, and C. Papageorgiou. 2013. Rising income inequality: Technology, or trade and financial globalization? *IMF Economic Review* 61:271–309.

Jayne, T., L. Rubey, D. Tschirley, M. Mukumbu, M. Chisvo, A. Santos, M. Weber, and P. Diskin. 1995. *Effects of market reform on access to food by low-income households: Evidence from four countries in eastern and southern Africa.* International Development Paper no. 19. East Lansing: Michigan State University Press.

Jayne, T. S., L. Rubey, M. Chisvo, and M. T. Weber. 1996. Zimbabwe food security success story. *Policy Synthesis* no. 18 (April). http://www.odi.org/resources /docs/5613.pdf.

Jelliffe, D. B. 1966. *The assessment of the nutritional status of the community.* Monograph no. 53. Geneva: World Health Organization.

Jensen, H., and S. Robinson. 2002. *General equilibrium measures of agricultural policy bias in fifteen developing countries.* TMD Discussion Paper no. 105. Washington, DC: International Food Policy Research Institute.

Jensen, R. T., and N. H. Miller. 2008. Giffen behavior and subsistence consumption. *American Economic Review* 98, no. 4:1533–1577.

———. 2010. *A revealed preference approach to measuring hunger and undernutrition.* Working Paper no. 16555. Cambridge, MA: National Bureau of Economic Research. http://www.nber.org/papers/w16555.

Johnson, D. G. 1975. *World food problems and prospects.* Washington, DC: American Enterprise Institute.

Johnson, Stanley R., Zuhair A. Hassan, and Richard D. Green. 1984. *Demand systems estimation methods and applications.* Ames: Iowa State University Press.

Johnston, W. 2003. Ireland's great famine, 1845–1849. http://www.wesley johnston.com/users/ireland/past/famine/index.htm.

Jolejole-Foreman, M., K. Baylis, and L. Lipper. 2012. Land degradation's implications on agricultural value of production in Ethiopia. Selected paper for the International Association for Applied Econometrics conference, Brazil, August. http:// ageconsearch.umn.edu/bitstream/126251/2/IAAE2012_JForemanBaylisLipper .pdf.

Judd, M. Ann, James K. Boyce, and Robert E. Evenson. 1987. Investment in agricultural research and extension. In *Policy for agricultural research,* ed. Vernon Ruttan and Carl E. Pray, 7–38. Boulder: Westview.

Kahkonen, S., and H. Leathers. 1997. *Is there life after liberalization? Transaction costs analysis of maize and cotton marketing in Zambia and Tanzania.* College Park: University of Maryland Press, IRIS Center.

Kaiser, J. 2004. Wounding Earth's fragile skin. *Science* 304 (June):1616–1618. http://search.proquest.com/docview/213604806?pq-origsite=gscholar.

Kakturskaya, M. 2003. Why aren't Russians having babies? *Argumenty I Fakty,* July 23. Reproduced in *World Press Review,* October. http://www.worldpress.org /europe/1486.cfm.

Kakwani, Nanak 1987. Lorenz curve. In *The new Palgrave: A dictionary of economics,* vol. 3., ed. John Eatwell et al., 243–244. New York: Stockton.

Kamrin, M. N.d. Environmental "hormones" pesticide information project. Lansing: Michigan State University. http://ace.ace.orst.edu/info/extoxnet/tics/env -horm.txt.

Kapoor, T. 2015. Is successful water privatization a pipe dream? An analysis of three global case studies. *Yale Journal of International Law* 40:157–192.

Karim, Rezaul, Manjur Majid, and F. James Levinson. 1984. The Bangladesh sorghum experiment. *Food Policy* 5:61–63.

Kates, Robert. 1996. Ending hunger: Current status and future prospects. *Consequences* 2, no. 2. http://www.gcrio.org/consequences/vol2no2/article1.html.

Katona, P., and J. Katona-Apte. 2008. The interaction between nutrition and infection. *Clinical Infectious Disease* 46, no. 10:1582–1588.

Keilmann, A. A., and C. McCord. 1978. Weight-for-age as an index of death in children. *Lancet* 311, no 8076 (June):1247–1250.

Kekic, L. 2007. The Economist Intelligence Unit's index of democracy. http://www.economist.com/media/pdf/Democracy_Index_2007_v3.pdf.

Kelly, Morgan, Joel Mokyr, and Cormac O'Grada. 2013. Precocious Albion: A new interpretation of the British industrial revolution. September 3. http://ssrn.com /abstract=2319855 or http://dx.doi.org/10.2139/ssrn.2319855.

Kendall, H. W., and D. Pimentel. 1994. Constraints on the expansion of the global food supply. *Ambio* 23:198–205. http://www.jstor.org/stable/4314199.

Kennedy, Eileen T., and Odin Knudsen. 1985. A review of supplementary feeding programmes and recommendations on their design. In *Nutrition and development,* ed. Margaret Biswas and Per Pinstrup-Andersen, 77–96. Oxford: Oxford University Press.

Kennedy, Eileen T., et al. 1983. *Nutrition-related policies and programs: Past performance and research needs.* Washington, DC: International Food Policy Research Institute, February.

Kennickell, A. 2006. *Currents and undercurrents: Changes in the distribution of wealth, 1989–2004.* Washington, DC: Federal Reserve Bank. http://www.federal reserve.gov/pubs/feds/2006/200613/200613pap.pdf.

Keusch, G. T. 2003. The history of nutrition: Malnutrition, infection and immunity. *Journal of Nutrition* 133, no. 1:336S–340S.

Keys, Ancel, et al. 1950. *The biology of human starvation.* Minneapolis: University of Minnesota Press.

Kienzle, J., J. Ashburner, and B. Sims. 2013. *Mechanization for rural development: A review of patterns and progress from around the world.* Vol. 20 of *Integrated crop management.* Rome: Food and Agriculture Organization. http://www.fao .org/docrep/018/i3259e/i3259e.pdf.

Kimbrell, Andrew. 2002. Seven deadly myths of industrial agriculture. In *Fatal harvest: The tragedy of industrial agriculture,* ed. Andrew Kimbrell, 49–66. Washington, DC: Island.

Kinealy, Christine. 2002. *The great Irish famine.* New York: Palgrave.

Kinzer, S. 2007. After so many deaths, too many births. *New York Times,* February 11.

Kirchick, J. 2007. Killing them softly: The other African genocide. *New Republic,* March 8. http://www.canada.com/story.html?id=8f31cab1-892e-4aad-8e8e -35489b646745.

Kluender, S. 2003. The Peace Corps in Zambia. http://peacecorpsonline.org /messages/messages/467/2018900.html.

Komlos, J. 1989. *Nutrition and economic development in eighteenth century Hapsberg monarchy: An anthropometric history.* Princeton: Princeton University Press.

Korpe, P. S., and W. Petri. 2012. Environmental enteropathy: Critical implications of a poorly understood condition. *Trends in Molecular Medicine* 18, no. 6:328–336.

Kremer, M. 1993. Population growth and technological change: One million B.C. to 1990. *Quarterly Journal of Economics* 108, no. 3:681–716.

Krick, Jackie. 1988. Using the Z score as a descriptor of discrete changes in growth. *Nutritional Support Services* 6, no. 8 (August):14–21.

Krueger, Anne, Maurice Schiff, and Alberto Valdés. 1991. *The political economy of agricultural pricing policy.* Baltimore: Johns Hopkins University Press for the World Bank.

Kuznets, Simon. 1955. Economic growth and income inequality. *American Economic Review* 65:1–28.

Ladha, J. K. 2014. Contributions of fertilizer nitrogen in global cereal production, soil organic matter status, and nitrogen balance. In *Proceedings: International symposium on managing soils for food security and climate change adaptation and mitigation,* ed. K. Heng, K. Sakadevan, G. Dercon, and M. L. Nguyen, 21–24. Rome: Food and Agriculture Organization.

Lakner, C., and B. Milanovic. 2015. Global income distribution: From the fall of the Berlin Wall to the Great Recession. *World Bank Economic Review* 30, no. 2:203–232.

Lakshmi, R. 2004. Opening files, Indians find scams. *Washington Post,* March 9.

Landes, M. 2004. The elephant is jogging: New pressures for agricultural reform in India. *Amber Waves,* February. http://www.ers.usda.gov/amberwaves /February04/Features/ElephantJogs.htm.

Landman, Lynn. 1983. China's one-child families: Girls need not apply. *RF Illustrated,* December. New York: Rockefeller Foundation.

Lashof, D., and D. Tirpak. 1990. *Policy options for stabilizing global climate.* Report of the US Environmental Protection Agency. New York: Hemisphere.

Laudermilk, B. 2011. China's one-child policy: Urban and rural pressures, anxieties, and problems. *World Report News,* September 13. http://www.worldreportnews .com/far-and-south-east-asiaaustralia-archived/chinas-one-child-policy-urban- and-rural-pressures-anxieties-and-problems.

Lee, John E., and Gary C. Taylor. 1986. Agricultural research: Who pays and who benefits? In *Research for tomorrow, 1986 yearbook of agriculture,* 14–21. Washington, DC: US Department of Agriculture.

Lee, R. 1968a. Problems in the study of hunter gatherers. In *Man the hunter,* ed. R. Lee and I. Devore, 3–12. Chicago: Aldine.

———. 1968b. What hunters do for a living, or how to make out on scarce resources. In *Symposium on man the hunter,* ed. R. B. Lee and Irven DeVore, 30–48. Chicago: Aldine.

———. 1969. !Kung bushmen subsistence: An input-output analysis. In *Environment and cultural behavior,* ed. A. Vayda, 47–49. Garden City, NJ: Natural History Press.

———. 1972. Population growth and the beginnings of sedentary life among the !Kung bushmen. In *Population growth: Anthropological implications,* ed. B. Spooner, 329–342. Cambridge: Massachusetts Institute of Technology Press.

Leggett, J. 2007. *Climate change: Science and policy implications.* Washington, DC: Congressional Research Service.

Lele, Uma J., and Arthur Goldsmith. 1989. The development of national agricultural research capacity: India's experience with the Rockefeller Foundation and its significance for Africa. *Economic Development and Cultural Change* 37:305–343.

Lele, Uma J., Bill H. Kinsey, and Antonia O. Obeya. 1989. Building agricultural research capacity in Africa: Policy lessons from the Madia countries. Unpublished working paper presented for the Joint TAC/CGIAR Center Directors Meeting, Rome, 1989.

Lemieux, T. 2006. Increasing residual wage inequality: Composition effects, noisy data, or rising demand for skill? *The American Economic Review* 96, no. 32:461–498.

Lentz, E. C., and C. B. Barrett. 2014. The negligible welfare effects of the international food aid provisions in the 2014 farm bill. *Choices* (Quarter 3). http://choices magazine.org/choices-magazine/theme-articles/3rd-quarter-2014/the-negligible -welfare-effects-of-the-international-food-aid-provisions-in-the-2014-farm-bill.

Lester, S. 2016. Is the Doha Round over? The WTO's negotiating agenda for 2016 and beyond. *Cato Free Trade Bulletin* no. 64 (February 11). Washington, DC: Cato Institute. http://www.cato.org/publications/free-trade-bulletin/doha-round-over-wtos-negotiating-agenda-2016-beyond.

Levinger, Beryl. 1994. *Nutrition, health, and education for all.* New York: United Nations Development Programme.

———. 1995. Critical transitions: Human capacity development across the lifespan. New York: EDC.

Lewis, W. Arthur. 1954. Economic development with unlimited supplies of labor. *Manchester School of Economic and Social Studies* (May):139–191.

Li, R., et al. 1994. Functional consequences of iron supplementation in iron-deficient female cotton mill workers in Beijing, China. *American Journal of Clinical Nutrition* 59, no. 4 (April):908–913.

Lim, S., et al. 2012. A comparative risk assessment of burden of disease and injury attributable to 67 risk factors and risk factor clusters in 21 regions, 1990–2010: A systematic analysis for the Global Burden of Disease Study 2010. *Lancet* 380 (December):2224–2260.

Lin, Justin Yifu. 1990. Collectivization and China's agricultural crisis in 1959–1961. *Journal of Political Economy* (December):1228–1252.

Lin, Justin Yifu, and Dennis Tao Chang. 2000. Food availability, entitlements, and the Chinese famine of 1959–61. *Economic Journal* (January):136–158.

Lipton, Michael. 1977. *Why poor people stay poor: Urban bias in world development.* Cambridge: Harvard University Press.

———. 2011. *Learning from others: Increasing agricultural productivity for human development in sub-Saharan Africa.* http://addis2011.ifpri.info/files/2011/11/Lipton_SSApaper.pdf.

Lipton, Michael, and Richard Longhurst. 1990. *New seeds and poor people.* Baltimore: Johns Hopkins University Press.

Lobine, E. 2000. *Waterwar in Cochabamba, Bolivia.* London: University of Greenwich, Public Services International Research Unit. http://www.psiru.org/reports/Cochabamba.doc.

López, R. E. 1980. The structure of production and the derived demand for inputs in Canadian agriculture. *American Journal of Agricultural Economics* 62:38–45.

Lowrey, A. 2012. When reality and perception part ways. *New York Times Policy/Debt-Reckoning,* December 21. http://www.nytimes.com/interactive/us/politics/debt-reckoning.html?ref=politics&_r=0#sha=40f845d4b.

Luo, Z., R. Mu, and X. Zhang. 2006. Famine and overweight in China. *Review of Agricultural Economics* 28, no. 3 (Fall):296–304.

Lutz, W., W. Sanderson, and S. Sherbov. 2001. The end of world population growth. *Nature* 412:543–545.

Lynch, Colum. 2008. U.N. warns of impending food crisis in Zimbabwe. *Washington Post,* June 19.

Lynn, R., and T. Vanhanen. 2002. *I.Q. and the wealth of nations.* New York: Praeger.

Ma, T., D. Wang, and Z. P. Chen. 1994. Mental retardation other than typical cretinism in IDD endemias in China. In *The damaged brain of iodine deficiency: Cognitive, behavioral, neuromotor, educative aspects,* ed. John Stanbury. Port Washington, NY: Cognizant Communication.

Mabbs-Zeno, C. C. 1987. *Where, if anywhere, is famine becoming more likely.* College Park, MD: World Academy of Development and Cooperation.

Mace, James. 1984. Historical introduction. In *Human life in Russia,* ed. E. Ammende, Cleveland: John T. Zubal.

Machmüller A, C. R. Soliva, M. Kreuzer. 2003. Methane-suppressing effect of myristic acid in sheep as affected by dietary calcium and forage proportion. *British Journal of Nutrition* 90:529–540.

MacMillan, M., D. Rodrik, and I. Verduzco-Gallo. 2014. Globalization, structural change, and productivity growth, with an update on Africa. *World Development* 63:11–32.

Maddison, A. 1995. *Monitoring the world economy, 1820–1992.* Washington, DC: Organization for Economic Cooperation and Development.

———. 2001. *The world economy: A millennial perspective.* Paris: Organization for Economic Cooperation and Development. http://www.j-bradford-delong.net /articles_of_the_month/maddison-millennial.html.

Malthus, T. R. 1803–1826. *An essay on the principle of population or a view of its past and present effects on human happiness with an inquiry into our prospects respecting the future removal or mitigation of the evils which it occasions* (1st ed. 1803, 6th and last 1826). London: Ward, 1890.

Mann, C. 1997. Reseeding the Green Revolution. *Science* 277:1038–1043.

Marshall, A. 1920. *Principles of economics, 8th edition.* London: MacMillan and Company. Available online at http://www.econlib.org/library/Marshall/marP.html.

Martin, A. 2008. Spam turns serious and Hormel turns out more. *New York Times,* November 14.

Martorell, Reynaldo. 1980. The impact of ordinary illnesses on the dietary intakes of malnourished children. *American Journal of Clinical Nutrition* 33:345–350.

———. 2001. Obesity. *Health and nutrition emerging issues in developing countries* no. 7 (February). Washington, DC: International Food Policy Research Institute. http://www.ifpri.org/2020/focus/focus05/focus05_07.htm.

Masibo, P., and D. Makoka. 2012. Trends and determinants of undernutrition among young Kenyan children: Kenya demographic and health survey. *Public Health Nutrition* 15, no. 9:1715–1727.

Masters, M. W., and A. K. White. 2008. The accidental Hunt brothers: How institutional investors are driving up food and energy prices. http://www.loe.org/images /content/080919/Act1.pdf.

Mataev, Olga. 2001. The time of trouble, as seen by Dutch merchant Isaak Abrahamsz Massa. *Olga's Gallery,* October 1. http://www.abcgallery.com/list/2001oct01.html.

Mauro, P. 1997. The effects of corruption on growth, investment, and government expenditure: A cross-country analysis. In *Corruption and the global economy,* ed. K. A. Elliott, 83–107. Washington, DC: Peterson Institute.

Maxwell, Simon J. 1978. *Food aid, food for work, and public works.* Discussion Paper no. 127. Brighton, England: University of Sussex, Institute of Development Studies, March.

Mayer, Jean. 1976. The dimensions of human hunger. In *Food and agriculture,* ed. Scientific American, 14–23. San Francisco: Freeman.

Mazumdar, D. 1965. Size of farm and productivity: A problem of Indian peasant agriculture. *Economica* 32 (May):161–173.

———. 1975. The theory of share cropping with labor market dualism. *Economica* 42 (August):261–271.

McCalla, A. 1998. Agriculture and food needs to 2025. In *International agricultural development,* ed. Carl K. Eicher and John M. Staatz, 39–54. Baltimore: Johns Hopkins University Press.

McDevitt, T. 2004. Contraceptive prevalence in the developing world. In *Global population profile, 2002.* Washington, DC: US Bureau of the Census, March. https://www.census.gov/population/international/files/wp02/wp-02005.pdf.

McDonald, S., M. Savy, A. Fulford, L. Kendall, K. Flanagan, and A. Prentice. 2014. A double blind randomized controlled trial in neonates to determine the effect of vitamin A supplementation on immune responses: The Gambia protocol. *BMC Pediatrics* 14:92. http://bmcpediatr.biomedcentral.com/articles/10.1186/1471-2431-14 -92.

McLaughlin, M. 1984. *Advocates for justice.* Washington, DC: Interfaith action for economic justice.

Mehta, A., and S. Jha. 2014. Pilferage from opaque food subsidy programs: Theory and evidence. *Food Policy* 45:69–79.

Meier, G. 1979. Family planning in the banjars of Bali. *International Family Planning Perspectives* 5:63–66.

Meinzen-Dick, R., and M. Rosegrant. 2001. *Overcoming water scarcity and quality constraints.* 2020. Focus 9 Brief no. 1 (October 2001). Washington, DC: International Food Policy Research Institute.

Mellor, John W. 1984. Food price policy and income distribution in low-income countries. In *Agricultural development in the third world,* ed. Carl K. Eicher and John M. Staatz, 166–188. Baltimore: Johns Hopkins University Press.

———. 1988, Global food balances and food security. *World Development* 19, no. 9:997–1011.

Mellor, John W., and Bruce F. Johnston. 1984. The world food equation: Interrelations among development, employment, and food consumption. *Journal of Economic Literature* 22:531–574.

Merrick, T. 1986. World population in transition, *Population Bulletin* 41, no. 2:1–52.

Meteorological Service of Canada. 2006. *Understanding atmospheric change.* Chap. 5. Ottawa: Environment Canada. http://www.msc-smc.ec.gc.ca/saib/climate/Climate change/SOE_95-2/sections/9_e.html#fig27.

Mincer, Jacob. 1976. Unemployment effects of minimum wages. *Journal of Political Economy* 84, no. 4, pt. 2 (August):87–104.

Miranda, M., and K. Farrin. 2012. Index insurance for developing countries. *Applied Economic Perspectives and Policy* 34, no. 3:391–427.

Mitchell, Donald O., Merlinda D. Ingco, and Ronald C. Duncan. 1997. *The world food outlook.* Cambridge: Cambridge University Press.

Mittal, Anuradha. 2002. The growing epidemic of hunger in a world of plenty. In *Fatal harvest: The tragedy of industrial agriculture,* ed. Andrew Kimbrell, 303–307. Washington, DC: Island.

Mokyr, Joel. 1985. *Why Ireland starved: A quantitative and analytical history of the Irish economy, 1800–1850.* 2nd ed. London: Allen and Unwin.

Mokyr, Joel, and Cormac Ó Gráda. 1999. Famine disease and famine mortality: Lessons from Ireland, 1845–1850. http://www.faculty.econ.northwestern.edu /faculty/mokyr/mogbeag.pdf.

Moore, M. 2006. As Europe grows grayer, France devises a baby boom. *Washington Post,* October 18.

Moses, S., F. Plummer, E. Ngugi, N. Nagelkerke, A. Anzalat, and J. Ndinya-Achola. 1991. Controlling HIV in Africa: Effectiveness and cost of an intervention in a high frequency STD transmitter core group. *AIDS: Official Journal of the International AIDS Society* 5, no. 4:407–412.

Moyo, D. 2009. *Dead aid: Why aid is not working and how there is a better way for Africa.* New York: Farrar, Straus, and Giroux.

Mudimu, G. 2003. Zimbabwe food security issues. http://www.odi.org/sites /odi.org.uk/files/odi-assets/publications-opinion-files/5613.pdf.

Mundlak, Yair, Donald Larson, and Al Crego. 1996. *Agricultural development: Issues, evidence, and consequences.* Washington, DC: World Bank.

Murray, C., et al. 2013. Disability-adjusted life years for 291 diseases and injuries in 21 regions, 1990–2010: A systematic analysis for the Global Burden of Disease Study 2010. *Lancet* 380 (December 15, 2012–January 4, 2013):2197–2223.

Mwanaumo, A., P. Preckel, and P. Farris. 1994. Motivation for marketing system reform for the Zambian maize market. *Journal of International Food and Agribusiness Marketing* 5:29–49.

Myles, I. 2014. Fast food fever: Reviewing the impacts of the Western diet on immunity. *Nutrition Journal* 13:61.

Nachtergaele, F., R. Biancalani, and M. Petri. 2011. *Land degradation.* SOLAW Background Thematic Report no. 3. Rome: Food and Agriculture Organization.

Nandy, S., M. Irving, D. Gordon, S. V. Subramanian, and G. D. Smith. 2005. Poverty, child undernutrition, and morbidity: New evidence from India. *Bulletin of the World Health Organization* 83, no. 3:210–216.

Nassar, M., et al. 2012. Language skills and intelligence quotients of protein energy malnutrition survivors. *Journal of Tropical Pediatrics* 58, no. 3:226–230.

National Academy of Science. 1989. *Recommended dietary allowances.* 10th ed. Washington, DC.

———. 2002. *Dietary reference intakes for energy, carbohydrates, fiber, fat, protein, and amino acids (macronutrients).* Washington, DC.

———. 2003. *Dietary reference intakes: Applications in dietary planning.* Washington, DC.

National Health Service, Birmingham Community Nutrition and Dietetic Service. 2006. *Treatment of undernutrition in the community: Including rationale for oral nutritional supplement (SIP) prescribing.*. http://www.dietetics.bham.nhs.uk/docs/final55975%20EBham%20Sip%20Feed2.pdf.

National Research Council. 2000. *Beyond 6 billion: Forecasting the world's population.* Washington, DC: National Academies Press.

National Science and Technology Council. 1995. *Biotechnology for the 21st century: New horizons.* http://catalog.hathitrust.org/Record/003052877.

Natsios, Andrew. 1999. *The politics of famine in North Korea.* Washington, DC: United States Institute of Peace, August. http://www.usip.org/sites/default/files/sr990802.pdf.

———. 2001. *The great North Korean famine.* Washington, DC: United States Institute of Peace.

Nelson, G., et al. 2010. *Food security, farming, and climate change to 2050.* Washington, DC: International Food Policy Research Institute. http://ebrary.ifpri.org/utils/getfile/collection/p15738coll2/id/127066/filename/127277.pdf.

Neue, H. 1993. Methane emission from rice fields: Wetland rice fields may make a major contribution to global warming. *BioScience* 43, no. 7:466–473.

Newbery, D., and J. Stiglitz. 1981. *The theory of commodity price stabilization: A study in the economics of risk.* Oxford: Clarendon.

Newton, S., et al. 2007. Vitamin A supplementation enhances infants' immune responses to hepatitis b vaccine. *Journal of Nutrition* 137, no. 5:1272–1277.

Nicol, Mark. 2003. Famine-struck North Koreans "eating children." *Telegraph,* June 9.

Nicolia, A., A. Manzo, F. Veronesi, and D. Rosellini. 2014. An overview of the last 10 years of genetically engineered crop safety research. *Critical Reviews in Biotechnology* 34, no. 1:77–88.

Nin, A., C. Arndt, T. Hertel, and P. Preckel. 2003. Bridging the gap between partial and total factor productivity measures using directional distance functions. *American Journal of Agricultural Economics* 85:937–951.

Nisbet, R. E., et al. 2012. Intelligence: New findings and theoretical developments. *American Psychologist* 67, no. 2:130–159.

North, D. 2005. The Chinese menu for development. *Wall Street Journal,* April 7.

Notestein, Frank W. 1945. Population: The long view. In *Food for the world,* ed. Theodore W. Schultz, 36–57. Chicago: University of Chicago Press.

Nunn, N., and N. Qian. 2011. The potato's contribution to population and urbanization: Evidence from a historical experiment. *Quarterly Journal of Economics* 126, no. 2:593–650.

OECD (Organization for Economic Cooperation and Development). 2012. Underweight and overweight. In OECD and World Health Organization, *Health at a glance: Asia/Pacific 2012.* Paris: OECD Publishing. http://dx.doi.org /10.1787/978926418390220-en.

———. 2015. Statistics on resource flows to developing countries. http://www.oecd .org/dac/stats/statisticsonresourceflowstodevelopingcountries.htm.

OECD (Organization for Economic Cooperation and Development) and FAO (Food and Agriculture Organization). 2007. *Agricultural outlook, 2007–2016.* Paris: OECD Publishing. http://www.oecd.org/dataoecd/6/10/38893266.pdf.

O'Gorman, M., and M. Pandey. 2010. Cross-country disparity in agricultural productivity: Quantifying the role of modern seed adoption. *Journal of Development Studies* 46, no. 10:1767–1785.

Olmsted, A., and P. Rhode. 2002. The red queen and the hard reds: Productivity growth in American wheat, 1800–1940." *Journal of Economic History* 62, no. 4:929–966.

O'Neill, Brian C., and Lee Wexler. 2000. The greenhouse externality to childbearing: A sensitivity analysis. *Climatic Change* 47:283–324.

Oram, Peter. 1995. *The potential of technology to meet world food needs in 2020.* 2020 Brief no. 13. Washington, DC: International Food Policy Research Institute.

Overpeck, M., H. Hoffman, and K. Prager. 1992. The lowest birth-weight infants and the US infant mortality rate: NCHS 1983 linked birth/infant death data. *American Journal of Public Health* 82, no. 3:441–444.

Overton, M. 1996. *Agricultural revolution in England: The transformation of the agrarian economy, 1500–1850.* Cambridge: Cambridge University Press.

Paarlberg, D. 1988. *Toward a well-fed world.* Ames: Iowa State University Press.

Paglin, M. 1974. The measurement and trend of inequality: A basic revision. *American Economic Review* 65:598–609.

Pardey, P., and S. Beintema. 2001. *Slow magic: Agricultural R&D a century after Mendel.* Washington, DC: International Food Policy Research Institute.

Pardey, Philip G., and Julian M. Alston. 1995. *Revamping agricultural R&D.* 2020 Brief no. 24. Washington, DC: International Food Policy Research Institute.

Parham, Walter. 2001. Degraded lands: South China's untapped resource. *FAS Public Interest Report* 54, no. 2 (March–April). http://www.fas.org/faspir/2001/v54n2 /resource.htm.

Parry, M., A. R. Magalhaes, and N. H. Nih. 1992. *The potential socio-economic effects of climate change: A summary of three regional assessments.* Nairobi: United Nations Environment Programme.

Parry, M., C. Rosenzweig, and M. Livermore. 2005. Climate change, global food supply, and risk of hunger. *Philosophical Transactions of the Royal Society B: Biological Sciences* 360:2125–2138.

Pattanayak, S., et al. 2009. *Bulletin of the World Health Organization* 87:580–587. http://www.who.int/bulletin/volumes/87/8/08-057422/en.

Pearson, N.O. 2007. Meat, sugar scarce in Venezuela stores. *Associated Press,* February 8. http://www.washingtonpost.com/wp-dyn/content/article/2007/02/08 /AR2007020801240.html

Pellet, Peter L. 1977. Marasmus in a newly rich urbanized society. *Ecology of Food and Nutrition* 6:53–56.

Pelletier, D. L., E. A. Frongillo Jr., and J. P. Habicht. 1993. Epidemiologic evidence for a potentiating effect of malnutrition on child mortality. *American Journal of Public Health* 83 (August):1130–1133.

Pelto, Gretl H. 1987. Cognitive performance and intake in preschoolers. In *Cognitive performance and intake in preschoolers,* ed. Lindsay H. Allen, Adolfo Chavez, and Gretl H. Pelto. Mexico City: University of Connecticut and Instituto Nacional de la Nutricion.

Penning de Vries, F. W. T., H. van Keulen, R. Rabbinge, and J. C. Luyten. 1995. *Biophysical limits to global food production.* 2020 Brief no. 18. Washington, DC: International Food Policy Research Institute.

Perkins, Sid. 2008. Disaster goes global. *Science News,* August 30. http://www.sciencenews.org/view/feature/id/35245/title/Disaster_Goes_Global.

Pettifer, J. 2001. The magic bean. *BBC News,* June 8. http://news.bbc.co.uk/1/hi/programmes/correspondent/1363320.stm.

Pfeifer, Karen. 1985. *Agrarian reform under state capitalism in Algeria.* Boulder: Westview.

Philippines Ministry of Agriculture. 1981a. *Food consumption and nutrition.* Memo to Minister of Agriculture Tanco. Manila: Ministry of Agriculture, National Agricultural Policy Staff, September 8.

———. 1981b. *Seasonal price indices of selected agricultural commodities.* National Policy Staff Paper no. 81-2. Manila: Ministry of Agriculture.

———. 1983. *National consumption patterns for major foods, 1977–1982.* Manila: National Food Authority, Special Studies Division, Economic Research and Statistics Directorate.

Philippines National Science and Technology Authority. 1983. Publication no. 82-ET-10. Manila: Food and Nutrition Research Institute, February.

———. 1984. *Second nationwide nutrition survey: Philippines, 1982.* Manila: Food and Nutrition Research Institute, October.

Phillips, Marshall, and Albert Baetz, eds. 1980. *Diet and resistance to disease.* New York: Plenum.

Pike, Ruth L., and Myrtle Brown. 1984. *Nutrition: An integrated approach.* New York: Wiley.

Piketty, T. 2006. The Kuznets curve: Yesterday and tomorrow. In *Understanding Poverty,* ed. Abhijit Vinayak Banerjee, Roland Benabou, and Dilip Mookherjee, 63–72. Oxford, Oxford University Press.

Piketty, T., and E. Saez. 2003. Income inequality in the United States, 1913–1998. *Quarterly Journal of Economics* 118, no. 1:1–39.

———. 2006. *The evolution of top incomes: A historical and international perspective.* Working Paper no. 11955. Cambridge, MA: National Bureau of Economic Research. http://www.nber.org/papers/w11955.

Pimentel, D. 1993. Climate changes and food supply. *Forum for Applied Research and Public Policy* 8, no. 4:54–60. http://www.osti.gov/scitech/biblio/5579867.

Pimentel, D., et al. 1994. Natural resources and an optimum human population. *Population and Environment* 15:347–369.

———. 1995. Environmental and economic costs of soil erosion and conservation benefits. *Science* 267 (February):1117–1123.

———. 1996. Impact of population growth on food supplies and environment. Presentation at the annual meeting of the American Association for the Advancement of Science , Baltimore, February 9.

Pimentel, David, and Mario Giampietro. 1994. *Food, land, population, and the US economy.* Washington, DC: Carrying Capacity Network.

Pingali, P. 1987. *From hand tillage to animal traction: Causes and effects and the policy implications for sub-Saharan African agriculture.* African Livestock Policy Analysis Network, Paper no. 15. Addis-Ababa: International Livestock Centre for Africa. http://hdl.handle.net/10568/4417.

———. 2012. Green revolution: Impacts, limits, and the path ahead. *Proceedings of the National Academy of Science* 109, no. 31:12302–12308.

Pingali, P., and P. Heisey. 1999. *Cereal crop productivity in developing countries: Past trends and future prospects.* Economics Working Paper no. 99-03. Mexico City: Centro Internacional de Mejoramiento de Maize y Trigo.

Pinkovskiy, M., and X. Sala-i-Martin. 2009. *Parametric estimations of the world distribution of income.* Cambridge, MA: National Bureau of Economic Research.

Pinstrup-Andersen, P., R. Pandya-Lorch, and M. Rosegrant. 1998. *The world food situation: Recent developments, emerging issues, and long-term prospects.* Washington, DC: International Food Policy Research Institute.

Pinstrup-Andersen, Per, and Elizabeth Caicedo. 1978. The potential impact of changes in income distribution on food demand and human nutrition. *American Journal of Agricultural Economics* 60 (August):402–415.

Pinstrup-Andersen, Per, and Peter Hazell. 1985. The impact of the green revolution and prospects for the future. *Food Reviews International* 1, no. 1:11.

Pinstrup-Anderson, Per, David Nygaard, and Annu Ratta. 1995. *The right to food: Widely acknowledged and poorly protected.* 2020 Brief no. 22. Washington, DC: International Food Policy Research Institute.

Pinstrup-Andersen, Per, et al. 1976. The impact of increasing food supply on human nutrition: Implications for commodity priorities in agricultural research and policy. *American Journal of Agricultural Economics* 58:137–138.

Pollitt, E., K. Gorman, P. Engle, R. Martorell, and J. Rivera. 1993. Early supplementary feeding and cognition. *Monographs of the Society for Research in Child Development* 58, no. 235:7.

Pope John Paul II. 1996. *Message to World Food Summit, November 13, 1996.* http://www.fao.org/wfs/index_en.htm.

Population Reference Bureau. 1970. *1965 world population data sheet.* Washington, DC.

———. 1987. *1987 world population data sheet.* Washington, DC.

———. 2013. *Africa and the demographic dividend.* http://www.prb.org/Publications/Reports/2013/africa-demographic-dividend.aspx.

Porter, J. R., L. Xie, A. J. Challinor, K. Cochrane, S. M. Howden, M. M. Iqbal, D. B. Lobell, and M. I. Travasso. 2014. Food security and food production systems. In *Climate change 2014: Impacts, adaptation, and vulnerability,* pt. A, *Global and sectoral aspects,* ed. C. B. Field, 485–533. Cambridge: Cambridge University Press.

Posner, R. A. 1986. *Economic analysis of the law.* 3rd ed. Boston: Little, Brown.

Postel, S. 1997. Dividing the waters. *Technology Review,* April 1997. http://www.converge.org.nz/pirm/water.htm.

———. 2003. Water for food production: Will there be enough in 2025? In *Global environmental challenges of the twenty-first century: Resources, consumption, and sustainable solutions,* ed. D. Lorey, 51–70. London: Rowman and Littlefield.

Prentice, A. M., G. R. Goldberg, and Ann Prentice. 1994. Body mass index and lactation performance. *European Journal of Clinical Nutrition* 48, supp. 3 (November):78.

Pustilnik, Lev, and Gregory Yom Din. 2003. Influence of solar activity on state of wheat market in medieval England. In *Proceedings of the International Cosmic Ray Conference*, 4131. http://arxiv.org/abs/astro-ph/0312244.

Qaim, M., and A. de Janvry. 2003. Adoption of Bt cotton in Argentina. *American Journal of Agricultural Economics* 85:814–828.

Qaim, M., and D. Zilberman. 2003. Yield effects of genetically modified crops in developing countries. *Science* 299 (February):900–902.

Quandt, Sara A. 1987. Methods for determining dietary intake. In *Nutritional anthropology,* ed. Francis E. Johnson, 67–84. New York: Alan R. Liss.

Ramachandran, P., and H. Gopalan. 2009. Undernutrition and risk of infections in preschool children. *Indian Journal of Medical Research* 130:579–583.

Ramalingaswami, Vulimiri, Urban Jonsson, and John Rohde. 1996. Commentary: The Asian enigma. In *The progress of nations,* ed., UNICEF, 11–17.Washington, DC: United Nations International Children's Fund.

Ranade, C. G., and R. W. Herdt. 1978. Shares of farm earnings from rice production. In *Economic consequences of the new rice technology,* ed. R. Barker and Y. Hayami, 87–104. Los Banos, Philippines: International Rice Research Institute.

Rand, W., R. Uauy, and N. Scrimshaw. 1984. Protein-energy-requirement studies in developing countries: Results of international research. *Food and Nutrition Bulletin Supplement* no. 10. Tokyo: United Nations University Press. http://www.unu.edu /unupress/unupbooks/80481e/80481E03.htm#5.%20Protein-energy%20interactions.

Ravallion, Martin. 1997. Famines and economics. *Journal of Economic Literature* 35 (September):1205–1242.

Ray, Anandarup. 1986. Trade and pricing policies in world agriculture. *Finance and Development* 23 (September):2–5.

Reardon, T., C. Barrett, V. Kelly, and S. Kimseyinga. 1999. Policy reforms and sustainable agricultural intensification in Africa. *Development Policy Review* 17, no. 4:375–395.

Rejesus, R., P. Heisey, and M. Smale. 1999. *Sources of productivity growth in wheat: A review of recent performance and medium- to long-term prospects.* Economics Working Paper no. 99-05. Mexico City: Centro Internacional de Mejoramiento de Maize y Trigo.

Renkow, M., and D. Byerlee. 2010. The impacts of CGIAR research: A review of recent evidence. *Food Policy* 35, no. 5:391–402.

Reuters. 1996. Tension in Jordan's Karak after bread riots. *New York Times,* August 16. http://www.nytimes.com/1996/08/21/world/in-jordan-bread-price-protests-signal -deep-anger.html.

Reutlinger, Shlomo, and Marcelo Selowsky. 1976. *Malnutrition and poverty: Magnitude and policy options.* Staff Occasional Paper no. 23. Washington, DC: World Bank.

Reutlinger, Schlomo, et al. 1986. *Poverty and hunger: Issues and options for food security in developing countries.* Washington, DC: World Bank.

Ricker-Gilbert, J., and T. S. Jayne. 2011. *What are the enduring effects of fertilizer subsidy programs on recipient farm households? Evidence from Malawi.* Staff Paper no. 2011-09. Lansing: Michigan State University, Department of Agricultural, Food, and Resource Economics.

Rivera, Juan, and Reynaldo Martorell. 1988. Nutrition, infection, and growth. Pt. 1, Effects of infection on growth. *Clinical Nutrition* 7:156–162.

Roberts, M. J., and W. Schlenker. 2013. Identifying supply and demand elasticities of agricultural commodities: Implications for the US ethanol mandate. *American Economic Review* 103, no. 6:2265–2295.

Rodell, M., I. Velicogna, and J. Famiglietti. 2009. Satellite-based estimates of ground-water depletion rates in India. *Nature* 460:999–1002.

Rodrik, D. 2008. Spence christens a new Washington Consensus. *Economists' Voice* 5, no. 3:1–3. http://cemi.ehess.fr/docannexe/file/2740/rodrik2008.pdf.

Rogers, Beatrice Lorge. 1988a. Design and implementation considerations for con-sumer-oriented food subsidies. In *Food subsidies in developing countries,* ed. Per Pinstrup-Andersen, 127–146. Baltimore: Johns Hopkins University Press.

———. 1988b. Economic perspectives on combating hunger. Presentation at the sec-ond annual World Food Prize Celebration, Washington, DC, September 30. [An ed-ited version of this paper is available in *Completing the food chain: Strategies for combating hunger and malnutrition,* ed. Paula M. Hirschoff and Neil G. Kolter, 122–126. Washington, DC: Smithsonian, 1989.]

———. 1988c. Pakistan's ration system: Distribution of costs and benefits. In *Food subsidies in developing countries,* ed. Per Pinstrup-Andersen, 242–252. Baltimore: Johns Hopkins University Press.

Rose, D., P. Strasberg, J. Jefe, and D. Tschirley. 1999. Higher calorie intakes related to higher incomes in northern Mozambique. *Flash* 17. http://www.aec.msu.edu/age-con/FS2/Mozambique/flash17e.pdf.

Rosegrant, M., R. Scheleyer, and S. Yadav. 1995. Water policy for efficient agricultural diversification: Market-based approaches. *Food Policy* 20:203–223.

Rosen, Sherwin. 1999. Potato paradoxes. *Journal of Political Economy* 107, no. 6:294–313.

Rosenzweig, C., and M. L. Parry. 1994. Potential impact of climate change on world food supply. *Nature* 367. http://www.nature.com/nature/journal/v367/n6459 /abs/367133a0.html.

Rosenzweig, C., M. L. Parry, G. Fischer, and K. Frohberg. 1993. *Climate change and world food supply.* Research Report no. 3. Oxford: Oxford University, Environ-mental Change Unit.

Rosenzweig, Cynthia, and Daniel Hillel. 1995. Potential impacts of climate change on agriculture and food supply. *Consequences* (Summer):24–32.

Rosset, P., J. Collins, and F. M. Lappe. 2000. Lessons from the green revolution. *Tikkun Magazine,* March. http://www.foodfirst.org/media/printformat.php?id=148.

Rountree, John. 1985. Computations done at the University of Maryland from data pro-vided by the Egyptian Ministry of Agriculture, the Central Agency for Public Mo-bilization and Statistics, and the Ministry of Supply.

Rowley, R. J., J. C. Kostelnick, D. Braaten, X. Li, and J. Meisel. 2007. Risk of rising sea level to population and land area. *EOS: Transactions of the American Geophys-ical Union* 88, no. 9 (February):105–116. http://onlinelibrary.wiley.com/doi /10.1029/2007EO090001/abstract.

Royal Society. 1999. *Review of data on possible toxicity of GM potatoes.* London. http://www.royalsoc.ac.uk/files/statfiles/document-29.pdf.

Ruddiman, W. 2005. *Plows, plagues, and petroleum: How humans took control of cli-mate.* Princeton: Princeton University Press.

Runge, C. F., B. Senauer, P. Pardey, and M. Rosegrant. 2003. *Ending hunger in our life-time: Food security and globalization.* Baltimore: Johns Hopkins University Press.

Sachs, J. 2005a. *The end of poverty.* New York: Penguin.

———. 2005b. A practical plan to end poverty. *Washington Post,* January 17.

Sagoff, M. 1997. Do we consume too much? *The Atlantic,* June.

Sahlins, Marshall. 1968. Notes on the original affluent society. In *Man the hunter,* ed. R. B. Lee and I. DeVore, 85–89. Chicago: Aldine.

Sahn, David E., ed. 1989. *Seasonal variability in third world agriculture: The conse-quences for food security.* Baltimore: Johns Hopkins University Press.

Sahn, David E., and Neville Edirisinghe. 1993. Politics of food policy in Sri Lanka: From basic human needs to an increased market orientation. In *The political economy of food and nutrition policy,* ed. Per Pinstrup-Andersen, 32–49. Baltimore: Johns Hopkins University Press.

Sahn, D., and D. Stifel. 2002. *Urban-rural inequality in Africa.* Ithaca: Cornell University Press. http://pdf.usaid.gov/pdf_docs/Pnacr742.pdf.

Salaff, Janet W., and Arline Wong. 1983. Report no. 12. *Incentives and disincentives in population policies.* Washington, DC: Draper World Population Fund.

Sala-i-Martin, X. 2002. *The world distribution of income (estimated from individual country distributions).* Working paper. New York: Columbia University, May. http://www.econ.upf.es/deehome/what/wpapers/postscripts/615.pdf.

Sampath, R. 1992. Issues in irrigation pricing in developing countries. *World Development* 20:967–977.

Samuels, B. 1986. Infant mortality and low birth weight among minority groups in the United States: A review of the literature. In *Report of the secretary's task force on black and minority health,* vol. 4, *Infant mortality and low birth weight,* 33–50. Washington, DC: US Department of Health and Human Services.

Sandburg, Carl. 1936. *The people, yes.* New York: Harcourt, Brace.

Sang-Hun, Choe. 2008. North Korea to widen access for aid workers; U.S. ship arrives. *New York Times,* July 1.

Santos-Villaneuva, P. 1966. The value of rural roads. In *Selected readings to accompany getting agriculture moving,* ed. Raymond E. Borton, 775–795. New York: Agricultural Development Council.

Schaal, B. 2003. Biotechnology, biodiversity, and the environment. Paper presented at the Conference on Biodiversity and Biotechnology and the Protection of Traditional Knowledge, Washington University School of Law, St. Louis, April. http://law.wustl.edu/centeris/Papers/Biodiversity/PDFWrdDoc/schaalfinal.pdf.

Schaible, U., and S. Kaufmann. 2007. Malnutrition and infection: Complex mechanisms and global impacts. *PLoS: Medicine* 4, no. 5:0806–0812.

Schemann, J. F., et al. 2003. National immunisation days and vitamin A distribution in Mali: Has the vitamin A status of pre-school children improved? *Public Health and Nutrition* 6, no. 3:233–244.

Scherr, Sara J., and Satya Yadav. 1997. *Land degradation in the developing world: Issues and policy options for 2020.* 2020 Brief no. 44. Washington, DC: International Food Policy Research Institute. http://ageconsearch.umn.edu/bitstream/16371/1/br44.pdf.

Schiff, Maurice, and Alberto Valdés. 1995. The plundering of agriculture in developing countries. *Finance & Development* (March):44–47. Washington, DC: World Bank.

Schiffler, M. 2015. *Water, politics, and money: A reality check on privatization.* New York: Springer.

Schnepf, Randall D., Erik Dohlman, and Christine Bolling. 2001. *Agriculture in Brazil and Argentina: Developments and prospects for major field crops.* Washington, DC: US Department of Agriculture.

Schoenmaker, C., et al., 2014. Cognitive and health-related outcomes after exposure to early malnutrition: The Leiden longitudinal study of international adoptees. *Children and Youth Services Review* 48:80–86.

Schuh, G. Edward. 1988. Some issues associated with exchange rate realignments in developing countries. In *Macroeconomics, agriculture, and exchange rates,* ed. Philip L. Paarlberg and Robert G. Chambers, 231–240. Boulder: Westview. http://agris.fao.org/agris-search/search.do?recordID=US8902946.

Schultz, T. P. 1999. Health and schooling investments in Africa. *Journal of Economic Perspectives* 13, no. 3:67–88.

Schultz, Theodore W. 1979. *The economics of research and agricultural productivity.* Arlington, VA: International Agricultural Development Services.

Scobie, Grant M. 1983. *Food subsidies in Egypt: Their impact on foreign exchange and trade.* Research Report no. 40. Washington, DC: International Food Policy Research Institute, August.

Scobie, G., and R. Posada. 1984. The impact of technical change on income distribution: The case of rice in Colombia. In *Agricultural development in the third world,* eds., C. K. Eicher and J. M. Staatz, 378–388. Baltimore: Johns Hopkins Press.

Scrimshaw, Nevin S. 1988. Completing the food chain: From production to consumption. Remarks presented at the second annual World Food Price Celebration, Washington, DC, September 30. [An edited version of this paper is available in *Completing the food chain: Strategies for combating hunger and malnutrition,* ed. Paula M. Hirschoff and Neil G. Kolter, 1–17. Washington, DC: Smithsonian, 1989.]

Scrimshaw, Nevin S., Carl Taylor, and John Gordon. 1968. *Interactions of nutrition and infection.* Geneva: World Health Organization.

Scrimshaw, Nevin S. and Vernon R. Young. 1976. The requirements of human nutrition. In *Food and agriculture,* ed. Scientific American, 26–40. San Francisco: Freeman.

Seck, P. 2007. *Links between natural disasters, humanitarian assistance, and disaster risk reduction: A critical perspective.* Occasional Paper no. 2007/15. New York: United Nations Development Programme. http://hdr.undp.org/sites/default/files /seck_papa.pdf.

Sen, Amartya K. 1964. Size of holdings and productivity. *Economic and Political Weekly* (February) 16: 323–326.

———. 1966. Peasants and dualism with or without surplus labor. *Journal of Political Economy* 74:425–450.

———. 1973. *On economic inequality.* London: Oxford University Press.

———. 1981. *Poverty and famines: An essay on entitlement and deprivation.* Oxford: Clarendon.

———. 1987. *Hunger and entitlements.* Helsinki: World Institute for Development Economics Research.

———. 1990. Public action to remedy hunger: Tanco memorial lecture. London: Hunger Project, August. http://www.thp.org/reports/sen/sen890.htm#n1.

———. 1999. *Development as Freedom.* New York: Knopf.

Shakir, A. 1975. The surveillance of protein-calorie malnutrition by simple and economic means (a report to UNICEF). *Journal of Tropical Pediatrics and Environmental Child Health* 21:69–85.

Shapiro, F. 2004. Plural of anecdote is data (Raymond Wolfinger). http://listserv .linguistlist.org/cgi-bin/wa?A2=ind0407A&L=ads-l&P=8874.

Shaw, A. 2000. Police, troops impose uneasy calm after food riots. Associated Press, October 19.

Sherman, Adria R. 1986. Alterations in immunity related to nutritional status. *Nutrition Today,* July–August.

Shorto, R. 2008. No babies. *New York Times Sunday Magazine,* June 29. http://www.nytimes.com.

Sicat, Gerardo P. 1983. Toward a flexible interest rate policy, or losing interest in the usury law. In *Rural financial markets in developing countries: Their use and abuse,* ed. J. D. Von Pische et al., 373–386. Baltimore: Johns Hopkins University Press.

Silent killer: The unfinished campaign against hunger. 2005. Scott Simon, narrator. KCTS/Seattle Public Television. http://www.silentkillerfilm.org/show_summary .html.

Simmons, George B., and Robert J. Lapham. 1987. The determinants of family planning program effectiveness. In *Organizing for effective family planning programs*, ed. George B. Lampham and Robert J. Simmons, 683–706. Washington, DC: National Academy Press.

Simon, Julian L. 1986. *Theory of population and economic growth*. New York: Blackwell.

————. 1996. *The ultimate resource*. Princeton: Princeton University Press. http://www.rhsmith.umd.edu/Faculty/JSimon/Ultimate_Resource.

Simon, N., M. Cropper, A. Alberini, and S. Arora. 1999. *Valuing mortality reductions in India: A study of compensating-wage differentials*. Working Paper no. 2978. Washington, DC: World Bank.

Singer, P. 1972. Famine, affluence, and morality. *Philosophy and Public Affairs* 1, no. 3 (Spring):229–243.

Singh, K. S. 1975. *The Indian Famine, 1967: A Study of Crisis and Change*. New Delhi: People's Publishing House.

Singh, R. B., P. Kumar, and T. Woodhead. 2002. *Smallholder farmers in India: Food security and agricultural policy*. Bangkok: FAO Regional Office for Asia and the Pacific.

Smith, L. C., O. Dupriez, and N. Troubat. 2014. *Assessment of the reliability and relevance of the food data collected in national household consumption and expenditure surveys*. Working Paper no. 008. Washington, DC: International Household Survey Network.

Snow, A. 2002. Transgenic crops: Why gene flow matters. *Nature Biotechnology* 20:542.

Solon, P. 2010. The human right to water and sanitation. Presentation of the permanent representative of Bolivia to the United Nations, July 28. https://pwccc.wordpress .com/2010/07/28/speech-the-human-right-to-water-and-sanitation.

Sommer, Alfred, et al. 1986. Impact of vitamin A supplementation on childhood mortality: A randomized controlled community trial. *Lancet* 327 (May):1169–1173.

Specter, M. 2006. The last drop. *New Yorker,* October 23.

Stackman, E. C., Richard Bradfield, and Paul C. Mangelsdorf. 1967. *Campaigns against hunger*. Boston: Belknap.

Steckel, R. H. 1995. Stature and the standard of living. *Journal of Economic Literature* 33:1903–1940.

Stein, A., H. Barnhart, M. Hickey, U. Ramakrishnan, D. Schroeder, and R. Martorell. 2003. Prospective study of protein-energy supplementation early in life and of growth in the subsequent generation in Guatemala. *American Journal of Clinical Nutrition* 78, no. 1:162–167.

Stein, Z. 1975. *Famine and human development: The Dutch Honger Winter of 1944–45*. New York: Oxford University Press.

Steindl, J. 1987. Pareto distribution. In *The new Palgrave dictionary of economics*, ed. J. Eatwell et al.:809–811. London: Macmillan.

Steinfeld, H. P. Gerber, T. Wassenaar, V. Castel, M. Rosales, and C. de Haan. 2006. *Livestock's long shadow: Environmental issues and options*. Rome: Food and Agriculture Organization. ftp://ftp.fao.org/docrep/fao/010/A0701E/A0701E00.pdf.

Stephenson, Lani S., M. C. Latham, and A. Jansen. 1983. *A comparison of growth standards: Similarities between NCHS, Harvard, Denver, and privileged African children and differences with Kenyan rural children*. International Nutrition Monograph no. 12. Ithaca: Cornell University Press.

Stevens, Robert D., and Cathy L. Jabara. 1988. *Agricultural development principles: Economic theory and empirical evidence*. Baltimore: Johns Hopkins University Press.

Stevenson, B., and J. Wolfers. 2008. *Economic growth and subjective well-being: Reassessing the Easterlin paradox.* Philadelphia: University of Pennsylvania Press. http://www.nber.org/papers/w14282.

Steyn, M. 2006. Salute Danna Vale. *The Australian,* February 15. http://www.freere-public.com/focus/f-news/1579787/posts.

Stiglitz, J. 1986. *Economics of the public sector.* New York: Norton.

———. 2002. *Globalization and its discontents.* New York: Norton.

———. 2015. *New theoretical perspectives on the distribution of income and wealth among individuals.* Pt. 1, *The wealth residual.* Working Paper no. 21189. Cambridge, MA: National Bureau of Economic Research. http://www.nber.org/papers/w21189.pdf.

Stone, Bruce. 1985. *Fertilizer pricing policy and foodgrain production strategy.* Washington, DC: International Food Policy Research Institute.

Stout, B. A. 1998. Energy for agriculture in the twenty-first century. In *Feeding a world population of more than eight billion people: A challenge to science,* ed. J. C. Waterlow et al., 69–87. Oxford: Oxford University Press.

Strategy Page. 2004. Korea. January 21. https://www.strategypage.com/qnd/korea/articles/20040121.aspx.

Strauss, J. 1968. Estimating the determinants of food consumption and caloric availability in rural Sierra Leone. In *Agricultural household models: Extensions, applications, and policy,* ed. Inderjit Singh, et al., 116–152. Baltimore: Johns Hopkins University Press.

Strauss, John, and Duncan Thomas. 1998. Health, nutrition, and economic development. *Journal of Economic Literature* 36:766–818.

Streeten, Paul. 1987. *What price food? Agricultural price policies in developing countries.* London: Macmillan.

Struck, Doug. 2001. North Korea food crisis intensifies. *Washington Post,* May 16.

Subar, Amy F., et al. 2012. The Automated Self-Administered 24-Hour Dietary Recall (ASA24): A research resource from the National Cancer Institute (NCI). *Circulation* 125, supp. 10:A029.

Subramanian, S., and A. Deaton. 1996. The demand for food and calories. *Journal of Political Economy* 104, no. 1:133–162.

Subramanian, U., and M. Cropper. 1995. *Public choices between lifesaving programs: How important are lives saved?* Working Paper no. 1497. Washington, DC: World Bank.

Summers, L. 1991. GEP [Global Environmental Policy] internal World Bank memo. December 12. http://www.whirledbank.org/ourwords/summers.html.

Survey Research Institute (SRI) International Network and Resources Center. 2016. Cornell University College of Agriculture and Life Sciences. http://sri.cals.cornell.edu.

Svedberg, P. 1999. 841 million undernourished? *World Development* 27: 2081–2098.

Swindale, L. D. 1997. The globalization of agricultural research: A study of the control of the cassava mealybug in Africa. ftp://ftp.cgiar.org/isnar/publicat/pdf/vision/swindale.pdf.

Tabarrok, A. 2015. The case for getting rid of borders—completely. *The Atlantic,* October. http://www.theatlantic.com/business/archive/2015/10/get-rid-borders-completely/409501.

Tang, A. M., et al. 1993. Dietary micronutrient intake and risk of progression to acquired immunodeficiency syndrome (AIDS) in human immunodeficiency virus type 1 (HIV-1)–infected homosexual men. *American Journal of Epidemiology* 138, no. 11 (December):937–951.

Tanner, J. M. 1977. Human growth and constitution. In *Human biology: An introduc-*

tion to human evolution, variation, growth, and ecology, by G. A. Harrison et al., 301–385. Oxford: Oxford University Press.

Tanzi, V., and H. Zee. 2000. *Tax policy for emerging markets: Developing countries.* Working Paper no. 00/35. Washington, DC: International Monetary Fund.

Telford, J., J. Cosgrave, and R. Houghton. 2006. *Joint evaluation of the international response to the Indian Ocean tsunami: Synthesis report.* London: Tsunami Evaluation Coalition. http://www.tsunami-evaluation.org/NR/rdonlyres/2E8A3262 0320-4656-BC81-EE0B46B54CAA/0/SynthRep.pdf.

Teshima, R., et al. 2000. Effect of GM and non-GM soybeans on the immune system of BN rats and B10A mice. *Journal of the Food Hygienic Society of Japan* 41, no. 3:188–193.

Thielke, Thilo. 2006. Kenya's deadly dependency on food aid. *Der Spiegel,* January. http://service.spiegel.de/cache/international/spiegel/0,1518,396031,00.html.

Thomas, F., F. Renaud, E. Benefice, T. de Meeus, and J-F. Guegan. 2001. International variability of ages of menarche and menopause: Patterns and main determinants. *Human Biology* 73, no. 2 (April):271–290.

Thomson-Wadsworth. 2003. 2002 dietary reference intakes (DRI). http://www.newtexts .com/newtexts/nutrition%20tables.pdf.

Timberg, C. 2005. In Zimbabwe, withholding of food magnifies the hunger for change. *Washington Post,* March 30.

Todaro, Michael P. 1980. Internal migration in developing countries: A survey. In *Population and economic change in developing countries,* ed. Richard A. Easterlin, 361–402. Chicago: University of Chicago Press.

Tollefson, J. 2015. Millennium Villages project launches retrospective analysis. *Nature,* August. http://www.nature.com/news/millennium-villages-project-launches -retrospective-analysis-1.18157.

Trabaquini, K., P. Galvao, M. Salgado, A. Formaggio, and L. Galvao. 2012. Estimates of land use and land cover change and soil loss in the Brazilian cerrado through geotechnology. Presentation at the Geoscience and Remote Sensing Symposium, Munich, July 22–27.

Transport for London. 2003. Congestion charging: Summary of week 6. Press release, April 1. http://www.tfl.gov.uk/tfl/press_cc_news_latest.shtml.

Trumbo, P., S. Schlicker, A. Yates, and M. Poos. 2002. Dietary reference intakes for energy, carbohydrate, fiber, fat, fatty acids, cholesterol, protein, and amino acids. *Journal of the American Dietetic Association* 102, no. 11 (November):1621–1631.

Tupasi, T. E. 1985. Nutritional and acute respiratory infection. In *Acute respiratory infections in childhood: Proceedings of an international workshop,* ed. R. Douglas and E. Kerby-Eaton. Adelaide, Australia: University of Adelaide Press.

UN Office on Drugs and Crime. 2007. *World drug report 2007.* New York: United Nations.

UN Population Division. 2005. *World urbanization prospects: The 2005 revision.* http://esa.un.org/wpp.

———. 2006. *World population prospects: The 2006 revision.*

———. 2012a. World population prospects: Assumptions underlying the results of the 2012 revisions of the world population prospects. http://esa.un.org/unpp/assumptions.html.

———. 2012b. World population prospects. The 2012 revision, New York: United Nations. http://data.un.org.

———. 2015a. *Probabilistic population projections based on the world population prospects: The 2015 revision.* http://esa.un.org/unpd/ppp.

———. 2015b. *World population prospects: The 2015 revision—Methodology of the United Nations population estimates and projections.* http://esa.un.org/unpd /wpp/Publications/Files/WPP2015_Methodology.pdf.

UN Population Information Network. 1995. *Population and land degradation.* Vol. 2 of *Population and the environment: A review of issues and concepts for population programmes staff.* New York.

UNAIDS (Joint United Nations Programme on HIV/AIDS). 2002. Global reports: Estimates end of 2001. http://www.unaids.org/html/pub/Global-Reports/Barcelona/TableEstimatesEnd2001_en_xls.xls.

———. 2014. HIV and AIDS estimates. http://www.unaids.org/en/regionscountries/countries/http://www.unaids.org/en/KnowledgeCentre/HIVData/GlobalReport/2008/2008_Global_report.asp.

UNCTAD (United Nations Conference on Trade and Development). 2011. *World investment report, 2011.* Geneva.

———. 2015. *World investment report,* 2015. Geneva.

UNDP (United Nations Development Programme). 2003. *Human development report 2003.* New York. http://www.undp.org/hdr2003/index.html.

———. 2006. *Human development report 2006: Beyond scarcity—Power, poverty, and the global water crisis.* New York. http://hdr.undp.org/hdr2006/pdfs/report/HDR06-complete.pdf.

———. 2015. *Human development report 2015.* New York. http://report.hdr.undp.org.

UNEP (United Nations Environment Programme). 1990. *The impacts of climate change on agriculture.* Nairobi.

UNESCO (United Nations Educational, Scientific, and Cultural Organization). 2006. *The 2nd UN world water development report.* New York. http://webworld.unesco.org/water/wwap/wwdr/wwdr2/table_contents.shtml.

UNICEF (United Nations Children's Fund). 1987. ORT and much more: Developing whole CDD programmes. Memo to all field offices. New York, January 15.

———. 1988. *State of the world's children 1988.* New York: Oxford University Press.

———. 1996. *Progress of nations.* New York. http://www.unicef.org/pon96.

———. 1998. *State of the world's children 1998.* New York: Oxford University Press.

———. 2001. *State of the world's children 2001.* New York: Oxford University Press.

———. 2003. *State of the world's children 2003.* New York: Oxford University Press.

———. 2007. *Progress for children: A world fit for children—Statistical review.* New York. http://www.unicef.org/publications/index_42117.html.

———. 2008. *State of the world's children 2008.* New York. http://www.unicef.org/sowc08/docs/sowc08.pdf.

———. 2011. Fact of the week, 59: In the developing world, 59% of children with pneumonia are taken to an appropriate health-care provider. http://www.childinfo.org/facts_1078.htm.

———. 2013. *State of the world's children 2014.* New York. http://www.unicef.org/sowc2013.

———. 2014. *Committing to child survival: A promise renewed—Progress report 2014.* New York. http://files.unicef.org/publications/files/APR_2014_web_15Sept14.pdf.

United Nations. 2008. *The Millennium Development Goals report 2008.* New York. http://mdgs.un.org/unsd/mdg/Resources/Static/Products/Progress2008/MDG_Report_2008_En.pdf.

US Census Bureau. 2008. Current housing reports, Series H150/07, American housing survey for the United States: 2007. Washington, DC: US Government Printing Office,

US Department of Energy (DOE). 2003. Residential energy consumption survey. Washington, DC. http://www.eia.doe.gov/emeu/recs/recs2001/detail_tables.html.

———. 2007. Research advances in cellulosic ethanol. http://www.nrel.gov/biomass/pdfs/40742.pdf.

US Department of State. 1976. *Clinical and subclinical malnutrition and their influence on the capacity to do work.* By G. B. Spurr, M. Barac-Nieto, and M. G. Maksud. Washington, DC.

US Department of Treasury. 2007. *Income mobility in the U.S. from 1996 to 2005.* Washington, DC. https://www.treasury.gov/press-center/press-releases/Pages/hp673.aspx.

US National Academy of Sciences. 1974. *Recommended dietary allowances.* Washington, DC.

USAID (US Agency for International Development). 2007. *Report on the first results of the Improved Road-Transport Governance (IRTG) initiative.* Accra: West African Trade Hub. http://www.watradehub.com/images/stories/downloads/studies/Report%20on%20first%20IRTG%20results,%20English,%20jw.pdf.

USDA (US Department of Agriculture). 1984. *The impact of wheat price policy change on nutritional status in Egypt.* By Ibrahim Soliman and Shahla Shapouri. Washington, DC.

———. 1988. *World food needs and availabilities, 1988–89: Summer.* Washington, DC.

———. 1991 *Food cost review.* Washington, DC.

———. 2008a. *U.S. biobased products: Market potential and projections through 2025.* Washington, DC. http://www.usda.gov/oce/reports/energy/BiobasedReport2008.pdf.

———. 2008b. *USDA agricultural projections to 2017.* Washington, DC. http://www.ers.usda.gov/publications/oce081.

———. 2012. Effects of ozone air pollution on plants. http://www.ars.usda.gov/Main/docs.htm?docid=12462.

———. 2016. U.S. bioenergy statistics. http://www.ers.usda.gov/data-products/us-bioenergy-statistics.aspx.

Usher, R. 1996. The Cadillac that moos. *Time,* April.

van der Zee, H. 1998. *The hunger winter: Occupied Holland 1944–1945.* Lincoln: University of Nebraska Press.

Vigen, T. 2015. *Spurious correlations.* New York: Hachette.

Viscusi, W. Kip. 1993. The value of risks to life and health. *Journal of Economic Literature* 31:1912–1946.

Viscusi, W. K., and T. Gayer. 2002. Safety at any price? *Regulation* 25, no. 3. http://www.cato.org/pubs/regulation/regv25n3/regv25n3.html.

von Braun, Joachim, and Eileen Kennedy. 1986. *Commercialization of subsistence agriculture: Income and nutritional effects in developing countries.* Working Paper on Commercialization of Agriculture and Nutrition no. 1. Washington, DC: International Food Policy Research Institute.

———, eds. 1994. *Agricultural commercialization, economic development, and nutrition.* Baltimore: Johns Hopkins University Press.

von Braun, Joachim, et al. 1989. *Nontraditional export crops in Guatemala: Effects on production, income, and nutrition.* Research Report no. 73. Washington, DC: International Food Policy Research Institute.

Walinsky, Louis. 1962. *Economic development in Burma, 1951–1960.* New York: Twentieth Century Fund.

Wallis, J. A. N. 1997. Brazil: The cerrados region. In *Intensified systems of farming in the tropics and subtropics,* 85–103. Discussion Paper no. 364. Washington, DC: World Bank.

Walsh, B. 2008. The farmer's bank. *Time,* January. http://content.time.com/time/magazine/article/0,9171,1708817,00.html.

Waterlow, J., D. Armstrong, L. Fowden, and R. Riley, eds. 1998. *Feeding a world population of more than eight billion people.* Oxford: Oxford University Press.

Waterlow, J., R. Buzina, W. Keller, J. Lane, M. Nichaman, and J. Tanner. 1977. The presentation and use of height and weight data for comparing the nutritional status of groups of children under the age of ten years. *Bulletin of WHO* 55:489–498.

Watts, J. 2007. Riots and hunger feared as demand for grain sends food costs soaring. *The Guardian,* December 4. http://www.theguardian.com/world/2007/dec/04/china.business.

Weiner, J. S. 1977. Nutritional ecology. In *Human biology: An introduction to human evolution, variation, growth, and ecology,* ed. A. G. Harrison et al., 400–423. Oxford: Oxford University Press.

Weiner, T. 2000. A farmer learns about Mexico's lack of the rule of law. *New York Times,* October 27.

Westcott, P., and J. Hansen. 2016. *USDA agricultural projections.* Outlook no. OCE-2016-1. Washington, DC: US Department of Agriculture, February.

Westcott, P., and R. Trostle. 2013. *USDA agricultural projections to 2022.* Outlook no. OCE-131. Washington, DC: US Department of Agriculture, February. http://www.ers.usda.gov/media/1013582/oce131d.pdf.

White House, President's Science Advisory Committee. 1967. *The world food problem.* Vols. 2–3, *Report of the panel on the world food supply.* Washington, DC.

Whitney, Eleanor N., and Eva Hamilton. 1990. *Understanding nutrition.* St. Paul, Minn.: West.

WHO (World Health Organization). 1985. *Energy and protein requirements: Report of a joint FAO/WHO/UNU expert consultation.* Technical Report no. 724. Geneva.

———. 1996a. *Investing in health research and development: Ad hoc committee on health research relating to future intervention options.* New York: United Nations.

———. 1996b. *State of the world's vaccines and immunization.* New York. http://www.who.ch/gpv/tEnglish/avail/sowvi.htm.

———. 1997. *World health report 1997.* Geneva.

———. 2001. *Iron deficiency anaemia: Assessment, prevention, and control.* Geneva. http://www.who.int/nutrition/publications/en/ida_assessment_prevention_control.pdf?ua=1.

———. 2002. *Diet, nutrition, and the prevention of chronic diseases.* Technical Report no. 916. Geneva.

———. 2003a. Progress towards global immunization goals, 2001. http://www.who.int/vaccines-surveillance/documents/SlidesGlobalImmunization_2002update.

———. 2003b. Water supply, sanitation, and hygiene development. http://www.who.int/water_sanitation_health/hygiene/en.

———. 2007. *Assessment of iodine deficiency disorders and monitoring their elimination.* 3rd ed. Geneva. http://www.who.int/nutrition/publications/micronutrients/iodine_deficiency/9789241595827/en.

———. 2008. *Worldwide prevalence of anaemia, 1993–2005.* Ed. B. de Benoist, E. McLean, I. Egli, and M. Cogswell. Geneva. http://whqlibdoc.who.int/publications/2008/9789241596657_eng.pdf.

———. 2009. Child growth standards and the identification of severe acute malnutrition in infants and children. http://www.who.int/nutrition/publications/severemalnutrition/9789241598163_eng.pdf.

———. 2014. Progress towards global immunization goals, 2013: Summary of key indicators. http://www.who.int/immunization/monitoring_surveillance/slidesglobalimmunization.pdf.

————. 2015a. Millennium Development Goal 4: Reduce child mortality. http://www.who.int/topics/millennium_development_goals/child_mortality/en.

————. 2015b. Obesity and overweight. Fact Sheet no. 311. http://www.who.int/mediacentre/factsheets/fs311/en.

————. 2015c. The global prevalence of anaemia, 2011, WHO. Online at http://apps.who.int/iris/bitstream/10665/177094/1/9789241564960_eng.pdf?ua=1&ua=1.

WHO (World Health Organization) and UNICEF (United Nations Children's Fund) Joint Monitoring Program. 2015. Progress on drinking water and sanitation: 2015 update and MDG assessment. http://www.who.int/water_sanitation_health/monitoring/jmp-2015-update/en.

WHO (World Health Organization) and United Nations. 1997. Micronutrient and trace element deficiencies: General information. http://www.who.org/nut/micr/micrgen.htm.

Wild, Alan. 2003. *Soils, land, and food: Managing the land during the twenty-first century.* Cambridge: Cambridge University Press.

Williamson, J. 1990. What Washington means by policy reform. In *Latin American adjustment: How much has happened?* ed. J. Williamson, 5–20. Washington, DC: Institute for International Economics.

Wines, M. 2007. Caps on prices only deepen Zimbabweans' misery. *New York Times,* August 2.

Winick, M., K. Meyer, and R. Harris. 1973. Malnutrition and environmental enrichment by early adoption. *Science* 190 (December):1173–1175.

Wittwer, Sylvan. 1995. *Food, climate, and carbon dioxide: The global environment and world food production.* New York: Lewis.

Wolfenbarger, L., and P. Phifer. 2000. The ecological risks and benefits of genetically engineered plants. *Science* 290 (December):2088–2093.

Wood, S., J. Henao, and M. Rosegrant. 2004. The role of nitrogen in sustaining food production and estimating future nitrogen fertilizer needs to meet food demand. In *Agriculture and the nitrogen cycle,* ed. A. R. Mosier et al., 245–260. Washington, DC: Island. http://www.worldwatch.org/press/news/1996/07/27.

World Bank. 1975. Land reform sector policy paper. Washington, DC, May.

————. 1982. *World development report: Agriculture and economic development.* Washington, DC: Oxford University Press.

————. 1984. *World development report 1984.* New York: Oxford University Press. https://openknowledge.worldbank.org/handle/10986/5967.

————. 1986. *World development report 1986.* New York: Oxford University Press. https://openknowledge.worldbank.org/handle/10986/5969.

————. 1990. *World development report 1990: Poverty* https://openknowledge.worldbank.org/handle/10986/5973.

————. 1993. *World development report 1993: Investing in Health.* Online at https://openknowledge.worldbank.org/handle/10986/5976

————. 1994. *Enriching lives: Overcoming vitamin and mineral nutrition in developing countries.* Washington, DC.

————. 1997. Does better nutrition improve academic achievement? Yes. *World Bank Policy and Research Bulletin* 8, no. 2 (April–June):1–3.

————. 2001. Private-sector development strategy: Issues and options. http://documents.worldbank.org/curated/en/2001/06/2478269/private-sector-development-strategy-issues-options.

————. 2007. *World development report 2008.* Washington, DC http://web.worldbank.org/wbsite/external/extdec/extresearch/extwdrs/0,,contentMDK:23062293~pagePK:478093~piPK:477627~theSitePK:477624,00.html.

————. 2008a. *China quarterly update.* Washington, DC, February. http://site

resources.worldbank.org/intchina/Resources/318862-1121421293578/cqu_jan_08_en.pdf.

——. 2008b. *World development report 2009*. Washington, DC. http://web.worldbank.org/wbsite/external/extdec/extresearch/extwdrs/0,,contentMDK:23080183~pagePK:478093~piPK:477627~theSitePK:477624,00.html.

——. 2015a. *World development indicators 2015*. Washington, DC http://data.worldbank.org/data-catalog/world-development-indicators.

——. 2015b. *World development report 2015: Mind, society, and behavior.* Washington, DC. http://www.worldbank.org/en/publication/wdr2015.

——. 2015c. World income distribution. http://econ.worldbank.org/wbsite/external/extdec/extresearch/0,,contentMDK:22261771~pagePK:64214825~piPK:6421 4943~theSitePK:469382,00.html.

——. 2016. Macroeconomics and growth. http://econ.worldbank.org/wbsite/external/extdec/extresearch/extprograms/extmacroeco/0,,menuPK:477883~pagePK:64 168176~piPK:64168140~theSitePK:477872,00.html.

World Bank and UNDP (United Nations Development Programme). 1990. *A proposal for an internationally supported programme to enhance research in irrigation and drainage technology in developing countries, Vol. 2*. Washington, DC: World Bank.

World Food Programme. Where we work—Zimbabwe: Food security overview. http://www.wfp.org/country_brief/indexcountry.asp?country=716.

World Future Council. 2013. Sharing the experience of the food security system of Belo Horizonte. http://www.fao.org/fileadmin/templates/FCIT/Meetings/Africites/presentations/WorldFutureCouncil_experience-Belo-Horizonte.pdf.

World Resources Institute. 2000. *World resources 2000–01: People and ecosystems*. Washington, DC. http://www.wri.org/publication/world-resources-2000-2001.

Worldwatch Institute. 1996a. Cropland losses threaten world food supplies. Press release, July 27. http://www.worldwatch.org/press/news/1996/07/27.

——. 1996b. Worldwatch Institute urges World Bank and FAO to overhaul misleading food supply projections. Press release, May 1. Washington, DC.

Yang Jisheng. 2012. *Tombstone: The great Chinese famine, 1958–1962*. London: Allen Lane.

Yao, Shujie. 1999. A note on causal factors of China's famine in 1959–61. *Journal of Political Economy* 107, no. 6:1365–1372.

Ying, Yvonne. 1996. *Poverty and inequality in China*. Washington, DC: World Bank. http://www.worldbank.org/html/prddr/trans/ja96/art2.htm.

Zeigler, D. J. 2012. Protein and protein deficiency. In *Food and famine in the 21st century*, ed. W. A. Dando, 339–346. Santa Barbara: ABC-CLIO.

Zhang, X., and X. Cai. 2011. Climate change impacts on global agricultural land availability. *Environmental Research Letters* 6, no. 1, article 014014.

Index

445

About the Book

The fifth edition of *The World Food Problem* reflects nearly a decade of new research on the causes and potential solutions to the problems of producing and distributing food in developing countries.

With extensively updated data and new case studies throughout, this edition includes new or expanded discussions of such issues as:
- genetically modified food
- the impact of climate change
- the quality of agricultural land and water
- the significance of globalization
- implications of changes in demographic policy, such as the reversal of China's "one-child rule"

The result is an accessible, comprehensive text, as well as a provocative assessment of prospects for the future.

Howard D. Leathers is associate professor of agricultural and resource economics at the University of Maryland, College Park. The late **Phillips Foster** was professor emeritus of agricultural and resource economics at the University of Maryland, College Park.